971.0086912 Lan

The land newly found.

PRICE: $45.00 (3559/wi   )

Books of Merit

The Land Newly Found

The
LAND NEWLY FOUND

▼ ▼ ▼

Eyewitness Accounts of the
Canadian Immigrant Experience

▲ ▲ ▲

NORMAN HILLMER

J. L. GRANATSTEIN

Thomas Allen Publishers
Toronto

Library and Archives Canada Cataloguing in Publication

Hillmer, Norman, 1942–
The land newly found : eyewitness accounts of the Canadian
immigrant experience / Norman Hillmer, J.L. Granatstein.

Includes bibliographical references and index.
ISBN 13: 978-0-88762-249-6
ISBN 10: 0-88762-249-6

1. Immigrants—Canada—History—Sources.
2. Immigrants—Canada—Biography.
I. Granatstein, J.L., 1939–   II. Title.

FC104.H55   2006   971'.0086'912   C2006-903880-5

Editor: Janice Zawerbny
Jacket and text design: Gordon Robertson
Jacket image: Brad Maushart / Veer

Published by Thomas Allen Publishers,
a division of Thomas Allen & Son Limited,
145 Front Street East, Suite 209,
Toronto, Ontario M5A 1E3 Canada

www.thomas-allen.com

Canada Council
for the Arts

ONTARIO ARTS COUNCIL
CONSEIL DES ARTS DE L'ONTARIO

The publisher gratefully acknowledges the support of
the Ontario Arts Council for its publishing program.

We acknowledge the support of the Canada Council for the Arts, which
last year invested $20.0 million in writing and publishing throughout Canada.

We acknowledge the support of the Government of Ontario through the
Ontario Media Development Corporation's Ontario Book Initiative.

We acknowledge the financial support of the Government of Canada through the Book
Publishing Industry Development Program (BPIDP) for our publishing activities.

10 09 08 07 06   1 2 3 4 5

Printed and bound in Canada

To the Hillmers, the Goodrows, the Heiligs,
the Granatsteins, and the Gellers, and to all the others
who were fortunate enough to find Canada

Contents

The Land Newly Found

Introduction

When Michaëlle Jean became governor general of Canada in the early autumn of 2005, she carried with her two quite different immigration narratives. The first was celebratory. She was an acclaimed black woman immigrant. At the age of eleven, she had come with her family from a brutal Haitian dictatorship "draped in barbed wire from head to toe," in her poet uncle's evocative phrase. She had risen far and fast, becoming among other triumphs the first black host of a Quebec television program. She was said to embody modern Canada, a multitude of races and cultures working and living together harmoniously. The Toronto *Globe and Mail* editorialized that Jean and the millions of other new Canadians were making the country's "unprecedented diversity into an unrivalled success, one the rest of the world watches in awe."

This happy message was contradicted by Michaëlle Jean's own immigrant past. Her journalistic career, to be sure, was studded with achievement, but she felt unusual, a curiosity, just as she had been growing up in Thetford Mines, Quebec. "Nigger, nigger, take a bath," people had yelled at the young girl returning home from school along the railway tracks. "Here I was in this hostile land," she recalled in her husband's documentary film *Tropic North*, "and hearing those hostile words for the first time." She was different, and Canada did not allow her to forget it. "The same winter which shapes the Québécois has shaped me too. When people look at you, they see black. When you look at yourself, you see black. For them you were an accident of history—or worse, a part of the problem . . . for them you are a stain on a white landscape." Little wonder that she bristled when a reporter asked if she was a "token" governor general, appointed for what she was and not who she was.

Both of Michaëlle Jean's immigration stories have their truth. Large numbers of Canadians, surveys of opinion demonstrate, agree that immigration is a positive force in community development and in the strengthening of the national cultural fabric, and that large numbers of immigrants ought to be welcomed into the country. Canada *is* diverse, and proudly so. "What is truly remarkable is the ethnic profile of immigrants to Canada," writes public affairs commentator Gwynne Dyer, "which is unique in how closely it matches the global distribution of the human population." A quarter of Canadian immigrants are from East Asia, another 25 percent from South and Southeast Asia, 20 percent from Europe and the United States, and 10 percent each from Africa and the Caribbean and from Latin America. "Look into the face of Canada," Prime Minister Paul Martin exclaimed in welcoming Michaëlle Jean to Rideau Hall, "and you will see the world."

Canadian multiculturalism, embedded in government policy and practice since the 1970s, keeps the world ostentatiously in Canada. That is its explicit aim: each of the country's varied cultures and races are to be respected and promoted, not homogenized and forgotten. Some European parties and politicians thrive on attacking immigrants; in Canada, no leader can do so with impunity. Nor, it follows, may multiculturalism itself yet become the subject of serious criticism or debate. It has taken its place alongside other totems of tolerance as one of Canada's bedrock ideals.

Yet Canada's immigration history is anything but multicultural. In 1920, a doctor and McGill professor, Andrew McPhail, captured a common sentiment when he wrote that "immigration is war,—war by the new comers upon those already in possession." That had consequences, he reported. "In the more civilized parts of Canada, one may have lived in a settlement for forty years, and yet be described as a foreigner, or as an imported man." Immigration policy was then more restrictive than it had been at the turn of the twentieth century, and it would become more so before circumstances at the end of the Second World War opened Canada up to a tide of immigrants and refugees. Polls taken over the period from the 1950s to the 1970s, however, showed that only a third of the population believed that Canada needed immigrants, while more than half thought that it did not.

The country and the policy changed after that, of necessity. An overwhelmingly white Canada and its often racist past were swept away by a rhetoric that championed immigration from Asia, the Middle East, and the Caribbean. Early in the palpably multiracial Canada of the twenty-first century, studies of public opinion apparently revealed a new ease about immigration. Just beneath the surface, however, substantial anti-immigrant sentiment remained, particularly in Ontario and British Columbia, the places with the most new arrivals. It seemed less evident that immigration was a Canadian success story. Newcomers concentrated in crowded Vancouver, Montreal, and Toronto, and they struggled to find work that would meet their qualifications and their family's needs. Meanwhile criticism mounted that immigration policy was not getting the immigrants Canada's economy most needed.

Complaints about immigrants and immigration have been as habitual as fear of change and hatred of difference. *Bloody Foreigners* is the title of a good book on centuries of immigration into England and it captures the sentiment nicely. In the late eighteenth century, Québécois worried about the English-speaking Loyalists who fled after the American Revolution, and Upper Canadians in 1805 resented Americans crossing the border. The British North Americans of the 1840s fretted over the rough Irish, rushing away from the potato famine. Sturdy east and central Europeans were favoured immigrants in the 1890s and the early 1900s; Jews, Blacks, Asians, and southern Europeans were not. Even the desirable, however, found disfavour when established Canadians saw strangers among them, looking and sounding odd, eating different foods, accepting lower wages, and sticking together like glue. Especially bothersome, related a Russian observer in 1899, were "their slovenliness, secrecy, distrustfulness, and constant self-deprecation, which the English find totally incomprehensible." Early in the twentieth century, an anti-Asian exclusion movement flourished, while seventy years later the National Citizens Coalition mounted a campaign against Vietnamese boat people, the hapless refugees of war-torn Indochina. If immigration is war, it is more often fought against the newcomers, not by them.

In this book of personal accounts of the Canadian immigration experience, our interest is primarily in the newcomers themselves. Their separation from family and place of birth. Their reasons for coming to Canada, and leaving what they knew. Their attempts at adaptation, their search for security, and their willingness (or not) to be assimilated. Their encounters with exploitation and racism— and sometimes with goodwill. Their strategies of mutual assistance, and their ethnic persistence. Their hard work, their difficulties of language and employment, their failures, and their successes. Their response to Canada, and Canada's response to them. Itself made up of immigrants, Canada was often an unusually reluctant host, to adopt the expression of immigration historian Donald Avery. The welcome on occasion could be warm, but even that was usually conditional. The Women's Institutes in the rural Canada of the 1930s, for example, or the International Institute of Metropolitan Toronto in the 1950s assisted immigrants with energy and compassion. They expected to Canadianize their clients in return.

The arduous journey to belonging can never be complete. We were struck from the beginning by Neil Bissoondath's telling phrase "the land left behind, and the land newly found." Both are part of the immigrant's puzzle: "left behind" cannot be divorced from "newly found." The desire to reunify families or return home runs through the decades of stories we print here; it is testimony to immigrants' need to recreate or retrieve what they have lost. The longing for what has been left behind was eloquently described by the English woman Susanna Moodie as she observed 1832 Upper Canada: "a strong and overpowering grief. One simple word dwelt for ever in my heart, and swelled it to bursting—'Home!'" Yet home was almost always very far away from Canada, particularly before modern travel made the world a small place. "If only dear homeland," cried a Hungarian emigrant of the 1920s, "were not so unreachably distant." A friend concurred, adding that the Hungarian "plain is calling us, and so do the sad sighs of our elderly parents, the smell of the blooming acacia trees, all are throbbing in our restless hearts. We'll go home." For an early-twentieth-century Mennonite whose village in Russia had been destroyed or a refugee from Cold War communism, going back was out of the question. That made it all the harder, and all the more likely that home would become an unattainable ideal that Canada could never match.

Lineage is indelible. Immigrant life does not begin in Canada, but in Scotland or Ukraine or Vietnam. Or, in Andrej Potocký's case, in the pre-First World War Austro-Hungarian Empire. He arrived in British Columbia in 1910 at the age of sixteen. He never returned to his native land, but he remained haunted by its pines, rivers, streams, mountains, and meadows and governed by "my Slovak conscience as a true son of our nation in a distant country." Adriana de Gouvêa's voyage from Brazil to Canada took place almost a century later. It was more straightforward. She came from a cosmopolitan family, spoke English fluently, and could fly back to her family fairly readily. Quickly she felt comfortable and "at home." Nevertheless, as she testifies here, getting used to Canada was easier than getting used to living without Brazil. Indeed, her Brazilian identity began to matter much more to her than it had when she could take it for granted. When she went through the moving Canadian citizenship ceremony, she felt thoroughly Canadian—and yet Brazilian too. Ken Wiwa's inventory of belonging is similarly complex, an expedition to Canada filtered through an African youth and the murder of his famous activist father in 1996 by the military regime in Nigeria. And for Stephen Eaton Hume, the grandson of industrialist and peace activist Cyrus Eaton, there was the ironic, bittersweet finality of "I was home," the concluding words of his essay on arriving in Canada from the heartland he had left behind, the southern United States he had grown up to know.

Ancient loyalties can overwhelm everything. We have examples of that, when allegiances stubbornly remain elsewhere. Sometimes immigrants lose both their countries, finding themselves stuck between two worlds, unable to go back but unable to embrace their adopted land. At best, however, the old and the new are integrated, as they have been in the lives of János Máté and Helmut Walter Ott, two more of the newcomers to whom we were introduced in the research for this book. For János Máté, the transition from revolution and anti-Semitism in Hungary to the relative tranquility of British Columbia was much harder than even he knew at the time. Only after fifty years in Canada, and the death of his mother, was he fully able to reconcile his Hungarian roots and his Canadian present. With that came the understanding that his family's norms and traditions had become a part of Canada's history. He was no longer an immigrant. Helmut Ott rejected his Austrian heritage as an immigrant boy but found it as a man, and found it indispensable. "Periodically, I need to relive those early memories: to climb the Austrian hills and think about my ancestors, where they lived and what their way of life was like. Then I reaffirm where I came from. I get in touch with a part of myself and give it legitimacy." He sees the immigrant experience as the entwining of two cultures, so that each is enriched, transformed, and revitalized. "We immigrants are bridge builders. We construct spans that join cultures."

Immigrant children and the children of immigrants absorb the novel and are absorbed by it much more quickly, but they are also unformed and vulnerable in ways that adults are not. Hartley Janssen, an emigrant from Holland in 1953 at the age of ten, did not understand what "foreigner" meant, but he knew that the epithet stung. He and Karishma Kapil, arriving in the 1980s at the same age, were met by patronizing teachers and the assumption that immigrants must be far behind Canadians in their education and development. Lori Weber's teacher, perhaps inadvertently, conveyed an awareness that having a German father in the aftermath of the Second World War meant that she was different—"something that one has to apologize for, to be embarrassed of even"—even though her family had been resolutely and bravely anti-Nazi. The irony was that Germans fit more easily into the Canadian mainstream than her Italian or Jewish or Filipino friends; what Weber found herself envying were the ties of blood and ethnic identification she did not have and could not feel. Andrew Chung, the son of a respected Chinese doctor and a Newfoundland mother, did not have it in him to be different as a child. So he did his best to conform, in the pattern of immigrants everywhere, and he does still. But conform to what, since he is neither accepted as white or Asian "in a state of immigrants where nations are so clearly defined."

Canada was slow to fill up with immigrants. Geography got in the way. The land was huge, uncompromising, difficult to settle.

The earliest immigrants were as likely to be the result of sponsored programs as they were to come for opportunity or escape. Not until the late eighteenth century did large-scale immigration take hold. After the American Revolution, the Loyalists arrived in their tens of thousands, escaping the newly republican United States, which had confiscated their property and had worse than that in store for those who would return. They were followed by the "late Loyalists," substantial numbers of American settlers who moved to Upper Canada in search of cheap land before the War of 1812. Then, swamping all those who had gone before, almost a million immigrants flooded into British North America from Britain and Ireland between 1815 and 1850. They were pushed out by severe conditions at home and pulled into coming to Canada by the hope of a better life.

Immigration was an essential cog in building the nation of Canada, formed in 1867 and soon stretching west to the Pacific and north to the Arctic. Immigrants were needed to fill the vast spaces of a country in the making; to clear the land and to hew farms out of the bush; to open mines and cut the timber; to build towns and villages and eventually raise cities to be hubs of commerce; to construct roads, canals, railroads, and factories; and to produce, ship, and buy the goods that came from farm and factory. Eventually immigrants or their children would be needed to fight their country's battles, sometimes against the nations from which they sprang.

Yet the new Canada seemed to bleed more emigrants to the United States than it could attract from overseas. The *Toronto Daily Mail* argued in the 1890s for an open immigration policy, decrying the common view that the only immigrants who should be welcomed were those from the mother country of Britain. The only possible objection to immigrants who were not British, the newspaper stated, was that they were not British. That was not objection enough. "If Canada depends for population upon the natural increase, or upon a movement from the United Kingdom, our territories will not be peopled in the next half century. . . . It will be found, moreover, that the next generation of these people will be as thoroughly English as any other part of Canada, and in half a century from now the language which they bring to the Dominion will not be used at all." Francophone Canadians like the eloquent Henri Bourassa had other ideas, fearing in his words that one of "the two original races in this country" would be swamped.

Conditions had turned favourable by the time the opportunistic Clifford Sifton, the government minister in charge of immigration from 1896 to 1905, came on the scene. The great American West had been largely settled by the end of the nineteenth century, while Canada still had huge tracts of open and available fertile land. Markets at home and abroad grew, and economic conditions improved in Canada. Jobs and opportunity pulled the immigrant westward. Europe's oppressive regimes and rigid social hierarchies meanwhile pushed the less advantaged out. Of the Doukhobors, religious dissenters from Russia who had negotiated a special deal to come to Canada under advantageous conditions, the *Daily Mail* said that "these people come to Canada as the result of persecution. Their language and their native land remind them only of suffering and sorrow, while their new homes and the English language will recall to them the beginning of peace and prosperity."

Doukhobors were a particular favourite of Sifton's, but he and his successors watched certain others very carefully. Chinese immigrants initially were subject to a $50 head tax, raised a few years later in 1903 to $500, a staggering sum. Canadians believed that they were an immoral "yellow peril." Emigrants from Japan were even worse, because their country was industrializing and becoming powerful; the Japanese, it was feared, were more intelligent—and hence more competitive—than other Asians. Japan was a respected world power and a friend of Britain, and so the restrictions had to be more sophisticated, but restrictions there were. Because Chinese and Japanese immigrants, those who somehow found Canada despite the barriers raised against them, settled in British Columbia, the hostility there was greatest.

This hostility was also directed at East Asians, Sikhs, and Hindus from the Indian subcontinent. In 1914, the *Komagata Maru*, a Japanese ship carrying Sikh immigrants, was refused entry to Vancouver and escorted out to sea by Canada's fledgling navy, notwithstanding the fact that India was a British colony. Canada was a white man's country. The preferred settlers were Britons, white Americans, and northern and east-central Europeans. Immigration and shipping agents struck quiet deals with Ottawa to select and transport immigrants, ideally all farmers; the railways were themselves major immigration entrepreneurs, making up the rules as it suited them. Americans poured into Alberta. Many were tenant farmers who realized their sole chance of acquiring land of their own was in "the last, best West."

The Canadian government greatly preferred farmers to "mechanics." Farmers would be dispersed across the Prairies, breaking the sod and generating agricultural produce that would fill the grainhoppers on the railways. That development, that wealth was good for Canada, Sifton said, and therefore only farmers need apply. Workers, he believed, would congregate in the cities. Some would bring radical ideas from abroad and stir up trouble. But workers came in any case. Some of them, especially the eastern Europeans and British, would make themselves heard, so terrible were working conditions in the factories of Quebec and Ontario. A polyglot labour force suited some employers very well. It was best "to have a mixture of races," a B.C. mine operator noted. "They are the strength of the employer, and the weakness of the union." Organized labour disliked immigration, shrewdly observing that it did nothing to strengthen the workers' hand.

Many immigrants also came to Canada without the intention to stay. These sojourners hoped to earn some money doing the back-breaking work of the fields or the forest or the railway, and then return to the Old Country to better their family's conditions. Some did go back, but many found that Canada had changed them. They put down roots, bringing their families over if they had them and establishing families if they did not. Sometimes it took a long time to re-establish a family separated by oceans, especially when the war of 1914–1918 disrupted everything.

Native-born Canadians put up with the farmer-immigrants, perhaps because they didn't see them often. There was scant tolerance for immigrant city-dwellers, and the opposition to them—and indeed to all immigration—was strongest in Quebec. Immigrants cooked with garlic, spoke undecipherable languages, and prayed to different gods.

The shops that catered to them had Cyrillic or Hebrew characters on their signs. Could these "sweepings of Europe" ever be turned into a nation?

Not that the British immigrants were viewed with any kinder eye. It was fine if Lord So-and-So's third son wanted to try ranching in Alberta or fruit farming in British Columbia. British workers, however, had incomprehensible dialects and some seemed to believe they were "entitled" to good treatment in Canada. They weren't, and Sifton's successor as minister of the interior, Frank Oliver, called them a "drag on the labour market from misfortune, incompetence or indifference." The troublesome and the ill could be, and were, deported back to England and Scotland when the boom tailed off into depressed economic conditions before the Great War.

Between 1867 and 1902, immigration had exceeded one hundred thousand in only the three years from 1882 to 1884. Between 1902 and 1914, immigration was well above that number in every twelve-month period. In 1910, there were 286,000 immigrants, in 1911, 331,000, and in 1912, 376,000. Four hundred and one thousand came in 1913, a number that has never again been matched in the country's history. Canada, according to the census of 1911, had 8 million people; to take in 5 percent of the population as immigrants in a single year was extraordinary. Between 1900 and 1914, Canada's population was transformed from an almost strictly Anglo-Saxon and French Canadian one into a mixture of European peoples with small numbers of Asians and blacks. Those of British origin still predominated, with French-speaking Canadians making up 37 percent of the rest, but Canada had become a multi-ethnic society. One-third of the west was no longer British or French.

The Great War years fuelled ethnic tensions. "Enemy aliens," including some who had been in Canada for many years, were interned. When the War Time Elections Act came into force in 1917, immigrants from enemy countries were disenfranchised, a deliberate and successful attempt (matched by giving the vote to women relatives of soldiers) to tilt the election results toward the government. Once the war was over and men returned to take their jobs back, the antipathy to "foreigners" who had filled the factories in places like Winnipeg boiled over. The Winnipeg General Strike of 1919 was in part galvanized by the opposition of veterans to the newcomers who had taken their positions. The strike itself seemed to be populated by immigrants, and the federal government, putting down the labour strife, promptly acted to deport as many of the strike leaders as it could.

Deportation was a common enough tool of government, one that could be used with a very broad brush and to punish many sins— immorality, radicalism, illness, even indigence. One young Jewish immigrant from Poland found herself unwed and pregnant. She was placed into a mental asylum until her baby's birth, and then promptly shipped back to Poland as an undesirable. Her family in Toronto, unable to resist the state, felt a continuing secret shame and guilt. That the deportee eventually was killed in the Holocaust only added to the family's sense of responsibility for the tragedy.

Immigration chugged along in the 1920s, although at levels below the pre-war years. The Empire Settlement scheme allowed a hundred thousand assisted British immigrants to enter the country. At the same time, the railways, anxious to carry immigrants from the east coast to their new homes and wanting an increase in population to increase their business, pressed Ottawa to open the door to Europeans. The government struck arrangements with the Canadian Pacific and Canadian National Railways in 1925, allowing the companies to recruit farmers from eastern and southern Europe. Some 185,000 immigrants arrived under the Railway Agreement by the end of the 1920s. The Great Depression, however, effectively put an end to immigration. The Conservative government of R.B. Bennett, responding to public demand and to rising nativism, sharply curtailed new arrivals, a policy that remained in place through the decade and the Second World War. Deportation was again a convenient weapon. Twenty-eight thousand of the recently arrived were hustled out of the country.

The Jews of Europe, fleeing from Europe ahead of Adolf Hitler's Nazis, suffered most grievously from Canada's narrowly defined immigration policy. Canada's door was closed to almost all immigrants in the 1930s. It was shut even more tightly to Jews. They were unlikely to be farmers and, in the eyes of the bureaucrats handling immigration questions in Ottawa, "their habits" did not allow for assimilation. Nor would they stop until boatload after boatload of them had been admitted to the country. Opposition in Catholic Quebec was especially strong, but there seemed little support for Jewish immigration anywhere in a Canada caught up in the Depression. Other nations took much the same attitude. European Jewry all but perished in the Holocaust.

"Orientals" remained another prominent target for restriction and discrimination. In 1923, the Chinese Immigration Act effectively barred emigration from China, an action that Chinese Canadians then and after regarded as a humiliation. An agreement between Japan and Canada later in the decade slowed Japanese immigration to a trickle. The community of Canadian Japanese, some 23,000 strong by the Second World War and predominantly living in British Columbia, nevertheless prospered, but they were viewed with hostility by the white population. The war in the Pacific fed this racism and led to the forced evacuation of Japanese Canadians to the B.C. interior and Alberta. Their property was confiscated and sold at fire-sale prices. Toward the end of the war, Ottawa had plans in hand to deport the entire group to Japan, a country in ruins and one that most of the Canadian Japanese had never seen. Some of these "throw-away citizens" (as one Canadian-Japanese woman described herself) were deported, but public and governmental opinion eventually forced a more humane approach.

By war's end, Canada had begun to gear itself up for new waves of migration. The feared economic disruptions of the reconstruction period did not occur, and Canada boomed. The Mackenzie King government took pains to say that no one had a "right" to come to Canada and that Canadians did "not wish . . . to make a fundamental alteration in the character of our population." Ottawa sent teams overseas to recruit "displaced persons" from refugee camps, to choose from among the soldiers who had fought in the war, and to search in shattered Britain and France for potential immigrants. Almost 70 percent of Canadians opposed the drive for more immigration, but business cheered it on, to keep the economy rolling forward. The agriculturalist class of immigrants shrank, as did the amount of land available. Most new Canadians went to the big cities, with skilled workers and professionals increasing as a proportion. One observer, while complaining of "the great unassimilated foreign communities," had to admit that "its new polyglot life . . . gives Toronto a colour and fascination which it could not otherwise possess."

Another post-war change was the birth of a new category, the sponsored immigrant. Why should the mother, father, sister, brother, or aunts and cousins of someone already established in Canada need to wait on the regular processes to immigrate to Canada? Why not short-circuit the queue and admit members of a family? Family life was a virtue, and the family members in Canada would surely absorb some of the initial costs of settlement. As a result, sponsored immigrants constituted the majority of those coming to Canada by 1959. Although the number dropped in the next years after a tightening up of the rules, still more than a third of migrants were sponsored.

When the Hungarian Revolution of late 1956 erupted and the Soviet Union crushed it, tens of thousands of refugees fled across the Austrian border seeking freedom. Pressured by international observers and community groups to do its share, Canada stepped in, put aside the usual rules, and welcomed some 40,000 Hungarians. Immigration minister Jack Pickersgill had the right under the 1952 Immigration Act to move decisively when he saw fit, and, encouraged by Canadians across the country, he grabbed the moment with great energy. The 1952 act, however, was clear. It declared that immigration was only for British subjects and those of French or American origin, unsponsored immigrants from Western Europe, sponsored relatives, and a residual category designed to restrict Asian immigration. Between 1945 and 1961, 2.1 million immigrants came to Canada. British and Americans were still the biggest contingents, but large numbers of immigrants were coming from countries such as Italy and Portugal.

A colour-blind immigration system was not far off. The Diefenbaker government of the early 1960s began the move away from the standards of national origin or ethnicity, and in 1967, a "points" system came into use, with independent applicants ranked on criteria of skills, education, and resources. The new policy began to shift the sources of immigration to Asia, Latin America, and Africa, a trend continued by the Immigration Act of 1976. Hong Kong, India, the Philippines, and Neil Bissoondath's Trinidad now led the list of places supplying immigrants to Canada. The Trudeau government's 1970s implementation of multiculturalism, ethnicity within a framework of bilingualism, enshrined Canada as a nation of many peoples.

Indeed it was already that. The 1971 census revealed that a quarter of the population was not of French, British, or Aboriginal ancestry, and the Canadian Charter of Rights and Freedoms a decade later pledged "the preservation and enhancement of the multicultural heritage of Canada," giving newcomers equal rights with citizens. The bad old days of racist immigration policies seemed gone forever, and nothing demonstrated this more than the eagerness with which Canadian governments, individuals, and churches cooperated to bring in more than 50,000 Vietnamese refugees in the aftermath of the fall of South Vietnam to the Communist North. There was opposition, but it was minimal.

The global unrest from the 1980s onwards increased the flood of refugees. Doubts arose. Were they really refugees? Or were they "economic migrants" seeking a better life in Canada? Should they not join the line with other immigrant applicants? The issue was unresolved and irresolvable, but Canadians tended to become more cautious in their attitude to immigrants and refugees. Government policy, spurred by security concerns, was toughened repeatedly. The number of refugee claimants in 2005 was at its lowest, approximately 17,000, since the late 1980s, when the average was just under 30,000 a year. Legal scholar Anna Pratt, who has a piece in this book, stipulates that the "denigration and distrust of refugee claimants, heightened anxieties about crime, security and fraud, and efforts to fortify the border and deflect risky outsiders" are old impulses in immigration enforcement. The regime of the gatekeepers, she argues, has been tightened in the aftermath of the September 11, 2001, terrorist attacks on New York and Washington.

We have tried to capture the history of Canadian immigration in all its generous and less generous aspects. As we did in our previous volumes in this series, *First Drafts* and *Battle Lines*, we have emphasized the personal and the immediate, the rawer and closer to the bone the better. Small changes of punctuation or spelling in the various accounts have occasionally been made in order to clarify the meaning or to streamline the text. The chronological arrangement is deliberate, in order to demonstrate the movements of peoples and ideas over time. The book begins in earnest with the Loyalists of the late eighteenth century, but we have tried to give hints of the making of Canada from the 1600s onwards. The literature of Canadian immigration contains some wonderful works of fiction, such as David Bezmozgis's *Natasha*, but we have decided not to include any of that writing in the book. The one exception is some lines from Ralph Connor's *The Foreigner*, which is embedded in a recollection of that author's 1928 encounter with a group of Polish Canadians in Winnipeg.

We are aware of some of the pitfalls of our endeavour. Historians are schooled to consider the source, but the provenance of immigration evidence can be particularly difficult to nail down. In *First Drafts*, we used an Irish famine diary that we now know to be fictitious. It was written many years after the event by a Canadian journalist without the intent to deceive, but it got around as the real thing, fooling even the Irish government, which used it in their schools. We rejected a good many sources that did not seem to us, or to experts we consulted, to be credible. We do include a 1920s saga of Hungarian immigrants on the Prairies that has undergone careful scholarly examination but cannot be absolutely verified because names and places are not identified. The manuscript might have been embellished, the more so since the author had a clear message he wished to convey to prospective European immigrants. This exposes a larger problem. Some immigrants will only tell their story if their privacy is respected, meaning that their reminiscences are cloaked in anonymity. Many immigrant accounts, moreover, were written either to encourage or discourage those who would come after, and they need to be read as such.

We have been the beneficiaries of a great deal of generosity. We particularly thank the scholars of Canadian immigration who have helped us: Estelle Bouhraoua, Wendy Cameron, Janice Cavell, Milly Charon, N.F. Dreisziger, Vadim Kukushkin, J.I. Little, Lillian

Petroff, Bruno Ramirez, Patricia Roy, Angelika Sauer, M. Mark Stolarik, Tova Yedlin, and Stacey Zembrzycki. Dr. Cavell and Dr. Kukushkin carried out crucial research for the book, as did Michael Ryan and Ryan Shackleton. The Multicultural History Society of Ontario is an invaluable repository of immigration history, run cheerfully and on a shoestring; the staff there, led by Dr. Petroff, was exceedingly helpful.

At the Dominion Institute, Rudyard Griffiths has innovated with the *Passages to Canada* project, one of the best of a myriad of websites that give immigration a human face. We also salute Stephen Davies's Canadian Letters and Images Project. Ronald Brown taught us about the Scottish Highland Clearances. Bruce Elliott drew the counterfeit famine diary to our attention, as well as alerting us to the Irish Emigration Database at the Centre for Migration Studies. Other advice and assistance came from Stephen Azzi, Melvin Baker, Andrew Burtch, Alan Cumyn, Greg Donaghy, Tina Edan, Suzanne Evans, Charlotte Gray, Christine McIvor, Ann McVeigh, Philippe Lagassé, Pierrette Landry, Hector Mackenzie, Bina Mehta, Stephen Hoogenraad, H. Blair Neatby, Peter Neary, Richard Newport, Davene Palvetzian, Joshua Prowse, Laura Ruptash, Rebecca Sampson, Jessica Smart, Boris Stipernitz, and Susan B. Whitney.

As she has done with our previous books, Trista Grant expertly assembled the manuscript and made many good suggestions about its content. Wendy Thomas was an imaginative copy editor, under the pressure of the tightest of deadlines. Edna Barker proofread the book, cheerfully and proficiently. Linda McKnight is our formidable agent and friend, and Janice Zawerbny our resourceful editor. A very good friend, William Kaplan, first suggested the idea of such a volume. Thomas Allen publisher Patrick Crean continues his commitment to the publication of fine and distinctively Canadian books.

Multicultural and multiracial Canada is so different from the country of a century ago, and so much better for it. Canada takes in more immigrants as a percentage of its population than any other nation. More than 20 percent of the overall population is foreign-born, a figure twice as high as that of the United States. Canada's diversity is unparalleled. Not even Australia, another great immigrant-receiving country, draws on such a geographical range.

A poll conducted by Solutions Research Group in the summer of 2005 revealed the strong allegiance of immigrants to their new land and demonstrated how this could be reconciled with a similar attachment to their cultural heritage. In Toronto, the destination of more than 40 percent of all immigrants, the mosaic of students in the public schools is heartening, as are the attempts to understand racial difference and defeat prejudice. Listen, however, to Michael Valpy's warning near the end of this book. Complacency would be fatal.

NH
JLG
Ottawa and Toronto
July 1, 2006

The Land Newly Found

Quebec: Canada's Main Path

SAMUEL DE CHAMPLAIN

> *In 1608 Champlain founded Quebec, the first permanent settlement in North America. His challenge, demonstrated in these documents written a decade into the enterprise, was twofold: to make the case for his nation-building to reluctant authorities back home, while establishing the rudiments of a colony in his new home. Historian of New France Cameron Nish writes that Champlain's "choice of Quebec decided the main path of Canadian history. His writings, and efforts, kept a flagging French interest alive to the potential of Canada. He used the lure of wealth, and the desire for souls, as means to implement his vision of Canada."*

To the Kings and the Lords of His Council

The Sieur de Champlain represents to you most humbly that for sixteen years he has toiled with laborious zeal as well in the discoveries of New France as of divers peoples and nations whom he has brought to our knowledge, who had never been discovered save by him; which peoples have given him such and so faithful report of the north and south seas that one cannot doubt but that this would be the means of reaching easily to the Kingdom of China and the East Indies, whence great riches could be drawn; besides planting there the divine worship, as our Récollet friars can bear witness, in addition to the abundance of merchandise from the said country of New France, which would be drawn thence annually through the diligence of the workmen who would go there. Should this said country be given up and the settlement abandoned, for want of bestowing upon it the needed attention, the English or Flemings, envious of our prosperity, would seize upon it, thereby enjoying the fruits of our labours, and preventing by this means more than a thousand vessels from going to the dry and green fisheries and for whale-oil. . . . The said Champlain most humbly entreats His said Majesty and the said Lords of his Council to grant him the means of strengthening and extending his design.

Statement of Persons to Be Brought and Maintained at the Quebec Settlement for the Year 1619

There will be 80 persons, including the leader, three Récollet Fathers, clerks, officers, craftsmen, and field labourers.

For every two persons there will be a mattress, a straw bed, two blankets, three pairs of new sheets, two coats apiece, six shirts, four pairs of shoes, and a cloak.

For arms, 40 muskets with their shoulder belts, 24 pikes, 4 wheel-locks four to five feet long, 1000 lbs. of fine powder, 1000 lbs. of cannon-powder, 1000 lbs. of balls for the cannon, six thousand-weight of lead, a puncheon of cannon match.

For the men, a dozen scythes with handles, hammers, and other tools, 12 sickles, 24 spades for turning up the soil, 12 pickaxes, 4000 lbs. of iron, 2 barrels of steel, 10 tons of lime . . . , ten thousand curved tiles or twenty thousand flat, ten thousand bricks for making an oven and chimneys, two mill-stones, . . .

For the service of the leader's table, 36 platters, as many bowls and plates, 6 salt-cellars, 6 ewers, 2 basins, 6 jugs holding 2 pints each, 6 pint-pots, 6 half-pints, 6 quarter-pints, all of tin, two dozen table-cloths, 24 dozen napkins.

For the kitchen, a dozen copper cauldrons, 6 pairs of andirons, 6 frying-pans, 6 gridirons.

There will also be brought two yearling bulls, heifers, and sheep; as much as possible of all kinds of grain for sowing.

Trying Newfoundland, 1622

EDWARD WYNNE

Early in the 1600s, the English established colonies in the Avalon Peninsula, building on their long-term activities in the New-foundland fisheries. Edward Wynne came to Ferryland, on Avalon's east coast, in 1621. His letter of August 17, 1622, its English modernized by scholar Peter Pope, was published in England as bait to entice immigrants. For that reason, it may have been cleaned up, and its optimism is to be suspected. The colony never attracted many more than 100 settlers. Not until the nineteenth century did a permanent settler population, drawn primarily from England and Ireland, take firm hold in Newfoundland.

We have wheat, barley, oats and beans both eared and codded [podded], and though the late sowing and setting of them might occasion the contrary, yet it ripens now so fast, that it carries the likelihood of an approaching harvest. We have also a plentiful kitchen garden of many things, and so rank, that I have not seen the like in England. Our beans are exceeding good; our peas shall go without compare, for they are in some places as high as a man of an extraordinary stature; radish as big as mine arm; lettuce, kale or cabbage, turnips, carrots, and all the rest is of like goodness. We have a meadow of about three acres; it flourished lately with many cocks of good hay, and now it is made up for a winter feeding. We hope to be well fitted with many acres of meadow against another year. Of pasture land, we have already to serve at least three hundred heads of cattle; and to all this, if it please God, a good quantity of seed ground shall be fitted, and such buildings as we shall be able to accomplish.

Now in the next place it may please your Honour to understand that touching this country, the summer time here is so fair, so warm and of so good a temperature, that it produceth many herbs and plants very wholesome, medicinable and delectable; many fruit trees of sundry kinds; many sorts of berries wholesome to eat and in measure most abundant, in so much as many sorts of birds and beasts are relieved with them in time of winter, and whereof with further experience I trust to find some for the turn of Dyers.

Our high levels of land are adorned with woods, both fair and seemly to behold, and green all winter. Within land there are plains innumerable, many of them containing many thousand acres, very pleasant to see to, and well furnished with ponds, brooks and rivers, very plentiful of sundry sorts of fish, besides store of deer and other beasts that yield both food and fur. Touching the soil, I find it in many places of goodness far beyond my expectation: the earth as good as can be, the grass both fat and unctuous and if there were store of cattle to feed it up, and with good ordering, it would become a most steadfast nourishment—whereof the large breed of cattle to our northern plantation have lately given proofs sufficient, though since, they have been most shamefully destroyed. The air here is very healthful, the water both clear and wholesome, and the winter short and tolerable, continuing only in January, February and part of March; the day in Winter longer than in England; the nights both silent and comfortable, producing nothing that can be said either horrid or hideous. Neither was it so cold here the last winter as in England the year before. I remember but three several days of hard weather indeed, and they not extreme neither, for I have known greater frosts, and far greater snows in our own country. . . .

It may please your Honour to understand that our salt-maker hath performed his part with a great deal of sufficiency, by whom I have sent your Honour a barrel of the best salt that ever my eyes beheld, who with better settling doth undertake to better this which he heath made already. I shall humbly also desire you to remember my last years suit, that our delicate harbours and woods may not be altogether destroyed, for there have been rinded this year not so few as 50,000 trees and they heave out ballast into the harbours, though I look on. It may likewise please your Honour to give express order, first, that such as be sent hither hereafter may be such men as shall be of good strength, whereof we stand in need of six masons, four carpenters, two or three good quarry men, a slater or two, a lime-burner and limestones, a good quantity of hard laths, a couple of strong maids that (besides other work) can both brew and bake; and to furnish us with wheels, hemp and flax and a convenient number of west-country labourers to fit the ground for the plough.

Secondly, that no more boys and girls be sent hither, I mean upon your Honour's charge, nor any other persons which have not been brought up to labour, for they are unfit for these affairs.

Thirdly, your Honour of necessity must send some guns and a gunner with his necessaries, for the place and time do require it. It is a durable chattel; they will command the harbour and secure all.

We stand also in need of another brewing copper [kettle], some clapboards, more iron and steel, brick, some lime and tiles for a beginning, whilst the slate-quarry is in fitting.

A complete magazine of all things will be necessary with victuals, linen, woolen for apparel and bedding, with better coverlets, shoes of wet leather, Irish stockings, coarse knit hose, coarse ticks, good flocks in cask, and instead of cloth, coarse mingled kersies, and no canvas suits, nor any ready made. But otherwise, it may please your Honour to send tailors, such as will help to guard the place, and do other things. The like of other tradesmen, and all to be furnished out of the magazine, upon account. . . .

It may please your Honour, that another iron mill, and two Bridewell mills may be sent hither, and then our bread-corn may be sent unground and if at any time it should happen to take wet, it may be dried again.

We want a dozen of leather buckets, a glazier, some glue, rats-bane, two fowling pieces of six foot in the barrel and one of seven foot, with a mold to cast shot of several sizes for fowling.

The last year I showed your Honour of much courtesy received from sundry masters; many this year have done the like, though some likes not our flourishing beginning and prosperity. Howsoever, I have proceeded with a great deal of care and respect unto your Honour's commandments, to use them with all humanity.

I hope you will be pleased to send us the plough next year and guns, for the time requires it. And so conclude, resting

Your Honour's most humble, thankful and faithful servant,

Edward Wynne,
Ferryland,
17 August. 1622.

The names of all those that stay with me this year.

Captain Powell.
Nicholas Hoskins.
Robert Stoning.
Roger Fleshman, Surgeon.
Henry Dring, Husbandman.
Owen Evans.
Mary Russell,
Sibell Dee, maide.
Elizabeth Kerne. } Girles.
Jone Jackson.
Thomas Wilson. } Smithes.
John Prater.
Iames Beuell, Stone-layer.
Benjamin Hacker, Quarry-man.
Nicholas Hinckson. } Carpenters.
Robert Bennet.
William Hatch.

Henry Doke, Boats-master.
William Sharpus, Tailor.
Elizabeth Sharpus, his wife.
John Bayly.
Anne Bayly, his wife.
Widdow Bayly.
Joseph Parscer.
Robert Row, Fisherman.
Philip Jane, Cooper.
William Bond.
Peter Wotton. Boats-masters,
Ellis Hinckson. } Boyes.
Digory Fleshman.
Richard Higgins.
In all 32.

Old France Into New, 1635–36

PAUL LE JEUNE

> *The Society of Jesus, the Jesuits, continued Champlain's experiment in New France. Paul Le Jeune, the superior of the Jesuits in Quebec during the 1630s, urged emigration from France as a means of strengthening the old land as well as the new and laid down strictures for potential immigrants, both the poor and those with considerable means.*

Would it not be better to empty Old France into New, by means of Colonies which could be sent there, than to people Foreign countries?

Add to this, if you please, that there is a multitude of workmen in France, who, for lack of employment or of owning a little land, pass their lives in poverty and wretched want. Many of them beg their bread from door to door; some of them resort to stealing and public brigandage, others to larceny and secret frauds, each one trying to obtain for himself what many cannot possess. Now as New France is so immense, so many inhabitants can be sent here that those who remain in the Mother Country will have enough honest work left them to do, without launching into those vices which ruin Republics; this does not mean that ruined people, or those of evil lives, should be sent here, for that would be to build Babylons; but if the good were to make room for the bad, it would give the latter an opportunity to escape the idleness that corrupts them.

Besides, if these Countries are peopled by our French, not only will this weaken the strength of the Foreigner,—who holds in his ships, in his towns, and in his armies, a great many of our Country-men as hostages,—not only will it banish famine from the houses of the multitude of poor workmen, but it will also strengthen France; for those who will be born in New France, will be French, and in the case of need can render good service to their King,—a thing which cannot be expected from those who dwell among our neighbours and outside the dominion of their Prince.

Finally, if this country is peopled by the French, it will be firmly attached to the Crown, and the Foreigner will come no more to trouble it. . . .

Now, there is no doubt that there can be found here employment for all sorts of artisans. Why cannot the great forests of New France largely furnish the ships for the Old? Who doubts that there are here mines of iron, copper, and other metals? Some have already been dis-covered, which will soon be worked; and hence all those who work in wood and iron will find employment here. Grain will not fail here, more than in France. . . . I will content myself by saying that it would be an honor and a great benefit to both Old and New France to send over Emigrants and establish strong colonies in these lands.

"La fécondité de ce pays"

JEAN TALON

New France was hanging on by its fingernails under the intendant, Jean Talon, its population under 4,000 in 1667. But Talon understood that increasing the birth rate could resolve the problem. To meet the shortage of women, he imported the "filles du roi," unmarried women from France who came out to marry—and bear children.

Monseigneur, . . . Toutes les filles venues cette année sont mariées à 15 près que j'ai fait distribuer dans des familles connues en attendant que les soldats qui les demandent aient formé quelque établifsment et acquis de quoi les nourir.

Pour avancer le mariage de ces filles, je leur ai fait donner, ainsi que j'ai accoutumé de faire, outre quelques subsistances, la somme de 50 livres monnaie du Canada en denrées propres à leur ménage.

La demoiselle Etienne qui leur a été donnée pour gouvernante par Mefsieurs les Directeurs de l'Hôpital Général retourne en France pour prendre la conduite de celles qu'on enverra cette année; si Sa Majesté a la bonté d'en faire pafser, auquel cas il serait bon de recommander fortement que celles qui seront destinées pour ce pays ne soient aucunement disgraciées de la Nature, qu'elles n'aient rien de rebutant à l'extérieur, qu'elles soient saines et fortes, pour le travail de campagne, ou du moins qu'elles aient quelques industries pour les ouvrages de main, j'en écrit dans ce sens à Mrs. les Directeurs. Trois ou quatre filles de naifsance et distinguées par la qualité serviraient peut-être utilement à lier par le mariage des Officiers qui ne tiennent au pays que par les appointement et l'émolument de leurs terres et qui par la disproportion ne s'engagent pas davantage.

Les filles envoyées l'an pafsé sont mariées, et presque toutes ou sont grofses ou ont eu des enfants, marque de la fécondité de ce pays.

Si le Roi fait pafser d'autres filles ou femmes venues de l'Ancienne en la Nouvelle France, il est bon de les faire accompagner d'un certificat de leur Curé ou du Juge du lieu de leur demeure qui fafse connaitre qu'elles sont libres et en état d'être mariées, sans quoi les

Ecclésiastiques d'ici font difficulté de leur administrer ce sacrement,
A la vérité ce n'est pas sans raison deux ou trois mariages s'étant ici
reconnus; on pourrait prendre la même précaution pour les hommes
neufs, et cela devrait être du soin de ceux qui seront chargés des paf-
sagers.

Counting Heads, 1671

ACADIA'S CENSUS

*As Talon tried to bolster New France, the handful of settlers in
Acadia, drawn from diverse homelands, were putting down
roots. The first census in 1671 found a population of European
origin that numbered 441, not counting the cattle and sheep.*

Jacob (Jacques) BOURGEOIS, Druggist, 50; wife Jeanne TRAHAN
40; children: Jeanne 27, Charles 25, Germain 21, Marie 19,
Guillaume 16, Marguerite 13, Francois 12, Anne 10, Marie 7,
Jeanne; cattle 33, sheep 24.

Jean GAUDET 96, wife, Nicole COLLESON 64; child: Jean 28,
cattle 6, sheep 3.

Denis GAUDET, 46, wife, Martine GAUTHIER 62; children: Anne
25, Marie 21, Pierre 20, Pierre 17, Marie 14; cattle 9, sheep 13.

Roger KUESSY 25; wife, Marie POIRIER 22; child: Marie 2; cattle 3,
sheep 2.

Michel De FOREST 33, wife, Marie HEBERT 20: children: Michel
4, Pierre 2, Rene 1; cattle 12, sheep 2.

Widow of Etiene HEBERT 38, children: Marie 20, Marguerite 19,
Emmanuel 18, Etienne 17, Jean 13, Francoise 10, Catherine 9,
Martin 6, Michel 5, Antoine 1; cattle 4, sheep 5.

Antoine BABIN 45, wife, Marie MERCIER 25; Children: Marie 9,
Charles 7, Vincent 5, Jeanne 3, Marguerite 1; cattle 6, sheep 8.

Olivier DAIGRE 28, wife, Marie GAUDET 20; Children: Jean 4,
Jacues, 2, Bernard 1; cattle 6, sheep 6.

Antoine HEBERT, cooper, 50, wife Genevieve LAFRAND 58;
Children: Jean 22. Catherine 15; cattle 18, sheep 7.

Jean BLANCHARD, 60, wife, Radagonde LAMBERT 42; Children:

Martin 24, Madeline 28, Anne 26, Guillaume 21, Bernard 18, Marie 15; cattle 12, sheep 9.

Widow of Francois GUDCIN, 26; Children: Anne 12, Marie 9, Jerome 7, Huguetta 5, Francois 2; cattle 6, sheep 3.

Michel DUPOUT, 37, wife Marie GAUTEROT 34; Children: Marie 14, Martin 6, Jeanne 4, Pierre 3; cattle 5, sheep 1.

Claude TERRIAU 34, wife, GAUTEROT 24; Children: Germain 9, Marie 6, Marguerite 4, Jean 1; cattle 13, sheep 3.

Germain TERRIAU 25, wife, Andree BRUN 25; Child: Germain 2; cattle 5, sheep 2.

Jean TERRIAU, 70, wife, Perrine RAU 60; Children: Claude 34, Jean 32, Bonaventure 30, Germain 25, Jeanne 27, Catherine 21, Pierre 16; cattle 6, sheep 1.

Francois SAVOYE, 50, wife, Catherine LeJEUNE 38; children: Francoise 18, Germain 16, Marie 14, Jeanne 13, Catherine 9, Francoise 8, Barabe 6, Andree 4, Marie 2; cattle 4.

Jehan CORPORON, 25, wife Francoise SAVOIE 18; Child: one daughter of 6 weeks; cattle 1, sheep 1.

Pierre MARTIN, 70, wife, Catherine VIGNEAU 68; Children: Pierre 45, Marie 35, Marguerite 32, Andre 30, Mathier 35; cattle 7, sheep 8.

Francois PELERIN, 35, wife, Andre MARTIN 30; Children: Hugette 5, Marie 3, Anne 10 months; cattle 3, sheep 4.

Pierre MORIN, 37, wife Marie MARTIN 35; Children: Pierre 9, Louis 7, Antoine 5, Marie 3, Ann 10 months; cattle 3, sheep 4.

Mathieu MARTIN, 35; Not married and weaver; cattle 4, sheep 3.

Vincent BRUN, 60, wife Renee BRODE 55; Children: Madeline 25, Andree 24, Francois 18, Bastien 15, Marie 12; cattle 10, sheep 4.

Francois GAUTEROT, 58, wife, Edmee LeJEUNE 47; Children: Marie 35, Charles 34, Marie 24, Rene 19, Marguerite 16, Jean 23, Francois 19, Claude 12, Charles 10, Jeanne 7, Germain 3; cattle 16, sheep 6.

Guillaume TRAHAN, 60, wife Madelaine BRUN 25; Children: Guillaume 4, Jehan-Charles 3, Alexandre; cattle 8, sheep 10.

Pierre SIRE, gunsmith, 27, wife Marie BOURGEOIS 18; Child: Jean 3 months; cattle 11, sheep 6. . . .

Halifax's "Poor Idle Worthless," 1749

GOVERNOR EDWARD CORNWALLIS

The founder and first governor of Halifax, Cornwallis had no illusions about the difficulties of creating a settlement. The human material he had available—in his jaundiced but hard-headed view—only added to the difficulties.

The number of settlers men, women, and children is 1400 but I beg leave to observe to your Lordship that amongst these the number of industrious active men proper to undertake and carry on a New Settlement is very small—of soldiers there is only 100—of Tradesmen Sailors and others able and willing to work not above 200 more—the rest are poor idle worthless vagabonds that embraced the opportunity to get privisions for one year without labour, or Sailors that only wanted a passage to New England. Many have come as into a Hospital, to be cured. . . .

Many of the Settlers are without shoes, stockings or shirts, I shall be obliged to furnish what is absolutely necessary, which they shall pay in work when we build storehouses Hospitals, etc. There are indeed many come over of the better sort who tho' they do not work themselves, are very useful in managing the rest. I have appointed two or three of these Overseers to each ships Company.

Displacing the Acadians—to Admit the English, 1755

GOVERNOR CHARLES LAWRENCE

As Britain and France began to fight the Seven Years War in North America, the Acadians of Nova Scotia seemed to be a potential threat to British control of the colony. Plans were thus laid to expel them. By order of the governor, the Acadian lands were to be held intact until plans could be laid to have "English Settlers" brought to Nova Scotia.

Last night a vessel arrived from New York, by which we have it confirmed that General Braddock was attacked by the French on the

9th of July, about 9 miles from Fort Duquesne, that his army was defeated, and that the General died of the wounds he received in the engagement, four days afterwards.

As it is hard to say what may be the consequence of this most unhappy affair, you cannot be too much upon your guard against any unforseen accident or surprise, and use your utmost endeavours to prevent, as much as possible, this bad news reaching the ears of the French inhabitants.

The Transports for taking off the Inhabitants will be with you soon, as they are almost ready to sail from hence, and by them you shall hear further, and have particular instructions as to the manner of shipping them, and the places of their destination.

I am hopeful that you will, in the mean time have accomplished the directions you had in my last with regard to the inhabitants. As there may be a deal of difficulty in securing them, you will, to prevent this as much as possible, destroy all the villages on the North and North West side of the Isthmus that ly at any distance from the Fort of Beausejour, and use every other method to distress, as much as can be, those who may attempt to conceal themselves in the woods. But I would have all care taken to save the stock, and the harvest upon the ground, which can be gathered in with any safety to the men; and prevent as much as possible the French fugitives & Indians from carrying off or destroying the cattle.

When the French inhabitants are removed, you will give orders that no person presume to take possession of any of the lands, until a plan of the whole has been laid before me, and terms of encouragement to English Settlers deliberately formed and made publick.

I hope you paid due regard to the direction you had in my last, for the seizing and securing all the French Vessels, and destroying the Villages about Tatmagouche and the French Vessels there.

As we cannot use too much caution for preventing the French from rising or joining together in any kind of body to our annoyance, I would have you give particular orders for entirely destroying and demolishing the Villages of Jediacke, Ramsach &c., and every thing they find about these quarters, from which any sort of support or assistance can be had by an enemy.

Fractious Loyalist Tendencies, 1784

GOVERNOR JOHN PARR

The American victory in the Revolutionary War sent thousands of Loyalists north. Some 30,000 came to Nova Scotia and, the governor moaned, instantly began to complain.

The final Evacuation of New York having taken place, closes the Emigrations from thence, as well as from other parts, with about 30,000 Souls added to this Province, all of which, except a few lately arriv'd, have got under tolerable Shelter for the Winter, and are accomodated as well as the nature of their situation would admit. yet, not withstanding that I have used every exertion, have done every thing in my power for them, some few discontented Rascals, at the most distant Settlements, begin to be clamorous and seditious, expecting more than possibly can be done in so short a time, jealous that more is done for one Township than for another, which is not the case, &c, &c, they threaten, and I am told have wrote complaints home against me, without having them made known here, whatever they may be, I am thoroughly well prepar'd to meet. their ungenerous disposition soon shewd itself, upon a late unfortunate change in Administration, which they thought might change their Governor, if he did not comply with every request they made, some of which were highly unreasonable, they gave themselves some airs, but they had no effect with me. there are several Sufferers among them, but at the same time there are many who have been enriched by the late War, and are in far better Circumstances, than they would have been, had there not been a War. Tho they plague me with complaints, and quarrel among themselves &c, I shall continue to render them every good office in my power, and may venture to assert with great confidence, that a *very great* Majority indeed, approve of my Conduct, but there are some not to be pleased or satisfied.

The Winter has not yet set in with any greater degree of cold, than you generaly have in England, at this time of the Year, which is a very fortunate circumstance for our late acquired Inhabitants, particularly for the Disbanded Soldiers, who went so late upon their Lands.

Rich Loyalist in Quebec

WILLIAM SMITH

> *If some United Empire Loyalists gave up everything when they left the United States, a few managed to make their way north with their possessions intact. An able, influential judge, William Smith would do well wherever he was. He wrote this letter from Quebec to his wife back in New York on October 28, 1786. He had been banished from the United States, but his family had been allowed to remain.*

I have heard of, but not seen the House recommended for our Mansion here—but however lodged, you will want a House Keeper & Cook *in one Character*, and a Female Hairdresser, with under Drudges, & two Men Servants (in Addition to the one I brought with me) with a Boy. Think well of this, & if you cannot find them at N York, let Mrs. Mallet have Directions to send them out to me with your Furniture, & direct her to contract firmly with them under the Eye of Mr Rashleigh or Mr. Watson; for as with you so here, the European Poor find so many of their own Condition, as to forget their Stations and Engagemts. There will be a Saving if you can supply yourself at NY. . . .

Perhaps your Orders to Mrs. M may not rise to the Sum comitted, & this will leave you Scope for a little Finery for the Girls of the newest Fashions of which Madam Mallet is no indifferent Connoiseur. The Ladies dress here much as in England when I left it, except that their Hair is not down yet into flowing Tresses, nearly as low as the Elevation made by what at Bath is known by the Name of the *brown Bristle*. It drop'd at a Ball & not one of a 100 Ladies could give it a Name.

I have ordered no Carriage out. So my Lord D advised, and yet he has his Coach, and this Colony is all Town upon the Banks of the River, 90 Miles below this, & 180 above it to Montreal. They use a Calash in Summer, which is a coarse Sort of Double Chair, and a Cariole in Winter or Chariot-Box upon a Slay. The Roads are so good, that the Calashes run 8 Miles an Hour, and are every where practicable for a Chariot in the Environs of this City, very beautifully disposed by Nature, & not meanly improved. But I can ill spare the Time for this Sort of Conversation. . . .

The Implements of Settlement

WILLIAM BELL

> *A Scots immigrant to Perth, Upper Canada, Bell was one of the few to detail populations and, most interestingly, the implements—including nails and a lock and key—provided by the government to settlers.*

Perth settlement being formed soon after the termination of the war with the United States, and at a time when a great reduction in the army took place, a great many discharged soldiers were induced to settle there. Indeed, when I came to the place, not less than two-thirds of the population were of this description. The privates settled upon their land, but most of the officers built houses in the village, and tended not a little, by the politeness of their manners, to render a residence here desirable.

It was expected that, in 1816, government would grant the same assistance to emigrants as in the preceding year; and, under this idea, many had prepared to leave home. No assistance, however, was afforded them on the passage, but they obtained land, implements, and rations for one year, the same as those who had arrived before them. Accordingly, in the course of the summer, the settlement received a great accession [. . .] population in both of emigrants and discharged soldiers. But provisions being enormously dear, and many being dissatisfied with the treatment they received from the new superintendent, left the settlement in the course of the following winter, and went over to the United States.

When I arrived, June 24, 1817, the population of the settlement was as follows:

	Men.	Women.	Children.	Total.
Emigrants,	239	111	366	
Discharged Soldiers,	708	179	287	
	947	290	653	1890

The implements granted to each settler were as follows: a spade, an adze, a felling axe, a brush-hook, a bill-hook, a scythe, a reaping-hook, a pitch-fork, a pick-axe, nine harrow teeth, two hoes, a hammer, a plane, a chisel, an auger, a hand saw, two gimblets, two files, one pair of hinges, one door, lock and key, nine panes of glass, one pound of putty, fourteen pounds of nails, a camp-kettle, a frying-pan, a blanket for each man or woman, and one for every two children. Besides these there were concession tools, which a number of settlers in the same neighbourhood had in common; such as a pit-saw, a cross-cut saw, a grindstone, a crow-bar, a sledge hammer, &c. An officer's allowance was just the above list doubled. But, indeed, the supply that any one received depended on how he stood with the secretary. Those who enjoyed his good graces obtained more, and those who had incurred his displeasure less. Complaints were often made. but they were generally unavailing. They were too numerous to be examined. Many of them were made without just cause, and those that were otherwise, seldom reached the governor; but, when they did, he never failed to cause the grievances to be redressed. Indeed, it is but justice to say, that government, both at home and here, have scrupulously fulfilled their engagements to the settlers, and even done more for them than was promised. It is true that the settlers have not obtained their deeds so soon as they expected, but it is hoped they will not be much longer delayed. The abuses committed in the settlement, I have reason to believe, were not only contrary to the intentions of government, but without their knowledge.

Island Evils, 1820

WILLIAM JOHNSTONE

A missionary and zealous advocate of emigration, William Johnstone was not one to gild the lily and promise an easy time, certainly not in Prince Edward Island.

Charlottetown, November 29, 1820.

But another evil no less ruinous is, when a man with his family has landed in time for attending to all these things, and yet who, after casting his eyes upon a scene altogether new to him, is so astonished at the unpromising appearance of the country, that his judgement is confounded, his resolution fails him, and after vainly wishing that it were in his power to return to his native country, he becomes so wavering and dissatisfied that he cannot bring his mind to fix upon any one spot he has yet seen, but always hopes to find a place better suited to his wants and inclination. Encouraged by this delusive hope, he is led to wander over the Island, perhaps spending in taverns and travelling, his little stock of cash, which might have procured himself and family many necessaries, till their new farm had become more productive, whilst his family are doing nothing but eating up the remainder of their provisions or money till the winter comes on; and before it is over, perhaps some of their clothing must be bartered for more, and next spring he has to enter upon a farm no better than one he might have entered to the week he landed. Every thing is therefore now to do, and nothing to do it with, unless by contracting debt, which must hang like a mill-stone about his neck for many years. This is not an imaginary picture I have been drawing but one which I have seen verified with my own eyes; for to hesitate in buckling to a farm as quickly as possible after landing, is, on the part of the emigrant, to waste his small remaining substance in a fruitless pursuit.

"Dirty, Gross, and Indolent"

JOHN HOWISON

> *John Howison, a doctor, lived in Canada for about two years. On his return to Edinburgh, he wrote his Sketches, published in 1821 and applying a cool Scottish eye to the Upper Canadian "peasantry."*

The Talbot Settlement lies parallel to the shore of Lake Erie, and consists of two great roads, which extend seventy or eighty miles, besides back settlements. The object in giving it such a longitudinal form was, that a road might be opened to the head of Lake Erie, and this has consequently been effected, much to the advantage of the Province in general. The tract of country in which the settlement lies, was placed by government under the superintendence and management of Colonel Talbot, and no one can obtain land there without applying to him. At first, lots, containing two hundred acres, were given to emigrants; but, when both roads were planted through their whole extent, the quantity was reduced to one hundred acres. The settler is obliged to clear ten acres of land, to build a house of certain dimensions, and to open one half of the road in front of his farm, within the space of three years;—regulations equally beneficial to the country in general, and advantageous to the occupier of the lot.

The first view of a new settlement excites pleasing emotions. It is delightful to see forests vanishing away before the industry of man; to behold the solitude of the wilderness changed into a theatre of animation and activity; and to anticipate the blessings which a bountiful soil will lavish upon those who have first ventured to inhabit its bosom. A new field seems to be opened for human happiness; and the more so, as those who people it are supposed, by the casual observer, to have been the victims of poverty and misfortune while in their native land. But a deliberate inspection will destroy all those Arcadian ideas and agreeable impressions. He who examines a new settlement in detail, will find most of its inhabitants sunk low in degradation, ignorance, and profligacy, and altogether insensible of the advantages which distinguish their condition. A lawless and unprincipled rabble, consisting of the refuse of mankind, recently emancipated from the subordination that exists in an advanced state of society, and all equal in point of right and possession, compose, of course, a democracy of the most revolting kind. No individual possesses more influence than another; and were any one, whose qualifications and pretensions entitled him to take the lead, to assume a superiority, or make any attempt at improvements he would be strenuously opposed by all the others. Thus, the whole inhabitants of a new settlement march sluggishly forward at the same pace, and if one advances in the least degree before the others, he is immediately pulled back to the ranks.

That this has hitherto been the case, in most settlements, can be proved by a reference to facts. The farmers of the Niagara district, many of whom have been thirty or forty years in the country, and now possess fine unencumbered farms, are in no respect superior to the inhabitants of the Talbot Settlement. They are equally ignorant, equally unpolished, and one would suppose, from their mode of life, that they were equally poor. Their minds have made no advance, and their ideas have not expanded in proportion to the increase of their means. Is it then to be supposed, that the people, who now fill the new settlements of Upper Canada, and carry with them similar ideas and prejudices, will make greater progress in improvement, than persons of the same description have done before them?

Few of the farms in the more improved parts of the Province retain their original owners, who have generally been bought out by people of similar habits, but greater wealth; and new settlements have hitherto almost invariably changed their inhabitants, within ten or twelve years after their commencement. It is to be hoped, that this will be the fate of the Talbot Settlement, and that its present occupants will henceforth gradually disappear, and be succeeded by a population of a superior kind. That this will be the case seems highly probable; for emigrants of some capital now begin to make their appearance in the Province, and most of them will of course rather purchase partially improved farms at a moderate rate, than expose themselves to the hardships and difficulties that attend the clearing and cultivation of waste land. The advantages which the Talbot Settlement presents, will induce many persons of this description to take up their residence in it, more especially, as a large number of the farms will soon be offered for sale, at a low price, by their present possessors.

The Talbot Settlement exhibits more visibly than any other part of the Province, these advantages, and that amelioration of circumstances, which Upper Canada affords to the peasantry who emigrate from Europe. Nine-tenths of the inhabitants were extremely poor when they commenced their labours, but a few years' toil and perseverance has placed them beyond the reach of want. All of them have rude houses and barns, also cows and oxen, and innumerable hogs. Some of the wealthier settlers feed sheep, but on most lots the quantity of cleared land is so small, that they cannot afford to lay much of it out on pasture. Most of the settlers might live much more comfortably than they do at present, if they exerted themselves, or had any ideas of neatness and propriety; but they follow the habits and customs of the peasantry of the United States, and of Scotland, and, consequently, are offensively dirty, gross, and indolent, in all their domestic arrangements. However, these, it is to be hoped, are temporary evils, and do not at all affect the conclusions that a view of this settlement must force upon every unprejudiced mind. It is evident, that the advantages to be derived from emigration to Upper Canada, are not altogether chimerical, as has been too generally supposed; but that, in so far as concerns the lower classes of Europeans, they are equally numerous and important, as some of our most sanguine speculators have represented them to be. No person, indeed, will pretend to say, that the settlers, whose condition I have described, are in a way to grow rich; but most of them even now enjoy abundant means of subsistence, with the earnest of increasing comforts; and what state of things can be more alluring and desirable than this to the unhappy peasantry of Europe?

Great numbers of emigrants, from the Highlands of Scotland, have lately taken lands in the upper part of the Talbot Settlement. These people, with the *clannishness* so peculiar to them, keep together as much as possible; and, at one time, they actually proposed, among themselves, to petition the governor to set apart a township, into which none but Scotch were to be admitted. Were this arrangement to take place, it would be difficult to say which party was the gainer, the habits of both being equally uncouth and obnoxious. However, the Scotch, notwithstanding their dislike to an American and Canadian neighbourhood, do not fail to acquire some of those ideas and principles that are indigenous to this side of the Atlantic. They soon begin to attain some conception of the advantages of equality, to consider themselves as gentlemen, and become independent; which, in North America, means to sit at meals with one's hat on; never to submit to be treated as an inferior; and to use the same kind of manners towards all men.

I resided many months in the Talbot Settlement, and during that time enjoyed abundant opportunities of acquiring a knowledge of its inhabitants, who form a democracy, such as, I believe, is hardly to be met with in any other part of the world. The difference in point of wealth, which exists among them, is as yet too trifling to create any distinctions of rank, or to give one man more influence than another; therefore, the utmost harmony prevails in the colony, and the intercourse of its people is characterised by politeness, respect, and even ceremony. They are hospitable, and, upon the whole, extremely willing to assist each other in cases of difficulty.—But the most extraordinary thing of all is, the liberality which they exercise towards emigrants, in immediately admitting them to live on an equality with themselves; for any poor starving peasant, who comes into the settlement, will meet with nearly the same respect as the wealthiest person in it, captains of militia excepted. The Scotch and English emigrants are frequently, at first, a good deal puzzled with the consideration with which they are treated, and, when they hear themselves addressed by the titles, *sir*, *master*, or *gentleman*, a variety of new ideas begin to illuminate their minds. I have often observed some old Highland crone apparently revolving these things within himself, twitching his bonnet from one side of his weather-beaten brow to the other, and looking curiously around, as if suspicious that the people were *quizzing* him. However, those who are at first most sceptical about the reality of their newly-acquired importance, generally become most obtrusive and assuming in the end; and it is a remarkable circumstance, that, in Upper Canada, the *ne plus ultra* of vanity, impudence, and rascality, is thought to be comprised under the epithet *Scotch Yankey*.

A deliberate inspection of a new settlement cannot fail to sink mankind lower in the estimation of the observer, than, perhaps, they ever were before. Human beings are there seen in a state of natural and inexcusable depravity, that can neither be palliated nor accounted for in any way, except by referring its origin to those evil propensities which appear to be inherent in all men, and which can be destroyed or counteracted only by the influence of reason, religion, and education.

The Perils of the Voyage, 1821

JOHN M'DONALD

The sea voyage from the British Isles was often terrible, but so too was the voyage from Quebec City inland to Upper Canada.

Having, with many of my countrymen, determined to embark for Canada; little dreaming, from the flattering accounts which had been so industriously published respecting that country, of the hardships attending such an undertaking, I left Glasgow for Greenock, to embark on board the ship David of London, for Quebec, along with nearly 400 other passengers, where, having gone though the necessary steps at the custom-house, we left the quay on the 19th of May, 1821. A steam boat dragged the ship to the tail of the bank, and the wind being favourable we immediately sailed, and in 28 hours lost sight of land. Having a fair wind for this space of time, with fine agreeable weather, we enjoyed the pleasure of walking on deck, and beholding the calm unruffled face of the deep, which, combined with the bold, rugged, and romantic appearance of the coasts bordering on both sides of the firth, presented scenes that were truly delightful. But alas! the picture was soon reversed. The wind rose, a heavy gale commenced, and the waves rolled mountains high, and made a mighty noise. To see a ship making her way in the midst of a storm, over these lofty billows, is both grand and awful. We now became like drunken men, reeling and staggering to and fro. To walk on deck was impossible, and the places where the pots were erected for cooking, tumbled down, so that we could not get any victuals made ready, and some of our associates were compelled to mix a little meal and molasses, and use this composition as a substitute for better fare. The comparative want of food, and the storm together, rendered us very weak. This storm continued nine days. The captain affirmed, that he had never witnessed a tempest of such long continuance at that season of the year. During the rest of our voyage, we had stormy days now and then, but none to be compared to the former, either in degree or duration. Several times many of our company got themselves drenched with the waves of a heavy rolling sea breaking over the deck, and which also entering the hatch-hole, wetted us very much. On this account, we were completely shut up in the hold. At the commencement of the storm the weather became very cold. This circumstance, providentially, was greatly in our favour, from our being so much crowded together, which in several respects was very disagreeable to our feelings. This cold state of the weather continued till we approached the mouth of the St. Laurence, when it became so warm, that I was nearly suffocated from the smell and heat below deck. I was consequently compelled to sleep on deck, together with many others, who were in a similar situation. Every favourable day the Captain ordered all his passengers to bring up their clothes and air them. The sick passengers were also all ordered above, those who were unable being assisted. The Captain was much afraid lest an infectious fever should get in amongst us, and he himself, after landing at Quebec, was confined for some time by severe indisposition. Four births took place during our passage, but three of the children died, and a boy of four years old; another fell from the deck into the hold, and broke his arm; and had not he fallen upon some persons who were providentially at that time in that place, the event would probably have been much more serious. Having entered the Gulph of St. Laurence, we found it necessary to obtain a Pilot. The weather now became warmer, and as the wind was a-head of us, our rate of sailing became slower, and we had to cast anchor several times. This change in our rate of sailing, was greatly in the favour of such passengers as were sick, as they all recovered quickly. This was a very happy circumstance, there being no impediment to prevent our landing: the surgeon having declared that there was no fever amongst us. We consequently got all in at once, and having anchored, the Captain and several of the passengers went ashore, having ordered the Mate not to suffer any ardent spirits to be brought on board. Nevertheless, some of the passengers who had gone ashore, returned with some rum, which was taken from them and thrown over board. This circumstance caused no small disturbance, and produced blows between the sailors and the passengers, and even also amongst the sailors themselves; and till the scuffle terminated it was indeed a very disorderly night. We arrived at Quebec on the 25th of June, when we were all inspected by the surgeon, and then passed through the custom-house.

We all slept that night on board, and by 6 o'clock in the morning the steam boat was laid alongside of us, when we all set to work to get our luggage on board of it. We continued all that day at Quebec, and then went off in the steam boat at 11 o'clock at night. As we were setting out, a tremendous storm of thunder and lightning came on, the most dreadful that ever I either saw or heard; the rain was also uncommonly heavy. There were nearly 400 people on board of the steam boat, the greater part of whom were obliged to sit on deck all that night. Reader, you may easily guess our situation. I can assure you, I myself and the greater part of all who were on deck were as thoroughly drenched as water could make us, and we all had to remain drenched as we were, in our wet clothes, till they dried on our backs. We had no alternative, access to our chests being impossible, as they were all locked up in the hold; and in this state we continued till we reached Montreal.

Here we arrived in 24 hours, a distance of 190 miles. Having stated our difficulties on the passage from Quebec to Montreal, I may add, that this was the first of our trials in going up the country; and I can safely aver, to my certain knowledge, that it was the source and cause of their trouble who are now no more in this world. Nay, to show you further our distress, the beds of those passengers who were stationed on the lee side of the boat, between the engine-house and the paddles, were made literally to swim with the rain water. Every thing was spoiled, our very meal and bread being reduced to a state of dough. We now began to carry our luggage from the steam boat, Government having provided waggons in abundance. We mutually assisted each other in loading them with the women and children; and all who were unable to walk got on the top of them as far as the village of La Chine, ten miles up the St Laurence from Montreal. Here we arrived on the 28th of June, and remained 4 days; till we got as many boats as we required. We then set out all together in 15 flat-bottomed boats. Our number amounted to 366 persons. Here a very difficult part of our journey commenced, namely, the passing the rapids of the St Laurence. Some of these have a very strong current, and as the stream is very shallow and stony, the boats sometimes grounded. Then all the men who were able were neces-sitated to jump into the river to haul the boats wading up to the middle of their bodies, and sometimes deeper. At these rapids the women and children were obliged to come out and walk; and in several places, the rapids run with such a force, that we were compelled to get 2 horses to haul every boat. None but those who have experienced it, can conceive the difficulty of ascending these rapids. To me it seems wonderful how they can surmount them. Many of our unhappy countrymen suffered extremely from these hardships, on account of the intense heat of the season, and drinking too freely of the river water. In addition to these difficulties, being destitute of dry clothes, we were obliged to continue in this uncomfortable situation night and day. Many of them took badly on the road, and were obliged to remain behind their families many days. This became a very distressing circumstance to them, in going up the river. When night came, we remained on the river side. Sometimes we got access to farm houses, and sometimes not. Others lay in the woods all night, where, having kindled a fire, they would have cooked their supper in the best way they could, and spread such clothes under them as they had, for a bed. In which situation I have found in the morning my night-cap, blankets, and mat, so soaked with dew, that they might have been wrung. One may easily conceive that this was very prejudicial to our health. Some of the passengers indeed got into barns, but by far the most part of them lodged out in fields for six nights, in which space of time we made our journey from La Chine to Prescot, which is 120 miles. There we had to pitch our tents in the best way we could, in the open field—wretched dwellings indeed! One may easily judge of our situation, from this circumstance, that frequently we were under the necessity, many of us, of spending the whole night in laying the water with dishes from around our tents, which literally ran below our very beds. Here we began soon to feel the effects of our river journey, and of our lying out in the fields. There were none, I believe, but felt these in a greater or less degree. Many were afflicted with the bloody flux, some also took fevers, and many died of a few days illness. Our situation now became very alarming, the people generally complaining of indisposition. I continued here three weeks. This was the end of our water conveyance. The cause of our delay here arose from the great multitude that were lying at this place before our arrival. Here we found one half of the passengers of the Earl of Buckinghamshire, all those of the ship Commerce, and including us, the passengers of the ship David of London, the whole exceeded 1000 people; and it took a long time to carry their baggage along a road of 74 miles to New Lanark. We all had, each society, to wait its turn in getting away. Many were obliged to remain here on account of sickness, and many died. William Purdie, agent for the Trongate Society, died here, and two families were left orphans; the one belonged to Bridgeton, the other to Bathgate, of the name of Dick. This man was bathing in the St Laurence, when he first stopped at La Chine. He had gone beyond his depth into the stream, and the velocity of the current swept him away. He left 9 or 10 children. The former family consisted of two children, whose mother died on the passage in the ship Commerce.

Getting Married

ABRAHAM GILL

> *The lack of a woman's companionship was a major concern of young male immigrants. Sometimes, as Abraham Gill remembered years later of his meeting and marrying Elizabeth in 1821–22, swains had to move quickly.*

Dear Children:

Having of late an impression on my mind that I shall not be much longer in this world, I thought I would write a few lines of my experience coming through this sinful world. The first, that my father and mother sent me to school to read the Bible, some of which I have in memory still, thank God for it. Since leaving school I have been tempest lost both in body and mind, but out of all the Lord hath brought me to the present time. The first heavy trial, the death of my sister. Next came the death of my mother—these were dear earthly friends. About this time I expected my father would do something for me that I might have a home of my own. I was then 25 years old but when I applied for some help from him, which he had plenty both money and cattle, he got into an enrage and declared that I was at first to get nothing and that got up a row, and then I said if you would give me £60 I would try to get my living in some other part of the world, and would not trouble him any more, so with much angry words and bad feelings, with the advice of my brother-in-law, he was persuaded to give me £35 and then to seek a home in some foreign land, so good Providence directed me to Prince Edward Island where the Lord has blessed me body and soul.

I did not at that time understand the Almighty power God has over us. At the time of leaving my native home, little thought I was bidding my kindred and acquaintance all this time, but God's ways are not our ways, nor His thoughts as our thoughts, so bidding them farewell, so I went off at once to Devon Port to get a passage, there was a large bark there belonging to Mr. Pope about to start in a few days. I had to go home for a few things to take with me. I asked the captain what he would charge for board and passage, he said he would if I mess with the men, for £6 as I had to go home first. He expected to get half then, but I did not know whether I could. When I arrived at Devon Port the vessel was just on her way out of sight, and I hired a man and his boat to put after them and the captain seeing we were making after them, hove too the vessel till I was safe on board, but the tossing of the boat made me very sick for three days I thought I should of died in an unprepared state. We left England April 15th 1819, and arrived Prince Edward Island 15th of June among strangers except Mr. Harvies family. I then began to enquire if there was a piece of land that I could get in the neighborhood: he said go to the agent, and he will let you know, and he said there was a piece of land, which I now occupy. Having obtained a piece of land, I began by the help of the Lord, to earn a living by the sweat of my brow, although late in the season I planted some potatoes among the windfalls and stumps, not many cattle that time so I made a rough fence and they grew well. I put them in a pit for the winter.

I hired for a month for the harvest. Donald McDonald, Tracadie, for £3 a month. The board and lodging was very different to what I had been accustomed to. I labored for many who paid me in horse labor. I was now lodging at Mr. Harvies, the first winter, in their loft and after a snow storm I had to shake off the snow before I put could put my clothes on. The Lord was very merciful toward me for I was not prepared at that time to leave this world for I did not understand the plan of salvation in Christ my Saviour. Soon as the winter began to set in to get timber to build a house the coming summer, so I worked away at it through the winter, quite a new thing that I was not accustomed to. I dressed the largest of trees in the wood and some of my neighbours hauled them out, and in the month of April 1820 we began to build on the land I had cleared, about 2 acres. Malcolm Forbes plowed it for me and it produced a very good crop for once plowing. The house we built was 30 feet by 18—this is something of the past. Log house built and covered in, two windows, 12 door, 10 paneled and then I went into the swamp for moss to put between the logs to keep out the cold, and now I began to think I had a home so I left Mr. Harvies to live in my own house to labor for myself and others all that summer, and to get along in the best manner I could, but good Providence was over me which I did not understand at that time, to take care of me or otherwise I should be lost forever.

It was good Providence which sent out a young women, that I had never seen or heard of in England, was going to see her Uncle at Antigonish, who coming with a family intending to winter on the Island and go over in the spring, so God sees different to what we see. So it came to pass in the fall of the year this family came to Charlottetown and from that to Georgetown. There was one of the passengers brought out a letter for Mr. Harvie, and he came to see me, so we talked till almost dark, he said he would lodge with me for the night—I said, "Very plain accommodations for a stranger, you should have brought a young person to help me," and I believe there is. "What is her name?" He gave me her name. "Where is she from?" Exeter. I thought a young lady from such a gay city would not be happy to make a home in the wilderness. I asked the man how long she would be in Charlottetown; he said two or three days. "Do you think I could see her before she goes to Georgetown or Antigonish?" He said if I would go with him tomorrow he would take me to her lodgings, so next morning off we goes to town and went to where a family she came out with so we knocked at the door and asked to see Elizabeth, and the old man after the old Devonshire way of talking, said, "I have brought you together make what you can of it." We were taken by surprise on the start by this audience as she was so lately come and her mistress looking after her had no time to spare for talk then, so I said, "If you come to Charlottetown before you go to your Uncle's at Antigonish will you come and see the locality?"—so we parted without any further conversation for the present. There were some emigrants came in the same vessel who were living in town about Christmas. I was in town and enquired if the young lady had gone over. They had just received a letter that she was coming to town for the remainder of the winter—it was then the latter end of January, and before she hired in town, came to see Little York in the year 1821, so we made up our minds to be joined in Holy Matrimony on the 7th of February—for better, for worse, for richer, or poorer, in sickness or health until Death doth us part, which was by God's goodness 42 years and about 2 months and God knows that I lifted neither hand nor foot to do her any harm.

Setting Up in the Woods, 1823

FRANCES STEWART

> Brought up in "all the refinement of high cultivation," Frances Stewart and her family found settlement in the Peterborough area of future Ontario made for a rough life. Her diary entry from April 5, 1823, recorded her optimistic determination.

I should have liked very much to have been here at the building of our houses because they are larger than log-houses usually are, and the logs are very large. Those which form the foundation are of cedar which is a very heavy and lasting wood, and will, I think, keep it perfectly firm and steady as long as we shall want it. In a few years T. intends to build a good stone house for we have plenty of excellent lime-stone on our land. T. is going to manufacture potash; the process is simple and as it sells well he thinks it will pay the expense of clearing the land. One must pay high for labour. The common wages for a chopper are twelve dollars a month.

We have no great variety in our food as pease-soup and boiled pork make our dinner every day. We have no potatoes yet, as all we can procure are kept for planting. At first it seemed odd to dine without them, but boiled pease, pea-soup, bread and sometimes turnips do very well. We have excellent bread, and in this respect are much better off than many people at first setting up in the woods, for I have heard of two or three families in our own class, who, for the first six months had no food of any kind except salt pork for breakfast, dinner and tea, without even bread. We have excellent milk, and plenty of it.

The arrowroot is a great comfort for Bessie, and I brought barley and rice here from Cobourg so we are very well off, and I never saw three more healthy children than ours. Indeed we all enjoy excellent health; I don't know when I had a headache. The air has a delightful smell and puts me in mind of dear Allenstown. Oh, if I had a few of my friends here it would be perfect happiness. . . .

But with all this interest and pleasure we have one great want here, that of a church. It is dreadful to be without a place of worship.

There is a most skilful doctor who lives about fourteen miles off. He visits every family in the neighborhood once a fortnight, and appoints places where he can receive messages. Our names are down on his list; every one he visits in this manner pays him *three dollars a year*! He is a Scotchman, young but clever.

New Brunswick Politics, 1829

J. MULLIGAN

> *Politics in New Brunswick, at least in the eyes of one Irish immigrant to the colony, was about fighting for the spoils. It was a tough game and one viewed with embarrassment by respectable folk.*

New Brunswick,
July 9th 1829

Dear Uncle

I suppose you feel very little interest in our political squabbles on this side the Atlantic. I take very little myself—so much so that I have not yet become a naturalised citizen though I might have enjoyed that privilege five years ago. As far as I can see it is not likely ever to be my wish to take any practical part in the politics of this country. Those who take the most active part in them and who are most successful in struggling for a few crumbs from the national treasury are generally men contemptible not only in the eyes of foreigners like me—but of all good & intelligent citizens—The fact is that the rude, the noisy, the arrogant, the unprincipled &c generally rule the roast [roost?]—And the prudent, moderate, and well informed and virtuous part of the community have to look on with as much equanimity as they can command. The present is a time of considerable pecuniary embarrassment here owing in a considerable degree to the failure of last years crop—Our manufacturers are nearily as loud in their complaints as those in England notwithstanding all the advantages which it was supposed they would reap from the late tariff.

"This Ultra-Republican Spirit"

SUSANNA MOODIE

> *Upper Canada was a major adjustment for well-born British immigrants. The locals, especially American settlers, were rude and coarse, and the "ultra-republican spirit" spread to the British immigrants. Susanna Moodie's crusty condescension faithfully reflected the prejudices of her class.*

Many a hard battle had we to fight with old prejudices, and many proud swellings of the heart to subdue, before we could feel the least interest in the land of our adoption, or look upon it as our home.

All was new, strange, and distasteful to us; we shrank from the rude, coarse familiarity of the uneducated people among whom we were thrown; and they in return viewed us as innovators, who wished to curtail their independence, by expecting from them the kindly civilities and gentle courtesies of a more refined community. They considered us proud and shy, when we were only anxious not to give offence. The semi-barbarous Yankee squatters, who had "left their country for their country's good," and by whom we were surrounded in our first settlement, detested us, and with them we could have no feeling in common. We could neither lie nor cheat in our dealings with them; and they despised us for our ignorance in trading and our want of smartness.

The utter want of that common courtesy with which a well-brought-up European addresses the poorest of his brethren, is severely felt at first by settlers in Canada. At the period of which I am now speaking, the titles of "sir" or "madam" were very rarely applied by inferiors. They entered your house without knocking; and while boasting of their freedom, violated one of its dearest laws, which considers even the cottage of the poorest labourer his castle, and his privacy sacred.

"Is your man to hum?"—"Is the woman within?" were the general inquiries made to me by such guests, while my bare-legged, ragged Irish servants were always spoken to, as "sir" and "*mem,*" as if to make the distinction more pointed.

Why they treated our claims to their respect with marked insult and rudeness, I never could satisfactorily determine, in any way that could reflect honour on the species, or even plead an excuse for its brutality, until I found that this insolence was more generally practised by the low, uneducated emigrants from Britain, who better understood your claims to their civility, than by the natives themselves. Then I discovered the secret.

The unnatural restraint which society imposes upon these people at home forces them to treat their more fortunate brethren with a servile deference which is repugnant to their feelings, and is thrust upon them by the dependent circumstances in which they are placed. This homage to rank and education is not sincere. Hatred and envy lie rankling at their heart, although hidden by outward obsequiousness. Necessity compels their obedience; they fawn, and cringe, and flatter the wealth on which they depend for bread. But let them once emigrate, the clog which fettered them is suddenly removed; they are free; and the dearest privilege of this freedom is to wreak upon their superiors the long-locked-up hatred of their hearts. They think they can debase you to their level by disallowing all your claims to distinction; while they hope to exalt themselves and their fellows into ladies and gentlemen by sinking you back to the only title you received from Nature—plain "man" and "woman." Oh, how much more honourable than their vulgar pretensions!

I never knew the real dignity of these simple epithets until they were insultingly thrust upon us by the working-classes of Canada.

But from this folly the native-born Canadian is exempt; it is only practised by the low-born Yankee, or the Yankeefied British peasantry and mechanics. It originates in the enormous reaction springing out of a sudden emancipation from a state of utter dependence into one of unrestrained liberty. As such, I not only excuse, but forgive it, for the principle is founded in nature; and, however disgusting and distasteful to those accustomed to different treatment from their inferiors, it is better than a hollow profession of duty and attachment urged upon us by a false and unnatural position. Still it is very irksome until you think more deeply upon it; and then it serves to amuse rather than to irritate.

And here I would observe, before quitting this subject, that of all follies, that of taking out servants from the old country is one of the greatest, and is sure to end in the loss of the money expended in their passage, and to become the cause of deep disappointment and mortification to yourself.

They no sooner set foot upon the Canadian shores than they become possessed with this ultra-republican spirit. All respect for their employers, all subordination, is at an end; the very air of Canada severs the tie of mutual obligation which bound you together. They fancy themselves not only equal to you in rank, but that ignorance and vulgarity give them superior claims to notice. They demand in terms the highest wages, and grumble at doing half the work, in return, which they cheerfully performed at home. They demand to eat at your table, and to sit in your company; and if you refuse to listen to their dishonest and extravagant claims, they tell you that "they are free; that no contract signed in the old country is binding in 'Meriky;' that you may look out for another person to fill their place as soon as you like; and that you may get the money expended in their passage and outfit in the best manner you can."

I was unfortunately persuaded to take out a woman with me as a nurse for my child during the voyage, as I was in very poor health; and her conduct, and the trouble and expense she occasioned, were a perfect illustration of what I have described.

When we consider the different position in which servants are placed in the old and new world, this conduct, ungrateful as it then appeared to me, ought not to create the least surprise. In Britain, for instance, they are too often dependent upon the caprice of their employers for bread. Their wages are low; their moral condition still lower. They are brought up in the most servile fear of the higher classes, and they feel most keenly their hopeless degradation, for no effort on their part can better their condition. They know that if once they get a bad character, they must starve or steal; and to this conviction we are indebted for a great deal of their seeming fidelity and long and laborious service in our families, which we owe less to any moral perception on their part of the superior kindness or excellence of their employers, than to the mere feeling of assurance, that as long as they do their work well, and are cheerful and obedient, they will be punctually paid their wages, and well housed and fed.

Happy is it for them and their masters when even this selfish bond of union exists between them!

But in Canada the state of things in this respect is wholly reversed. The serving class, comparatively speaking, is small, and admits of little competition. Servants that understand the work of the country are not easily procured, and such always can command the highest wages. The possession of a good servant is such an addition to comfort, that they are persons of no small consequence, for the dread of starving no longer frightens them into servile obedience. They can live without you, and they well know that you cannot do without them. If you attempt to practise upon them that common vice of English mistresses, to scold them for any slight omission or offence, you rouse into active operation all their new-found spirit of freedom and opposition. They turn upon you with a torrent of abuse; they demand their wages, and declare their intention of quitting you instantly. The more inconvenient the time for you, the more bitter become their insulting remarks. They tell you, with a high hand, that "they are as good as you; that they can get twenty better places by the morrow, and that they don't care a snap for your anger." And away they bounce, leaving you to finish a large wash, or a heavy job of ironing, in the best way you can.

When we look upon such conduct as the reaction arising out of their former state, we cannot so much blame them, and are obliged to own that it is the natural result of a sudden emancipation from former restraint. With all their insolent airs of independence, I must confess that I prefer the Canadian to the European servant. If they turn out good and faithful, it springs more from real respect and affection, and you possess in your domestic a valuable assistant and friend; but this will never be the case with a servant brought out with you from the old country, for the reasons before assigned. The happy independence enjoyed in this highly-favoured land is nowhere better illustrated than in the fact that no domestic can be treated with cruelty or insolence by an unbenevolent or arrogant master.

Grosse Île, 1831

HENRY DEAVES

> *Immigrants put into quarantine at Grosse Île, Lower Canada, frequently suffered greatly, as did the ship's captains, who had to feed the poor wretches out of their stores. The letter from Henry Deaves, captain of the* Mary of Cork, *was not published for three years, when it became part of a campaign to remedy the immigrant shipping trade.*

Grosse Island, May 27th, 1831.

I arrived here on the 18th, with three hundred passengers, forty of whom were sent to hospital on the 18th and 19th, more or less affected with measles and typhus fever. We lost seven on the passage, viz one man, by a fall, and six children, from the want of proper attention being paid them, their parents being sea-sick. I landed the remainder of them on the 20th, got the vessel cleaned and fumigated on the 21st, and the passengers were sent on board on the 24th. The poor creatures have been on board ever since, with only eleven beds between two hundred and fifty. The straw-beds which they had were thrown overboard, and they are now obliged to lie on the boards, without a covering, the greater part having nothing on the passage but their wearing apparel, which they are obliged to keep on to prevent the boards from cutting their hips. There are mothers and their children in this state. It is inconsistent with reason to expect them to remain healthy while they are in this state. There is no constitution able to bear such treatment in these piercing nights. There are fifty of my passengers in hospital at present, and the remainder must be soon there if something is not done for them.—The people ought to be kept on shore until the vessel is liberated for, while there is such a number together there will always be somebody complaining. Dr. Poole has reported seventy-eight in hospital. There have been six deaths and a few bad cases, but the greater part of them were very slightly affected; in fact there was nothing the matter with some of them. I think it advisable to allow the vessel to proceed immediately with the passengers she has on board, as there have been but two fresh cases of measles since they have been re-embarked—or allowed to re-land them and then proceed, provided their passage be found them to Quebec. It is a sad thing to detain the vessel here such a length of time. Dr. Poole expected I would be allowed to proceed last Sunday, but there is no likelihood of it. I stated our situation to the commandant, who said he could do no more than give me a little straw for them, when he gets it. He has also told me that I will have to victual the passengers, which is a great imposition.

The Cholera Came

JOHN AND ESTHER CHANTLER

Deaths in the Chantler family from cholera were discussed from two perspectives. Cousin John wrote a contemporary diary in 1832. Daughter Esther remembered the event 64 years later; she was 12 at the time of her parents' death.

[July?] 13th, Arrived at Montreal this morning: it is 180 miles from Quebeck. The town has a very dull appearance off the water; the first street being a parcel of Wooden Houses, mostly Warehouses, and in the spring and fall the roads are so bad that one may sink up to his knees in mud. Father and Uncle went to the bank for their money, and as soon as they came back they took their Passage for Prescott. We went on board the Batteaux in the afternoon, here we met with Henry Miles of Guildford, he has been here about 2 weeks, and is upon taking a mill about 3 miles from the town. As the mill laid about half a mile from the corner[?] he walked up with us. He advised Father to stop . . . Montreal and look about him, but it was too late as Father had paid our passage.

We reached Luschine [Lachine] in the evening, where we entered the River again. The next morning we were towed by a steamer to Cedars where we had to pass through another Canal. Cedars is 24 miles from Luschine. After we were through the Canal we came in sight of a strong rapid, where there is a lock for the Boats to pass through. We staid here for the night and Father hired a room at an Inn. They all slept there except Father and myself.

In the morning I was sorry to hear that Uncle had been very ill during the night of the Cholera. They sent for Father directly and he sent the Innkeeper for the Doctor who lived a few miles off. The Doctor ordered him immediately to be put into Hot water which relieved him of the cramps, and pains in the chest. When the Doctor came again he was much better and he told us he was in a fair way of recovery. He advised Father to send him in a cart to Coto-du-lac [Coteau-du-lac], and there he could rest a day or two until the boat came up, which Father did and put a bed into the cart and made it as easy as he could. Aunt, Cousins and I went with him. Uncle bore the journey very well till we were within 1 mile of the place, when he began to get worse, and we could perceive he was getting insensible.

When we reached Coto I enquired for a room at all the Inns, but they all refused. I then inquired if there was any outhouse in the Place; they all said no, and one had the cruelty to give me this answer, "We are all Canadians here and could not think of such a thing." I then asked what we were to do. Let the man die and you shift for your-selves, answered the Cruel Man. We were obliged at last to go out on the Wharf and get on the underside of the storehouse. We then took the Bed and laid Uncle on it who was quite insensible. I then covered him over with a large trunk[?] . . . and what boards I could find so as to keep the wet off. Uncle continued to get worse and to complete our distress [?] . . . came on to rain till 1/2 past 10. Then sat down and went to sleep. Not slept long when Aunt awoke me and said [missing] It was not till then I had the least Idea of fe[ar?] . . . now remembering the danger of being near a dead . . . affected with the Cholera, and also being wet thro[ugh] . . . spread such a chill over me that I sunk down . . . Boards almost insensible, but was soon rouse[d] . . . the distress of my poor Aunt and Cousins. We then . . . Place convinced that we do no more . . . we could find some shelter, after looking abou[t] . . . time we found a barge that would shelter us, . . . here till the boat came up in the morning. As soon as it was known a coffin was made and his remains were interred in the ground about 3 miles from Coto Du Lac. Neither of us followed the coffin to the Grave.

We staid here till the 18th when the boat came up. It was a very wet day and all the Passengers had to walk 3 miles so that by the time they reached Coto they were all wet through. Father thought it would be very imprudent to go on board the boat in such a condition as it was just going off with a good wind. He therefore took our passage in a Steam Boat for 40 miles. When we arrived at Cornwall we could hear no tidings of our boat. The captain gave Aunt her Passage free. We took lodgings here for the night and next morning hired a waggon to take us above the Rapids 22 miles, but we could hear nothing of the Boat. We slept in a Barn here for several nights in the morning sister Ann was taken ill and showed symptoms of the Cholera. We used the same means the doctor advised for Uncle which gave her great ease, and in the evening she was much better. Next morning Father and another Passenger went down to the River in search of the Boat, through the woods. Sister was taken with the cramps again in the morning but they soon ceased by bathing her in Warm Water and applying warm flannels.

22nd, Sister continued the same during the day. There is no doctor nearer than Prescot, and her complaint was so mild that we did not think she needed a Doctor.

23rd, Sister grew considerably worse about 11 o'clock her arms and legs turned Black and her breath was short. Father returned at one o'clock just in time to see . . . her last she was very quiet during the last ten minutes . . . departed with a sweet smile. Father buried her un[der] . . . at the water side and raised a heap of stones over her.

To My Dear Children from there Mother

My Children I know you have often wondered why I have had so little to say of my Childhood & early part of my life not that my People or Myself have comited any crime that I have been ashamed of. [M]y Parents were poor & I can remember my Father having very poor health & I also remember seeing My Mother shed tears when they talked of coming to America but did not realize it as I did after what it ment, but my history was so sad so filled with sad events on every hand that I avoided refering to it in every way that I could had I have been old enough to have given dates but my Parents died & was buried & I could not tell the day of the month or where there remains was laid as not a friend was present to drop a tear, & my dear ones you can imagine how I have been reminded when attending funerals ever since of the difference. I was to[o] young to describe the situation of the country & when my father was taken with that dreadful desease cholera of which he died[.]

I remember after leaving the ship at Quebec we traveled in boats drawn by horses up what was called the rapids & at night we all had to stop & the night my father was taken we was stoping at a house near the river—it might have been a house for travellers but I do not know where—but in the morning we had to leave the boats, had to go on. My uncle & family went on with the boats, but my mother, John Chantler & us little ones was left behind to take our sick father in a waggon; I think we was not alowed to stay there but the boats had gone on and our luggage so we came to a place called Coto [Coteau] du lac, but it was known we had Cholera among us [and] we was not alowed even a shed. Everyone was afraid of us, would not open there doors when we went to buy milk. I often think of it & what must have been the feelings of that dear Mother—a dying husband and five little children in a strange place where every one was afraid of us—& as a last resort our dying father was laid on the wharf

on a bed with no shelter but a cart turned over it & night coming
on. There was a boat tied at the wharf that us little ones got into.
John Chantler our cousin and our own dear Mother with a lantern
watched at the side of the dying bed. A storm came up I well remember & we were so frightened as the boat rocked about on the water;
the wind blew & the rain fell. Is it any wonder my dear ones that I
have not wanted to refer to those scenes of misery & sadness but that
heart rending seen [scene] seems stamped on my memory for life &
other sceens to[o] sad to pen can never be erased while life & con-
siousness remains. My uncle lost a daughter [Ann] with that desease
& had to dig her grave himself but I do not remember weather it was
before or after my fathers death.

After we were left little friendless orphans my pillow was often
wet with tears when none but god was near. I often prayed that he
would take my dear Little brother Nat that was so dear to me as my
own life, but I seemed to have so much trouble on his account, he
being only three years old when our parents died, & when he was
blamed or corrected for any thing it seemed to hurt me more than
him & being separated as I was from my other brothers. But through
all I never lost track of any of my brothers. I do not know about my
brother Joseph but that dear lady knew where my Mother had let
him go & to whom as there was no one else to tell my uncle when he
came to look after us in Toronto from a dream he had. He came said
he could not rest.

I have here got ahead of my sad story—the death on the wharf in
the storm and darkness. In the morning my fathers remains were laid
in a coffin & just as he died taken to his last resting place by strangers,
I know not where. If I remember right the boats came on by that
time that we came on, but the journey from there to Toronto is all
gone from me. My dear ones, I am about to take a journey to Kansas
with Sophia and have not time to copy any more of my sad history &
if not spared you will see that I had put it off to[o] long.

My dear children after an absence of nearly four months I was
permitted to return to my home but it was under very sad circumstances similar to what have occured in our family several times. To
stand at the death bed of another of our loved ones taken in the
prime of life with every thing seemingly to live for, as also was the

case of his dear sisters, & me that have almost lived out my usefulness left. But such is life & we must submit to him that doeth all things well. But the loved ones all left a full assurance of that peaceful happy rest in that home . . . hands eternal in the heavens where if faithful we can all meet them. & I will again commence my sad life. Our uncle and his family left us come up Young Street; we was then left alone among strangers in a strange land but my Mother understood the straw Millinery and found she could do well at that or at least would try it. I well remember her saying to me if I am spared & have my health I think I can do well here, but that dreadful desease was rageing then in Toronto & my Mother was asked to take charge of some rooms that was aranged for taking care of the homeless & friendless orphans & she had decided to do so. The Govener of Canadas man, Sir John Colbourn, his lady, & a sister of hers, a Miss Young, seemed to take great interest in that class and they both came to see my Mother. I well remember them, they was so nice, but dear ones how they found my Mother out & wanted her I cannot tell. It seemed to please my Mother to be able to get the situation but before any thing was done only the rooms ready & us in them my Mother was taken with the dreaded desease. I remember it was sabath day she had got up in the morning to dress & was taken with Cramps in her limbs. I went for a neighbour woman & a Doctor was sent for. Mother plead with him not to have her sent to the hospital. we lived not far from it & so few ever came out alive that went there, so she dreaded it, But I well remember her sufferings was terrible. I was not allowed in the room but it was a sad day for me & I watched every move with anxious fears that our all was to be taken & in the evening she was taken to the hospital on a bed. The Dr was so nice, seemed to do every thing to save her. My dear ones, young as I was I realized that our doom was sealed. I went to see how she was in the morning; she had changed for the better but did not let me see her. I can never forget the kindness of that Dr; he seemed to feel so sorry for me & after that morning one of my brothers and I was alowed to see her & she seemed quite better, could talk to us. I do not remember how the goveners lady knew my Mother was in the hospital but she sent Jelies & Wine & lots of nice things to nourish her, & I well remember, when we went to the hospital to see her each morning, we went to the Govenment house to tell her how she was & we was taken to her room by one of the girls & she would ask all about her. There are few such ladies as her & to wards the last of that week we was told to bring her Cloths in as she was going to get up. We took the cloths in, but she had a relaps instead & gradually grew worse & our hopes were blighted. We went on Saturday morning & she did not seem to know us, was verry ill & the next morning we was not alowed to see her. The Dr said she would not know us and in the afternoon I was laying on the bed crying & I heard the Dr ask where is Mrs Chantlers little girl her Mother is gone. He was a dear man, so full of sympathy for her little ones, not many Drs like him. I asked him if we could [see] her but he said that we could not. She was burned, I do not know where, none to shed a tear over her remains, all strangers & one of my brothers and I went to let that dear lady know that she was gone & her & her sister talked so nicely to us little orphans. How often I have thought of those dear ladies & there kind & loving words & often wish I could remember more about them but god [h]as long ago taken them to himself.

They asked if we had any friends & where they had gone, gave me to understand that we would be cared for, We was then under the care of a woman that took my Mother place, & the lady herself & sister came to see about our things as we did not know where our uncle & family had gone. So she said our things had better be sold & she would see that the money was put in the saving bank of us, but told me and the woman to keep our cloths out & to keep any little things that I wished out. She seemed to want to get good places for us. Our brother Joseph was not with us in that trying time; our Mother had got a place for him with one known to us as Captain Davis, near Lake Simcoe in the township of Oro. That Lady must have known where, as she was the only one to tell our uncle when he came to look after us from a dream that he had. He could not rest; if it had not been for that dream we might have been separated as many families at that time was, one here and another there, among strangers. But through a kind & all wise providence & that dear lady I was able to keep track of my brothers. She did not seem in a hurry to get places & seemed sorry that we did not know where our uncle had gone. But the dear

old man came, but not before our things had been sold & places had
been got for Henery & Alfred.

Travel Advisory, 1832

HIS MAJESTY'S CHIEF IMMIGRATION AGENT

> *His Majesty's Chief Agent for the Superintendence of Settlers
> and Emigrants in Upper and Lower Canada published this
> admonition to "the Emigrant arriving in Canada . . . addressed
> to him in the simplest possible language."*

Previous to disembarkation arrange your baggage in a small compass,
the fewer packages the better, but have them well secured—old dirty
clothing, large boxes, and other useless articles, are not worth the carriage. If you have any provisions left, such as oatmeal, potatoes, &c.
You can sell them at Quebec at a profit, and avoid the expense of
transport, and you can purchase baker's bread, butter, tea, sugar,
and other necessaries more suited for your journey. All sorts of provisions, may be bought cheaper, and generally of a better quality, in
Montreal and Upper Canada, than at Quebec. Dress yourself in light
clean clothing. Females frequently bring on sickness by being too
warmly clothed. Cut your hair short, and wash daily and thoroughly.
Avoid drinking ardent spirits of any kind, and when heated do not
drink cold water. Eat moderately of light food. Avoid night dews. By
attending to the preceding directions sickness will be prevented,
with other serious inconveniences. When every thing is ready for disembarkation, and, if the ship is lying at anchor in the river—take
care in passing from the ship to the boat; avoid all haste, and see that
your baggage is in the same conveyance with yourself, or left under
the charge of some friend, with your name on it. If the ship hauls to
the wharf to disembark, do not be in a hurry, but await the proper
time of tide when the ship's deck will be on a line with the quay or
wharf. Passengers are entitled by law to the privilege of remaining on
board ship 48 hours after arrival; and it is unlawful for the Captain

to deprive his Passengers of any of their usual accommodations for cooking or otherwise: you may therefore avoid the expense of lodgings, and make all your arrangements for prosecuting your journey, previous to disembarkation. Should sickness overtake you, proceed immediately, or be removed to the Emigrant Hospital, in St. John's Suburbs, where you will be well taken care of, and provided with every thing needful until restored to health. Medicine and medical advice can also be had at the Dispensary attached to the Quebec Charitable Emigrant Society. This Society will grant relief to all destitute Emigrants. In Montreal there is a similar institution for the relief of Emigrants. It is particularly recommended to Emigrants not to loiter their valuable time at the port of landing; but to proceed to obtain settlement or employment. Many have regretted when too late that they did not pursue this course, and take advantage of the frequent opportunities that presented themselves for settlement in convenient situatious [sic] in Upper or Lower Canada, instead of squandering their means and valuable time to looking after an imaginary Paradise in the aguish swamps of Illinois and Missouri, or other distant regions of the Western States. There is no portion of the American continent more congenial to the constitution or habits of Emigrants from the United Kingdom, or that offer a wider field, or surer reward for industry and good conduct, than the fertile districts of Upper Canada or Lower Canada. Many Emigrants will [find] employment in the city of Quebec and its vicinity, as also in and about Montreal. Single men in particular are advised to embrace the offer; but Emigrants with large families had better proceed without delay, to Upper Canada, . . . or, to situations in Lower Canada, particularly the Eastern Townships—and if they have sons and daughters grown up, they will find a sure demand for their services. Artificers, and Mechanics of all denominations, and farming Labourers, if sober and industrious, may be sure of doing well. Blacksmiths, particularly those acquainted with steam engine work also good Mill-wrights, Masons and Sawyers, by machinery, are much wanted in the Canadas.

"My Own Wish To Go," 1833

ELIZABETH WAINWRIGHT

A reassuring letter from Elizabeth Wainwright of Wickham, England, to her mother, full of the promise of a better life in Upper Canada.

My dearest Mama will be perhaps rather surprised after my having told her my loved husband was going to Sea, at the change we have made, his appointment was a matter of great uncertainty & the benefit another uncertainty—& to tell you the honest truth, I cannot bear to be separated from him in the way we must for him to get on, we have long considered the point & have actually come to the determination of going to York, John has made many enquiries, & has many friends there, & it is much more satisfactory to ourselves to do it at once, than potter on undecided, he has fixed to go himself first, & spy the land, his present intention is to buy a few acres within a mite of York, & build a house upon it, about five hundred pounds he finds will do this, & give us a garden & field or two for Cows, here we shall sit down with every comfort, near Doctors, nurses, &c, & we shall be able to keep two maids & a man, we are informed by those there, that we might live very well upon two hundred a year, but we shall have near *four* inconsequence if Mrs. Wainwright allowing some of her principle to go there, she will draw what she would receive were it in England from ours, & as hers will bring six per cent we shall gain three per cent upon that, which will not a little benefit us, & do her no harm, we shall be able to keep a sleigh & horse to go about in winter, & a poney for Johnny to go to school every day when old enough, the property that Government will give John he will let to people to clear, & in due time if we like to build a *Summer residence* upon it & go there for a few months for a *lark we can* & make our *Sugar & candles*, now I am sure dear Mama you will see the wisdom of all this, & not think it the wild scheme you did, we shall gain a livehood for ourselves & children, & in case of English disterbances maybe of essential use to others, if we do not like it, & England looks up again, there is no manner of harm done, we can sell our property for twice what we give & return, & we fully mean to take a trip in five years to see everybody—suppose dear Mama there is a rumpus in the funds why we are beggars at once, & would not have the power of going & every year things are increasing in price there, I have just had a letter from Mary Marshall & she tells me many very genteel people families are going from there this Spring—& it is much thought of it is you see quite impossible to get on here, dear John is expensive in nothing—I am as economical as possible in the house, & yet with all our care we spent 300 last year, 70 more than our income, mind we spent no principle it was all presents, but suppose these presents cease what should we do & children increase, & if John was at Sea I could not live anywhere here upon half what we have. I must give up this Cottage & live somewhere with only one Servant, & be ever divided from my loved husband. I have felt for some time the necessity of the step, & since we can now be near York & not in wild backwoods, I know you will not think of it as you did, my only drawback is the leaving my much loved Mother, but when I think how completely we are now divided, neither can come to either, & if we were to go for cheapness to Wales or Devonshire it would be just the same as Canada, & John says as I before said we will come & visit you all in five years. This in a great degree with my-self, as well as with you, brakes the pang of parting, & leaves it that in a few years we may *yet* spend many together, for my dear husbands sake I must possitively assure you it is *my own* wish to go, he told me before we fixed it if I had any compunctions about it, & would not like it, he would not go, but I feel our own & our childrens comfort so much depends upon it that I shall now be very sorry not to go, John will himself name it to Papa, soyez tranquille my dear Mama, all if for the best, I feel a wise & kind Provedence will guide our steps—that he will soften my Fathers heart about it & comfort my own beloved my own beloved Mother, John will tell you all the plans—& I am sure you will see how rational he is & how much he has the interest of his wife & children at heart, I can hear every month from you, & it is only three weeks at the longest going by New York to get there. You see so far from going to live wild with the

Indians, I shall have to take out some nice dresses, as the Govenor being a friend of Johns I may often be at his table, & balls given by him, in a year or two his back wood property will begin to produce plenty, & we shall get so rich that we may assist relations in getting children out, & John may be a *member* of *Parlement*, & in case the Govenor takes John by the hand, he may give him some good appointment he was an intimate friend of Capn Wainwright A supper was given a short time since by a Gentleman in York to two hundred gentle folks, off silver gilt, I must intreat you will make Papa understand it is my *own wish to go* & that John is not taking me against my wish, & that I just long to have a great farm, & make butter & cheese, we shall make our own white sugar from the Maple tree & all kind of things in due time, write to me dear Mama tomorrow if you can I shall feel very anxious to hear from you, as soon as possible. John will tell you he thinks of going in a fortnight & I may go in the Autum a family of the name of Burchal Son of Mrs. Burchal with Mrs. Shirers is coming very soon & likely to return in the Autum & if so I should go with them John meeting us as we *land*, at *New York*, we have an invite to their house, & if they stay all winter in England, they will lend us their house in York to live in, in that case & perhaps in any, John will return to fetch me. The Autum is a very favourable time for me to go, it would be before I weaned, which would be not a little comfort to the child, on the Voyage *Awhile I am as I am*, & when the packets have *very few* Emagrants therefore many additional comforts, I am going to write to Aunty I do not know what she will say. John will tell you all about baby—she grows such a darling—her arm was not larger than this ◯ but the Doctor considered her quite safe, the common people here get an idea that the Doctors to make the Cowpox *stronger mix* a little *small pox matter with* it is it not entertaining. If it is fine Mrs. Wainwright is coming in the Car with the girls for a week the week after this, we have the use of Aunt Anna's house, by so doing they will see baby & see John again before he goes—I think it a good plan, babys bowels are improving. I sometimes give oil sometimes magnesia & rhubarb but oftner enjections which answer famously she has got a little cold & just now her bowels are a little the other way—I long to show her to you, I have stated the plan to Papa & asked him to let me come in the course of the summer to Harley St I have not another minute accept The most affect love of your attached daughter

Ez W.
(Do write tomorrow)

As the Canada journey is really quite settled I know my dear Mama though repugnent to her own feelings will try & make the best of it to Papa.

Eliza Aug. 1833

American Money, Canadian Distances

SCOTTISH SETTLERS

> *In the Scottish-published volume from 1834,* Counsel For Emigrants, *a letter from Fort Erie, Upper Canada, sought to counter the perception that the United States was vastly more attractive than British North America. Another letter, from Montreal this time, demonstrated how Canada's vast distances could be explained away or transformed into a virtue.*

Fort Erie, 21st September, 1833.

I have now seen part of the States and part of the Canadas, and think that a man can live most comfortably in the latter. There is little doubt but that most money is to be made among the Yankees, but then an emigrant must keep his mouth shut when he hears his country despised. Improvements of every description get on in the States with double rapidity. The American machinery is much better planned for saving labour than ours, but in farming they are very far behind us. There is a farmer of the name of Dobie, from Scotland, who settled near this upon a farm a few years ago, without any original capital, and is doing remarkably well. He has only about eighty acres cleared, but raises more wheat than his neighbours do who have double the quantity. He is spoken of for twenty miles round as being the best farmer in the district. His average is never less than forty bushels of wheat an acre. Many of the farms do not produce more than sixteen bushels an acre, and if you saw their plan of farming, you would scarcely think it would give the seed. When they thrash their wheat, they cart the straw direct to the same field. There is a farm of 161 acres which I saw near the Falls for sale, at ten dollars per acre, and reckoned very cheap, considering the situation. Wheat is selling here for 5s. per bushel; oats, 1s. 3d. per bushel; butter, 6d. per lb.; eggs, 6d. per doz.; whisky, 1s. 6d. per gallon; beef, 2 1/2d. to 3d. per lb. Servants' wages, £2 to £2 10s. per month, with board. Tea, 3s. per lb.; green tea, 4s. 6d.; potatoes are selling at 1s. per bushel; 350 bushels is an average crop per acre.

These prices will give you some idea how a farmer may get on in this country. The price of beef will seem low to you, but as a farmer may keep as many cattle in summer in the woods as he inclines, at no expense whatever, I think the price pretty fair. In winter they must be kept upon hay and the tops of Indian corn. Two men can work a farm of a hundred acres with no assistance in harvest, or at any other time, from boy or woman. They are now busy cutting their Indian corn and buckwheat; most of their white wheat was cut in July.

The taverns in the Canadas are very inferior to those in the States. In their bed-rooms there is seldom a basin, or even some other things we reckon fully as necessary.

Game is most abundant here of all sorts, but the Americans, whom I have seen, are very bad shots. I have not observed one of them attempt to shoot upon wing, although the gun is seldom out of their hands.

A farmer can settle here in style with £500, and keep as good a table as any of our lairds, but of course must attend to his business and keep at home, as servants here are much less to be depended on than they are in Scotland. I have seen a few persons in the ague, but they seem to think little about it; those near lake Erie are more liable to it than those on the lower lake. Since I have arrived I have enjoyed excellent health, with the exception of one week after landing at New

York, and all the other cabin passengers were a little *troubled* in the same way.

Doctors charge here most extravagantly, say from ten shillings to three pounds a visit, but there are few that I would be inclined to trust my life with. If Mr. — turns his attention to making and selling quack medicines, he is sure of making a fortune. They sell here very high, and are used by almost every body. If Mr. — think of coming out, he ought to become a complete chemist. There are a great many doctors, but few of them of good education.

Montreal, 10th January, 1834.

I feel it a difficult task to explain the state of the country to you according to my promise. At home you have but one opinion as to the excellence of the Canadas, but on the spot you will find many who grumble excessively, and others who praise highly. I never will advise any one to emigrate; but, if they find they can't live at home, of course they must go where they can live. Those who are pretty well at home must judge themselves whether they may be better here; but those who have nothing at home must determine for some of the Colonies, and the Canadas, in my opinion, offer advantages preferable to any of the rest. For one reason, the distance is scarcely any object; for, by the time one is here a month, distance becomes a very relative idea. A tradesman, for instance, falls out of employment in Quebec. He comes to Montreal (one hundred and eighty miles) for 7s. 6d. and has a great chance of employment there. When there, he hears of stirring times in York, and gets there (upwards of four hundred miles) for, perhaps, £3 or less, certainly not more, and never thinks that he has gone but from one door to another. At home, if one goes even to Glasgow seeking employment, he thinks the distance so great that he almost resigns the idea of ever returning. But here, going a couple of hundred miles is like taking breakfast and walking a mile or two to dinner.

Highland Scots in Inverness Township, 1834

WILLIAM HENDRY

> *William Hendry, a victim of one of the many clearances from different parts of the Scottish Highland in the 1820s, established himself in Inverness Township, Lower Canada, in what is now Quebec. His 1834 letter, written in Gaelic to his mother and translated here by scholar Ronald Black, is a rare and important one that has attracted the attention of historians. It demonstrates vividly, historian J.I. Little points out, the warring emotions that erupted in Hendry and other Highland emigrants. The emigration from North Arran in 1829, like every other clearance, broke what Little calls "a tight and extensive web of personal relations, one that would only be partly (and often temporarily) reconstituted in the new world. But, limited as they may have been, social links to kin and former neighbours clearly did much to ease the transition to life in a radically new environment."*

October the fifteenth 1834.

My dear mother, brothers and sisters.

Dear mother, I am taking this chance to write to you to let you hear that we are all well at present, thanks be to God for His mercies to us, and that we would wish that you should have the same to say; and I had expected to send you a letter at the beginning of the summer, but I went for a short while to the States (about two hundred miles from this place, seventy miles the other side of the Line), and the work I had for part of the time was making bricks, and my cousin Uilleam Ruadh was with me and another five lads from the place; and we came home, but Peter Hamilton (a friend of mine) stayed, and he asked me, if I were sending word home to you, to tell his people that he was well, and he isn't coming home for a year if he gets on all right. And I have to tell you that Johnnie from Cuithe that used to be in Lochranza is dead. He died of sickness in Quebec. May the Lord prepare us all for that time. And there's a daughter of William Kelso's from Sannox that they think is in a consumptive sickness and another daughter of Baldie Calum's that isn't getting her health at all.

But then there's no place without illness, and my friends with whom I go around every day and my mother's brother and his family are in good health, those of them as are at home, but he himself is failing very much; and they have got on well since they came to this country. They have two cows and small beasts. This year they have as much as would be a considerable help to one or two families in addition to themselves, and he says that he would consider himself never to have been happier than he is now if he had his children gathered around with him. They send many greetings to you. And my cousin Janet is in the Minister's service at present; she sends you many greetings. And my friends that I am with send many greetings to you and to my grandmother and to my father's sister Katie. And my dear kinsman William Murchie has come home and he is well. He only stayed about one week and set off again yesterday on the way to the place he was in before, about six hundred miles from here. Before that they took six months coming down by raft to Quebec. And my dear cousin Uilleam Ruadh is well, he is sometimes employed as a carpenter and works the land the rest of the time, and he has some hopes that the rest of the family will come out, but he does not know, and I can well believe that they would be better here than where they are, and many other people besides, but I am not encouraging anybody to come at the moment, for many are coming who are not pleased with this place, and I'm none too pleased with this place myself as yet, but it may be very good for all that. But I know I would be far happier if yourself and the rest of the family were here and also the large number that came to this place at first. They came through many a trial after arriving that the folk who are coming now [are not] getting. . . . If I were expecting you to be coming here I would start preparing for you here and I would go away and earn for a year to help you come out. I don't know whether I am doing well by you to be staying here or not but it's [here] I'd prefer to be. You are showing your concern for me every time you get the chance to and [I] ought not [to be too] concerned about you. I am distressed that it has been so long since I have seen yourself and all my dear kinsfolk who are there, but I hope that I will see you either here or there before too long, if that is the Lord's will. This place is pretty tedious to be in sometimes, we can see nothing around us but the forest and the skies above. The winter here is just long and cold. We are having snow at the moment.

And I don't know any of my kinsfolk there who might not with His help do very well here once they were over. Some of the land is just fine and some pretty useless, some is very swampy, stony and rocky but a lot of it is very good for people's needs.

I send many greetings to yourself and to my grandmother and to all of my paternal and maternal uncles and to all my maternal and paternal aunts and to all my male and female kin though I can't mention them just now.

Virtues of Upper Canada

GEORGE MENZIES

> *A Scottish schoolteacher settled at Chippawa, in the Niagara area of Upper Canada (now Ontario), George Menzies offered a comparative view of the virtues and disadvantages of three likely areas of settlement. His comments on the "banditti" in Lower Canada were provocative.*

Chippawa, Nov. 30, 1834.

What place is the most eligible in general for a native of the British islands to emigrate to? I answer, unhesitatingly, Upper Canada— that, in my opinion, is emphatically *the* country for a poor man with "thews and sinews," aided by a willing mind and steady habits. In no other place will industry meet with a surer ultimate reward than in this section of the British empire; but let it be remembered that industry is a *sine qua non*. As I have no reason, however, to suppose, that the people for whom I write are to rely on the authority of mere assertion, I shall state the grounds of my preference for Upper Canada when compared with the Lower Province or the States. With regard to the former, the winters are longer and much more severe; and, in summer, the heat is perhaps more, certainly not less, oppressive. The harvests there, being from five to eight weeks later than here, necessarily render the crops much more liable to be injured by early frosts. Last year, I know that, from this very cause, they were all but a total failure. Having resided, during the summer of 1833, in the neighbourhood of the township of Leeds, from which you have some highly-coloured accounts in your "Counsel," &c. and which is, perhaps, one of the most flourishing settlements in the interior of the province, I am enabled to lay before you the true state of matters there. Now, I do know, that although a few of the older inhabitants, after years and years of toil and hardship and privation, such as a reasonable, though distant prospect of ultimate success alone could have enabled them to surmount, are just beginning to realize some of the fruits of their labour, in the shape of tolerable houses to dwell in, and, perhaps, nearly enough of such homely fare as the country produces to subsist upon; by far the greater number still remain in a state of destitution, equalled only by that which many of them left in their native Ireland. Many a family have I known to live for weeks exclusively on potatoes. It is to be hoped, however, that when the new Land Company commences its operations, some of the evils under which the settlers at present labour will be obviated by the opening of land and water routes of conveyance—for the latter of which the country possesses many facilities—and the consequent introduction of more intelligent and wealthy emigrants. Still there is one paramount drawback, which such a remedy will be long in reaching, viz, the precariousness of the climate. One other circumstance would have considerable influence in deterring me from settling in Lower Canada, and that is, that such of the old country people as have not joined that party in the province which is headed by Papineau, and the rest of the revolutionary *banditti* who compose the majority of the House of Assembly, have virtually no political existence. A jealousy of British people, and a bitter, now no longer disguised, but openly avowed, hatred of British supremacy, manifest themselves in a greater or less degree through every department of French Canadian society.

Between Upper Canada and the (so miscalled) republic in its neighbourhood, very few emigrants from Britain, I suspect, if they take a little time to "look on this picture and on that" before fixing on a final "location," will have much difficulty in choosing; for, however much we may have been accustomed to grumble at the unequal pressure of "tolls and taxes," and to shrink from "the rich man's contumely and the proud man's scorn," while we remained at home, we find, on a nearer examination, that universal suffrage, vote by ballot, voluntary churches, and all that sort of thing, do not make the people a jot more satisfied with "the powers that be"—do not turn *chucky stanes* into gold, nor earth into heaven, after all. Children as we are of the mightiest nation on the face of the earth, and proud as most of us are of the relationship, we do not feel very comfortable under the contempt of a set of upstart pretenders of yesterday to national, moral, and intellectual superiority. It is amazing to hear with what singular effrontery, and at the same time, be it observed, inconsistency, seeing they characterise the head of their own oligarchy—for such it in reality is—as the most despotic tyrant of modern times: it is amazing, I say, to hear how well educated, and, in other respects, intelligent men, will talk of the British as a nation of slaves, and predict, with oracular solemnity, the certain and speedy downfall of our own old indomitable island-home. Now, it is easy for people on your side of the water to philosophise about the absurdity of allowing such matters as these to fret one's temper; but when our native land has become to us but a fondly-cherished memory of the past, and the billows of a mighty ocean are rolling between us and the home of our earliest and best affections, you may rely on it we regard these things with very different feelings—but it is not sentimentalism you want.

I am far from meaning to insinuate, however, that all Yankees are disposed to underestimate you on account of your country, and I am aware that *all* old countrymen do not feel reproaches of that nature with the same degree of acuteness. Still, as many little jealousies do, in general, subsist between them, I would seriously advise every emigrant, as if he were my own brother, to "look before he leaps," as he may otherwise have occasion to "repent at leisure" having taken a step which it will then no longer be in his power to retrace. But this caution does not particularly apply to unmarried men, whose object is present employment, and not a permanent settlement. Such persons, and even married mechanics, may remain some time in the States, if they feel so inclined, and can meet with good encouragement; although of that the chances are at present more in their favour in Canada. To those, however, who intend purchasing land,

I repeat my advice to consult the "town-clerk of Ephesus." Only think of the probability of a war between the two countries; which I pray God may long avert, for the sake of both. Remember, in America, whether in the States or Canada, you must be a soldier.

Duty and Faith, 1837

ELLEN OSLER

Ellen Osler was thirty when she married Deacon Featherstone Lake Osler ("Fed") in 1837, in Falmouth, England. Two months later, they sailed from the coast of England for Quebec City and then made their way to Tecumseth, Upper Canada. The first section of this letter was written to Ellen's sister-in-law, Lizzy, on the ship when it was about to arrive at Quebec City; the second part was a product of Quebec City itself. Featherstone was to be appointed a minister of the Anglican Church and given charge of the parish of Bond Head, where his job would be to evangelize the pioneers. As a result of the research of historian Estelle Bouhraoua, we know that Ellen Osler went to Canada to help her husband because it was their godly duty to obey the orders of Featherstone's hierarchy. Although she was not happy to leave her beloved country as well as her family and friends, she made up her mind to make the best of her new life.

May 20th

My very dear Lizzy will not, I hope, object to her sister Ellen's crossing these lines so fairly written by her dear brother. I am not going to write any lengthy apologies, but if my scribble is so written as to be decipherable with difficulty, it is owing to the unsteadiness of the old *Bragila*. We have a brisk fair wind carrying us up the St Lawrence, and the ship rolls pretty much when there is anything of a breeze, yet I am willing to get on with my writing, as we may not have much time at Quebec. Long before you receive this I hope you may hear of our safe arrival there, as we purpose writing by post to your Mother and my Aunt. Our voyage has already been prolonged far beyond the time I had calculated. From 3 to 5 weeks I understood to be the time generally given, but find 7 is a common passage. The disappointment has made it much more tedious than otherwise. Yet we have not reason to complain. Free from sea-sickness since the morning after I left England is a cause for much thankfulness, and though for a fortnight we experienced very bad weather, and had no comfort by day, or rest by night, we received no damage to our ship or distress of any kind. He who is "the confidence of the ends of the earth and of those afar off upon the sea" will, I trust, bring us in safety to a quiet resting-place, which I think I shall enjoy, however humble it may prove; since that memorable day, Feby 6th, I have had little else than journeying by land and voyaging by seas. The latter has a tendency to make me very lazy, which spirit I hope will disappear before settling down at Tecumseth. My dear Fed rather encourages me by making the bed, tending me to dress, and in numberless little things. He means it as kindness; as such I receive too; only if the effect produced us to bring on bad habits, it will prove a sad thing, will it not? An account of our voyage you will have in F's letter to his Mother, so I need say but little. As expected, we find Scadding an agreeable addition. We were all disposed to like him the little we knew of him before leaving, but he improved much on a closer intimacy. We have nice chats about Canada, and thus will be likely to feel ourselves at home there much sooner. It is also pleasant for my dear Fed and him to talk about their College affairs: he speaks so highly of Mr Simcoe and family, with whom he usually spent his College vacations. Mr and Mrs Simcoe sent a book to each dear F and myself with their most kind regards and Christian love. Francis Tincombe is rather a more troublesome boy than we anticipated. He has no mind whatever, and is pleased when he can get amongst the men. I pity his mother, who most likely is looking forward to a son being with her able to conduct the business of the farm. Unless he vastly improves he will be no acquisition to her household. Alice Trupp proved just such one as her first appearance led to expect; a superior, confidential servant, she has only within a few days got over her sensitiveness, poor girl; but withal she has borne it very well, and says she shall now be prepared to undertake her homeward voyage, if spared to return, in 4 years' time. I have not needed her services, my dearest Fed is so close and kind an attendant. I find he has already mentioned the probability there is of my adding another to the family. You will, my dear Lizzy, be pleased at this. We neither of us felt over-anxious about the matter, though I believe I hoped I might not have children, yet now I feel no uneasiness of mind, and trust that all will be well with me. I am surprised to find myself so well under such circumstances, for which mercy I cannot be too thankful. Our gracious Lord is all-sufficient, and is able to help me through all; therefore in Him I will trust, committing my care unto him. Often, very often, do we talk and think of you. At this time I fancy you scattered, and the house closed; dear Aunt and Uncle Bath, with Henrietta, snugly settled at the Mumbles; you and your dear Mother at Portreath, and little Minny with Mary. Dear child, she was up in bed when we left, and we did not see her to give a parting kiss, which we both much regret. Our supply of oranges were a great luxury, and led us again and again to thank the kind donor. The time will seem very long till we hear from some of you, and our patience will be in full exercise. I trust that my dearest Charlotte has ere this recovered her spirits, and that they all get on better without me than they expected.

22nd There was so much motion in the vessel I was compelled to leave off on Saturday, and in the afternoon all of us felt the inclination to "turn in" for an hour. The Captain regularly takes a snooze then; the stewart was scrubbing out the cabin. All in a moment there was a great commotion on deck; the Captain flew up half asleep, the rest (except myself and Alice) soon followed. The ship had been running for 3 days with a fair wind, but the weather so very thick as to prevent them getting a sight of land or the lighthouse on the island of Anticosti. All at once land was seen, and so very close as to occasion a little alarm, but they quickly put the ship about and all was well. We discovered that we were a considerable distance farther than we thought. Yesterday morning we took a pilot on board, and are now at the entrance of the river, not more than 170 miles from Quebec, but with a foul wind, against which and a strong current it is impossible to beat. We have land on either side, the river 25 miles across. The same parts are visible now that were in sight yesterday morning, so judge of our progress. Dear F or myself will conclude his when at Quebec, if spared in the meantime. I have to write two or three others, and am with most affectionate love,

Your friend and Sister,
Ellen

Quebec, May 31st, 1837. My dearest Fed is so fully employed that he will not be able to write near so much as he intended; therefore, dear Liz, you and Henrietta must excuse your letters not being finished by him. We are detained in this place a week at least, the Bishop having purposed to admit F to Priest's Orders next Sunday, when Mr Scadding will be ordained Deacon. They have to attend to-morrow at ten, for examination. The Bishop has asked F to preach a charity sermon on Sunday evening, and he has much trouble about getting all the luggage from the ship to a suitable place till we leave, which will be by the first conveyance next week. Many have called on us, and these calls must be returned, or they will have little opinion of English politeness. Fed's time is therefore fully taken up. I can't say I enjoy my solitude at the inn, but I bear it patiently as I can, often wishing that you and others of my beloved friends were with me. We are quite pleased with the city of Quebec. The houses in Upper Town are good, and those we have visited furnished with every comfort. The roofs of the houses are covered with tin cut in squares as our slates. It had a beautiful appearance when the sun reflects on them, being just like burnished gold. Most of the people are Roman Catholics, and kept by the Priests in great ignorance. Mr Vachell, an itinerating clergyman, spent an evening with us, and lamentable was the account he gave of their destitute state. He, dear man, "preaches not himself but Christ Jesus the Lord," and the blessing of the Lord has followed his labours in very many cases. He has convened a meeting at his lodgings this evening of as many clergy and good men as he can muster for prayer and profitable conversation. He is going to visit the villages down the river, and may make some stay at St André, where Howard lives. By mistake we brought away this book, supposing it to belong to Mary. Please return it with our kind love and hope ere this she has recovered even more than her usual health.

The weather is very beautiful but warm, and I fear that going up the river and canal we shall find it *more* than warm. We did not calculate on being so long on our passage or should have left out summer as well as winter clothing. Beseech the Lord for me, my dear Lizzy, that I may be fitted for all there is before me to do and bear. He has said, "My grace is sufficient for thee," but my faith is weak.

May He bless and keep you is the constant prayer of yours sincerely,

Ellen

Women's Work, 1841

ROBERT MCDOUGALL

> *"The work is neither servile nor at all heavy," McDougall told young Scottish women in his emigrant's guide to North America, greatly exaggerating the virtues of domestic and farm work in the New World.*

I think that it is my duty, in the beginning section, to mark out who is, and who is not, suitable for the journey and for the country about which we speak, and that is Upper Canada; for it is the area of the country which I am observing at present. I am so eager to give good directions in this matter that I will address the young women first.

For young girls, and for spinsters, I do not know, although it is a great claim, if there is a land as good as America. Both work and marriage are easy to be had for them there; and the work is neither servile nor at all heavy. There is no mention of creel or hoe, of the strand or peat bog in that place; and it is not fashionable for women to be working outdoors there, at least no farther than to bring a water pail or firewood through the door. Poor service is the custom of the country, and four *dollars* a month is the common wage a servant receives. I would advise every young woman, who is neat, and who has permission to travel, to do her utmost to get over there without delay. She need not take a bundle of shoes with her, for footwear is as inexpensive over there as it is here; but let her take plenty of clothes with her, if she is able, particularly of that sort that her mother and grandmother used to make, which some call *stuth* while others say *camlet*. This clothing is exceedingly useful in the winter, for it is warm and snug, and it is not prone to catch fire like cotton clothing. The spark which jumps from the fire (for there will be sparks as large as a pullet's egg exploding now and again from the fire in America) will go through a cotton gown as quickly as a musket ball would go through a winnowing-fan; but it will fall away from the *stuth* as if it met a coat of tempered mail.

Before I bid farewell to the young women, I say freely and clearly to the one who decides that she will not be obedient and useful to her mistress, or to her own husband (if one accidentally falls for her deceit), that she not go over there to deceive the unsuspecting; let her remain where they know her, and her ways. If she is not respected over here, she will not be any more valued over there, once they come to know her; and flitting from one residence to another every month is too troublesome and too costly in America.

Much Better Off

JAMES THOMSON

> *James Thomson was a Scottish baker's apprentice who came to Canada in 1844, when he was in his early twenties. The first letter is written to his wife, Mary, shortly after he arrived in Quebec; the second is addressed to his father twelve years later, informing him of his infant son's death and furthering plans for his family to join him in Edwardsburgh, Canada West, now Ontario. A postscript was added to sister Helen. Alexander, or Sandy, was James's brother; he seems to have been a blacksmith, like his father.*

June 26, 1844

Dear Mary

I thought when I left Scotland that by this time I would have been able to give an opinion as to whether it would be advisable for a person to emigrate, but I have seen too little of this country and I feel that I have far too little experience to say anything decided on important a matter where so much depends on the individuals own disposition and exertions. A person who intends to emigrate should be fully resolved in his own mind that he can leave home and friends, and at least for some time put up with fatigue and disapointment but on no account get disheartned, always hope the best. There is no doubt cases of poverty and suffering in this country, but I can safely say that so far as I have seen the great mass of the people are much better off than in Scotland. Tradesmen in Montreal are much better paid than same classes in Aberdeen and farm servants in the country are better too. As to settlers with small capital I have not seen any of them yet but I believe that with industry and economy they can in a few years better their condition vastly more so than in Scotland. At least those who have families have a much better prospect of seeing their children provided for in a decent way. When you write you might mention whether Sandy says anything about coming to this country. If he were resolved to come I should be most happy to do all in my power to give him advice and assistance. There is not a better paid trade in Canada than a blacksmith.

Edwardsburgh June 24th 1856

Dear Father

Yours of 27th May has arrived. I am sorry to learn by it that Sandy is still so weak as to be unable to come with you to Canada.

I am also sorry to inform you that on your arrival in this country you will not see your little grandson. He who while on earth took little childern in his arms and blessed them, has called the spirit of our little boy home to heaven before it had time to be tarnished by sin. We bow with humble submission to the Divine will knowing that the Judge of all the earth will surely do right. Our loss will be his eternal gain. Henry Alexander was a fine healthy child, I may say he never had a days sickness until the third of this month when he was attacked with Scarlet fever, which terminated fatally on the morning of the eighth. Had he been spared he would have been twelve months old tomorrow, but he is gone. He cannot return to us but we shall go to him.

By the time this reaches you, you will likely have your arrangements for crossing the Atlantic pretty nearly completed. At all events I do not think that I could tell you anything about that but what you already know. I shall therefore say nothing about that but endeavour to give you some information as to how to proceed when you get to this side of the ocean. On your arrival at Quebec it may be that your ship will not at once get to a wharf but may have to anchor in the river. In that case if there are many passengers it might be well for one or two of them intelligent and active men to go to the office or go on board some of the Montreal Steamboats and make arrangements for all those who wished to go to Montreal. By so doing it is probable that they might send a Steamer alongside your ship to take off passengers and Baggage which would save going ashore in small boats and carting to Steamboat wharf. The Captain of your ship might do something in this matter as it is his duty to see you landed.

If you want any information or have any grievance to complain of you best apply to Mr Buchannan Emigration Agent. He or some of his clerks will likely come on board your ship on her arrival. When you get to Montreal you will find plenty of Steamboats ready to carry you up the river. The Kingston Mail boats or the Ogdensburgh boats are either of them good and come from Montreal to Matilda in from sixteen to twenty hours. As they do not come through the Matilda Canal, they do not have any stopping place here. Those boats that come through all the canals and stop here are a smaller and slower class, unable to go up the rapids, whereas the fast Boats go up all the rapids except at two places. I think it would be well for you to have a few lines ready addressed to me and when you get to Quebec and find out when you are to start for Montreal, pencil down the time and drop in Post office. You might do the same at Montreal and it is probable that I might get word in time to meet you at Matilda. If not, on your arrival at the latter place you might put your luggage in the Store house on the wharf and go to Gordon Brouse or some other Tavern Keeper and they would bring you up here—about five miles.

When you leave the ship you will require to have your luggage in as handy a shape to lift about as possible. Keep them as well together as you can and recollect how many pieces or packages you have. You will be one night between Quebec and Montreal and one between

Montreal and Matilda So that you will want some of your bed clothes as the night air may be cool. You will probably have to sleep on top of your luggage, or among boxes and barrels, that is if there is a crowd of Passengers. Write when you engage your passage and know when you are to leave Aberdeen. Wishing you a safe prosperous and pleasant voyage I must bid you good night

> Your affectionate son
> James Thomson

Dear Sister

In reply to your enquiry about bringing blankets and pillows, Mary thinks you had better bring what you can conveniently unless you can dispose of them to good advantage at home, as such blankets as you have would cost high here and feathers are scarce. Only mind and not burden yourselves with too much luggage. When at sea you will require considerable bed clothes as it is sometimes very cold. Your chamber and cooking utensils will have to be tin ware as far as possible, and you will have to keep your provision chest well packed in case of rough weather. A tin can (with narrow mouth) large enough to hold your daily allowance of water would be very convenient. The children will likely be sick at first but they will soon get over it.

> Hoping soon to see you I remain your
> Brother James Thomson

"So Many Joyous Beings"

AN IRISH OBSERVER

> *An Irish chronicler contrasted the joyous immigrants aboard a German ship with the despicable conditions prevalent on the Irish emigrant vessels that fled the famine.*

All of them without a single exception, comfortably and neatly clad, clean and happy. There was no sickness among them, and each comely fair-haired girl laughed as she passed the doctor, to join the group of robust young men who had undergone the ordeal.

As we repassed the German ship, the deck was covered with emigrants, who were singing a charming hymn, in whose beautiful harmony all took part; spreading the music of their five hundred voices upon the calm, still air that wafted it around. As the distance between us increased, the anthem died away until it became inaudible. It was the finest chorus I ever heard—pleasing to see so many joyous beings, it made me sad when I thought of the very, very different state of my unfortunate compatriots.

The Maritimes Labour Market, 1849

REVEREND JOHN MULHOLLAND

Immigrants arrived in North America expecting to find work at once. But in a seasonal economy, jobs were scarce and "labor in the country is indeed hard."

Collegiate School
Windsor, NS
March 21, 1849

My Dear Geo Kirkpatrick,
    . . . Emigration is a difficult part to speak upon. I should wish I could say something satisfactory on this point in order that you might communicate it & those who feel inclined to seek for support in a land less distracted than by our poor native land. I can only speak of Nova Scotia & New Brunswick. What I have strictly investigated. When a workman or labourer comes to either of these provinces he may get work almost regularly from April 15 to nr. [November] 25 perhaps later at 3/6 to 5/- per diem currency i.e. 2/- British being equal to 2/6 currency in dry season he can get £5 per month = £4 British. If honest & industrious he can get 24 to 26 currency per annum paid monthly—(the usual engagement) & his board in a family. I pay mine 24 & his board & I could not get one for less, & I must have a

man to cut & chop the wood for the fires & attend the cows & farm
of 18 acres which are attached to the establishment. Again during
the winter i.e. from Nr. 25 to April 15 a labourer may or may not get
work—It requires tact & skill to chop & fell in the woods & as a man
is paid by measurement A native can do more in 1/4 day than a new
comer can do in a day conseqently can earn wages—the general way
a colonial—a poor man I mean—acts is this—he works for others
from April to Nr.—he gets a bit of land & during the winter clears it
that is cuts down the trees to a level with the snow which may be 2–3
or 5 feet high—he then leaves the stumps & when the snow has gone
off he scrapes or tears ruffly up the ground between the stumps sows
his grain & leaves it till Autumn—This is what is called clearing
ground, but the stumps begin 3 to 6 or 8 years before they are rotted
when a fire is put in them, & what remains is easily torn up by leavers
& crow-bars—These appeared strange to me at first but even now I
am become accustomed to them & think nothing of seeing whole
acres on fire, by which it sometimes happens the fire spreads, [deso-
lates?] for miles—Travelling from here to Halifax there are more than
2000 acres of bear poles sticking out of the ground to a great height, so
caused by the spreading of fire. I think thru the south of the states—
New Orleans is the best place, but not by any means New York or
Philadelphia which are overtaken already, & those who have been
induced to go hence to them have returned. All work is done cheaply
there & consequently cant afford high wages—besides an ordinary
laboring man can do only in the fields & must move backward—but
how do this if he have not the means—I fear too many leave Ireland
expecting people to be on the quays offering them work on landing
whereas the poor people have to look for work & wait even for it.
The very day we landed at St John a vessel full—300 passengers
landed, & they thought they had nothing to do but go to work—so
far from it for weeks they did not get work, & a clergyman Dr Gray
told me afterwards—a subscription had to be raised for the poorest
& those who could went off to the states in search of work & money.
But again if a man can work & is willing to work & not be contami-
nated or enter into leagues with the workman throughout the provinces for high wages, he will do very well. I shall be very happy to

find out & communicate any information I can if it be desired [for?] persons about to emigrate—the advice I would venture to give viz— Let them choose whether they will work in the agricultural parts or in the towns for they are totally distinct & different. Labor in the country is indeed hard, & owing to the long winter, when no farm work can be done, the spring work is urged on with severity to keep pace with the rapid growth. Now not a blade of grass is in the fields & a month or 6 weeks hence & all will be luxuriant, & every flower in bloom.

A Plea for Black Emigration to Canada, 1852

MARY SHADD

Mary Shadd was a black Quaker-educated writer and journalist, writing for the "information of colored emigrants," and publicizing Canada's virtues as a country of settlement. There was increasing anti-slavery sentiment in Canada, she argued, and no hope for the abolition of the institution of slavery in the United States.

The population of Canada consists of English, Scotch, French, Irish and Americans; and, including coloured persons, numbers about 1,582,000. Of the whites, the French are in the majority, but the increasing emigration of Irish, Scotch, English and other Europeans is fast bringing about an equality in point of numbers that will be felt in political circles. In Canada West the French are in the minority.

The disposition of the people generally towards coloured emigrants, that is, so far as the opinions of the old settlers may be taken, and my own observation may be allowed, is as friendly as could be looked for under the circumstances. The Yankees, in the country and in the States adjoining, leave no opportunity unimproved to embitter their minds against them. The result is, in some sections, a contemptible sort of prejudice, which, among English, is powerless beyond the individual entertaining it—not even affecting *his circle.* This grows out of the constitution of English society, in which people are not obliged to think as others do. There is more independent thought and free expression than among Americans. The affinity between the Yankees and French is strong; said to grow out of similar intentions with respect to political affairs: and they express most hostility, but it is not of a complexional character only, as that serves as a mark to identify men of a different policy.

Leaving out Yankees—having but little practical experience of coloured people—they (the French) are predisposed, from the influence alluded to, to deal roughly with them; but in the main benevolence and a sense of justice are elements in their character. They are not averse to truth. There is a prevailing hostility to chattel slavery, and an honest representation of the coloured people: their aims and progressive character, backed by uniform good conduct on their part, would in a very short time destroy every vestige of prejudice in the Province. . . .

Coloured persons have been refused entertainment in taverns (invariably of an inferior class), and on some boats distinction is made; but in all cases, it is that kind of distinction that is made between poor foreigners and other passengers, on the cars and steamboats of the Northern States. There are the emigrant train and the forward deck in the United States. In Canada, coloured persons, holding the same relation to the Canadians, are in some cases treated similarly.

It is an easy matter to make out a case of prejudice in any country. We naturally look for it, and the conduct of many is calculated to cause unpleasant treatment, and to make it difficult for well-mannered persons to get comfortable accommodations. There is a medium between servility and presumption that recommends itself to all persons of common sense, of whatever rank or complexion; and if coloured people would avoid the two extremes, there would be but few cases of prejudice to complain of in Canada. In cases in which tavern keepers and other public characters persist in refusing to entertain them, they can, in common with the travelling public generally, get redress at law.

Persons emigrating to Canada need not hope to find the general state of society as it is in the States. There is, as in the old country, a strong class feeling—lines are as completely drawn between the different classes, and aristocracy in the Canadas is the same in its mani-

festations as aristocracy in England, Scotland and elsewhere. There is
no approach to Southern chivalry, nor the sensitive democracy prevalent at the North; but there is an aristocracy of birth, not of skin,
as with Americans. In the ordinary arrangements of society, from
wealthy and titled immigrants and visitors from the mother country,
down through the intermediate circles to Yankees and Indians, it
appears to have been settled by common consent, that one class
should not "see any trouble over another"; but the common ground
on which all honest and respectable men meet is that of innate hatred
of American Slavery.

The conclusion arrived at in respect to Canada by an impartial person is that no settled country in America offers stronger inducements
to coloured people. The climate is healthy, and they enjoy as good
health as other settlers, or as the natives; the soil is of the first quality;
the laws of the country give to them, at first, the same protection and
privileges as to other persons not born subjects; and after compliance
with Acts of Parliament affecting them, as taking oath, they may
enjoy full "privileges of British birth in the Province." The general
tone of society is healthy; vice is discountenanced, and infractions of
the law promptly punished; and, added to this, there is an increasing
anti-slavery sentiment, and a progressive system of religion.

Trapped in Quebec

JOHAN SCHRØDER

> *An 1860s warning to potential Scandinavian emigrants centred
> on the port of Quebec City, "the worst den of robbers an emigrant
> may be trapped in."*

For the Norwegian who sets out to leave the narrow valley of his forefathers it is difficult to know what is fact and what is pure invention
in the many accounts of the New World that are pressed upon him. It
is therefore high time that something be done to help him to distinguish between truth and falsehood in matters that are of vital interest
for the emigrant and his family.

At home the emigrant who seeks advice on where he should settle in America faces prejudice from all quarters. If he goes to the bookstore and demands guidebooks for these to-him-unknown territories, he will as a rule be given accounts published by public or private landowners and speculators who all praise the glories of their own land and recommend the cheapest and fastest route to these unequalled treasures. Should the emigrant wisely decide to disregard these biased and generally untruthful accounts, his only recourse is to seek information on the spot—in America. But on his arrival in Quebec he will soon discover that he has far too limited means to act independently and, consequently, that he again is forced to rely on the accounts and advice of others.

No truth-loving person can deny that for many years Quebec has been and still remains the worst den of robbers an emigrant may be trapped in. Early each spring the agents of railroads, steamship companies, and land speculators assemble here. In advance they have fought viciously among themselves, but now they come to co-operate in sharing the bounty. At sea the emigrant has observed the ability and authority of the ship's captain. He has learned to appreciate him and trust him, and will in most cases be inclined to follow his advice on how to travel farther west from Quebec. So agents and runners concentrate on the captain and seek by all means to bring him to their side. In nine of ten cases even the best of captains will be ensnared by them and, directly or indirectly, he is bribed to persuade the emigrants to buy tickets for one particular route. After much hustle and bustle the reloading is completed and the emigrant can continue on his westward journey. Along the way, however, land agents do their best to lure him to those lands they are commissioned to sell, and the emigrant will often interrupt his journey and acquire land far from his original destination. Not until he has gained experience and is able to evaluate his own situation does he realize that he has come to the wrong place and that he has lost time in labour that will yield less profit.

When a group of emigrants leave Quebec or another port the agent for the railroad or the shipping company will inform his headquarters by telegram about their expected arrival. But their representatives will often wait in vain and eventually discover that the emigrants will never arrive since they have been detoured by agents of competing companies and sent off by another route.

The emigrant will either have a definite place in mind where he will find family or friends, and then he will be well taken care of on arrival, or he is simply looking for suitable land. In the latter case he is again exposed to unnecessary expenses and runs the risk of making mistakes. In effect he cannot claim that his journey is at an end before he has found the spot where he will live and work.

The Settler's Life, 1881

EDWARD FFOLKES

> *Ted ffolkes's* Letters from a Young Emigrant in Manitoba, *covering the early 1880s, were immediately published by his mother and uncle as a down-to-earth primer for prospective settlers in the Canadian west. ffolkes was the son of an English churchman. He left home at the age of eighteen and wrote this letter of December 15, 1881, to his mother.*

As I know you are a thirst for knowledge of the settlers's life, I will try and give you all the points worthy of discussion, so that you may be able to form both your plans and your advice for my future advantage. I. As regards money; II As regards time; III. As regards housekeeping.

I. Money. It is beyond the possibility of a doubt, that the first year the settler must have money enough to buy the necessities of life—oats for his horses, if he has any, (a wise settler will have oxen the first year, as it advisable to put nothing in but potatoes, as the ground never mellows properly with a crop the first year); also he has to buy tools, window frames, stove, cooking utensils, waggon sleigh, horserake for his hay, pigs, cow, lumber for the flooring of his house, etc. Shingles for his roof—they are like slates, only made of wood. Having told you, in a rough way, what he has to buy, I may now hint at the different methods settlers adopt of getting the necessaries. I know all the settlers around here, and they, without exception, have adopted one of three methods. 1. The older ones have some money of their own. The younger ones are given it by relations, who take an interest in their welfare. This is the easiest, and need I say it, as far as their farm goes, the best. 2. Are those who spend their summer up here, and have also some business down below (in Canada), either pig-smoking, or something of that sort. These are only the older people, who have a profession. 3. Are those who work in partnerships in twos. One goes and works on one of the railroads which are being made, in Manitoba, and the northwest, and makes money, which he sends to be laid out by his partner to their mutual advantage. This, I may add, is a method adopted by common labourers; no educated person could possibly stand the company of navvies, such as are employed in the far west, truly, the scum of the earth—Yankees, Irish, and Scotch, chiefly, who are used to spend their money, and any one else's they can get hold of, in drink, and other articles as useless. I have met one or two this summer, who tried the experiment, and gave it up as hopeless. It pays to get your land cleared by someone else the first year—cost $4 an acre,—since oxen are useless, as far as ploughing is concerned, to those not used to managing them. This I have direct and unanimously from the settlers about here. The settler will have plenty to do—geting ready for winter, building his house, etc. The greatest amount cleared in the settlement for the whole three years, is thirty-six acres; and to me, who am utterly untutored in rough carpentry, house and stables and cattle-shed will take an enormous time to put up. Log to draw out and hew; the latter, of course, I could not do, though cutting them down and drawing them out of the bush I could. Hew, is to chop into a square. So I should take three years at least before turning over a cent to my advantage, and the fencing my land in will take some time. I can cut the rails out in winter, but of course I cannot stick them up, on account of hardness of the ground. Suppose I *do* get twenty acres broken, there are only two months, May 15th to July 15th, for breaking, and back set it in the fall. I can raise twenty acres of grain the second year; say 15 acres of fall wheat, 2 1/2 of oats, 2 1/2 barley—

	Dollars	Cents
15 acres of wheat, at 20 bushels to the acre, = 300 bushels, at 75 cents per bushel	225	60
2 1/2 acres of oats, at 40 bushels to the acre, = 100 bushels, at 60 cents per bushel	48	75
2 1/2 acres of barley, at 30 bushels to the acre, = 75 bushels, at 65 cents per bushel	$333	75

out of which I must feed my horse, buy my groceries and sundries, besides seed. I may have a calf, and some pigs; the latter I shall eat. I may have some potatoes to sell, but not many.

II. Time. There is little of this for a farmer to spare, on that which is not actual farming. In summer he is on the run all day. In winter the day lasts from eight till four; very short. He is employed in summer getting up his crop; breaking new land, and changing work with his fellow-settlers. There is very little hiring here; everybody changes work, i.e. settlers come and help you to do something—get in a field of grain, bind, shock, and draw it in; then you go and help these in their turn. In winter you are drawing out logs for new buildings, and for fencing new clearings, etc. I mention this, to show you it does not pay to raise butter, milk, etc.; you have not time. In summer you have to bake at night. The seasons are short here. It is light in summer from 3.30 till 9; and with so few hands, it is impossible to do a variety of things.

III. Housekeeping. May be divided into three divisions: 1. Marry; 2. Sisters or young brother well versed in such things; 3. Bach it.

I have to do with the third. The bachelor lives on pork and bannocks, as a rule; never sweeps his house out, or very seldom; generally hoes the floor once a month. It is the most expensive way, because he has no time to make bread often, or even butter, in summer, or puddings, or soups with vegetables, which saves the meat—and meat is expensive, pork being 11 cents per pound; and he also has to eat syrup instead of butter. I am now quoting incontestable truths; therefore my advice to the settler is, *marry*. Every girl is pounced on directly she puts her face inside the settlement. Young fellows get so sick of the monotony of baching. I hope to get Frank out, after a year or two, to help me; or marry—some young lady well versed in scrubbing, washing, baking, dairying, getting up at 3.30 in summer, 5.50 in winter; strong nerves, strong constitution, obedient, and with money. Where can I find the paragon? Ever since I have been up here, I have been studying the whole thing; walking a mile and a half after tea, to have a talk with one settler and another, to get advice, and gain information, with the full intention of starting on my own hook, by hook or crook, in the coming spring. Now to come to the point. The universal advice is, if you have the money, buy some discontented man out, and start where he left off, thus gaining three years. Now, here is the curious part of it: everybody round here declares *he* has the best farm in Manitoba; he would not part with it, or trade, for worlds; everyone seems as content as possible, with one exception. About a mile and a half from here, is the best, but it costs $1 an acre more to clear, either in hire or trouble, which makes $5. He has a house, 24 ft. by 20 ft., staircase, five windows, upstair room, etc., not finished yet, but when finished, which he agrees to do before spring, $450; stable, to hold two teams, $100 cow-stable, to hold cow and calves, $80: total, $790; besides fences, etc. He will get the deed and hand over with the property. He has been on the land for four years, and wants $2,500—about £520. Now for the reasons I tell you this. Four years' start would be worth £500 at least; and I find there are no lots now, which have not been granted to the different railways, within a reasonable distance of markets. Another fellow wants to sell half his lot, 320 acres, with improvements, for $4,000, which is the current price of land here now, in fact what some has actually been sold for. But to return: $2,500—half now, half this time next year, i.e. £260 on the 1st of April, 1882, £260 on the 1st of April, 1883, without interest. The property here increases in value monthly, on account of the railways coming through; and all the lots were handed over to the railway the week before last, I hear, and they are going to charge $5 an acre. It seems to me a pity to go far west, if it possibly can be helped, when the land can be got safely here, with the value rapidly increasing. Now, is it possible to borrow £500 at 6 per cent. and give the deed as security with leave to recover it when the money is paid in full, plus the interest from date of borrowing—interest paid half yearly? Now, the deed is, of course, more than security, as the value of land always increases. I should be able to put in crops enough to pay the interest and my second half-year's living, thus making the business pay the first half year, having the advantage of another man's four years' work. The man is about to marry, if he can sell out, for the wife won't come up to Manitoba. Directly I heard of this extraordinary bargain I told Boulton, who merely said, "The man always was a fool," and also said that the land is as good as any he has seen. He helped to get off the crops, this year, and saw the place thoroughly, and advises me to buy it, if I can possibly raise the money; he also added that if he had the money he would buy the land for speculation. Now I don't really suppose that I can get enough money, but this will show you, and give you an instance, how a settler can turn over money and double it, with money at his disposal to pick up a chance at the right time. The settlers here range from English gentlemen to common labourers; all nations, sects and classes. Write and tell me your plans as regards myself, as soon as possible. If you don't wish me to start on my own account just yet, I shall employ my time from spring outwards at some trade, in a town such as Winnipeg, where wages are high; since one can't get steady wages on a farm out here, as nobody has enough money to hire men, even if they had enough steady employment for a man to work at. I have now spent a year and a half at farming, and I feel sure I could pull for myself. I am afraid you will find this letter rather unamusing, but I hope you will reflect on what I have said. I meant to have put in some news of my daily life, but it is ten o'clock, and I must go to bed, my only time for writing being after tea. Mail goes to-morrow. I am very anxious to hear about Aunt Mabel, and I have not had a letter for two weeks; they are forwarded from Eastwood to Bob, then he reads them, and forwards them. I hope, dear mother, you are recovering your late fatigue, for I know it is no light work planning for a lot of thoughtless boys. Some day I hope you will stand at the door of my house, with the stock wandering harmlessly round you, and the yellow grain, glistening in the morning sun, bending in the light breeze. What a happy visit it would be! Always remember me, dear mother.

Please Decide

WILLIAM WALLACE

William Wallace, his brother Andrew, and their father, Peter, arrived in Manitoba from Scotland in early 1881, at a time of a land and immigrant boom. "I think the whole world will soon have flocked into Manitoba," wrote William. In frequent letters to his sister, Maggie, who had remained in Scotland, he urged her to join them. He was frank both about his affection and the uses he wished to put her to as a housekeeper. In 1904, Maggie and her husband came to live nearby. When he died, she kept the home of her brothers, who never married.

I was especially glad to have your ideas with regard to coming out, but these have still one fault—they are not conclusive. . . . You say that you fear there is no great necessity for you coming out. Well, I must state that there is a very great necessity. For two years now we have been working and cooking. At first, and for some time, I rather liked the housework—now, however, I am heartily sick of it. After one has been working hard outside and then requires to come in, kindle the fire, and prepare the dinner or supper, it takes away all the

relish of a keen appetite. It gives one the impression of working continually—even the eating appears labour. Besides, it takes up a large
quantity of valuable time. An hour at least extra at midday and the
evening is occupied pretty much with washing dishes and mending
garments. Heretofore we have been able to spare the time, but next
autumn, even the whole summer, the outside work will hardly have
sufficient attention [even] though we should occupy the whole of
our time with it. What you write with regard to bad housekeeping is
all rubbish—we are all of us qualified, or think we are, to teach.

The other objection you write of—as to being in the way should
there be any marital intentions, has also no weight. Should such an
event occur, you would neither be in the way or dependent, each of
us with farms containing 320 acres. The government insists upon a
house and etc. being erected on each of them, to be resided in at least
six months in the year, and in view of that Papa would be more independent with you to keep his house—meantime our plan is to flit
from one to the other so as to secure each claim.

My great fear in view of this objection is that your independence
would quickly manifest itself by being tempted away by some neighbouring pioneer to keep his house. Young ladies are rare here. . . . To
delay the reunion till the August of next year, I do not approve of it—
what with hurried bad cooking, hard work and [?] we would be all
invalids by that time and I do not see any great end it would serve.
You do not say, but I presume you will be entitled to a full certificate
before the holidays in June. After that I would consider you were
independent anywhere—even in Manitoba. Here such a good certificate would get you employ if at any time should you discover that
you did not like the farm work. And so far as you assisting us with
money is concerned, we hope to be in possession of as much as will
satisfy our wants from the fruits of our next labour, and each year will
in the same way, I expect, satisfy our increasing wants. Just now is our
worst time, just between the spending period and the earning, so you
must set this idea aside from your calculations. The decision however
must be come to by yourself.

Andrew and I were differently circumstanced when we proposed
coming, where our situation then was not the most lucrative one,
besides it was a very dependent and precarious one. Comparing our

position then with what it is now there is all the difference in the world. Now we have no limit to our hopes of what we may yet be, so that we have reason to be pleased with the change. . . .

Do not for a moment think that by stating this I want to influence your feeling—far from it. I cannot express to you our sorrow at your not joining us last spring. All along, I have since that time been calculating the months that would intervene before you came out, and I think I would for very joy become foolish, outrageously hilarious when you did come. In my imagination I have met you times innumerable and conveyed you to all the picturesque points from which to see our unrivalled scenery, and conjured up your looks of astonishment and words of wonder. But still I would not entice you to do anything you might afterwards regret. . . .

Now bear in mind when deciding, that you are to leave us outside of consideration. We, when we left you in the old country, did what we considered best for ourselves—now you must do the same with regard to yourself. And mark you, if you decide against coming out we will require to debit your account in our books with the wages of an old squaw, or else you may get out of the difficulty by engendering in some nice quiet good-looking accomplished young lady a desire to emigrate to Manitoba and address her to my care and guidance—but joking aside, if you have really a longing to come out that seems to overmaster your desire to remain, just make up your mind. . . . We unite in sending you our kindest love, and no matter how you decide, I will ever remain

> Your affectionate brother
> Willie

"Don't Send Any More"

MANITOBA FREE PRESS

> *Jewish refugees from Russian pogroms looked for any country willing to take them, and some came to Canada. The local newspaper in Winnipeg, the* Manitoba Free Press, *commented on the arrival in that city of a first group of 19 on May 26, 1882, a second group of 247 on June 1, and a third group a week later.*

Warmth and helpfulness towards the immigrants turned to skepticism over how badly immigration was being managed by the government.

May 27, 1882

Jewish refugees from Russian persecution, who were stated, in a late number of the *Free Press*, to be on the way to this province, arrived yesterday. The party consists of 15 men and the wives of four of the number, making in all 19; besides whom four in charge of baggage have not yet arrived. Accommodation was provided for them at the Government Immigration buildings on Fonseca Street West. There is among the men three carpenters, one blacksmith, one cabinet maker, one painter and one dyer, the remainder of the number being farmers. They are all young, none of them being over 30 years of age, and they are stalwart looking and evidently intelligent. They are able and willing to work and ready to avail themselves of any opportunity that may be afforded them of earning an honest livelihood. The members of the Jewish community here are doing all in their power to provide for the immediate wants of the people, as they are entirely without means; but, as the community is small, embracing only eight families, they would be glad of the assistance of any who may be able to help, especially in finding immediate employment for the strangers. Those who desire to do so can apply at the immigrant sheds, where the agent in charge or the caretaker will be able to interpret for them. Of course, none of the party can speak English, but as they have all some knowledge of German, no great difficulty will be found in obtaining the assistance of persons able to converse with them.

June 2, 1882

Supper was furnished them by the Jewish residents of the city, and it was clear to the spectators who happened to be present that the kindness was well-timed. The travellers ate as if famished, and their evidently destitute condition touched the sympathies of those who saw them. Scarcely had they finished eating when the men were informed that if they liked to go to work immediately and work all night, they might all do so, and that their wages would be paid at the rate of 25 cents per hour. This noble offer was made to them by the firm of Jarvis and Berridge, and the work with which the immigrants began their experience in Manitoba consisted in unloading two rafts of lumber which had just been brought down from Emerson by the S.S. Ogema. It is said that the people almost wept when the offer was interpreted to them. With the promptness of a company of soldiers, they fell into line and marched to the bank of the Red River, a little south of Broadway Bridge, where they were soon at work. At a late hour 37 of them were laboring industriously and showing that they were neither averse nor unaccustomed to work. They impressed their employers and others who saw them, very favorably, were regarded as intelligent looking and of good, strong, physical constitutions, and were thought to give promise of making hard-working and valuable settlers of this new country.

June 9, 1882

With the exception of a blacksmith, a shoemaker and six students, they are farmers, and they have come to this country with the sole desire of cultivating farms of their own. Half a dozen of them have means sufficient to enable them to start in an economical way upon farms; also to assist about a dozen more to do the same thing. A little judicious and prompt co-operation on the part of the Dominion Government would enable them to establish a hopeful colony, and be the means of influencing thousands of their fellow-men to come and fill up this vast country with an industrious population. Matters have not, however, been managed with a view to this desirable end, and the consequence is that prompt measures have been taken to stop any further immigration of these people to Manitoba. There are 10,000 Jews now congregated at Brody, on the frontier of Austria, anxious to emigrate, but not knowing where to go. Many new countries will be glad to obtain such settlers, but owing to mismanagement of immigration matters, the message has to be telegraphed from Manitoba. "Don't send any more here," and those who have arrived have to write their friends saying: "Don't come to Manitoba."

Quarantine Island

VERA VELICHKINA

The last of the four 1899 Ottawa-sponsored contingents of Doukhobor immigrants travelled on the steamship Lake Huron *out of London, England. The passengers tried to cover it up, but Canadian inspectors discovered smallpox aboard ship and placed everyone in quarantine on Grosse Île, near Quebec City. Vera Velichkina, a medical doctor, accompanied the Doukhobors and wrote these sympathetic reminiscences for a Russian newspaper,* Russkija Vedomosti.

The quarantine where we were to spend twenty-one days was situated on a rather large island named *Grosse Île* (about 6.5 km long), lying at the mouth of the St-Lawrence River, about 35 kilometres from Quebec City. What a paradise it seemed to us after the ship! Even before disembarking we admired the picturesque group of Doukhobor women and children who had gone to the island first and who had spread themselves out along the shore to wash all their clothing and underwear in the water—finally, fresh water! The little children took great delight in playing and running through the grass around their mothers.

In the meantime a ceremonial welcome awaited our party in Quebec. Representatives of earlier Doukhobor emigrants had come, along with delegates from the Philadelphia Quaker committee. But they were not allowed to meet with us. Three Doukhobors came to see us in quarantine and stayed with our party for the whole month, while the Quakers sent a welcoming letter to Grosse Île, expressing fervent brotherly sympathy. . . .

Part of the island, about a kilometre square, had been sectioned off for the ship's passengers. At the other end of the island was a general hospital and the smallpox dormitory. Most of the island was covered with a splendid forest. In the middle of it stood the employees' houses and the house of the quarantine director, Dr Martineau. At our end of the island there were eight large, bright dormitories and a fairly spacious old kitchen, which was not being used as in addition to that there was a new kitchen with well-appointed stoves and pantries. Besides the kitchen, the Doukhobors could use the bakery to make bread and in one of the dormitories there was even tap water, and bath-tubs.

Those escorting the party and the ship's crew were housed in a splendid large building called an *hôtel*, which was divided, like the ship, into first and second classes, with rooms appointed in the fashion of ships' cabins. At first the crew hoped that they could spend the quarantine period on the ship itself, but this proved inconvenient, and a few days after us they moved in. This rather restricted the Doukhobors, since they were no longer able to freely come and see us in this building.

About twenty paces from the hotel were the quarters of the sergeant who ran this part of the island, and next door to them was a small room where smallpox vaccinations were administered. Next came the disinfection chambers, and beyond that was the cabin of an English physician, Dr Church, whose whole job was the inspection of ships.

There was no pharmacy nor walk-in clinic on this part of the island, nor was there any doctor to service them, since it was assumed that all serious cases of illness would be treated at the hospital. During the quarantine I became convinced even more than on the ship of how important it was to equip one's self with all kinds of medications and instruments.

Upon my arrival on the island, I went to see the chief physician of the district, Dr Montizambert, suggesting that I carry on my work during the quarantine. He was very happy [about this] and said that everyone would gladly help me if I needed it.

As to the medications, I was obliged to go see our quarantine director, Dr Martineau. I immediately made up a list of required medications and bandaging materials—a rather modest list—and while my requests were never directly refused, what I got was either not delivered on time, or delivered in such small quantities or in such a disordered state that I have never, anywhere, suffered so much from a lack of medicines as on Grosse Île. I had, for example, [to deal with] a multitude of minor surgical cases—burns, cuts etc., and in response to my request for bandaging materials I received a huge quantity of cotton batting and only *three* bandages. Then several people showed up with a rash; I prescribed sulphuric ointment, and they sent me *two ounces*. . . . During the second half of our stay in quarantine I began ordering medicines from Quebec myself, but this did not happen often.

The individual smallpox vaccinations began right from the first day the Doukhobors began setting foot on the island. No official interpreter had yet been brought in; K. had his hands full looking after the Doukhobors' living arrangements, and so right from that very first morning I offered to help the quarantine doctors in this work.

After the vaccinations the quarantine doctors made their daily rounds of all the dormitories, seeing to it that sanitary regulations were being observed and watching for the appearance of new cases of smallpox, which, thankfully, didn't happen.

Then a curious incident took place. The quarantine authorities were not quite sure that the Doukhobors' escorts had not taken part in covering up the smallpox on the ship. At one point Montizambert expressed his doubt to K., adding, half-jokingly, that this was subject to a fine of 800 dollars and six months in prison. K. told that to the Doukhobors.

Then on one of my rounds I found in one of the dormitories a very lively meeting taking place. I asked what was going on.

"Yes, haven't you heard, Vera Mikhajlovna, about the trouble that has befallen us?" replied Pavel Planidin, one of the most influential Doukhobors in the party. "The doctors say that because of us, because of our mistake, our escorts may be put in prison. We cannot allow that to happen, and we have got together and want to go to see the doctors. We'll tell them to take all of us instead of the escorts, since they didn't have anything to do with it. If we wish to hide (something), nobody, not even the doctors, no matter how much they inspect the dormitories, will ever find anything." And in fact they followed through on their intention and spoke about this to Montizambert.

But the main activity of the quarantine doctors was, of course, the disinfection of all the baggage and the ship itself. They really had a lot of trouble doing this. Those accompanying the ship were also obliged to expend no little energy convincing the Doukhobors that this was essential, and that without disinfection of their baggage they would not be allowed to leave the island. Our party had brought a fair number of possessions with them, including reminders of their previous days of wealth, and the Doukhobors greatly feared that this would all be spoilt by the disinfection. There were many doubts, questions and negotiations at first, but then little by little the matter was resolved, the Doukhobors became convinced that everything would remain safe and unharmed, and not only did they calm down themselves, but they also tried to write letters to calm the fears of those who were in hospital. The latter, for their part, also wrote cheerful letters [back] to their relatives to the effect that nothing was . . . taken away from them or burnt, as they had previously supposed, but that on the contrary, their needs were being well looked after and the food was splendid. In fairness to the quarantine personnel, it must be said that they were actually very attentive and careful with the Doukhobors' baggage.

Baggage already disinfected was identified by labels with the sign of a red cross. Here another misunderstanding arose. The Doukhobors were greatly troubled upon seeing the crosses and asked that a different sign be used. They apparently took these crosses as a violation of their religious beliefs. One of our escorts, B. went to see Montizambert and asked him to resolve the misunderstanding in some way. He replied that [the inspectors] were obliged to attach this label, but that if the Doukhobors didn't like it they could scrape it off. The Doukhobors soon realised that there was no attempt to violate their beliefs here.

I myself took no part in the disinfection and didn't even have time to observe it. . . . After receiving patients I made my rounds of the dormitories. I was almost never able to complete this before lunch, and so continued with it after lunch. Later, if there were no serious cases to attend to, I would go to my cabin to rest for a couple of hours, prepare medications and talk things over with my colleagues. Then before supper I would once again open the doors of my clinic, and make a second tour of the dormitories in the evening. But I doubt I was able to follow this schedule to the letter much of the time, especially when there was a lot of work.

My evening reception hours began stretching to almost 11 o'clock at night, so I tried to get in the second tour of the day somewhat earlier. When there were more serious cases, I would have to visit the more distant dormitories as often as three or four times a day. Often secondary activity—writing letters for the Doukhobors, mediating as an interpreter between them and the Canadians—would take [time] away from my purely medical work. I tried to avoid such activity as much as possible during the quarantine, since in addition to K., who had a good command of both English and French, we did have an official interpreter. But the Doukhobors knew that I too spoke the language that was foreign to them, and they often turned to me for help in this.

Before long an epidemic of dysentery broke out on the island. It turned out that at one end of the island, not far from two dormitories which stood some distance off to one side, was an old blocked-off well, alongside a huge abandoned cemetery containing the graves of some 3,500 people who died on this island from cholera and smallpox in the 1840s. To avoid going further afield—i.e., to the river—the Doukhobors in these dormitories unblocked the well without telling anyone and began drawing drinking water from it. The quarantine guards noticed it two days later, but the dysentery had already managed to infect almost all the residents of these dormitories and spread even further. At one point there were so many people ill that it seemed that there were scarcely any healthy people left.

Even in that desperate situation I was constantly lacking the [needed] medicines. . . . True, there were few fatal cases. Altogether we lost seven people during the quarantine. Five very old people died—one of them from dysentery, the rest simply of old age, without getting sick. Then a small child died of lung inflammation, and one middle-aged man from dysentery.

Finally Dr Church offered to help me in all cases where there were complications. He was a very good, experienced physician who was really a great help and support for me at this difficult time. Sometimes during the worst weather and in the middle of the night he would go with me without a word of complaint, and I felt much calmer in the presence of such an experienced senior colleague.

At this time in the dormitory furthest away a child became sick with inflammation of the lungs, which required very careful attention. My own condition was such that upon seeing me, Montizambert at once suggested the hospital. He insisted that I send all the dangerously ill patients there. I objected, saying the Doukhobors would be most reluctant to agree to that. But he continued insisting, saying that I could no longer go on working in my condition, that I would faint from fatigue. "*Qu'allons-nous faire, si vous crevez de fatigue?*" he would say.

In the end Montizambert persuaded me to tell the Doukhobors that this was his order. Of course I realised that in the large, splendid hospital they would receive a hundred times better care than from me.

I selected three to be transferred: an old man, who was lying in the kitchen, the child with inflammation of the lungs, who had taken ill just the day before, and Larion *Tarasov*, who had a typhoid form of dysentery. As I had expected, they all agreed very reluctantly. And I felt sorry to send them away, simply wanting to save myself extra work. But on that same day Kh. was released from the smallpox dormitory and after disinfection she set about taking care of these patients in the hospital.

The day went quietly, but the following night I was awakened and called to the telephone. Usually our telephone made the voices sound muffled during the day, but they were clear at night-time, and I heard Kh.'s voice distinctly telling me that Larion Tarasov had passed on, the child after him, and soon the old man would die. The relatives had to be notified.

These three deaths all at once were a sudden shock to me. I had to go to work as soon as day broke, but my former cheerfulness and energy were gone, and I was very glad when, after the old man's death, K. returned to us and was able to share the load. I must admit that during these latter days of our quarantine I was quite willing to let her take care of the whole task of receiving patients. In the meantime the epidemic had subsided.

The quarantine itself was finally lifted, the doctors withdrew, but our party still remained on the island, as the trains that were to take us to the north-west were not yet ready, because of some national holiday the Canadians were celebrating. The Doukhobors were terribly bored and anxious to get out to their sites as quickly as possible. Finally a small ship was hired which was able to take our party to Quebec, one group at a time.

Again we went with the last party, having seen all the Doukhobors aboard. As they passed through a gate onto the ship, they had to hand in their certificates showing that they had been vaccinated and had taken a bath. Dr Martineau carefully looked each one in the face as they walked by, so as not to let pass anyone with smallpox. We were obliged to be present at this inspection to resolve any misunderstandings that might arise.

The procedure did not pass without a few comic scenes. One woman, for example, had a child in tow whose face was covered in freckles, and Martineau looked at him suspiciously. Noticing this, the woman explained: "*Konopatyj on*, understand? *Konopatyj!*" ["He's speckled!"] Of course neither Martineau nor even the interpreter understood the word *konopatyj*, and even I didn't catch on at first. "*Ko-no-PA-tyj!*" the woman repeated. General consternation.

Finally, after all the concerns and alarms, the last group ceremoniously thanked the doctors and boarded the boat, and we went along too. I must admit I felt a tinge of sadness at leaving the island, where I had done so much work and gone through so much for my patients, all the more so since I myself now had no idea where I was going, for how long, and what would be awaiting me in this new and unfamiliar land.

The Battle of the Pioneer

SIR CLIFFORD SIFTON

> *In the 1920s, a decade when earlier policies were being questioned, the minister responsible for the interior in the Laurier years vigorously defended the philosophy that had guided his period in office from 1896 to 1905.*

People who do not know anything at all about the policy which was followed by the Department of the Interior under my direction quite commonly make the statement that my policy for Immigration was quantity and not quality. As a matter of fact that statement is the direct opposite of the fact. In those days settlers were sought from three sources; one was the United States. The American settlers did not need sifting; they were of the finest quality and the most desirable settlers. In Great Britain we confined our efforts very largely to the North of England and Scotland, and for the purpose of sifting the settlers we doubled the bonuses to the agents in the North of England, and cut them down as much as possible in the South. The result was that we got a fairly steady stream of people from the North of England and from Scotland and they were the very best settlers in the world. I do not wish to suggest that we did not get many very excellent people from the more southerly portions of England, but they were people who came on their own initiative largely, which was the best possible guarantee of success. . . .

When I speak of quality I have in mind, I think, something that is quite different from what is in the mind of the average writer or speaker upon the question of Immigration. I think a stalwart peasant in a sheep-skin coat, born on the soil, whose forefathers have been farmers for ten generations, with a stout wife and a half-dozen children, is good quality. A Trades Union artisan who will not work more than eight hours a day and will not work that long if he can help it, will not work on a farm at all and has to be fed by the public when his work is slack is, in my judgment, quantity and very bad quantity. I am indifferent as to whether or not he is British-born. It matters not what his nationality is; such men are not wanted in Canada, and the more of them we get the more trouble we shall have.

For some years after the changes in policy which followed my retirement from office, Canada received wholesale arrivals of all kinds of immigrants. . . . Particularly from the continent it is quite clear that we received a considerable portion of the off-scourings and dregs of society. They formed colonies in Ottawa, Montreal, Toronto, Winnipeg and other places and some of them and their children have been furnishing work for the police ever since. . . .

I have a very emphatic opinion, based on my observation of something like thirty years, about the class of settlers that are not wanted in Canada. It is said there are millions of town dwellers, artisans, small

shopkeepers, laborers and so forth on the continent of Europe who
are anxious to come to Canada. Everyone will sympathize with their
condition and desire that they should find a place where they will lead
a happier life; but we do not want them in Canada under any conditions whatever. These people are essentially town dwellers. They
have no idea in the world of going out in a country like Canada and
fighting the battle of the pioneer. If they come here they will swell the
ranks of the unemployed; they will create slums; they will never go
upon the land; they will not add anything to the production of the
country and we shall have an insoluble problem and festering sore
upon our hands which, if the experience of the past is any guide, will
remain as long as Canada endures.

Recruiting Americans, 1901

J.E. BLUM AND J. GRUMPPER

*At the turn of the twentieth century, ads were appearing in thou-
sands of Canadian and American newspapers as the government
in Ottawa trolled for immigrants.* The Manitoba Morning
Free Press *published a full-page advertisement on July 27, 1901,
under the signature of the minister of the interior, proclaiming
in bold headline: "The Canadian West. Homes for Millions."
"Free homesteads," it continued. "Cheap lands to purchase in
all districts." A dozen testimonials followed, one from Michigan
farmers appointed by their peers as delegates to examine what
Canada had to offer. The Canadian Pacific Railway, a most
interested party, paid their transportation north.*

Winnipeg, 15th July, 1901.
J. Obed Smith, Esq.,
Commissioner of Immigration,
Winnipeg.

Dear Sir:
    As delegates from Manchester Washtenaw Co., Michigan, we vis-
ited the Northwest Territories with a view to ascertaining whether the

reports in circulation as to its being a good field for settlement were reliable and true or not. We trust from our report that anyone reading same may find something that will encourage them to come and partake of the good things offering in this great territory. This is certainly the only term we can apply to it, after a rather lengthy trip of some three weeks' duration.

We left home on the 24th of June, and having decided that it would be advisable to look over the country thoroughly before returning, advised you to this effect on our arrival at Winnipeg. We were furnished by the railway company, at your request, with transportation to Edmonton, in Alberta, and Prince Albert in Saskatchewan. Our first point of inspection was Didsbury, Alta. This part of the country seemed to be more particularly suitable for ranching and dairying. We visited a number of the farmers in this district amongst others a Mr. Shantz, one of the good old Pennsylvania stock, although he came recently, some seven years ago, from Ontario, with $24 in his pocket. He has certainly prospered, as he now owns over 70 head of cattle, has a good log house framed over, also a good barn, and in all respects looks a thrifty and well-to-do farmer. He had some good crops of oats and barley. We very much regret, that owing to the wet weather, we could not move around as we could have desired.

Edmonton was our next point of view. We met a large number of well-to-do settlers there. Wheat and all other grains and garden produce looked splendid, and promised a heavy crop. Owing to the great distance to vacant lands, we did not decide on anything there. We returned to Calgary and looked around this beautiful ranching centre, the splendid herds of cattle and sheep; however, we saw very little farming. Returning to Regina, we looked around the country north to Lumsden and Balgonie, where the crops looked very promising and heavy; continuing up to the Regina and Long Lake road, we came to Saskatoon, on the crossing of the South Saskatchewan river. The country there pleased us better than any we have seen. We drove out eighteen miles in a north-westerly direction through the Smith settlement. This is a wonderful district; the growth was splendid, all kinds of grain and roots were perfection. The older settlers had good buildings of all kinds and looked very prosperous, in fact, we came to the conclusion, that we had found what we were looking for—a good country. While the nature of the soil changes, and is in some parts light, in others stony and again heavy, generally speaking it leaves nothing to be desired. Hay and water are also in abundance, and wood can be found along the river slopes and islands. We have decided to locate there, and shall certainly advise our friends to do likewise. We also trust that this report may have the effect of drawing the attention of land seekers to this district, and can honestly advise all such to locate there. They will find a good thing. As farmers ourselves, from a good district in Michigan, we have come to the conclusion that properly farmed the Canadian Northwest will grow almost anything. Your servants.

J.E. Blum,
J. Grumpper.

The Dojack Family

THOMAS S. AXWORTHY

The lives of the Dojack family from Bohemia in the Austro-Hungarian Empire (later Czechoslovakia) became entwined with the Prairie immigrant experience. Tom Axworthy married Roberta, the daughter of Charles Dojack.

The history of the Dojack family of Winnipeg is, in microcosm, the history of Prairie immigration. The Golden Age of Prairie Immigration, from 1896 to 1914, saw the Dojaceks (the family changed the spelling in the second generation in Canada) arrive from Bohemia. As the pioneer years receded and the Prairies matured, the Dojack family became instrumental in serving as a bridge between the traditions of the Old World and the prospects of the New. Finally, the work of integration done, as the third generation of the family grew up in the 1960s, they assimilated into the wider Canadian mosaic. The immigration experience became an aspect of their heritage, instead of forming the core of their lives.

Starting in the ancient Austro-Hungarian Empire, the story begins with the birth of Franz Dojacek in 1880 in the town of Vlasim, not far from Prague. His father died when Frank (as he became) was a child; one of five children, he was sent to Vienna to learn tailoring. In 1903, he joined the tens of thousands who decided to leave their homelands and come to the Canadian West in the early years of the twentieth century. He arrived in Winnipeg to practise his trade as a tailor, but within a year, he was showing the entrepreneurial drive that characterized his life. Winnipeg was the "Chicago of the North," a bustling city, the gateway of the great Prairie expansion. As historian Gerald Friesen has written, "To descend from the train at the CPR station in Winnipeg was to enter an international bazaar."

Fluent in seven languages, Frank Dojacek became a major figure in Winnipeg's international bazaar. He was a source of assistance and advice to many fellow immigrants, easing the transition from old country to new. He often acted on behalf of immigrants as an interpreter at court appearances. (His son, Charles, carried on this tradition, once interpreting for the Russian national hockey team during a game in Winnipeg.) In 1904, Frank married Rosa Misera, who had been in service in Vienna and who joined him in Winnipeg. Eventually, all of Frank's siblings (except for one brother, Karl, who stayed in Bohemia) emigrated to Canada. The extended Dojacek family moved beyond the initial Winnipeg home to settle in Regina and Edmonton. The parents of Paul Dojack, the Canadian Football League head referee, arrived in Canada in 1912, eventually moving to Regina in 1924 to establish a branch of the family's music business.

Frank sold bibles and Czech, Polish, and Ukrainian books on a bicycle in the city and by horse and buggy across the Prairies from 1904 to 1906. Then he purchased the stock of John Bodrug, one of the first importers of books from Eastern Europe, and established a Ruthenian, Polish, and German bookstore on Main Street, in the heart of Winnipeg's north end. Now recreated in the national Museum of Civilization's Canada Hall as an exhibit on Western Canadian history, the Ukrainian Booksellers and Publishers, as the business was later known, became a magnet for new immigrants. Dojacek carried a wide array of publications useful to new Canadians. He sold books in a dozen languages, including Czech, Slovak, Ukrainian, Polish, Hungarian, Croatian, and German. The most popular publications were Ukrainian-English dictionaries (still printed today), self-help books, and education primers. Other needs were also catered to, including Polish, Ukrainian, and German greeting cards; baptismal and marriage certificates; records, radios, iceboxes, and then refrigerators. One could even purchase patent medicines—Persian Balm, Florida Water, or the Lapidor tablet. Virtually every central European immigrant to Western Canada visited his store to purchase supplies, converse in their native language, or seek Frank's counsel.

In the 1920s Ukrainian Booksellers flourished and Frank Dojacek expanded his enterprises in two directions, and these expansions became the core of the business lives of two of his sons. The initial bookstore on Main sold musical instruments, and, in time, this part of the business became even larger. During the 1930s, Ukrainian Booksellers and Publishers moved to its final location at Main Street and Henry, where it was renamed Winnipeg Musical Supply. By then Frank had moved beyond his store to enter the world of ethnic publishing. He was president of National Publishers, Ltd. and publisher of *Der Nordwesten* (German), the *Canadian Farmer* (Ukrainian), and *The Croatian Voice*. Now, as well as selling foreign-language books, he was printing them and publishing weekly newspapers. He printed the strikers' newspaper in the Winnipeg General Strike of 1919 and also printed labels for another immigrant family of Manitoba—the Bronfmans. *Der Nordwesten*, the oldest German newspaper in Canada, had the largest circulation of National Publishers' papers. Newly arrived immigrants were given free subscriptions to the paper and books printed in German, called "Canada, Your New Home." Through these ventures, National Publishers became the largest ethnic publisher in Canada.

Frank Dojacek never forgot the land of his birth. Before and during the First World War, he worked with the patriots who were trying to free Czechoslovakia from the Austrian Empire. This brought him into contact with the creator of Czechoslovakia, Thomas Masaryk. Frank was bitterly disappointed when Czechoslovakia lost its freedom to the Nazis and then again to the Communists in 1948. Members of the family were denied entry to Czechoslovakia while it was under the Communist regime. Finally, with the fall of the Berlin Wall and the coming of the Velvet Revolution, the third generation of Dojacks was able to make contact with Karl's family.

Der Nordwesten was at one time a supporter of the Conservative Party, but Frank soon broke that link, and the Dojack family began a life-long identification with the Liberal Party. Prime Minister Mackenzie King conducted a regular correspondence with Frank Dojacek; his son Charles became a strong supporter of Paul Martin, Sr. The Liberal Party always had a keen appreciation of the immigrant community, and the Dojack family reinforced that political connection. Religious affiliation, as well as political allegiance, was passed on from Frank to his family. He was a man of strong faith, active in the Baptist Church. He was the Sunday School superintendent of McDermot Avenue German Baptist Church for twenty-four years, played a role in Tabernacle Baptist Church, and founded the Czechoslovak Baptist Mission, spending his weekends in its service. He also helped found the Czech Baptist Church in Toronto. When he was felled by a stroke, he was away from Winnipeg, preaching.

In 1951, when Frank Sr. died, the family carried on his legacy. Frank Jr. took over Winnipeg Musical Supply, and Charles managed National Publishers. Winnipeg Musical Supply was a fixture on Main Street, and Frank Jr. became president of the Main St. Merchants' Association. Once the center of Winnipeg commerce near the busy CPR station where Frank Dojacek first arrived, the street saw its fortunes wane as immigration lessened, the CPR moved out, and urban rot set in. Frank and the Merchants' Association fought the trend, but after his death in 1982, the store closed. Charles, the youngest of the five Dojack children, was an original member of the Winnipeg Symphony orchestra and joined the Canadian Army Show in the Second World War, with composer Robert Farnon and comedians Wayne and Shuster. The cello was his instrument. He gave up his first love, however, to take over his father's publishing business. National Publishers was the only ethnic-language publisher to send a correspondent to the Ottawa Press Gallery and, in 1967, Charles organized the first tour of fifty-eight ethnic press editors to Quebec, followed by a visit of seventy-two French-Canadian editors to the West.

Immigrants still come to the Prairies, but now they are from India,

China, Vietnam, or the Philippines. However, the legacy of Frank Dojacek endures, even though no one in the third generation took on the challenges of Winnipeg Musical Supply or National Publishers. Frank's career and that of his family show the attraction of Canada and the value of immigration. From the relic of the Austro-Hungarian Empire, he emigrated to seek a land of opportunity and freedom. He found it, and he and his sons spent the rest of their lives working to make sure that others could enjoy the same opportunities. It is a tale of enterprise, devotion, and civic duty. And it has a happy ending— the Dojacks thrived, and so did their new land.

"Blue Sky Ahead," 1903

JOHN QUTLE

> *Optimism was a prerequisite for life in the Northwest Territories, in an area that is now Saskatchewan. The railways and land prices were measures of that spirit. So too, for an Irishman writing home and his wife Florrie, was the abundance of game birds.*

Saskatoon
N.W.T. (North West Territories) Canada
30th October 1903

My dear Alex

The reason for my not writing sooner was that I was very anxious to be able to say that I saw blue sky ahead before doing so, & I am now more than thankful to say that I do, & feel satisfied that with a little luck we are going to do well, at all events I think it will be my fault if I do not succeed better than I could ever hoped at home.

This place I feel sure, is going to be a pretty big countre we are told that within the next year we will have two railways if not three which you understand means a very big thing to a growing town, anyway the value of town lots which measure 25 feet frontage & one hundred in depth have more that doubled since the spring, the owners of them are a very big financial Stockbroking firm in Montreal Winnipeg

& they are I understand about the best informed people in Canada.

You will have heard from Florries letters that I am working with Acheson the leading Lawyer here, he is an Irishman from Galway & a very nice man we are getting along tip-top & I have little fear of the future now. I am sure you would laugh if you saw me splitting wood, I can tell you it is great exercise & good for the arms, but not for ones temper, when you snare a notty old gentleman the swearing begins.

I made many examinations of the Flax crop here & from what I can see it is thicker & stronger in the stalk than Irish Flax & would make good yarn, but the question of labour in pulling knocks the bottom out of any chance of sending it to Ireland I am afraid, however I am going to see next year what can be done with the Russian settlers who work in communities for their general welfare, they may tackle it, but no one else. . . .

You will have to take a couple of months holiday next autumn & come out to pay us a visit & get an idea of the vastness of the Territories it is really terrifying at first when you get out on the prairies Florrie looses herself & points out Saskatoon where probably no house comes between her & Hudson's Bay, & gets very indignant when I laugh.

We both been nearly living on Game for the past two months Duck Teal Widgeon Wild Geese & Prairie Chicken. . . . The chicken . . . are twice as big as Grouse & bigger eating half an one does us for meal. The Geese are fine birds running up to 12 lbs in weight & their flesh is not strong. . . .

Yours sincerely
John Qutle

Providence's Choice

HENRI BOURASSA

> *Henri Bourassa, the leading French-Canadian nationalist of his day, dissented from the view that American and European immigration ought to be encouraged. Confederation, in this 1907 vision, was based on an alliance of British and French peoples,*

*and that ought to be the face of the Canadian west. Foreigners
from other lands had nothing in common with "the two original races in this country."*

I [do not] state . . . that the people from Scandinavia, Russia, or
Germany are not a splendid race of people, a people animated by
high national traditions, and a people actuated by a deep sense of
civilization.

I am not claiming that we are the best people in the world; that
our civilization is the highest form of civilization; but I do claim that
our present civilization suits us, and it is that which we have set ourselves to improve. Our social system, our political system, our religious system, are those which we have inherited and under which we
are trying to improve ourselves.

Possibly a Chinaman is a better man than an Englishman. Let the
Englishman answer for that himself; a Japanese may be a better man
or a Russian may be a better man than the Englishman; I say nothing
about that, he may be a much better man, but he is not one of us; and
inasmuch as he is not one of us he is not helping us to develop along
those lines that Providence has chosen for us, or that we have chosen
for ourselves. His presence is a hindrance and not a help. . . .

I hear it often said by men who at other times will try to stigmatize
us as disloyal, as racial or religious zealots, that it does not matter from
what country settlers may come, that all the Americans who want to
come here are welcome. To a certain extent I agree with them. Let all
good, moral, intelligent people come to this country. That we must
seek a large influx of American population may be from a purely
monetary point of view, sound policy; but if there be any sincerity in
the so-called loyalty of those who argue this way, you cannot say it is
in accord with your sense of British citizenship that you should open
this country wide to the influx of American population, capital and
ideas. It is all very well to say that the Americans who go west are
satisfied with the laws of Canada. They do not come here to study law
but to make money, and because they find the conditions at present
in Canada better for making money than in the United States. But
when they have grown two or three generations, when they have
reached a higher stage of civilization, and when they will form the

majority of the people of this country, are you quite sure they will be so much attached to British institutions as you claim, and that the simple fact of having so many British flags hoisted on schools and elsewhere is going to make them British? Are you sure, when you discriminate against the farmers from Quebec, Ontario and the maritime provinces going to settle in the west, that the newcomers will be as safe and sound with regard to British connection and Canadian citizenship as you say they will? Are you quite sure that mingled with those foreign elements, neither British nor American, but who will always have a natural attraction for the larger and wealthier country to the south, a country independent by itself—which has always a greater prestige in the eyes of foreigners than a colony—are you quite sure that these foreign elements will be attached to British connections in such a way that if it comes to a choice between their British connection, between their connection with the rest of Canada, between the unity of confederation, and their economic interest; that they will not ten times rather break the British connection, ten times rather break the Canadian confederation, than endanger or damage their economic or their business prospects? It may be that my view is wrong, it may be that I am a pessimist in this; but I claim that this is a point of view which cannot be dismissed by a simple laugh at Little Canadianism.

A Harsh Initiation

LESLIE H. NEATBY

An impractical English doctor, Andrew Neatby, collided with his first Saskatchewan winter in 1906–1907, at Earl Grey, north of Regina. Among his seven children were historians-to-be Hilda Neatby and her brother Leslie, the author of a memoir of Prairie immigrant pioneering from which this passage is taken.

The prolonged and bitter winter of 1906–07, still discussed among the oldest of oldtimers, gave our parents a harsh initiation to the New World. The Earl Grey district was not the bald prairie we were soon to know, but parkland liberally sprinkled with aspen groves. A thicket of these grew within a stone's throw of our house, and from this, with Yorkshire thrift, our father cut his fuel. It was poor economy both in a business sense and in terms of human comfort. This middle-aged English physician and his two sons, aged twelve and eleven, must have spent hours in loose snow and bitter cold to accomplish what an experienced axeman would have done in half-an-hour, and they probably did it in inadequate English clothing. Poor Kenneth, not yet seven years of age, was enlisted to help drag in the firewood. He used to howl because of the cold and was rewarded by rebuke and the threat of a thrashing from a parent in whom pity was smothered by his own acute discomfort. There is nothing so dehumanizing as cold hands and feet. Cutting our own wood made us unpopular with the men about town who felt cheated out of the odd dollar they reckoned on earning by supplying the doctor with fuel.

The 1907 Anti-Asian Riot

VANCOUVER *DAILY NEWS ADVERTISER*

British Columbians in the early twentieth century, as historian Patricia Roy writes, "firmly believed that theirs should be a white man's country." On September 7, 1907, a year that saw an influx of immigrants from Japan, an anti-Asian riot erupted in Vancouver; it was the subject of dramatic front-page coverage the next day in the Vancouver Daily News Advertiser. *The mayor hoped that it would not detract from the campaign to restrict "Oriental immigration." In fact, the disturbance aided the cause, leading directly to an agreement between the Canadian and Japanese governments to limit severely the number of labourers and domestics who could immigrate to Canada from Japan. The spectre of another immigration riot hung over Canadian politicians for years thereafter, reinforcing their bigotry and their caution.*

Vancouver last night bubbled and boiled with anti-Asiatic sentiment, culminating in a riot which threatened to leave Chinatown and the Japanese quarters a wreck. Fortunately, the trouble got no further than a very considerable and destructive window smashing, which, however, was damaging enough.

To the credit of the men who organized last night's parade and addressed the meeting in City Hall, it must be said that the lawlessness was no fault of theirs as they strongly counseled moderation and constitutional methods, but a gang of hoodlums took advantage of the occasion and, while the meeting at the City Hall was in progress, marched down [to] Chinatown and through the Japanese quarters, waving banners they had captured by force, and breaking every window in sight. . . .

Seen at an early hour this morning Mayor Bethune expressed his deep regret and indignation that the good name of Vancouver should have been injured, as it undoubtedly has been by the disorder and rioting last night. "In regard to our efforts to restrict Oriental immigration," said His Worship, "such conduct cannot fail to prejudice our cause and that view has been expressed to me to-night by many of our best citizens. The citizens can be assured that the authorities will do their best to preserve order, and I am convinced that should the necessity arise many citizens will come forward to assist the police in doing that. Doubtless claims for compensation will be made on the City by those whose property has been damaged. Again, I can only express my deep regret that such disorderly acts should have occurred."

It was a peculiar coincidence that Mr. Ishii, the special envoy of the Japanese Government, sent here to investigate the question of Japanese immigration to this continent, should have arrived in the City last evening. Certainly his impression of the treatment his countrymen were receiving could not be very favourable.

En Partant de Saint-Pierre et Miquelon

SOEUR YVONNE LANDRY

> *In her memoirs, Yvonne Landry, a nun, described her family's emigration from Saint-Pierre and Miquelon and her arrival in 1908 Montreal as a little girl. Her father's store in St. Pierre had fallen on hard times, and he was scooped up by Quebec's immi-*

gration agent, who had come to the nearby island in search of French-speaking immigrants. To the Landrys, used to small-town life where everyone knew and helped one another, the big city was a shock. "I didn't meet anyone I knew," Yvonne's grand-mother said sadly after returning from a walk.

Depuis quelques années, les affaires de mon père déclinaient. Un de ses proches, homme ambitieux à qui mon père pardonna dans la suite, lui enleva son bon patron de goélette. Au dernier moment, mon père dut prendre un autre homme. Celui-ci utilisait la goélette pour faire du sport plutôt que pour faire la pêche. La saison terminée, il revint annoncer à mon père, en pleine nuit, que la pêche avait été presque nulle. Alors, cette année-là, les dépenses en salaires, etc. furent plus élevées que les recettes. Et il en fut ainsi les années suivantes, de sorte que mon père dut vendre la goélette et liquider le magasin. C'est ainsi qu'en 1907, un agent d'immigration, le docteur Brisson de Laprairie, Québec, étant venu à St-Pierre chercher des émigrants, mes parents décidèrent de venir au Canada. . . .

A St-Pierre, tout le monde se connaissait, et ma bonne grand-mère était revenue d'une course en ville en disant: "Dire que je n'ai rencontré personne de ma connaissance." Dans les tramways, elle engageait facilement la conversation avec la personne assise à côté d'elle. Les gens n'étaient pas toujours aimables, ce qui la mortifiait. On raconte qu'une Madame B., une St-Pierraise venue à Montréal à un âge assez avancé, avait demandé à un facteur, rue Ste-Catherine, s'il avait des lettres pour elle. Aussi qu'un jour, prenant le tramway St-Denis, elle avait dit au conducteur: "Je m'en vais chez Girouard." "Quelle rue?" demande le conducteur. "Comment, vous ne connais-sez pas Girouard? Mais ça fait dix ans qu'il est à Montréal."

"How Wisely Should We Care for the Immigrant!"

J.S. WOODSWORTH

Preacher-politician J.S. Woodsworth was a future leader of the Cooperative Commonwealth Federation, the first national democratic socialist party of Canada. In 1909, he was director of the All People's Mission in the north end of Winnipeg, where there was a substantial immigrant population. Out of that experience grew Strangers Within Our Gates; or Coming Canadians, *a volume that balanced sympathy for the immigrant with a warning that the government must be selective in its policies and assimilationist in its intent. The "incoming armies of foreigners" had to be turned into "loyal British subjects." Here Woodsworth combined a first-hand immigrant account with his reflections.*

The following letter was written as a composition exercise in February, 1908, by one of the boys in the night school at All Peoples' Mission; we have made only slight corrections:

It was the '03–'04 winter in Russia. I, in a business school, and my brother, in a technical school, were living ten miles from our parents who lived in a small country town where my father had kept a general store for eight years. (This was three months before the Russian-Japan war.) When we came to our home for Christmas vacation we found our father thinking to exchange his form of life. None of us liked store-keeping. For a long time we had thought of farming. A year and a half before my father had written to the Government of Russia asking permission to buy some land. (The Hebrews have not liberty to buy land in Russia.) The reply came in the negative. Then my father thought to emigrate to Palestine—the Holy Land of Zion. But this was not so easy. It required a large sum of money. Then we thought about the Argentine where the Jewish Colonization Association had founded some colonies. To obtain information my father went to another city to a man who came from Argentine. He explained that it is a fair country where there is a lot of good land, and there is a company which sells it on credit. My father came back thinking to emigrate in the spring to Argentine. But a little later he decided to exchange Argentine for Canada, because the latter is a more educated country, and Englishmen are much better than Spaniards. We were all glad to leave Russia and emigrate to Canada.

On the 13th of June my father went to Fort Qu'Appelle, Sask., where there was a Roumanian Jewish colony two years old. There were a few Russian Jews who came a couple of months before my father. My father's letters were very favorable. They were full of poetry; the green grass, the fresh air, the woods, the ponds, the birds—and one hundred and sixty acres for ten dollars. He did not tell us about the poverty of the farmers, or about their very cold houses; so we thought that the farmers lived a very comfortable life in their new colony.

We had to sell two stores on the town market, and a house communicating with a two hundred dollar grocery store, situated on the other side of the town. As the town was small we could not get rid of the stock till the middle of '05 winter. Then came a great disaster. Our house was burned. We had to rent a house to live in till spring when we expected to go to our father. We did not write to him about the fire. A month later we gave my uncle fifty dollars to help him to go to Canada, too. After this we sent father one hundred dollars. Then we had some payments to make, and three hundred dollars to collect. Of this we did not collect one-third. We thought by selling the property to have enough money for the journey. But in a small country town in war time it is not so easy to sell properties. We remained till the 18th of June. Not being able to sell the properties we left Russia with only one hundred and fifty dollars (three hundred Russian roubles). A man lent us one hundred dollars. By the time we had reached Canada he had sold the stores, but would not mind to send us the difference money.

We expected to get cheap tickets from London, but to our dismay we did not find any society with cheap tickets for poor immigrants. We were obliged to stay in London nine weeks till my father had sold his cattle and sent us one hundred and fifty dollars.

In London we had a very bad time. I will never forget the wretched journey. In the three days' train ride from Quebec to Qu'Appelle we had nothing to eat. It was very hard on my dear mother, because it is the worst time for a mother when her children are hungry. Only one day, we thought, and we will be at our new home with our dear father! But we had to wait more than a day for we found that the colony is forty miles from Qu'Appelle. In Qu'Appelle we met a Hebrew boy who lent us two dollars. Oh, glorious moment! After a fast we enjoyed our dinner! Next day we engaged a man who took us to the colony. But there we did not find what we expected. We thought a colony would be as in Russia—two to four hundred houses together. Here we found a small shack, occupied by a Hebrew farmer, who explained to us what the colonies are in Canada. He had no place for us for the night, but he directed us to another farmer one mile further. We went, and to our delight found he was a friend from the Old Country. He explained to us that our father was working for a farmer, and that all farmers were poor enough yet. So we had to wait a week more till our father came to see us. It was the 30th of October, 1905.

The winter of '05–'06 we lived in another farmer's house, because ours was not ready for the winter. My work was to feed five head of cattle, cut wood, bring in wood, water or snow. So I was busy all day at home, and my father and brother in the bush, because we had no other income to keep us alive. It was a hard time. Four dollars a week cannot keep well a family of eight. But we did not care much for it. We were very glad to be in Canada, and have a farm.

In the spring of '06 we moved to our farm where we had a two-story lumber house which we had to plaster. On the farm we had two good cows, and so had more to eat, and our life was more comfortable. The plastering of the house was very hard work for us, as we were not used to such work. We mixed clay and water, and put it on the walls. But we did our work well, and we have a very comfortable house. Just as hard was the bush work in summer, or the building or plastering of the big stable. But we always did our work with pleasure. The best work was our garden. We planted it carefully, and for our labor had quite a lot of vegetables. My mother and sister were busy with the chickens. In the middle of July we started the nice haytime. It was very agreeable work to cut hay around the ponds. In the autumn we gathered our vegetables down the cellar. Our autumn work was to get wood for the winter and for sale. Every day my father and I went to the bush, and came back with a large load. After autumn came the severe '06–'07 winter. To keep us alive my father or brother used to go twice a week to town with wood or hay. I had the same kind of work as the winter before—to feed eight head of cattle and cut the wood, and carry water and snow. But everything has an end, and that strong winter ended.

Living on the farm I had no chance to learn English as I wanted to do. In the free time I used to copy from an old primer, but I did not understand the meaning of the words. At last I asked my parents to go to Winnipeg to work and to learn. They let me go. With thirty-five cents in my pocket I went to Winnipeg, but arrived without a black cent. This was the 24th of April, 1907. I had an uncle here. He found me some work in a factory where I worked for a short time. Then I started to work in a grocery store where I worked till the 10th of November. Now I am working in the G.N.W. as a messenger boy. I did not have any lessons in English till I started to your school. To it, I am obliged for whatever I know of the English language.

This may be taken as a typical story of the experiences of a family of immigrants—the dissatisfaction in the old land—the dreams and plans about the new—the father going first to prospect and pre-pare—the sacrifice made in leaving the old home—the anxieties and hardships of the journey—the hopes that buoyed them—the disap-pointment in reaching the land of their dreams—the struggles to gain a foothold—the privations of the first few months or years—the gradual making of the home—the move of the young men to the city—their struggles. How much one can read between the lines! With variations, this is the experience of immigrants from all coun-tries. Thousands of families scattered all over the prairies can tell such tales.

Such stories give us hope for the future. Such courage—such endurance—such struggles cannot but develop a high type of char-acter. Compare such experiences with the easy-going, self-satisfied, narrow, unprogressive lives of many who are hardly holding what their fathers gained! These latter, with their little round of petty plea-sures, despise the poorly clad "foreigner" with his broken English and strange ways; but the odds are largely on the side of the immigrant. It required no little decision of character to undertake to change the whole course of his life. It required no little management to carry this through successfully. Then what an experience in the long journey and in the coming to a new land! A year in Europe is sometimes con-sidered, by the wealthy, a liberal education. These immigrants have that kind of liberal education which can come only by experiencing two very different kinds of life, and really entering into the second. We must also think of the powers of adaptation that are necessary in fitting one's self to the new conditions. In this again the immigrant has the advantage. Of course, there is the other side—the long, hard struggle for life that crowds out many of the things that make life worth living—the uprooting of lifelong associations, and the difficulty of taking root again in a strange soil—the sudden emergence into freedom unknown before, and the difficulty of training the children for the new life—the strain of rising in a few short years through degrees of well-being that ordinarily would take generations. Such are the trials. How wisely should we care for the immigrant! What will become of this Jewish boy who has told us his story? Full of the highest possibilities he runs most serious risks. His ambition will save him from many evils. Will he become a money-making sceptic? Or will he become a man of high ideals and noble life? That depends— well, upon what?

"The Case of the Negro," 1909

WILLIAM J. WHITE

> The Canadian government discouraged black settlement proposals, but individual blacks could and did legally cross the border. William White, the inspector of United States Agencies for the Immigration Branch in Ottawa, reported to the minister on a 1909 trip to Oklahoma, the home of blacks whom he feared might be headed northwards.

I have just returned from a five day trip through Oklahoma as per your instructions. . . .

The population of Muskogee, Okmulgee and Cowetz is largely coloured and considerable of the business is carried on by them,—the negro and Indian negro. Certain districts in all of the towns is given over to them, while other districts are devoted to the business of the "whites." Immediately you step from one to the other the difference comes upon you like a flash. There is about the former a carelessness and indifference even greater than a prejudiced person might expect to see. The tumble-down buildings, the ill-kept and badly ventilated shops and stores have nothing about them to indicate the business courage and enterprise of those that lie just beyond the demarcation line, where the "whites" business is conducted. Laziness is abundant and seems to have put its hall-mark everywhere. . . .

I became alarmed when I thought we might get an influx of these people. I saw five or six of their pastors, and after a talk with three of them I felt satisfied that they had been advising their people to remove to Canada. Before I left them I believe I satisfied them that Oklahoma was a much better place and I do not think their influence in future will be exercised in the same direction as I think it was in the past.

My reference here is as to the general conditions. With the colored people as with others, there are exceptions. We have already a number of them in portions of Western Canada and I believe them to be superior to most of these I saw in the south, and if there is any best, I think we have secured the best, and secured only those who will make good citizens, but the risk of the emigration of a large number who would prove undesirable is so great that I feel it would be wise to take such action as would prevent any more of them making homes in Canada. Again I say they are as a class looked upon as undesirable in the territory in which they have been born and raised, and my own observations bear out the statement. There was nothing about the conditions or surroundings in which they have lived to give the faintest hope that by their removal to Canada they would adopt any other than the indifferent life they have been living. They retard the healthy growth and prosperity of the community, and by keeping out the settler whose aim is a life beyond the level of the negro's comprehension. Right in Oklahoma where the settlements are made of whites, there is a marked difference to that where the settlements are colored, although the laws of both are of the same quality. In the former there [are] good homes with . . . well-kept yards and well-tilled farms, the abundance of thrift everywhere discernible. In the latter, there has been but little change in over quarter of a century. The tumble-down buildings to-day have done service in the same tumble-down fashion for thirty years, and the rotting and broken fences are worse to-day if anything than they were twenty years ago.

I wish to point out that the colored population of the portion of Oklahoma that I visited is different altogether from the colored population of Ontario, and without one has some knowledge of both it is unfair to the former to make any comparison. There is so much of the Indian blood in the colored man of Oklahoma, carrying with it all the evil taints of a life of rapine and murder, that it will not easily assimilate with agrarian life.

The railroad companies of the south are anxious to replace the colored man along their lines with a white population and they direct their efforts by inducing him to go north. . . .

Notwithstanding our very best efforts to guard carefully the class of people, who go to Central Canada, we find the case of the Negro probably the most difficult to deal with. If given a free hand and the privilege to absolutely refuse to give a certificate entitling him to the settlers rate, we could meet it. Whether it is advisable to refuse the colored man this certificate is a question that bothers us considerably. There is a fairly large colored vote in Eastern Canada, most of which is liberal, and if it came to their notice that their people were discriminated against, it might lead to their opposition. On the other hand, I know that the people in the West do not care to have them in their neighborhood.

There are some settlements of them now, and, as far as I can learn, they are prosperous, law abiding and, with the exception of their color, may be looked upon as good citizens.

In some cases, where we have thought it safe, we have absolutely refused to give certificate; in other cases we have advised them of special rates, which can be secured on certain days and which they can take advantage of. This, however, is only a makeshift and is also likely to be resented.

I would not have brought the matter to your attention, but at almost every office I find application from these people, and, while the number who are likely to go to Central Canada may not be very large, it is a question whether The Department should become a party to assist them in emigrating to Canada. I wish you to bear in mind that the refusal of The Department to help them to secure a rate will not keep them from going. Their friends send back such splendid reports of the country that, even if they had to pay the full fare, they will go. At times, as I have said, they can reach there without paying the full fare and without the Government certificate. Instances have come to my notice where they have gone up with Land Companies and in one case the Canadian Pacific Railway Irrigation Branch, which uses a certificate, has given to Tennessee colored people a certificate, which secures them the low rate at the boundary.

Macedonian Self Help

LILLIAN PETROFF

> *Macedonian workers countered Anglo-Canadian indifference and hostility by relying on themselves. Research on this subject, historian Lillian Petroff recalled, "was made extremely difficult because of the scant official records and limited written accounts by the Macedonians themselves. I conducted and made liberal use of oral interviews to record 'memory culture,' and I unearthed parish records, municipal documentation, directories, letter-writing manuals and dictionaries, the last offering a compendium of useful phrases that immigrants could memorize in order to rent a room or ask for a job. In this way I sought to reconstruct the life of Toronto's Macedonians in transition from poor peasant migrants to proud members of a self-conscious community."*

Given the indifference and not infrequent hostility of Anglo-Canadian citizens, "caretakers," and employees, Macedonian workers came to rely heavily on internal sources of information and assistance. Men frequently secured jobs on the railway and in the factories through the services of the padrone, or labour agent. A description of a Greek padrone fits the Macedonian case as well: "This designation runs all the way from the petty faction leader who happens to know English and acts for a few, or some unscrupulous exploiter of his people who has got the upper hand, to the really great and enterprising contractor. The 'agent,' however, defies exact definition because of the manysidedness of his agenthood."

Many Macedonians obtained jobs at Kemp's Manufacturing through the efforts of two company employees, Lazo Evanoff and Staso Filkoff. Among the earliest of Macedonian employees, these two carefully learned the manpower needs of the factory's departments and then directed compatriots to them. It is not clear whether Evanoff and Filkoff profited in more than reputation and status for playing this role—or whether the company encouraged them as a means of imposing social controls on the recruitment of labour. As if to dehumanize the men who turned to them for work, the padroni at Kemp's also renamed the new immigrant employees. A Macedonian immigrant states simply: "Lazo Evanoff told them [the employers] my name 'Charlie' because English people . . . don't want the foreign people of those days. Proper names [such as Dono] they don't want. They want names that are easy for them. I was called, 'Charlie Johnson.'" As long as he remained at Kemp's, this immigrant was known to his friends and employers as "Charlie Johnson."

Jobs on the railway were, similarly, obtained through the good offices of the padrone. Andrew Dimitroff and James Georgieff, partners in a dry-goods store on King East, acted as labour agents for railways. The padroni at Kemp's were said to offer their services without fee. In contrast, Dimitroff and Georgieff required job seekers to pay one dollar and purchase their "railroad clothes," such as boots and overalls, from the bosses' store. Railway jobs were also available through the elusive "man from Florina"—Chris Tipton. Macedonian labourers believed that Tipton was an agent of the Grand Trunk Railway. He was an important figure, a go-between with much informal power, but little is known about him. Tipton travelled north from Toronto taking gangs of Macedonians, Bulgarians, and men of other nationalities to jobsites along the route.

Other sources aided Macedonians in their search for work. Railway navvies in the United States and Canada from the village of Buf in Macedonia received funds to tide them over and were kept informed by villagers about seasonal and permanent jobs in Toronto; in Columbus and Mansfield, Ohio; and in Detroit and Ann Arbor, Michigan. The Toronto steamship and banking agency Slave Petroff and Co. offered the services of a labour office especially for all those whose migration it brokered and to the Macedonian community. The Baptist church in Toronto also established a labour exchange and information bureau at its East End Macedonian and Bulgarian Mission Hall. The reluctance of many Anglo-Canadians to perform certain tasks opened opportunities for "less fastidious" immigrants. Macedonians accordingly found jobs at the "smelly factories," the fur and dye works of the Frederick Schnaufer Co., or the W. Harris Co., which made, imported, and refined vast quantities of "Glue, Fertilizers [and] Tallow Greases." Canadian experience also gave men the confidence to search for and obtain jobs. After he "learned the trick" of making soap at the John Taylor Soap Co., one Macedonian found greater benefits as an experienced workman at the rival Palmolive Soap Co.

The guidebooks of the 1910s reflected a decade or more of work and experience in the New World and made job-hunting and dealing with authorities much easier for sojourners. Malincheff/Theophilact's *Dictionary* (1913) aimed to protect Macedonian newcomers from undue hardships by enabling them to comprehend the nature of potential work. It showed the men how to ask a foreman or a company representative, in English, for a job: "Good morning, sir. Have you any work for me?" Macedonians then learned how to ask about wages:

> How much do you pay per hour for this work?
> How much do you pay per day for this work?
> How much do you pay a week for this work?
> How long will this work last?
> Fifteen cents per hour
> Dollar and a half per day
> Nine dollars a week
> I am satisfied with this wage.

Also: "How many hours do we work a day? Is there overtime?" Formal phrases dealt with job advancement and employees' privileges:

> Dear Sir:—
> As my present work with the _____ does not give me an opportunity for advancement. I regretfully beg to make application for a change to some other kind of work . . .

Men learned how to request a day off because of illness or to attend a relative's funeral.

Nedelkoff's *Letters* (1911) and Yovcheff's *Letters* (1917) offered more detailed and comprehensive instruction and assistance. Nedelkoff's volume presented sample letters requesting financial compensation or an occupational adjustment for injured employees. Varied levels of directness and intensity allowed men to choose the form that most suited their temperament and predicament.

In the best tradition of such industrial critics as Upton Sinclair, one such letter boldly demanded restitution from an insensitive corporation: "I appreciate that a corporation is a soulless being, and hence what I ask, I do not ask as a matter of charity, but as a matter of justice. Neither do I expect to gain a fortune therefrom. You will agree with me that as I lost my finger at your work, it is nothing more than fair for your company to allow for this loss, at least the twenty-five days of labour, which I so unwillingly lost, and amount, at $1.75 per day, to $43.75. I hope you will see way clear to grant this petition of mine."

In contrast, a request for a change of occupation because of after-effects from a work-related injury was humble in tone: "I recently applied at your plant for re-employment and secured my old job. However, even the first day, my head began to ache, my eyes got dim, and I was forced to quit. In a few days, I tried again with the same results, in fact, I was dizzy and unable to work. I am a poor man, without means of support with a wife and [three children] to keep. I must work. Will you be kind enough to find me a different place in the plant, where it would not require so much lifting and exertion as at moulding? Anything you may do for me will be appreciated."

When an industrial accident killed a Macedonian worker, quick provision had to be made to notify kinfolk and countrymen. Yovcheff's model telegram—"Nestor Parmakoff was killed in a coal mine yesterday. Funeral March 10. Please notify his relatives and friends"— provided his readers with a brutally simple and efficient example. The guidebooks also dealt with such combustible and delicate issues as relations with co-workers of other ethnic origins. Nedelkoff's guide contained a form letter of protest over the preferred position of Italian navvies in a railway camp.

The three guidebooks/dictionaries became popular with Canadian Macedonians and their families. They were invaluable compilations of collective wisdom and experience—one of the community's first public expressions of its sense of its place in Toronto and in the New World. They occupied a special place in each household and were consulted frequently, if not acted on, by one and all. However, Macedonians were quick to grasp their limitations. These guides could only alleviate the heavy dependence on go-betweens, both in and outside the group. People met the need to provide for themselves, in what we would now call social insurance and workers' compensation, by creating a range of community institutions.

"Life Was Different Here"

ANDREJ POTOCKÝ

> *Andrej Potocký's point of departure was the village of Sedliacká Dubová, Orava country, Upper Hungary (Slovakia). He progressed via Hamburg by ship to Ellis Island, New York, and then by rail to Chicago, St. Paul, Minnesota, and Spokane, Washington, finally coming to Nelson, British Columbia, in 1910. The Slovaks originated in the dual monarchy of Austria-Hungary, which was allied with Germany during the First World War, causing them to be branded as "enemy aliens" by the Canadian authorities.*

My three older brothers already lived in British Columbia. Jozef, the eldest, was there from 1900. The second brother, Peter, returned home after six years in December, 1909. He prepped me for the trip to Canada. At that time the Magyar [Kingdom of Hungary] government did not easily grant passports. Therefore, thousands of Slovaks left illegally, without passports. From Orava they generally crossed over the Beskidy mountains into Poland.

I left home on June 23, 1910, without a passport or birth certificate. Jozef Michna led me from the village at 12:30 A.M. over our Magura mountain to the village of Erdutka. Mother packed into my backpack one change of clothes for my month-long trip into a strange land.

In Erdutka a certain Mr. Červen, a forester for the landlord of Orava castle, found me a youngster who guided me over the Beskidy mountains into Poland. After that I was on my own. I described my trip to Canada in the *Kalendár Kanadskej slovenskej ligy* (1953).

In Nelson, B.C., I spent the night of June 17, 1910 in the home of Ján Svoboda, my brother Jozef's godfather. I arrived at Westley, B.C. in the morning of June 18. My two brothers were already there. Jozef was the foreman of the railroad workers. He was like a father to me until his death. He was married with two daughters. Three weeks later the stork brought him a third. My brother Ján was also there since 1907. Wesley is about 30 miles from Nelson on the Columbia River.

I started working on July 23, 1910. We worked on the railroad for ten hours a day. Newly-hired workers earned 15 cents an hour. One had to buy one's groceries, clothes and repay one's parents for the trip with such earnings. The trip cost 450 gold coins (Hungarian). One gold coin was worth two Hungarian crowns. It was a bloody and callous-making 15 cents an hour. It was also extremely hot—85 to 115 degrees Fahrenheit. From this heat I suffered nosebleeds three to five times a day. My brother Jozef worried that I would not be able to take it. The only drinking water was from the Columbia River. My shirt was covered with salt from the evaporating sweat.

In those days railroad workers in British Columbia had to feed themselves. Six of us lived in a wooden shack. One of us cooked, another baked, the others carried water uphill from the Columbia River. We took turns each week. We also washed our own clothes. One had to learn to darn, sew, cook and bake. One also had to take care of one's own bed, which consisted of straw or pine boughs laid across bare boards.

For breakfast we cooked oatmeal for 30 minutes and washed it down with coffee mixed with milk. We also fried some bacon. For supper we had baked beans. In the morning we soaked the beans in water and baked them in the evening. That's what we ate for two years, except on Fridays. On Fridays, instead of bacon we had yellow cheese. One pound of bacon cost 35 cents, but you had to buy a whole slab that was dry and covered with mould. Eggs were 30 cents a dozen, and half were rotten. A hundred pounds of flour cost $2.10. We baked bread thus: in the evening we made some yeast and in the morning we kneaded the dough and let it sit and rise on our bed, covered. When we returned home from work, we baked it.

Wesley had a large sawmill which had burned down in 1908. Nothing remained except one store and a few houses watched over by a young Englishman. Apart from seven workers and a foreman with his wife, no other people worked on the rails. The store supplied settlers along the Columbia River, upon which plied stern-wheelers.

For the last two years it was impossible to buy some meat. There was no place to refrigerate it in that heat. Ice could not be had and refrigerators did not yet exist. If one wanted to have meat, one had to go to Nelson for it.

My first two pairs of shoes from the Eaton's Catalogue in Winnipeg cost $1.75 a pair. Dress shoes cost $5.00 a pair. Work pants cost $1.50. Those $1.75 shoes lasted me for ten hours. When it rained, the shoes got soaked and fell apart like paper. My daily wage was exactly $1.75.

After a week of work I injured my knee and it swelled up. The elder Jozef Kurčinka advised me to massage it, that it would heal by morning. His hands were as hard as tin. He massaged the leg with Carbolic Liniment. He poured it on and it burned so much that you could see my veins. My brother Ján took me to the hospital in Nelson. I rested there for two weeks and one more week at home. At that time my cousin Pavol Potocký was also in the hospital because he had lost a leg while dynamiting some boulders that had fallen on the tracks. There were many such incidents. Three of our Slovaks lost their legs, and their lives.

In Castlegar one locomotive was always on duty. It helped push trains up Farron mountain; then it returned. In 1911 this locomotive quietly passed by our shack at around 4:00 A.M. It was early March and the ground was covered with snow. As we walked to work, not quite a mile from West Robson, we noticed some gloves on the rails. About 150 feet further down we found a person's head, as if cut off by a sword. In West Robson we found a man without a head laying beside the tracks, covered with blood. Since I was the youngest in our gang, I had to clean up the blood. Never in my life has my heart been so heavy with worry that this could also be my fate.

Who that was and what was his nationality I do not know. They carried the body to the CPR station, which was only 200 feet away. In those years there was no road, only the railroad track. Whoever went looking for work had to carry his bedding and backpack on his back—they weighed 60–70 pounds.

For the winter the "roadmaster" sent us a letter, announcing how many men were to be laid off. Only two were to remain at work, those who had the greatest seniority. Since I was the youngest, my brother Jozef gave me his place, because he was sure that he would get a job in Castlegar in their sawmill, which they were just constructing. Jozef Kurčinka returned to the Old Country and left his place to Peter Bajdík. It was a very cold winter. He was a strong 34 year-old and I was only 17. In the winter the rails often cracked from the cold. We had to replace them with new ones that weighed 700 pounds, and that was very hard on me.

That first winter our little rail-wagon, on which we went to work, was struck from behind three times by a freight train that suddenly appeared from behind a curve. We were lucky to have jumped from our wagon just in time.

In the winter snow often completely covered the tracks. That's when they attached a plow to a train, to push it aside. On January 1, 1912, one of these plough trains jumped the tracks just above a tunnel. It killed a foreman from South Slocan. On the next day a locomotive set out from Nelson to investigate. Jozef Kurčinka was killed at that same spot. He had returned to Canada for a fifth time. He came from the village of Dlhá nad Oravou. My brother Jozef then claimed his job, which he got at the end of March. Since they needed more men, I moved to my brother's place in South Slocan. It is 12 miles south-west of Nelson.

There were three power dams around the Kootenay River in 1912. Today there are six. Here life was different. The region resembled our Orava. Near the tracks were farms with fruit trees. Today the Douk-hobors live there. They call it the "Beautiful Valley." Here one could buy fresh eggs and meat for cheaper prices. We didn't have to pay for the fruit. The local farmers were generous to us and we reciprocated. Since there were no roads yet, we often gave them a ride. Eight passenger trains passed through South Slocan to Grand Forks, Trail, Rossland and Slocan City. One could catch nice fish in the Kootenay River. After work one of us cooked and the other went fishing. Here, too, we had to look after ourselves. We lived in the wagon. It had only one window and door. One could stretch out only in the centre of the wagon.

While I lived in Wesley a Syrian priest came to Castlegar for Easter services. Above the store and post office was a hall where he celebrated Mass and heard confessions with the help of cards written in various languages. He came once a year and people came from all over to fulfill their Easter duty. It was different in South Slocan. In Creston Valley, about three miles from South Slocan there stood a large sawmill and above the store a hall. The chief cook at the sawmill was a Slovak, Michal Sitek from Podbiel, Orava, and he was still single. There were three French-Canadian families, one Croatian called Kocejančik and in Glade one Italian family. Every month Father John came from Nelson. He celebrated Mass in the hall and all the Slovaks attended. Michal Sitek then treated us to some coffee and cookies. I will always be grateful for his generosity. He is buried in the United States of America.

Most of the railroad workers were Slovaks, Ukrainians, Italians and Swedes. During World War I, the CPR received orders to fire all workers from enemy countries who were not yet Canadian citizens. Most of us had not been in Canada long enough to take out citizenship, and many of us came only for the earnings. From Proctor to Midway there was one superintendent and four bosses of various backgrounds. Whoever worked under the English boss retained his job. But the Swede fired everyone. The same goes for the Italian. I was lucky enough to keep my job. Our Slovaks, the brothers Ján and Peter Šutaj, lost their jobs.

During the war in South Slocan 18 men worked in three places. Half were Slovaks and the rest Ukrainians. The Ukrainians declared that they came from Russia and kept their jobs. Our Slovaks were fired. Hundreds of our Slovaks walked south to the USA before it entered the war. No one knows how many of them died. There were no roads and they had to walk through unknown forests. Many ended up in concentration camps. The Slovak Juraj Šuty, who tried to cross the border, was arrested.

One day's wages per month were confiscated for the war effort. To this day I have these receipts from the CPR. Only in 1916, when there was a shortage of labour, did they begin to release people from the concentration camps. They sent them where needed. My older brother Peter worked for two years for room and board only at Ján Svoboda's in Nelson. I, too, considered fleeing across the border, but was able to avoid being sent to a concentration camp.

Since a daughter was born to my brother Ján in Eholt, Jozef and I were invited to the Christening. It was to be on a Saturday in August of 1913, on our return trip. There was a tunnel where the passenger train and the freight were supposed to separate, on a siding. The freight was late and the passenger train was supposed to wait on the siding. But, instead, it went into the tunnel, which was three-quarters of a mile long. The trains almost collided—ours stopped only two feet from the freight. Since then the trains have to turn on their front lamps, to avoid collisions. As a memorial to our near-death experience, Jozef wrote to our parish priest in Sedliacká Dubová and had a painting made showing two trains on a collision course, with our Guardian Angel separating them. To this day this painting hangs in the rectory of our village. I have a photocopy.

. . . As the Great War continued, I decided to move to Fort William. I left South Slocan on April 17, 1918 and went to join my countryman Martin Štrbavý. I spent the first night at his place and then started to board at the home of František Bachlieda Ťapák. I found employment at the CPR coal dock, where I worked for 40 years, until my retirement in 1958. During the winter I worked in the shipyards.

In the fall of 1918 [1919] I was struck down by the Spanish flu and spent a month in the hospital. It was a terrible disease. In 1929 I had three head operations within two weeks, due to some disease. I was in the hospital from November 15 to March 1. My right hand and left leg were paralyzed after the operation and I lost all the hair on my head. Today they treat such illnesses with injections. The hospital and the doctor sent me a bill for $1,480, not counting nursing services. I had to pay it on the installment plan.

. . . Besides having served in various city positions and also as a warden of our church, in 1935 I became the Supreme Secretary of the Canadian Slovak League. I held this position until 1954. It was a very demanding but interesting job. With God's help and with the assistance of my lodge brothers and sisters, the Canadian Slovak League grew and prospered, in spite of the fact that it was the Great Depression. In this position I not only learned a lot, but made many good friends, with whom I still correspond, and who still send me greetings or who come to visit me. I am truly grateful.

. . . I will not speak of whatever I accomplished as an organizer, whether on a national or cultural basis. That you will find in the minutes of fraternal, parish and cultural organizations. I acted according to my Slovak conscience as a true son of our nation in a distant country, although I left it as a youth of sixteen. Since then I have not seen my native land. In spite of that, my native river Oravienka still appears before me, as if I had left it only yesterday. Not just the Oravienka, but all those sweet, beautiful Slovak pines, rivers, streams, mountains and meadows still haunt me from afar in all of their majesty.

In Steerage, 1910

AN ENGLISH TRAVELLER

This account of a trip from Liverpool to Montreal was written by a young Englishman. His 1910 article in the Montreal Star *ended with stark conclusions about the immigrant process.*

We cast off at 7 P.M. on a Saturday, and a glance around the forward and after compartments of the steerage accommodations revealed a strange conglomeration of nationalities—Russians, Roumanians, Poles, Hebrews, Scandinavians, Germans, Swiss, French, and Italians, comprised the foreign element, while the major portion of the steerage complement were English emigrants, women with children going out to rejoin their husbands, who had preceded them; young men seeking their fortunes in Canada, some capable, many not; whilst a bevy of young women . . . completed the number.

Slipping down the Mersey, the first meal of the passage is announced by the ringing of a bell, and in vain I scrutinize and taste the food placed before me in an endeavor to find fault with it. It is good plain wholesome fare, exceptionally well cooked, and undoubtedly, in many cases, far superior to that obtainable by the emigrant at home.

Take the following menu as an average example:—Breakfast, 7 a.m.: Oatmeal porridge and milk, bacon and eggs, fresh baked bread and butter, tea, coffee. Dinner, 12 a.m.: Soup, roast beef, potatoes and vegetables, fresh bread and biscuits, plum pudding and sweet sauce, ice cream, fruit. Tea, 5:30 p.m.: Red herrings, fresh bread and butter, jam, marmalade, currant buns, tea. Supper: 8 p.m.: Biscuits, cheese, gruel.

I figured out the cost of my passage across from England to Quebec, and third class railroad fare to Montreal, roughly speaking, at $27.00. The distance is close on 2,700 miles and on the basis of these figures it works out at one cent per mile. Compare this with a railroad journey from Montreal to Vancouver, where you have to provide your own food.

I slept in a four berthed room, and had for my mates an Anglo-Canadian, who had been across to the Old Country to place his mother away in her last long sleep.

An Irish horse breaker, (a broth of a boy) and a Cockney never-do-well from the Slums of London, who was being sent out by some charitable (?) society.

Don't think I am hard on the Londoners out of narrow minded prejudice (I was born within 12 miles of Westminster Abbey), but of all the dirty, shiftless, grumbling, growling guys I ever struck, he was the limit. I happen to know as I practically lived with him for nine days, and had him sized up in nine minutes. This is the class of emigrant Canada can well do without, and to protect herself from such, is making her emigration laws more stringent and severe every year.

The greatest care is exercised by the Steerage Head Steward in keeping the various nationalities together. For instance, the foreign element (single men) were berthed forward and excepting on the occasion of concerts and sports were barred from coming aft. This is a very wise and necessary precaution.

Any complaint made receives immediate attention and if a legitimate one is when possible remedied.

The bane of a sea voyage, especially in dirty weather (and we had it pretty rough until we reached the Straits of Belle Isle) is mal-de-mer. I have never been sea-sick so cannot describe the horrible sensation, but judging from the terrible condition of those who were, should say it is pretty tough.

It is not my intention to discuss the merits or demerits of Vaccination as a preventative against smallpox, but as Canada insists upon her immigrants who have not undergone this simple operation, to have it performed by the ship's doctor prior to their landing I see no cause for complaint in this direction. A good deal of unnecessary drivel has been written on this subject by Canadian settlers and others who have returned to the Old Country for Canada's good. Canada pays the piper and has a right to call the tune.

Some of these feather bed Colonists would squeal if they had to experience ship life 20 years ago. Things are getting better all the time. Steerage is now as good and better than second cabin was a few years. Some steerage passengers get angry because their rooms are not so nice, nor food not so various (it is a near thing regarding the quality) as the passenger, who pays twice as much for his passage. I paid £5 10 0 to come across plus 13-9 railroad fare and got good value for my money, and courteous attention thrown in.

It is impossible to time the arrival of a liner at her destination like a railroad train and for this reason, no doubt, can be attributed the long wait of three hours on a bitterly cold frosty morning, for the arrival of the immigration authorities on our disembarkation at Quebec. Put a bit of gold lace on an ignoramus, place him in the position of a Government official, and a "Bowery tough" is a lamb in comparison. I don't care what nationality a man is, if he is worthy of the name of a man, he merits treatment different to that received by many whilst passing through the Immigration sheds. Think of it: three and a half hours herded together in a stuffy room, the atmosphere of which you could cut with a knife, and not allowed to move. I sat next to a quaintly dressed woman and her family from one of the tribes of Northern Russia, where they never wash for fear of getting pulmonary trouble. When I stretched my legs and endeavored to get near the key hole for a breath of pure air, I was asked if I did not feel well by a supercilious individual. Being afraid to open my mouth for fear of the odor suffocating me, I shook my head, when I was told to take my seat, and gently, but firmly, pushed into it again. Talk about the Black Hole of Calcutta, it was a fool to it.

There is need for reform in this department, also in the way the railway sidetracked us on the journey to Montreal. Thirteen hours from the time of leaving Quebec until we arrived at the Montreal depot. I had a headache I shall not forget in a hurry, and a taste in my mouth I would not have given to a dead rat.

Carefully reviewing the incidents of my passage across, I arrived at the following conclusions, based on actual experience not supposition.

First. The second class emigrant liners naturally are not so well fitted—fitted mark you—(they are victualled on the standard lines of the company whose flag they hoist, and the food is as good, wholesome and plentiful, in addition to being well cooked), as the more modern and newer liners. The older boats, which are fast making way for the newer and larger ones, make a bath on the trip across for the steerage passenger almost impossible, which to a clean living man or woman is a distinct hardship, although if it were possible to provide a bath for every passenger, my experience is that not ten out of every hundred would avail themselves of the privilege. One individual with whom I berthed, did not wash his face on the way across and he was not the only one by a long chalk.

Second. The companies are too ready to overcrowd the third class accommodation of their liners to the discomfort of their passengers and make it doubly hard for the stewards to give that courtesy and attention which many of them find a pleasure in doing, on the return trip.

Thirdly. A very minute investigation should be made as to the bona fides of the so-called charitable and colonising societies who dump useless and undesirable emigrants into Canada and profit considerably thereby under the cloak of charity.

Fourthly. Certain officials of the immigration sheds should be made to understand they are dealing with human beings, in many cases far superior intellectually and physically to themselves, and either hand out reasonable treatment to those whom they are paid to pass through their hands, or quit.

Lastly. Anyone suffering from tuberculosis in any of its dreaded stages should not be allowed to land. Canada is quite able, unfortunately, with other countries, of raising her crop of consumptives, a disease far too prevalent here to admit of raw recruits and seasoned veterans in this sad direction, being added to the ranks. She has neither time nor room for constitutional cripples and it is alarming the number of physical emigrants, with neither health or money, who flock across in a futile endeavor to find both, to this country's cost and detriment.

"I Thought Only of the Music"

ANTONIO FUNICELLI

Antonio Funicelli gave a typical and vivid itinerary of life as an artisan-labourer, capturing the Italian love of music in his life trajectory and the tension—so clearly rendered here—between "dream" and "reality."

I came from a town called Alife, in Campanie. I arrived in Montreal in May 1911—I was 18 years old then. The boat had left from Naples; it then stopped at Palermo to take other passengers. Afterwards it stopped in Portugal, and from there it travelled to Boston. On the boat there were not only Italians, but also Greeks, Portuguese, Sicilians. We passed the medical in Naples, just before boarding; we were also vaccinated.

On our arrival in Boston, I had the impression of being among stray sheep—some going this way, the others that way. Some officials checked our papers and saw that we were headed directly to Montreal, so they let us pass. I remember when we got down on the dock there were Italians who were selling bananas. In Italy, they had bananas, but who ever saw them? They were for the rich. You could find them in Naples, but not in the villages. So my mother bought a large bread and a bunch of bananas. Let me tell you: I never ate so many bananas in my life! Then we took the train for Montreal. We travelled the whole night.

My father was already in Montreal, as was one of my brothers and a sister. An aunt who owned a grocery store in Montreal had helped them come over. Then it was me and the rest of my family. We were going to live next to my aunt, not far from the parish of Saint Cuné-gonde. Other Italians lived there, but they were scattered—some lived in Saint Henry, others in Ville Émard or Côte Saint Paul, or at Lachine. A good number of them came from the Marches and Campobasso. They had already opened a few groceries, shoe-shops, bakeries, and so on.

I began working at ten cents an hour at Canadian Car. I was a labourer. It was not very difficult to find work, but I did not speak the language. The foreman called us all "Joe": "Hey, Joe, come here, you!" There we were mixed up with all nationalities. We lifted the iron on the freight cars to send them to the foundry. Labourers like me were hired by the week. We started at ten cents an hour, and afterwards our pay was raised to fifteen cents. At that time life was less expensive, but you had to make ends meet. If you went to a bar for a beer it cost five cents. Eight cents for a 22 ounce bottle. Two bottles cost 15 cents, and you could save a penny.

I stayed at Canadian Car for nine months. I was not made for this kind of work. It was not a craftsman's work: "Take this debris, bring it there, load that, bring them here." Those who could speak a bit of the language were better treated than those who just arrived. And then we did not know which language we should learn, English or French.

I was a trained shoemaker. So, when I had made some economies, I decided to open a small shop to repair shoes. It was not difficult because I knew my trade well; also because you needed little capital, there were no machines involved. Bit by bit, I established a clientele. Even though I did not speak the language well, I was able to tell them the price: "75 cents, 50 cents, one dollar" and they understood. My shop was on Notre Dame Street, near the parish of Saint Cunégonde. I had found a little shack, and it sufficed.

I had learned my trade in my village; I also studied music. There, there was a master shoemaker who had his own shop, and took in boys as apprentices. He taught me how to make a pattern, how to cut the leather, how to put it on the shoe form; we did this all by hand. He was strict, and how! We did not know sports. We went to school then after school we learned the trade. By the age of 15 or 16 I had learned my trade and I was capable of making a pair of shoes a day. I remember that my shoes were on display in the shop window. But we worked night and day. The master had his customers; they came and we made their shoes to measure.

But my passion was music. In my village there was a municipal brass band, and the *maestro* taught music to the boys, to have enough students for the village band. We were given uniforms and when we played, they paid us. At the start, my father did not want me to learn music; he thought musicians were vagabonds. He said: "They never work, they just play." He was hard on musicians because in his trade he worked with iron and wood—hard work! For him, all the musicians did was to march in procession, caress their instruments, and then go home after the performance. I was forced to study my music in hiding, because I was strongly attached to music, it turned me on. I played the trombone in our brass band, but I also learned to play the mandolin. I was also taught theory . . . even today I write music. . . .

In Montreal, at the start, I wanted to return to Italy to study music, but my mother would scream at me, cause my brothers and sisters were still too young and they needed my income. So I studied here. With the savings I made as a shoemaker I was able to pursue music. I gave my shop to one of my brothers, and I dedicated myself to music. I studied night and day, for two or three years. I studied the violin at the Canadian Academy of Music on Sherbrooke Street. There were many professors who taught different instruments and gave courses in singing. My violin professor was Mr. Albert Chamberlain. That is how I managed. I studied and I became a professional musician.

At the age of 23 or 24 years I began to play the violin with a small group of musicians. We played in the movie theatres because at that time the films were silent, and it required accompanying music. The owner of the theatre gave us a sheet with the theme and we made the arrangements for the different instruments. We were a part of the Musicians' Union. It was a well organised union, and affiliated with the United States. If someone needed a musician or a band, they phoned the union and they arranged everything. We came from all nationalities. There were a lot of Italians. The union president, Charlie Molinari, was Italian, and he spoke three languages.

Meanwhile I married and started a family. My wife was born here, but her parents were Italian immigrants. When we were married my band came to the church and played the entrance march and the exit march, with a violinist who played in my place—a Belgian: he played so well!

At this time there was an Italian brass band. The conductor was Giuseppe Agostini—he played many instruments and also taught the piano. He was a sculptor by trade. I played several times in this band. We played processions at Notre Dame de la Défense, with fireworks, just as we had celebrated in Italy. With this I earned a few dollars. During the First World War when a group of Italians were headed off to fight, we would go to the Windsor Station and play the Royal March, with the Italian flag. It lasted an hour, and we were paid a few dollars. It was organised by a committee and the Italian Consul. They asked Maestro Agostini to gather 20–25 musicians to play the Royal March. Most of these young men who departed, never returned. Others returned mutilated, having lost an arm, another a foot.

With my training as a shoemaker I could have lived in my village. But my father decided to sell his shop. My father, he was a coach builder. He built coaches. He was an artisan—he worked in iron and wood. The wheels, the springs, the chassis, he made them all. Our village was an ancient Roman fortress, surrounded by walls. We had some contact with the neighbouring villages, because this region was rich in water and produced lots of vegetables to sell in the neighbouring villages. Some *paesi* [villages] were so close we could easily walk to them. We also celebrated religious festivals, we went with the brass band, during the season, in spring or the summer—there was a festival here, another there, that way we could get around quite well. In winter, each went back to their own work, because we musicians had several trades—one was a tailor, or a barber, yet another a shoemaker. . . . But there was never enough work—not enough money either. My father in his trade was paid with sacks of potatoes, or a sack of beans, or even a small lamb; that was how we were paid.

Many people from my village emigrated to the United States, Brazil and Argentina. They came back after two or three years with a few thousand dollars. And when the money ran out, they left again. They left their families in the *paese* [countryside], sending money and coming and going. So my father also decided to leave. When he arrived here, he did not take up his trade, but worked at Canadian Car and worked as a blacksmith. He stayed a bit of time, and started to age, for the work there was so hard.

For us musicians also it was hard. When the talking pictures arrived in Montreal, they installed the machines in the theatres and many among us could no longer find work. I foresaw the depression because I had read the papers and when talking films were developed I told my musician friends: "The day will come when we will no longer work with our instruments, we must turn to another trade." "Oh, you are talking foolishness," they would tell me. But it was like that. They began to install these machines in the theatres, and we had trouble finding work. The Musicians' Union went bankrupt. So I took up my trade again as a shoemaker.

In the beginning, when I attended the Academy of Music in Montreal, I thought to make a career as a concert musician, but who could make it? It took lots of money, or have someone to help me climb those difficult mountains. Some succeeded; others made it half-way.

Writing Back to Newfoundland, 1912

JOHN SPARKS

John Sparks, writing home from Vancouver in 1912 to the editor of the Bay Roberts Guardian, *hit classic Newfoundland themes. Newfoundland, then not a part of Canada, could be a paradise on earth if only resources were properly developed and people were treated decently. After all, the argument went, look at how well Newfoundlanders did elsewhere when they were given a fighting chance.*

Dear Mr. Editor:—Kindly allow me space in your valuable paper to pen a few words re your comments in the developing of Newfoundland, and which you say could be a great deal better than it is. Yes, I must agree with you on this subject, as I feel sure that Newfoundland as a country can be extended to a far greater prosperity than she now is if only her people, or we may say, her leading men that hold the reins would throw off that yoke which is put upon the working-class and pay them the value of their labor things would not be as they are today in Newfoundland.

Think of it, Mr. Editor, a man with a family working from dawn until midnight and only getting from $1.25 to $2 a day. What does it all mean? Is it not asking the blood of the working man and giving it to the few that can lay back in their chairs and laugh at these poor working-class people. Now why cannot these Upper Ten, as we may term them, compare the system of the working call with other countries, and see the development that is brought about, which is due to good judgment and paying the laboring man what he is worth and not keep them going along in the same old rut as they have been going all the time. I for myself know that a country cannot develop itself as long as the working classes are kept bound down to a certain standard. Newfoundland has its own prosperity, but it is only two or three that has the control of the whole thing, and it is those that are keeping it as it is, and who are afraid to put their money to uses that would go the development of the country. No, they go to a certain extent and no further, and finally, it is the same thing over and over again, and therefore no room is allowed for development.

Why not open up our little Island. It can be done, and it has the class of people to do it, as the word Newfoundlander is enough for any country where I have been, and surely he is worth as much in his own country as he is in any other country. There is not a country where a Newfoundlander has gone but he is far better situated than he would be if he had stayed at home. But the whole trouble is that he had to leave it, and that is what many are still doing, and the whole thing is due to the system under which the working class are being kept down to a certain stage and not allowed to get ahead.

Now what can we find in a Newfoundlander when he is away and living in a country which is based on the right system of working. Take, for instance, here in Vancouver. Why, almost all the building propositions are supervised by Newfoundlanders. And again we may mention the halibut fishing. It is almost wholly commanded by New-foundlanders. Capt. A. Dawe, who as you know is a Bay Roberts man, and who for many years was in charge of one of Vancouver's halibut steamers, and whose ability and skill placed him in a position with the Government as captain of the Government dredge. We will mention other Newfoundlanders who are at present in command of steamers sailing out of this port, viz: Capts. Churchill, Freeman, Barry and Keough. And we may put Capt. Churchill as head of the fleet, having headed all the others in the catch this past season, while Capt. Freeman's tact and energy has placed him in the position he occupies and likewise Capts. Keough and Barry. I could mention many others, but time will not allow me.

Now, Mr. Editor, where is the problem of all this to a Newfound-lander in Newfoundland. Is it not the fault of the capitalist? Let them put up their money in circulation and pay the working call what they are worth. Invest in land, open up farms, etc., and not keep their money tucked away in old stockings where it will do nobody any good. Let the working class force those industries and get down to business, and Newfoundland will be as well as any other country and her men will be able to get a living at home.

Now, Mr. Editor, I will not take up any more of your space, but trust that things will come to a greater stand than they are at the present time. Thanking you for this kind permission, I am yours from the old town of Bay Roberts,

Rugged British Columbia

DAISY PHILLIPS

> *Daisy Phillips and her husband, Jack, were hopeless English*
> *farmers who planted apple trees in the wrong place. Daisy loved*
> *the rugged life in British Columbia. Her husband did not. He*
> *was relieved when war broke out in 1914, giving him an excuse*
> *to return to the homeland. He was killed and she never returned*
> *to Canada, though she had left everything behind, including*
> *all of her underwear neatly folded in the closet. She scrimped a*
> *living in Oxford and spoke of their days on their B.C. farm as*
> *the happiest in her life. This letter was written by Daisy to her*
> *mother on August 15, 1912, from Athalmer, B.C.*

Dearest Mother,

Here I am again, Thursday, and my home letters not touched, but the days slip away and when you have done tea you must wash up, and then Jack calls, "Come and give me a hand!" And so we go on. Your daughter's latest accomplishment is sawing down trees! We have got a crosscut saw and are clearing the trees in front of the verandah on the slope so as to get a better view up to Mount Hammond. Jack cuts a wedge-shaped piece out of the tree with the axe and then we begin to saw, one at each end of the saw with a swinging movement, till we get within two inches of the cut. Whoever gets there first calls out "Two inches," and if the other side is not so near *you* only saw easily. Then a crack, then a call, "Timber!" and down she comes. Don't think I shall get killed! There is heaps of time to get out of the way and I am getting quite expert at knowing which way it will fall. We fell one tree each day directly after breakfast. Very fine exercise, and it makes me ache all round my ribs! This morning I set to and bottled more rhubarb in cold water, as old Patterson down in Athalmer (who is an "old timer" and has a tiny shack and a small garden *full* of rhubarb) gave us two sacks full, so we have two dozen "quart sealers" ready for the winter. One cannot possibly get fresh fruit or vegetables until next May as the summer season is late because of the night frost, although the days may be warm. I find that people here seem to bottle about 60 quarts of fruit and think nothing of it. Of course, we shall when we get fruit of our own, but this year we have to buy it and we have so many expenses. I have only my camp stove. All the same, I am going to try and bottle a dozen bottles of plums next week. You make a thick syrup and slightly cook the fruit in it and bottle without more cooking, as far as I can make out. I must try and get to see Mrs. Cuthbert tomorrow and she may be able to help me, but at present I have no weights or scales to help me as that Stores box is not unpacked yet and the barn is brimming over!

A thunderstorm is now raging and rain pelting down. It is very sad as our rye is just cut and the last few days have been so sunny and warm. Another stroke of bad luck, Jacks calls it, but that is because the plasterer has not yet come to the house. When we go to the Company, they always say, "The lime will be up by the next boat." In fact, everybody always tells you, if you are out of anything you want, it will be in by the next boat! When we first came we believed them, now we do *not*. I have quite given up worrying about things. It is no good as here you are perfectly helpless to help yourself and just take what comes or what the Stores have got and are very thankful! On Sunday we walked across to see a Dr. and Mrs. Turnor. I don't know the number of the lot, but quite close to Wilmer, about 300 feet above. We cut across country so it was only about two miles and a half. I had met Dr. Turnor and he had lent Jack some papers on chickens and we went to return them. Being good walkers Jack and I find it is the best way to go and see people. They are always pleased to see you, and are not all as energetic perhaps as we are. Mrs. Turnor was very nice, and there are two girls of about 12 and 13, and a little boy about 5. One little girl is rather lame. They have got ten acres on top and the rest of the land is much too steep to cultivate and runs down to the Wilmer Road. Another doctor was staying with them for a month. He had been ill and came from England for the trip, but it does not suit him very well because it is too high. I met Mr. Marples on the road yesterday and he has asked us to go up to see him on Sunday. He is going home in a week's time to fetch his wife and two children, and his house is being built meanwhile. He said he would take us on an awfully nice walk to a big ranch that is over the other side of Toby Creek. It belongs to Jim Johnson. We have heard a lot about his ranch but thought it too far to go until we got a horse. Mr. Marples has found a short-cut, across country, I expect, and that means jumping and climbing over many tree-trunks. The only tracks one finds occasionally are pony trails and then it is easier going.

Did I tell you I had got some Waterglass and am trying to preserve eggs when I can spare a few to put down? I am always afraid how things will turn out, as I am afraid I have diluted the Waterglass too much. Many thanks for the recipe for treacle pudding. I hope to get suet sometimes in the winter, and could get it now had I a kitchen to cook in. Many thanks, too, for the *Daily Mails* you have sent. I cut out the recipes for scones in the last one. All recipes without many eggs are useful, and things in the cake line will be a great deal wanted, also at any time if you see recipes for "doing up" stale tough beef and suchlike. Tonight we have curried haricot beans and stewed rhubarb, and last night we had scrambled eggs and *peas*, the first we had picked, and they were a real treat although boiled without mint! The Waring books have come and are most useful. It is such fun opening these things when they arrive, and we both grab the *Lady Pic.* and *Punch.* I have forgotten to tell you that Mr. and Mrs. Hamilton drove up to see me yesterday afternoon. Mr. Hamilton is a financial secretary and manages the Company's affairs, and I should say Mrs. Hamilton manages *him*! She is a bossy bouncing female and might be a Suffragette if in England, and is followed about by a fox-terrier and a wolfhound, who wandered about the barn. I took him over the house but they would not stay to tea as they were going on to Mrs. Young, but brought me some recent numbers of the *Illustrated London News.* Jack does not like *her.* She has too strong views on "women's rights," so when we are in the house and she comes my husband will be very busy indeed. This happens when people do not interest him, and I find, entre nous, there are a good many of these!

Friday. This morning we have received most terribly sad news by cable. Kenny [Jack's brother] caught by machinery and killed. My poor old Jack is awfully cut up about it, and it does seem hard lines but we must wait for more particulars. He and Jack were evidently great pals, and Jack has always so looked forward to Kenny's weekly letters. He had left Chesterfield and was working with his brother-in-law at Stafford, and he and Ada were living at an hotel. His last letter was full of a pretty house with a nice garden that he was going to take and things financially were looking more promising. . . . Poor Ada, it is terrible for her. You may have heard before you get this. But as usual when you wrote to Jack about his father you said just the right thing, not too much, but in that case I am afraid he had no regrets.

I have been making some enquiries about Parcel Post, and I believe things will come alright during winter without extra cost. If you can declare a parcel as value under a dollar we have nothing to pay either. The silver things from Ways were splendidly packed and arrived in *perfect* condition, the case too, but it was a good strong one. . . .

I have ordered my onions and carrots for the winter and they will be put in the root cellar out of reach of Jack Frost. Our meat is hung up to freeze outside—I expect, suspended from a tree! More or less of a carcass, I suppose, and Jack the butcher, but I don't suppose we shall recognize the joint! The great thing here is to have a Wellbanks cooker, and we shall get one out from the Stores next year, I expect, but it is too late now. It is the same sort of thing as a Warrens cooking pot. You steam the meat and then just finish it off in the oven. You will see these in the Stores list, also the cross-cut saw, also a thing you hang on the wall of the kitchen for drying towels, with many arms and when done with folds up flat. . . .

We have got nearly all our picture frames fixed up now and new glasses, so don't worry any more about them as I have rubbed the furniture with linseed oil and I think we can mend all easily, except the little table. Jack is not a great carpenter at present. He much prefers making a wide path in front of the verandah and working with pick and shovel! But in the winter I think he will prefer the house more, if we ever *do* really get into it. You talk about my brown skirt being dyed! I only wish you could see it. Camp life has done for it completely and it has a *darn* of brown wool right across the front where I caught it on a tree trunk! But I use it for cooking and washing and am so very thankful I had it with me. It is hard wear on my underclothes and nightdresses too, and I have only *two* of everything going and have had to darn a "nighty" in one or two places. This was lighting the fire when Jack was ill, so don't say anything about it. You see, we stroll out of the barn quite happily in these nether garments. . . .

No more news as I want to write a line to poor Ada. Jack is not able to sleep and is frightfully down. He says if this had happened a year ago he would have felt absolutely alone in the world. When letters come they will be rather upsetting, and I am afraid he will get one from Kenny tonight. Much love to all. It will soon be a case of one post a week, I expect, and then perhaps you and Freda could take it in turns, and it would not be quite such a tax if you had not much time. You always, both, write such a lot, but I love the letters and I often see no other woman for a week at a time!

Your affectionate child,
Daisy

The CPR's Rough Treatment

IVAN HUMENYUK

> *Ivan Humenyuk returned to Russia after several months of working as a navvy for the Canadian Pacific Railway. From his home village in the province of Volyn, he sent a petition to Sergey Likhachev, the Russian consul general in Montreal, complaining about the rough treatment of immigrant labourers by the CPR and asking for assistance in obtaining the wages that he claimed the company had denied him. During the First World War, there were frequent conflicts between immigrant labourers from Austria and Russia, stirred by wartime nationalism. Humenyuk referred in his petition to a meeting with the governor of one of Russia's provinces; this is almost certainly fiction.*

On the 29th day of March, we, Russian immigrants, came from Russia to Halifax on the steamer *Birma*. At debarkation, Canadian immigration authorities charged each of us ten dollars for railway transportation through Canada to the place of our work, and gave us some sort of tickets, which later turned out to be contracts. There were over a thousand immigrants, but nobody knew that they cheated us this way into taking contracts. We were carried locked up in the cars like criminals; at the stations where the train stopped, CPR policemen with handguns and other weapons surrounded the train and did not let anyone out, and those who did come out were beaten like criminals with handguns and some other weapons and driven back into the car. This way they carried us for five days and brought us to a parkway in Saskatchewan, and there they divided us into work gangs.

I began to work in early April, and on the 15th of May I got my first paycheque for fourteen dollars for twenty-one days of work. The rest of the money—more than ten dollars—was again deducted to cover my rail transportation. I worked in gang no. 6 for three months and twenty-two days, but then I was forced to quit my job because of the Galicians, who would not leave us Russians alone, and went to work in gang no. 8, where I worked for three months. Altogether, I worked in two CPR gangs for almost seven months.

In the autumn, on the 26th of October my comrade Yakov Kadeyka and I had to leave our jobs and go back to Russia by the order of the legitimate Russian administrative authorities. We both took out our "times" on the 26th of October and went to Moose Jaw to the superintendent's office to get our pay. We went to the superintendent many times but got nothing. We got interpreters and paid them but nothing helped. The superintendent just kept saying: I won't give you any money, go back to work in the gang. So we tried to get our money for ten days but did not get it, and we sold both "times" to a Galician man by the name of Andrey for thirty dollars, even though [the company] owed the two of us sixty dollars. And in the evening of November 4th, I bought a ticket in Moose Jaw to Brody, Austria, for $82.70. My name on the ticket is written as Fred Huminik. And Yakov Kadeyka bought a ticket to Montreal for $42.35. In the morning of November 9th, we sailed from Montreal to France. In Warsaw, I had an occasion of meeting a governor, whom I told everything that had happened to me and also showed him the [CPR] contract. The governor gave me your address and told me to write a petition to you and ask you to get at least some of my money from the CPR. Because they secretly cheated us and gave us contracts, none of us immigrants knew absolutely anything, and they did not ask us anything, only looked at some cards that we had received in Libava and copied our names from these cards onto the contracts.

Labouring in British Columbia

ZINOVY PESHKOV

> *In 1904, at the age of twenty, Russian Zinovy Peshkov immi-grated to Canada, where he worked several years as a labourer. Later he fought for France in both world wars and represented that country as an ambassador.*

Mountains, mountains, mountains everywhere. . . . High mountains with spiked tops, covered with wild forest. Water swiftly runs down the mountains, forming sparkling foam at the bottom and turning into currents, whirling and roaring in the rapids. Trees, brought down by time and winds, get in the current's way, and it hammers wildly at the bodies of these forest giants, seeking another way and forming a sharp bend. Nature is mighty but harsh here; there is no softness or tranquility in it. Only deer and moose, which abound in the moun-tain forest, bring life into this place with their graceful moves and looks.

This mountain chain in British Columbia has a pass called Crow's Nest. There is a valley below, and in the valley there is a town popu-lated by people who dig coal from the mountains. . . .

The forest around the small town is cleared, but bare and charred stumps are left here and there, standing as reminders of magnificent trees that once grew here. Around the town, huddled on the moun-tain slopes, are shacks made of logs and boards. At one end of the town, across the fast-flowing Elk River, there is a whole settlement of shacks, all black, covered in smoke and soot. . . . The settlement is called "New York" and its residents are Russians. Most are peasants from Grodno and Minsk provinces but there are also Little Russians from Podolia. Italians live at the other end of the town. There are also the French and the Swedes. The English and the Scots live in one-storey houses inside the town.

Opposite "New York," at the foot of the mountain across the Elk River there is a row of long brick ovens, where coal is made into coke. . . . Fire burns in them night and day without stopping. The Elk takes in the firelight and refracts it strangely in the water. Men bustle around the ovens day and night, turning the red-hot coal with huge iron pokers. Their crouched backs are under great strain—it looks as if they carry long spears, fighting some invisible and mysterious enemy.

There are more than a hundred ovens, with three hundred *puds* of coal thrown into each oven. The coal burns three days and three nights before the fire is put out. With large shovels, the steel-coloured coke is moved out and thrown into railway cars. Then the ovens are again filled with coal, and again it burns. . . .

Night and day, soot falls on the town squeezed on all sides by the mountains. When wind blows from the town, all the soot is carried to the mountain slope with the shacks of "New York" huddled on it. When wind blows from the Elk River, trouble awaits the town, which is filled with coal dust and ashes. Heat blows into people's faces—sweet, acid heat. You turn away and cover your face with your hands but nothing can save you from large flakes of soot flying everywhere.

All the houses are black and the water in the ditches beside the streets is black too. Everything, everything, everything.

And that is in the town. Near the shacks that are clustered on the hill so close to the ovens, the soot and smoke are much worse.

"When we go to a well to get some water, we have to pour water from the first two buckets on the ground. There is no water in there, just black sludge. Only after that it gets cleaner. But still we never drink clean water here," say some men.

"Why'd you even drink that water when we have whisky and beer! You down a glass of that vodka, then help it through with some beer—and then you can even eat the coal *ol rait* [all right]!" say others.

"Ten years ago, nobody at home knew about America, and now whole villages are leaving," some say.

"You'll get all dirty here, but you'll make some good dollars," others say.

And they do get dirty. And they do make dollars.

The labourers' shacks are black both on the outside and the inside, as if these were not human dwellings but square chunks of coal. Everything inside is permeated with coal dust. Black tables, black benches, a black water bucket. The black beds are hay-filled sacks with black blankets thrown over. The floor is soft, slippery, covered with a thick layer of mud. And the men. . . .

Men from Grodno province live in especially dirty conditions. These are not humans but some primitive creatures. Illiterate and superstitious, they are thrifty and quiet until their first drink but turn rowdy and unruly when they are inebriated. They live the same way as they lived at home, with the only apparent difference being that here they have coal dust and mud instead of cattle manure. They even eat the Russian way, making pickled cucumbers and cabbage. In a large pot, they cook borscht that lasts them three days, and make buckwheat *kasha* and peas. And they drink, and drink, and drink. . . .

They drink on every occasion:

"You see, a fellow from home has arrived. . . ."

"Two fellows are going back home. . . ."

"How can you not have a drink on payday?"

But the worst drinking happens on Russian Orthodox Church holidays. They are strictly observed here.

Peasants from the village of N. from Pruzhany district, Grodno province, had a holiday and all men from that village drank for three days. With brawls, tears, fights, cursing and hugging. They played harmonicas, balalaikas and violins. They sang, they danced, and they remembered the homeland:

"Oh, what a holiday they are now having at home! Oh my Lord, what a holiday! And how they must be drinking! Oh, boys, what are we doing here in this God damn Canada?"

All men have left the village.

"To make some money, some dollars."

And they make money. . . .

The men live here for about two or three years, some even five.

Wives and children stay at home. Young lads are told to go by their fathers:

"Listen, son, our house is falling apart, and it would be good to add some land to our plot. . . . Go with Stepan to Canada to work on the coal. Our men are making good money there. . . ."

And the son goes to work "on the coal."

But the young folk rarely send money home. They spend it on drink and women.

The workers get paid twice a month. The money is put in a sealed envelope. The men carry the envelopes home unopened. Only when inside the shack, they open the envelopes and count the money. They put it first in one pocket, then another. Some hide the money away in their chests but then take it out again to count:

"How much would it be in rubles?"

And the money is counted in rubles.

This is how they drink whisky: they boil it with hot pepper, or if they do not boil it, then they put pepper in the drinking glass.

"This [Canadian] vodka doesn't smell good," they say. "With pepper it sure is stronger but the smell goes away."

They drink from tea glasses. The shack probably has about twenty men, and each man's chest has a ceramic jug, which can hold about five bottles of whisky.

After a drink on payday, the young start a conversation like this:

"So, shall we go to the whores in a while?"

And everybody's eyes become oily.

The older men spit and say:

"That's all you care about, damn you. . . ."

Even though the married men drink and have a good time too, they still save money.

They earn three dollars a day, and after three or four years they manage to save a thousand or more.

"America is like a drug," the men say. "What kind of life do we have? Neither here nor there. . . . The wife and kids are by themselves, and we are by ourselves. We work hard, but when you get back to Russia and live there for half a year or so, you want to go to America again. America draws us. . . . Think about this, my friend: at home I work fifteen hours for a contractor or a landlord for seventy kopeks, and here I make six rubles. Six rubles is not seventy kopeks, my friend. We have little land, and what land we have is mostly sand. Not much grows on our land. Now our wives and kids mind the farms. They hire help, too. If a soldier comes home on a leave or if there is an older man who still has strength, they hire them."

"Don't your women miss you? And the kids must have a bad time without their fathers too?"

"The kids are fine. They are even better because they don't get spanked as often, but the women are doing badly, that's true."

Toronto's Jewish Community

JOSEPH B. SALSBERG

Eleven-year old Joseph Salsberg arrived in Quebec City by ship from Poland in 1913. He and his shipmates had paper tags, with their destination written on them, attached to their lapels. The tags worn by Joseph, his mother, and sister read "Toronto," the city that he described in this 1978 interview as a magnet for Jews of smaller Polish communities.

Our haven of safety was on Cecil Street, near Spadina Avenue, at the time, a considerable distance from the old Jewish quarter which was located in the area now known as Dundas Street, from University to Yonge and then known as Agnes Street. The first Jewish community centered around that area, and the streets running off it; Chesnut Street, Centre Avenue, Elizabeth Street, Tawraley which is now Bay Street. Those were Jewish areas and as the immigrants arrived, they all found quarters there. It was an area of old small houses, many of them still framed and I found later that some of them had their toilets, the wc's, in the yard in the back of the house. They were water closets all right, but they had been added later after those cottages had been built, and they were located, they looked like the privies that we see pictures of on the farm. But they were in the backyard, and they didn't have the modern plumbing that we find in bathrooms now. Water flowed only when you sat on the seat and it stopped when the seat rose, and there were lead weights attached to the seat so that when you got up, it immediately flew back and therefore turned off the water. But I learned also that you had to learn to do it very fast, otherwise you got a wallop. The seat flew up before you managed to sidestep.

So that the community was there, the first little synagogue, the first Jewish institutions, organizations, were all centered there. The Yiddish theatre was on the corner of what was then known as Tawraley and Agnes, and which is now Bay and Dundas. The northeast corner had the Yiddish theatre. A beautiful little house, I think it had been a church a way back before, but it had a balcony and it had a gallery which was called the Family Circle group, whereas the orchestra and the balcony had individual seats. The family circle had no individual seats but benches, and the theatre management didn't even sell tickets, ordinary theatre tickets for the family circle because first come first serve, whereas the others were reserved. So you got a stiff ticket, with cardboard, and you went up and you rushed to grab a seat. However, that's where Jewry began adjusting to the new life. When my father bought the small house on Cecil St., he was among the first to move westward, the trend to cross University into the area between University and Spadina was then underway. So he already bought a house and that's where we lived when we arrived. As a matter of fact, my mother remained on the same street for 50 odd years, and she moved not from that little house because later we bought in the same block a bigger house because the family grew, and the old one was too small, so she lived there until about the last 8 years of her life. My father had passed away there, she refused to give it up, and finally we, the children, sort of insisted on bringing her up to the new area, now north Toronto, north of Eglinton.

Three Hundred Barbadians

DUDLEY MARSHALL

> *Dudley Marshall came to Canada the year before the beginning of the First World War. Born in Barbados in 1895, he lived most of his life in Toronto, but he started his Canadian life in the coal*

mines of Nova Scotia, a common destination for the few black
immigrants of the era. "The entry of black immigrants," histo-
rian Agnes Calliste writes, "was severely restricted except when
there was an urgent demand for their labour."

Down in Nova Scotia, we worked in the coal mines. That time after
the war started they needed men; so, they asked us to send and get all
our friends, anybody we knew that wanted to come out. So, we got
three hundred Barbadians over to Nova Scotia at that time. In fact,
you will find most of the descendants of people that came out at that
time. They went off to work in the mines. They came, they paid their
way. After working for a year and paying their expenses, they were
free to go any place they wanted to.

The Komagata Maru, *1914*

VANCOUVER SUN

The freighter Komagata Maru *arrived at Vancouver in May*
1914, hoping to land its 376 Punjabi passengers for settlement in
British Columbia. The Canadian government had admitted
2,000 South Asians a few years earlier, but was determined there
would be no more. At the time, Canadians called East Indian
immigrants "Hindus" or "Hindoos," even though almost all of
them were Sikhs. Komagata Maru *was carefully watched for*
two months, preventing any disembarkation. On July 20, when
this report in the Vancouver Sun *was published, the Canadian*
navy cruiser Rainbow *arrived on the scene. Three days later,*
the Komagata Maru *was dispatched from the harbour.*

The Dominion government yesterday instructed Superintendent
Reid, of the immigration department here, to take firm steps at once
to bring the Hindus on the Komagata Maru to subjection, and send
the steamer on her return passage to the Asiatic coast. All the power
and resources of the government are placed at Mr. Reid's disposal and
the telegram from the government declared that the laws of the coun-

try would be enforced if possible without using extreme measures, but if needed then forcible means would be employed. The telegram commended the Vancouver police and the special officers of the immigration department for not having used firearms in yesterday morning's encounter, and complimented everybody who took part in it for their behaviour.

It is reported that the first-class cruiser Rainbow is being made ready for use against the Hindu mutineers. The ship was taking on fuel yesterday. . . .

Owing to the possibility that the shore Hindus might make an attempt to take arms and ammunition off to the Komagata last night, the big tug Sea Lion . . . joined the gas cruiser Winamac and the launch Jessie Ellen in doing picket duty around the Komagata. The Sea Lion carried the special police in the service of the immigration department, 35 in number, armed with Ross rifles. The crowds . . . assembled on the Burrard street overhead way and along the waterfront, hoping that another attempt to get aboard the Komagata would provide them with some excitement. Nothing was done or will be done until tomorrow or the next day. When another attempt is made to get the ship out of port, it will be done properly, so as to leave no doubt of success. It will be planned with the utmost care and skilfully carried out.

Wives Left Behind

AGAFIA KOVAL

Many peasant men from Ukraine, Belarus, and other areas of the Russian Empire came to Canada in the early twentieth century to work in Canadian industries. They had no plans to take root in Canada, and they left their families at home, expecting to return in two or three years with a nest egg. But the First World War and Russian revolutions intervened, trapping the men in Canada and inflicting many hardships on wives and children, who had to spend years without their husbands and fathers. The first letter is from Agafia Koval to her husband, Afanasy, and was written on October 8, 1915. The second is to Vasyl Dohvan from his wife, who was illiterate and had to dictate her letter. Her name is unknown.

To my dear husband Afanasy from his wife Agafia. In the first lines of my letter I hurry to inform you that through God's kindness I am alive and well, and I wish you the same from our Lord. I received your letter of 1st October, for which I kindly thank you. My dear husband Afanasy, I am not very satisfied with your letter because you write that you will not come home but want me to come to you. I would go with great pleasure if I knew that I would cross the border all right. Find out if it is possible to sneak through the borders at this time and then send me a ticket. If you are going to send me a ticket, then tell me what to do with the land, whether to give it up for good or not and so on.

Your brother Demian was drafted on August 15 your nephew Stefan was drafted in May and now, that is on October 1st, he was wounded but I do not know where the wound is. His wound may be dangerous and hard to heal. We have had one bad thing after another; one month we had a big fire and 13 houses were destroyed, from Evdokim Baby to Demian Melnychuk. This year we have terrible news, it must be that God is punishing us. If these bad times last for another two years, then God knows what we will do. To till the land is very expensive but the harvest is not always good. For example, this year I had very little rye, not even enough for seed. And I only have one-half of a desyatina [1.85 acres] and I need to pay the tax and till the land—but how and for what? This crop is not worth working for. This is not life, only torture, but if I abandoned the land (did not work it), I would be ashamed of people.

You write that people live well there, and I see here that some people also live well. But if I knew that you live so well there, I would leave everything and go there. May God save anybody from a life such as mine; and I would never wish you such a life. And later it will probably be even worse. Boots that used to cost 5 rubles are now 20 rubles. I am writing you the whole truth but if you do not believe, that is fine. It is good that I am by myself here, because even though the boots are 20 rubles, I can save for them somehow, but those who have big families are doing poorly because you won't go without boots. My dear husband Afanasy, I ask you with my heart to respond after you receive my letter. I have no more news. With this,

Good-bye,
Remaining alive and well and wishing you the same,
Your wife Agafia

My dear and much respected husband! In the first lines of my letter I hurry to inform you that the children and I are alive and well but we miss you very much. The children especially miss you. I often have no time to be home. I am sent by Russian authorities to dig trenches and the children stay alone at home and cry. But I cannot refuse to go. We are now considered free citizens, we have no tsar now and we have citizens' rights. The war is going on, troops are stationed in all villages and all are happy. But I am unhappy and lonely, and I live in tears. Everything is expensive. I cannot buy anything and I have no strength to reap the field and tend to the garden because I am too exhausted. And our daughter Dunia misses you so much. I had 7 soldiers stationed at our house, and when they were leaving, she cried badly. She had got close to one of them and kept calling him "Daddy." I could not calm her down. I beg you to come back and give the children and myself some relief.

I have no more money at all and I have nowhere to get it. The recruits' wives are not sent to dig trenches, only the Americans' wives are. Because you are away, I am suffering here. The land that your father gave you was sown one year and stayed fallow the next year because everything is expensive and there is no seed. Someone wanted to buy it and I wanted to sell but Mother would not let me. And now it cannot be sold so it stays empty.

Our neighbour Sylvester gives me the hardest time. He tells everyone that I encourage the soldiers to dig his potatoes. And he maligns me and wants to see me driven away from here. He thinks that you are dead, and Andrey does not tell him anything. Earlier he used to be afraid of you but now he thinks he can do what he wants because you are away, and he tells people stupid things. Your mother married off a daughter and only goes to visit her and has forgotten completely about me. She thinks you will never come back. Your brother Afanasy is drafted to the army. He had been declared unfit three times but was drafted the fourth time.

We have a lot of news here but the man who is writing this does not understand me and I cannot explain anything to him. When you come, you will see everything yourself. If you are going to come soon, we are waiting for you impatiently, but if you cannot come soon, then send us money, because everything is expensive and I cannot buy anything for the winter and I have nothing.

With this, goodbye, dear husband, the children and I bow to you deep down, send you a kiss and cannot wait for you to come. And if you cannot come, then take me to live with you. I cannot live without you.

Picture Bride

TAMI NAKAMURA

> *Japanese picture brides saw their husbands-to-be only in photographs. When the women arrived in Canada, life was not often as advertised. Tami Nakamura found a good man waiting for her, but a stern life.*

In those days, nobody worked even if they'd graduated from girls' school. A woman just got married. If you said you were going to be a working woman, you got laughed at. In the Hiroshima area, some women became schoolteachers, nurses, or telephone operators. But that was just until they got married. I used to see young women walking past our house morning and night, going to work. They were all wearing *hakama* (Japanese-style divided skirts). If women had been free to work, like today, I would have tried it too, without getting married. But I just went to girls' school where all they gave you was a bride's education. So when I graduated I was like everybody else;

I took lessons in sewing and the *koto* [a Japanese harp]. If I started wanting to go overseas, it was because of a silly reason.

I've never told anybody about this before, but . . . It's because I wasn't good-looking. That isn't very flattering to my husband, but there it is. Besides my face, there's my frizzy hair, as you see, and it's dreadful. It's thin now, so it isn't noticeable, but it's terribly kinky. When I was a young girl in Japan, the fashion was smooth upswept hair, they had different pompadour styles, and my hair wasn't right for any of them. I suffered so much, I got to feel that I couldn't get married, and that's why I started wanting to go overseas.

One of my classmates had gone to Hawaii, and said to come, because she'd look after me. At the time I didn't like the idea of Hawaii very much. I must have had a vague dream of going to a place like the United States or Canada. So I wasn't unwilling to emigrate, in fact I really wanted to come here. I didn't care what my husband would be like. I didn't even have marriage in mind. As long as I could go, that was all I wanted. I just wanted to go to a foreign country, because I wouldn't have to wear a pompadour. Nowadays, you're lucky to have frizzy hair even in Japan; you don't need a permanent, but in those days it just wouldn't do. That was my reason for wanting to leave Japan.

At the time, you couldn't come over unless you were married. No matter how much you wanted to, it was impossible to come alone. Any husband would do, so all I had to do was get married. Two or three years after I graduated, my father became ill and died, and my mother had to make do with an officer's pension, and take care of the household. If I got married, that would take some of the burden off my mother. Besides, I could work overseas and send money back to her. I was the oldest of five children, my brothers and sisters were at home, and I came to realize how hard life was, so I felt I wanted to help out, if only a little. If my father had been alive, I think he would have been against the idea.

Just then an acquaintance of my mother's came along, saying that a certain man she knew wanted a wife. He was a farmer in Canada, and according to his father, he was doing well, so I wouldn't have to do anything but housework. So I thought, well, maybe I'll get married, and agreed. The arrangements went ahead. My father-in-law was pleased with me and took the trouble of coming to our house, and said he wanted this marriage to happen. So the discussions went ahead and I got engaged. I didn't meet the man; I just saw his photos.

Then we exchanged letters for six months. My husband often wrote, but there's nothing special that I remember. I don't remember anything of what I wrote, either. I do remember that his letters gave me the impression that he wasn't a bad person. Anyway, it was my feeling that I could get married to anybody, so I wasn't particular about details. I thought that if I were to live in a town in Canada, I could work too and send at least a little money to my mother. When I arrived, I found he was very, very poor and there was no question of sending her any.

My husband grew up in Hiroshima City, actually a place on the coast called Eba-cho about a mile from the centre of the city. It was a place where they harvested laver and oysters, and his family did a little fishing along with the farming, and they had a nice house. They were on the prosperous side, I think. My father-in-law was working, without expecting any money from overseas. It seems my husband had thought of going abroad from the time he was a child, and he left the village with a friend when he was 17. A lot of immigrants went from the Eba area to Hawaii, intending to make a success of themselves. They say quite a few went to the U.S. mainland, too.

So it seems he went to Hawaii first, worked for about six months on a sugar-cane plantation, and then came to Canada in 1907. He worked in road construction, and sawmills, and learned English by working in a hotel. At the time he came over his dream was to own a farm, so he saved everything he earned, he says. With the little money he saved by practically starving, he went west, from the area of Vernon in the interior of British Columbia, walking around looking for farmland. That was the third year after he came to Canada. He got 20 acres of uncleared land in Mission. He cleared it, and finally by the time he sent for me he was growing a few strawberries on it.

The marriage talks had gone ahead, and our parents had approved, so I had entered my husband's family register and was living at their house. When I got registered, all we did was to decorate the place with my husband's photo, invite relatives and neighbours, and hold a sort of mock marriage ceremony. I didn't bring anything with me, and lived with my in-laws without doing anything. Six months after I had married into the Nakamura family, my passport was issued. I left Japan in October 1916.

I was 21 and when time came to set out, I got happier and happier because at last I was going off to a place I'd been dreaming of for so long. There was no reason to learn about what kind of man I had married. I wasn't afraid, thinking that once I got there it would be all right. The only slight worry I had was, he was a farmer, while I had grown up in the city. I was right to worry. I came to a farm, and had a hard time of it. As a housewife I worked from sunup to sunset, cooking, washing, and bringing up the children; eventually more than 10 people were living in that farmhouse all the time, including people we brought over from Japan, and the hired men, so my work never ended.

I left Japan from Kobe, and my mother-in-law saw me off. I was already the bride, so my father-in-law paid for everything: the passage and expenses. I even got spending money. He was very nice and encouraged me all he could. I made friends with two other brides going to Canada from Kobe, just like me, and the three of us had a lot of fun; it was just like a school outing. One of them had married a man who was farming on Vancouver Island, but she had built him up too much in her imagination, and after she got to Victoria, she cried, saying she didn't know her husband was such an old man. There was no going back, but she didn't want to get off the ship either, so it was a problem. That was the peak of picture marriages, so the boat was full of brides, and we made a lot of commotion. It was a small ship called the *Sadomaru*, and it took two weeks to get to Victoria.

My husband had come to meet me from Mission in the country and later I was told that he had gone to a movie in Vancouver. It was so interesting that he wanted to see it again, and when he did, he missed the ferry to Victoria, so he came alone after the others. I didn't mind that he wasn't there, because all the brides were looking at the men, saying "whose husband is that?" Anyway, the whole ship was full of brides and they were terribly excited.

When I saw him for the first time, I thought his face was quite a bit nicer than in the photos. He was smiling a big smile. Well, it was our first meeting, so he must have been happy. As for me, I wasn't especially glad. I didn't think the marriage was good or bad. I thought "Well, this is the man I've married." For his personality, just as I had thought, he was a nice man and I had nothing to complain about. We stayed at a hotel for one night, and the next day we took the ferry to Vancouver. I got new Western clothes made from head to toe and wore them all the way to Mission.

Mission is on the north shore of the Fraser River, 40 miles from Vancouver. We took the train there and at the station a horse and wagon came for us. I'd been imagining that my husband was a big farmer with 20 acres of land in Mission, but as I was taken along into the mountains I wondered what kind of place Mission was, and where we were going. There were certainly some big fields, and houses too, but it was much wilder than I had imagined it in Hiroshima. It was real frontier country. . . .

At the end of the first season, and as the second year was coming around, I understood that we were poor, so I gave up the idea of making money and going back to Japan. I wanted to see my mother and brothers and sisters, but every year, I felt more and more resigned, and I got used to feeling like that. I had baby after baby, and Japan seemed further and further away. A farmer has land, so you get tied down to it and you settle in.

An East Indian's Loneliness

A.P. LEDINGHAM

> *A sympathetic United Church minister, charged with Christianizing the East Indian population of British Columbia, described his sad encounter with a man separated from his family on a particularly important day in 1917.*

One day shortly after my coming I said to one man whose hair was an iron gray Well—are you living fairly comfortably in our land? He hesitated but finally said Well Sahib with no wife to cook my food and keep my house tidy and no children to make merry—It is not much comfort a man can have without these. On further talk it turned out that his son was that very day being married in India and the father was not there to oversee the festivities and hospitalities of such an occasion. There is not a heathen civilization on the face of the earth so far as I know that makes a law that comes in and separates the father and husband from the children & wife. That is reserved for Christian Canada. The family relationships of the whole round earth cries out against this kind of stupidity and inhumanity—and we are slowly it may be but none the less surely blackening our national name and our Christian name in the great land of India.

Life in an Internment Camp

PHILLIP YASNOWSKYI

> *An Austrian citizen working in northern Ontario when the First World War broke out, Phillip Yasnowskyi was interned as an enemy alien by the Canadian government.*

For the winter, the internees were issued good army boots, flannel shirts, warm underwear, warm pants, and waterproof mackinaws. Those who worked in the bush felling trees were also supplied with warm mitts. The army garb served to drive home our state of captivity.

At the end of the month, everyone received a book of thirty coupons, each worth ten cents. These coupons could be exchanged in the canteen for tobacco or oranges.

The snow continued to fall without a letup. In a few days, it was knee-deep. Every day, it got deeper and deeper. The temperature dropped to thirty and forty degrees below zero. Notwithstanding the deep snow and the bitter cold, the men, guarded by soldiers armed with rifles, continued to cut brush in the woods.

One redeeming feature of the winter was its short days. Before it got dark, all the men quit their work and returned to the barracks. After a skimpy supper, they livened up the barracks with chatter and amusements.

In all, there were over 1,300 men in the camp. The majority of them were young men, between twenty and thirty years of age; the rest were from thirty to fifty years old. One-third of them were Ukrainians from Galicia, and the others were Croats, Poles, and Hungarians.

There were also a few hundred Turks, but they were lodged in separate barracks.

In the evenings, it was very easy to tell the Ukrainians from the others. When the day's work was done and they had free time, they would get together for a singsong. There seemed to be no end to the number of songs they knew. I joined in, too, to take my mind off our imprisonment, at least for the time being. In the other barracks, the Ukrainians made music on different instruments and danced the *kolomyika* and the *hopak*. In one barrack, the young fellows were learning their parts for a theatrical performance. They were rehearsing *Swatania na Honcharivtsi*. One could not help admiring their perseverance in such an undertaking under such adverse conditions. When the play was staged, I went to see it. It went off well even though the fellow who played the role of the young lady could not, for the life of him, change his voice to sound like a young woman's, and neither the skirt he wore nor his wig of braided hair were of any help. . . .

We had only one newspaper, the Polish *Dziennik Ludowy*. But we could not learn much that was of interest from this paper. We were permitted to write letters, even to the old country, but no one ever received an answer. We complained to the major about not receiving letters from our families though we had been writing to them frequently. The major replied, "We see to it that your letters are sent overseas, but it is not our fault that the Germans sink the boats."

Maybe our letters had been sent out, but we did not ask him how many boats had been sunk. There must have been quite a number of them, since not one of us had ever received a single answer to his letters.

Slowly but surely, the winter was drawing to an end. In the clear spaces where trees had been cut, one could see stumps three to four feet tall, and a mass of felled trees resting on these stumps. It was a dreary spectacle. Only an occasional raven winged his way over this desolate scene. The sky remained overcast, but one could detect a breath of warmth in the air. In the camp, there was anticipation of Easter.

Finally Easter Sunday came, gray and dull. And it went by like any other Sunday with one significant exception—there was no work for us that day. To hold a service of worship was out of the question as there was no priest. The men sat the day out in the barracks, silent, depressed, and wrapped up in their somber thoughts. Only now and then someone would softly strike up "*Khristos Voskres.*" Each one was weighed down by his own misery. The thought that gnawed most fiercely at all of us was "How long is our punishment going to go on? When are we going to be out of here, free once again?"

Unworthy Persecution, 1918

PHILLIPS THOMPSON

> *An Oakville, Ontario, labour activist wrote the editor of the Toronto* Globe *in March 1918 protesting the internment of "enemy aliens."*

In striking contrast with the contention that Canadians are fighting for freedom, democracy and the observance of national obligations, is the mean and unworthy spirit of persecution displayed towards the so-called "alien enemies" who are quietly attending to their own business here. These people are here on our invitation. For many years successive Governments, both Liberal and Conservative, despite the protests of the labor unions, have spent millions of dollars in scattering over Europe invitations to men of all nationalities to settle in Canada, where they would be free from military despotism and be accorded equal opportunities with our own people. They took us at our word, came by the hundred thousand, and were made welcome and regarded as desirable accessions to our population. Suddenly on the outbreak of the war they found themselves ostracized. They were deprived of their employment, not allowed to leave the country, and many of them interned on any display of natural resentment, or on the merest suspicion. Those who were guilty of the "crime" of sending money to their starving wives and families at home were sentenced to terms of imprisonment. Our courts have almost invariably dealt harshly with any man of alien birth accused of minor offences, inflicting heavy penalties frequently accompanied with coarse and brutal insults from the dispenser of alleged justice.

Bear in mind that the great majority of these people are only enemies in a technical sense, being about as loyal to Hohenzollern or Hapsburg as a Sinn Feiner is to the British Empire. The growing scarcity of labor has somewhat ameliorated their condition, but latterly a systematic crusade bas been set on foot to drive them from the factories where they are employed in productive labor and compel them to work for mere subsistence wages. They are making too much money, it is said. I think you will admit that the manufacturers may be trusted to see to it that they earn not only their wages, but enough in addition to enable their employers to realize a substantial profit. It is quite beside the question to urge that Canadians found in Germany have been, or would be, worse treated. The cases are not parallel. Germany never invited Canadians to go there and cast in their lot with the German people.

"They Hated the Germans"

BERTHA KNULL

> *Bertha Knull was a Russian German who had been in Alberta for over a decade when her new country went to war with Germany in 1914. During the Second World War, anti-German sentiment in the province would be less pronounced; however, the Mennonites and Hutterites, mostly German-speaking and pacifist, suffered significant prejudice as they long had. German government attempts in the 1930s to enlist support for Nazism had failed in Alberta, but found support in other parts of Canada.*

The war years were difficult years for the Germans. They were not allowed to speak German in public, but some of the people couldn't speak English, so they spoke German, anyway. One time I was talking to my husband in German in a restaurant and they came over to tell me to stop. I was about to answer them when a lawyer we knew, came over and said that I shouldn't say anything. In the countryside it was different. It wasn't too bad in Leduc, but we heard that it was bad in Edmonton. They hated the Germans there.

Three Hungarians on the Prairies

SÁMUEL ZÁGONYI

> *After the First World War, travelling alone without their families, three Hungarian emigrants became acquainted on an ocean liner from Hamburg to Halifax. When they met six years later in order to compare their experiences in the Canadian west, their reminiscences were grim. Complained one whose work experience had been more positive, "What do we have in this country beside toiling? A sparsely populated, endless, strange land all around us. Seven months of awful cold and snowdrifts in the winter, followed by unbearable summer heat full of inhuman work with dubious results. School makes strangers of our own children. For whom do we live, and why?" This piece is a distillation of their recommendations to future immigrants.*

They agreed that the agriculturalist who immigrated to Canada should not consider settling down permanently or buying any land until he familiarized himself with local conditions, which would take at least three or four years. The only way to do this is for the immigrant to work as a farmhand for a year after his arrival; and it is advisable that he work for a non-Hungarian, English-speaking, old-time settler with a good reputation.

The rights and duties of both parties should be put down in a contract—two copies—signed by four witnesses. One copy should be kept by the employer, the other by the worker. To avoid language problems, the services of an interpreter should be requested from the local sheriff. The interpreter's name should also be recorded in the contract.

In Canada, farmers use every minute of the workday during the summer, from early morning till late evening. Everybody has to be prepared for this. The winter season is slower, but when working outside one always has to be wary of frostbite. It is advisable to learn from the old settlers different ways of protecting the hands, feet and ears against the cold.

Each immigrant should make learning English his primary goal. Younger immigrants can achieve this in 1–1 1/2 years if they live among [native English speakers]. It is especially true if they use their spare time for language learning. With a good working knowledge of English, the immigrant can get along much easier than the one who, lacking this skill, depends solely on his relatives [who can take advantage of the situation].

If permanent settlement is the immigrant's ultimate objective, his own personal experiences in the first year and reliable information about past circumstances usually give him an adequate picture of the area's economic conditions. If these conditions are sufficiently tolerable, the immigrant enters into contract with one or more farmers for the second, third and fourth year. If the conditions are unfavourable, he ought to move on and relocate at least a couple of hundred miles away. There is no limit on distances in Canada.

He can repay his passage money out of his first year's salary. The following year he can bring his wife over, if conditions will allow. The couple's hard work in the third and fourth year may yield enough income so that they can begin to farm on their own without taking an unreasonably burdensome debt. Even so, the beginning is very hard, and 15–20 years will pass, full of hardship and inhuman toil, before the settlers can call their sufficiently equipped homestead their own property.

This is not to say that such a goal must be, or can be, attained by everyone. Nor is it denied that fortunate cases do and can exist— cases in which bigger or faster results are achieved. As elsewhere, this is simply a matter of luck.

Even in the most optimal case one should ask, however, whether the result was worth the sacrifice. You have to leave the familiar culture of the old country. The distant foreign land you travel to will remain foreign to you forever. Still, decades of hard labour will tie you inescapably to the strange soil. Since you cannot sell your property, you are condemned to stay for a lifetime. You exchange your usual way of life and your children's, your ancestral language and customs, for a cycle of never-ending work. . . .

Most unfortunate is the situation of those immigrants in Canada who have been duped into investing some money in advance of their arrival in an unknown place, among unfamiliar conditions. By doing so they deprive themselves of the freedom of movement [and expose themselves to exploitation]. One can never warn immigrants enough against the dangers of such practice.

Those immigrants who possess considerable capital and come to Canada to increase it, must keep in mind that in this country everybody is an entrepreneur and businessman who possesses not only the language but also the knowledge of local conditions—indispensable for capitalizing on business opportunities.

A Home Boy's Shame

ALBERT O. LEE

> *Just short of 100,000 British boys and girls, residents of homes for the poor and orphaned, were brought to Canada as farm workers or domestics in the years from 1873 to 1930. Historian Joy Parr concluded that child migration was "more like British transportation and indentured service policies of the seventeenth and eighteenth centuries than the private and voluntary population movements of the nineteenth and twentieth." In 1913 Albert Lee was placed in the St. Anthony's Catholic Home for Boys in Middlesex, England, at the age of five, after his parents had gone to India, leaving their children behind. Seven years later, the Home dispatched him to Canada, without his parents' consent. He recalled the exploitation and abuse, but most of all the stigma attached to being a "Home Boy."*

I can honestly say that I was never happy being a British child immigrant. Except in Western Canada, we were ridiculed wherever we went. I don't think we were all that bad. Most of us said very little. After we lost our English accents, there were fewer problems. Learning to speak French certainly helped me lose my accent much sooner. What was worse than the ridicule, however, was the fact we were victims of society. We were exploited and abused; and there was a definite lack of understanding and proper supervision by those in authority. I'm not bitter now that it is all over, but there were times when I was terribly unhappy.

My life improved tremendously once those early years of farming were over, and my life in Canada was great. I often thought that Britain and Canada should have united to make some arrangement to send all those children still alive on a free trip back to England. I am very sure many of us did earn it.

To this day, my children do not know about my early years in Canada as a child immigrant. There was a stigma attached to being a "Home Boy." As much as I wanted to tell them, I could never speak about it. Perhaps this account of my life will help them understand.

"Why Orientals Should Be Excluded," 1922

W.G. MCQUARRIE

> *A British Columbia member of parliament for New Westminster argued for the exclusion of "Oriental aliens" and gave his reasons. McQuarrie was a Conservative, but that didn't matter. The entire bloc of thirteen B.C. MPs was united in the cause. They were backed by a nationwide campaign, which got its way when the 1923 Chinese Immigration Act in essence ended emigration from China to Canada.*

Mr. W. G. McQuarrie (New Westminster) moved:

That, in the opinion of this House, the immigration of oriental aliens and their rapid multiplication is becoming a serious menace to living conditions, particularly on the Pacific coast, and to the future of the country in general, and the Government should take immediate action with a view to securing the exclusion of future immigration of this type. . . .

The question which naturally presents itself is, why should orientals be excluded? I have put down certain reasons in brief and concise form. I will read them to the House:

1. They cannot be assimilated. They will always exist as a foreign element in our midst. The real test of assimilation is intermarriage. The divergence of characteristics of the two races is so marked that intermarriage does not tend to perpetuate the good qualities of either race. The races are fundamentally different.

Their morals are different, and language, heredity, religion and ideals will militate against and prevent even sociological assimilation of orientals. . . .

The standards of living of the Japanese are certainly lower than ours. They live in a different way altogether, and in British Columbia they do not conform to our customs to any great extent. They are a foreign settlement in our midst, and they cannot be assimilated.

2. If their peaceful penetration is allowed to continue it will eventually lead to racial conflict and international unpleasantness.

In this connection I would again point to the Vancouver riots in 1907, and say that if some action is not taken by this Government, riots just as bad or worse are likely to happen.

3. Their standards of living are lower than those of our people.

4. Our people cannot compete with the Japanese and Chinese in certain lines.

5. Unemployment will be decreased.

6. They are responsible, to a certain extent, for the drug traffic.

7. They cannot become good Canadians because of their dual citizenship. Even if they become naturalized, they do not divest themselves of their allegiance to their own emperor.

8. It is desirable that we should have a white Canada and that we should not become a yellow or mongrel nation. This is a great national question and our future progress and prosperity are at stake.

An Immigrant Pastor

EDUARD DUESTERHOEFT

A Russian citizen of German origin, Eduard Duesterhoeft emigrated from Volhynia to Saskatoon in 1925, in order to be trained as a Lutheran pastor.

West Canada was a field of the United Lutheran Church. It was settled at the end of the last century and at the beginning of this century. To provide ministers for this field, it started a theological school in Saskatoon to train men for the field, where "German" was yet the language for most of the settlers. Till this school was to be able to supply the need for this field, men from the Old Country were recruited. That is how my friend, Luetkehoelter, and myself did come to Canada to serve the Church. We belonged to the fortunate group amongst the immigrants after the first World War. We knew, while leaving the Old Country, where to go, and the field wherein we would be employed. . . .

After graduation and ordination for the ministry, I was placed as Vicar to serve St. Paul's Lutheran Church at Ellerslie, south of Edmonton. This was in May, 1925. What impression did the country, the people, and conditions make upon me? I will answer in the words of a saint, who, in a rapture, had been elevated to heaven. Asked how it was in heaven, he answered: *Totaliter aliter* (Everything entirely different). And so it was.

The membership of St. Paul's Lutheran Church at Ellerslie was made up by immigrants from Poland and Volhynia. I felt right at home with them. And they regarded me as being one of them, in spite of the fact that I spent many years in Germany, which were decisive in moulding me as a person. As a pastor, I was paid about a thousand dollars per year. That is what they paid the teachers and the pastors. Of course, the pastor also had a house and a garden.

What impressed me most favourably was the progress the colonists had made within a period of thirty years. When I came, the congregation in the Leduc district counted about four hundred families. Later there were some six hundred and twenty families. They were all Germans from Volhynia, some were from the Volga area. Very few families came straight from Germany. They came in 1896, 1904, and later in the 1920's. They had settled on one hundred and sixty acres of bush. The early years were not easy. Most of them admitted they would have returned to the Old Country within the first year, if the means would have been available.

Jobs Canadians Didn't Want

NELLIE O'DONNELL

Nellie O'Donnell, writing under an assumed name, described her hard life as an Irish domestic in Ontario.

It was 1927 when I left Ireland for Canada. I was twenty. We had to take the train from Tipperary to Belfast. My father stayed overnight to see me onto the boat which was leaving the next morning. When I got on the boat this minister came up to me and was lecturing me about going to another country and about my church and about this and that. The things he'd come out with! I looked at him and I said, "I'm Catholic." And he said, "Why didn't you tell me that before!" And he just snatched the papers out of my hand and took off. I thought: Oh my God, is that what it's going to be like out in the world? The boat coming over was packed. Young people, the cream of the land coming out. When we started to separate off the boat everybody got kind of sad because we were all going in different directions.

I arrived in Montreal and then I took a train to Toronto where my step-father's sister lived. The first thing my step-aunt said to me when I arrived in Toronto was that I was halfways across the Atlantic before she found out that I was not her brother's child. I was coming through the Immigration and there had to be somebody in Canada that would sign papers for me. She wanted nothing to do with me. I would have to pay the extra fare—they gave me the impression that I would be deported. I thought: Oh my God, have I brought that all the ways to Canada with me? I didn't want anybody to know I was illegitimate after I got here.

Canada was on the verge of the Dirty Thirties—the Big Depression—when I arrived. Nobody knows what it was like, only them that lived it like myself. They were putting us in awful jobs. Bringing boatloads of us out—farm help and domestic help—from Ireland or wherever they could pick them up. And the Canadians were disgusted. As soon as they'd find out you were an immigrant, they'd swear at you. We had nothing to do with it because they used to put big posters on our railroad stations over in Ireland about the land of the milk and honey over here. All the money! You'd swear to God you just had to get up on a bush and shake it down and pick it up off the ground, the money was so plentiful. I found out that wasn't so.

I found Toronto hard to cope with. I got into domestic work, like most Irish women. Domestic work was a hell of a job in some of these places. I was a maid in one of the big houses where they had a cleaning woman, a laundry woman and a nursemaid. I was the waitress on the table as well as the cook. They made me stand at the table and I had to take the plate from one side and served from the other. Then I had to stand at the end of the table, wait while they ate, and serve the next course. That job wasn't too bad but one day I took a fit of sneezing. They watched and when everything was all over and her company was gone the woman of the house said, "You Irish people don't know what germs are like over there!" She let me go. I had to go out on the street with no money at nine or ten o'clock at night. It was during the Depression, when people were working for practically nothing. They knew they could go to the hostel any time and get domestic help.

There was discrimination in Canada back then. I got another job with a doctor answering his phone, but he said my Irish accent was so bad that his patients couldn't understand. He said he had to let me go for that. Even now people think I have quite an Irish accent. After the British were pulled out of Ireland and we got our freedom, they were getting us back to speaking Gaelic, but I was all mixed up then with the Gaelic and the English language. I was in a turmoil. I knew what I was saying but they were complaining about the reception of my voice on the phone. Of course, we didn't have phones in Ireland and I wasn't used to talking on the phone. I thought I was speaking the King's English, but they didn't understand it.

Oftentimes Irish Catholics were called "Dogan." Sometimes they'd call you "a bloody Irish Dogan," when they'd get mad. That's what they called us in Toronto. Later on they called us "Micks." It was mostly Protestants who called us such names, but other people would get it in there too. In Toronto, the 12th of July was a big day for them Orangemen. It was terrible. If you were Catholic you had to keep the hell out of there when the Protestants were marching on the 12th.

Then I got into a lot of problems with the jobs they placed me in because there was sexual abuse in Canada in them days. I worked in one place where the husband was a businessman. Used to have to sleep in the attic. He used to have meetings about once a month and his wife was away a couple of times while I was there. After the men were gone, he used to come upstairs to try to get into my room. There was no lock on my door, but there was one of them big old-fashioned sewing machines which I used to pull up against the door to keep him out. He'd pound, wanting to come in. "Let me in, Nellie. Let me in!" This night I'd had enough of being put in these kind of jobs, so I told him, "You'd better get away from me. I've got my window opened!" We were on Dundas Street in Toronto and I was going to holler for help. He said some abusive word back to me. I left that job.

Then I found a job in a laundry. If you really wanted you could find jobs that the Canadian people didn't want. It was hard work in the laundries in them days. We had to clean curtains, but they weren't nylon like they are today. They were lace curtains that had to be dried on wooden rods and adjusted to the same measurement as the curtain before it was washed. And then they had to be pulled out and folded. Maybe I was getting $12 or $13 a week for working in the laundry. I worked there from eight o'clock in the morning to six o'clock at night, and overtime you just got straight time for it. I was doing very well and my forelady was very, very nice to me. But then I was getting letters from the Immigration authorities, telling me that I hadn't filled my contract because I left domestic service and went into laundry work which I was not supposed to do.

So I got married. The reason I got married was because I was afraid of being deported. I wasn't going to be able to pay the fare. I was afraid that they would contact my parents and I'd have to go back home. That's the last place I wanted to go. I saw myself getting out of it through marriage. My maiden name would be gone and Immigration wouldn't be able to find me, I thought. But somebody, in the meanwhile, reported me for doing it even though I was married. Immigration kept telling me they wanted that money because I didn't fulfil the contract of staying in the domestic jobs. They kept asking me for the extra fare but I couldn't give it to them because the wages were terribly poor.

"There Weren't Many Blacks"

HARRY GAIREY

Born in Jamaica in 1898, Harry Gairey moved with his family to Cuba when he was very young and came to Canada for the first time at the age of sixteen.

There was a cigar factory on Front Street, between Yonge and Bay, by the name of Androse, I can remember well. They wanted a cigar maker, and I was one, I learned back home. I saw this sign in the window, "Help Wanted," and then I saw it in the paper. When I went into the factory it didn't take me long to see that it was all white there. But I applied. They says, "No, we have no job for coloured people." Then I saw a job advertised for on one of the boats. For help. I went down to the employment place, where the people phone in for help. The girl phoned up and then said, "No, they don't want you." That was in the early twenties. And when I got the job on the road, I never turned anywhere else. Never bothered, because I knew I was blocked everywhere I went; it was no use to butt my head against a stone wall; I'd have a railroad job and I'd make the best of it.

My first job was dishwashing, and in the kitchen, for the Grand Trunk. There was a chap named Joe Bailey. From a third cook he'd worked himself up to chef on a café car—it was a half-parlour car and it had about twenty seats for serving and a small kitchen. Bailey took me down to the Grand Trunk and got me the job with Mr. Harry Burnet. He was from Michigan, and he was the travelling chef.

My first night, they were coming from Montreal, going on to London. They took me down from here to Cobourg because the train was late. I had to wait in the station until about two in the morning. I went right through to London that night, and the next day we went to Windsor.

Toronto was our headquarters. We started out here at nine in the morning to Montreal and we arrived between five or five-thirty. Then we would come back the next morning and go right through Toronto to London. Get to London, Ontario at approximately ten P.M. Clean up the kitchen and then we went to the quarters—Grand Trunk provided us with quarters at London. The next day we serve lunch and go to Windsor, stay there till four P.M. and back on to Toronto. Go home, Grange Avenue. And then the next morning we repeat it over again, over and over again, same story. Every morning we have to go somewhere, every day. Thirty dollars a month. If the train was late you didn't get any overtime. You would work actually around the clock. There was no union. No day off. It was just a continuing thing. If you stay on there all night and all day, you get thirty dollars a month. Thirty-one days, you still get thirty dollars a month. But it was good pay at the time. There's nothing you could do; if you protested against this—I wouldn't have anyway—then you had no job. You're in a strange land, you have to keep going.

One thing, I always like to advance up. Some people like to stay dishwashing all the time but I always experiment, you know. I watched the cooks; they never showed you anything, but I look over their shoulder and see what they're doing. I went on early. I usually put in extra hours because it was to my advantage. Now the second cooks were getting forty-five dollars a month and the chef cook, like Joe Bailey on the café car, he would be getting seventy-five dollars a month. And in the dining car they would be getting around eighty, eighty-five dollars a month because they fed more people.

Now the chef on a dining car doesn't do as much work because he has a good second cook. I worked with a chef, MacGregor, and when I became his second cook, I had to do all the work. He planned the menu and I prepared all the meals. It took me about a year and a half to get a chef's job on a buffet car. So I was in the higher bracket at the time. And then I went into the dining room, waiting on tables, and I liked that very much. Because you see, the waiter was getting thirty dollars a month, same as a dishwasher, but they made tips. They made maybe fifteen, twenty dollars a day at that time in tips. So that was very good.

There weren't many Blacks here at the time. Not more than five thousand, if that many. At one point I knew most every Black family in Toronto. (At that time, they were called "coloured" people. If I called them "Black" they'd have run me out of town.) In the 1920s there wasn't any West Indian settlement as such in Toronto. A few coloured people lived on Adelaide Street, a few on Queen Street, some in Cabbagetown and on University Avenue. The Simpsons had a large house on University Avenue between Dundas and Queen.

Maybe there were Black leaders, but not that I know of. Because at that period, the Blacks were almost just emerging. At that period we, the Blacks, were nothing you know, and you just almost gave up and said, "What's the use?" It's not like now; they were ashamed to identify, they weren't proud of themselves.

You couldn't go to Eaton's and ask for a job, or to the Bell Telephone. It was unheard-of to go to a restaurant or a public dance. You wouldn't go there because you knew you weren't welcome. That's a known fact, you see.

The Brain Drain, 1927

W.A. IRWIN

> *W.A. Irwin, the associate editor of* Maclean's, *picked up on a common immigration theme of the 1920s when he questioned why the federal government was spending millions of dollars to bring immigrants to Canada when almost as many Canadians were emigrating to the United States. Irwin sent out a questionnaire to the "exiles," asking them why they left.*

One thousand graduates of universities representative of all sections of the Dominion, now resident in the United States, were selected at random and asked to give the reasons that actuated their departure from Canada. They were told that they could speak freely under a promise of anonymity. Two hundred and three of the thousand responded—a remarkably high return, as anyone who has had anything to do with questionnaires will admit. The replies came from thirty-four states of the Union and the District of Washington. The writers were representative of all the common, and many of the un-common, professional classes known to modern society—doctors and dentists of all sorts . . . ; pharmacists and chemists; physicists and metallurgists and engineers; clergymen; college professors, journalists and school teachers of both sexes; lawyers; financiers, men of commerce and industrial executives. There was even the odd millionaire or two and an extremely odd self-confessed failure. A thoroughly representative list, and one so widely distributed geographically as to be worth analysing.

And what did they have to say?

Naturally, many of them gave more than one motive for their leaving Canada, but a more or less arbitrary classification of reasons works out, on a percentage basis, as follows:

Economic advantage	57%
Better opportunities for advanced education and a wider field for the specialist	20%
Health and climate	9%
Family and personal reasons	5%
Objection to political, social and intellectual conditions in Canada	5%
The lure of the unknown	2%
Miscellaneous	2%

. . . Listen to this from a graduate of Toronto, who is now head of the chemistry department in a Mississippi Valley college:

"My reason for leaving Canada may be briefly stated: a desire to improve my economic condition. After graduation, and while pursuing post-graduate work at the University of Toronto, I was asked by a Toronto firm to organize an analytical and research laboratory for their factory. This was done. The analytical routine was quite a success. The individuals concerned worked hard and soon had the purchases of raw materials and the sales of finished product conforming to definite standards. The research program was a dead failure. The manufacturer was unwilling to wait for results. Even in connection with the most complex problems on which the best scientific brains in that industry had spent years of study and investigation with only partial success, he expected and demanded that they be solved overnight. Instead of encouragement, he gave nothing but complaint. He was always generous with his praise concerning the results achieved in standardizing his purchases and his products. He could not understand, however, why it was we could evaluate a raw material in a few hours and could not solve a manufacturing problem in an equal period of time. Naturally I became discouraged and when I was offered my present position here—to train research workers—at double the salary, I accepted." . . .

And here's a word from one of the millionaires, now the vice-president and general manager of a realty company which controls $50,000,000 worth of property in California:

"I have been to Canada at least a dozen times in the last twenty years, and can see the great contrast. It appears to me that young men of good character and ability can receive much better financial assistance in the United States than they can in Canada."

Assimilation: A Dissent

FREDERICK PHILIP GROVE

> *The prominent novelist-commentator Frederick Philip Grove made an early missionary appeal that Canada become a meeting place of many races. Maclean's advertised Grove's views on the assimilation of the foreign-born immigrant as "different," but pointed out that they were "those of the foreign-born immigrant himself." Grove advertised himself as a Swedish immigrant of the 1890s. Instead, he was almost certainly Felix Paul Greve of Germany who came to North America just before the First World War. The subterfuge was probably the result of his criminal record in Germany and anti-German sentiment in Canada at the time of the war.*

Mr. Canadian Citizen, let me tell you a few truths about yourself as well as about your guests; for, since you have invited the newcomers, they are plainly your guests, entitled to all the privileges which we commonly accord those whom we thus honor.

What, at the present moment, do you, the average citizen of this country, do in order to make the newcomer feel at home? Anything or nothing? First of all, you call him a "foreigner"—a title of honor, indeed, since it implies that likely he has seen more of the world than you have seen—unless you have traveled. But it is well-known that this title, within the British Isles, has from time immemorial had a sinister sound. A strange thing to say, seeing that the population of Great Britain is itself a mixed population, compounded of many different racial strains. Yet, if the national status of Canada means anything at all, then it surely means this, that here, in Canada, we cultivate or at least mean to cultivate an attitude toward life and its various phases, economic, intellectual, spiritual, distinct from that of a mere British Crown colony. In such Crown colonies the foreigner may be tolerated; *we* invite him.

. . . What, Mr. Citizen, do you do in order to welcome the "foreigner" whom you invite? Oh, well you assign him 160 acres of land in the bush or a job in a factory or work on the road-bed of a transportation line, and therefore you leave him icily alone. He meets with other "foreigners"; and if they are farmers, there is soon a "foreign settlement"; if they are factory hands, there is a "foreign quarter" in some city; if men of the pick and shovel, there is a "foreign gang." The adults in settlement, quarter, or gang are very apt to hang on to their vernacular; they have little opportunity to acquire any other, especially the women. They have no desire for isolation; but it is forced on to them.

Their ways may be strange and even repulsive to you; so are your ways to them.

. . . And now the crucial question. Do you, Mr. Canadian, want to assimilate these people? Do you want them to give up what is theirs and to adapt to your vaunted "high standard of living" which is only a high standard of waste? Do you want them to eclipse themselves and to drop their good as well as their evil? But the question itself is sheer nonsense. It posits as possible what is an impossibility. There is no such thing as a one-sided assimilation. Don't forget that these people who come among us have pluck and enterprise; or they would not be here. Do not forget that they have brains; for most of them were the underdogs in Europe; and it is precisely the underdog who develops his brains. Look at your rural schools in mixed districts: which children lead their classes, yours or those of these "foreigners." No, assimilation can only be mutual. Only if you take from them, will they take from you.

Ralph Connor's Injustice

JOHN MURRAY GIBBON

> *John Murray Gibbon was a passionate proponent of the idea of a Canadian multicultural mosaic, and he claimed the famous novelist Ralph Connor (the pen name of the Reverend Charles William Gordon) as one of his converts.*

The vivacious and graceful dancing of a Polish group at the New Canadian Folk-Song and Handicraft Festival held in Winnipeg in 1928, had a marked influence on the attitude taken by Anglo-Saxons towards the foreign-born in that city. When that Festival was being organized, I was told quite frankly by a number of those whom I met there that the Canadian Pacific Railway was doing the wrong thing in encouraging these people to retain their old customs. In the course of conversation it usually developed that the critics were influenced by a novel written twenty years before by Ralph Connor, the popular Canadian novelist, entitled *The Foreigner*, a somewhat lurid melodrama of the shack-town which had grown up on the skirts of this mushroom city:—

> "With a sprinkling of Germans, Italians and Swiss, it was almost solidly Slav. Slavs of all varieties from all provinces and speaking all dialects were there to be found: Slavs from Little Russia and from Great Russia, the alert Polak, the heavy Croatian, the haughty Magyar, and occasionally the stalwart Dalmatian from the Adriatic, in speech mostly Ruthenian, in religion orthodox Greek Catholic or Uniat and Roman Catholic. By their non-discriminating Anglo-Saxon fellow-citizens they are called Galicians, or by the unlearned, with an echo of Paul's Epistle in their minds, 'Galatians.' There they pack together in their little shacks of boards and tar-paper, with pent roofs of old tobacco tins or of slabs or of that same useful but unsightly tar-paper, crowding

each other in close irregular groups as if the whole wide prairie were not there inviting them. From the number of their huts, they seem a colony of no great size, but the census taker, counting ten or twenty to a hut, is surprised to find them run up into hundreds. During the summer months they are found far away in the colonies of their kinsfolk, here and there planted upon the prairie, or out in gangs where new lines of railway are in construction, the joy of the contractor's heart, glad to exchange their steady, uncomplaining toil for the uncertain, spasmodic labour of their English-speaking rivals."

I had attended the rehearsals and knew how much time and trouble these New Canadians had put into their contributions to the programmes, and was therefore disturbed by the slim attendance at the opening afternoon concert. As Ralph Connor was an old friend, I got in touch with him and asked him to come and see the show. It happened that a Polish group danced some measures from the Mazur at the concert he attended. They were beautifully dressed in white satin, trimmed with ermine, and their dancing was as finished as one could expect from the best professionals. At the close of the performance, Ralph Connor went behind to speak to the dancers and found them to be as simple as they were charming.

"This is a revelation to me," he said, when he came back. "I always looked on the Poles as husky, dirty labourers whose chief entertainment was drink, but these are delightful, cultivated people. I feel that I have done them an injustice in my book. What can I do to make amends?"

The penance that I suggested was that he should go home and telephone to all his friends to come and see the remaining Festival performances, and to show a good example by coming himself. This he did, and the result was a noticeable change of attitude. By the fourth and last day, all Winnipeg realized that this New Canadian Festival was well worth while, and at the final performance in the Walker Theatre there was "Standing Room Only."

A Word of Warning, 1928

H. DENKERS ET AL.

In January 1928, a group of Dutch immigrants wrote to a news-paper in Holland of their disappointments: "We wouldn't rec-ommend anyone to emigrate to Canada."

Dear Mr. Editor,

Considering that the conditions in Canada are not as rosy as are being represented by the various paid agents of the steamship lines and Canadian railways, we want to inform our fellow countrymen of the following:

Due to the great flow of immigrants to Canada in 1927, unemployment is so great that the majority of the new arrivals are walking around without work and if there is work the Canadians and English get preference. Even the Dutchmen who have been here a long time and know the language well can't get any work. Occasionally an individual is lucky enough to get work, but then the wages are also so low that it isn't worth the effort to leave the homeland for that. Great big sturdy guys work for $10 or $12 a week in a factory and many can't even get a job on a farm for just room and board. Many, who have earned a little in the summer have to collect the money with the help of a lawyer. As a result, in Chatham alone—a city with 17,000 inhabitants with many big factories, in which there is nothing to do—there are so many unemployed that the streets are black with them and they are forced to eat up the pennies that they managed to save up from the summer, if they have them, or else live on poor relief. Three weeks ago, a half starved Hollander without a decent place to sleep was found in the fields. He wasn't placed in the poor house but thrown into jail instead and will now be sent back to Holland. Three months ago a Hollander committed suicide due to despondency and poverty and there'll be more. A lot of people suffer from poverty here, not only just among our people, but also among the Canadians who, after all, are citizens here. There's always a lot of boasting here about the tobacco harvest. But there are a lot of people walking around with worried minds because they can't even sell it. A great number of people, who had a few pennies, grew tobacco for half shares of the profits. They ate up the money they had and are now waiting for the profits from the crop that they can't even sell. The farmer tries to steal your half from you with all kinds of mean tricks. They don't leave one stone unturned. A couple of examples: 3 men from Friesland had ten acres of tobacco on half shares and 3 acres of potatoes. The potatoes have been sold and the farmer won't give them their half share: 60 times 90 lbs. are still on the land and he won't give up their share of that. And now he's trying to steal their half share of the tobacco. All three together worked about 50 days for that farmer and now that they ask for their money, he won't pay. Another example: One person had a whole farm on half shares. The boss was quite accommodating in the beginning and advanced him some money. When the harvest was ready, he suddenly asked for the payment of the advance. The man couldn't pay immediately and he put it up for a sheriff's sale which was to take place at two o'clock in the afternoon. The boss and a notary public arrived at 9 o'clock in the morning when there were no other buyers. An immediate sale was concluded and the boss bought everything for a third of the price. Naturally this was all done in a premeditated fashion. So this man and his family worked hard the whole summer and are now put out on the street. He was also falsely accused and shoved into jail. There are more like that here. There's also another here who works in a factory as an ordinary labourer for $10 a week. Here, $10 is not like 25 guilders there but more like 10. Such people don't want their stay-at-home relatives to know that they are so very poor here. It's difficult for married people to save the money for a return passage in order to go back home. There are a lot here who would very much like to return to Holland. It's a little different for single young men, but we wouldn't recommend anyone to emigrate to Canada. We're talking about the province of Ontario, which is the best of the bunch, as many who were in the West jumped on the buffers of the trains in order to get here to the East. This is not exaggeration, but the pure truth about the past year and this year will certainly not be any better considering the cheap passages that are being offered. We ought to be able to get such cheap tickets for the return passage, then hundreds, yes thousands would go back to the old country. We think that our countrymen are thus well informed and we advise them to think things out well before they begin to think about going to Canada. This is to safeguard our fellow countrymen from the disappointment which we ourselves have experienced.

Colonial Canada

PHYLLIS KNIGHT

Phyllis Knight was born in a working-class district of Berlin in January 1901. She arrived in what she thought a narrow Canada in 1929, the year after her husband, Ali.

Ali was already in Canada and I was recuperating [from a miscarriage] in Berlin. We wrote cheerful letters to each other. Although we both read between the lines and saw that things weren't working out, as we hoped. It was only later that we both learned exactly how miserable a time each of us had had.

While we knew something about Canada, we read up about the country to check the impressions we had. The basic outline of our knowledge wasn't that far wrong. By the time we were seriously reading about it we had already decided to emigrate to Canada and it would have taken some pretty drastic exposé to change our minds. Once we had started thinking about that step it sort of crystallized in our minds and almost anything we learned could be fitted in as something good or as something to be avoided. But the basic decision to go seemed to make itself.

We didn't expect to get rich and we didn't think the streets were lined with gold. But we figured one could lead a pretty good life in Canada, if you worked and after you got settled in. Of course, we didn't figure on the depression. Moreover, we half expected that you would be less surrounded by restrictions in Canada. I guess it was the feeling of getting a new start, corny as that may sound.

I think what attracted us most was that Canada was still a big country with a lot of open space and nature left but that at the same time it was civilized and orderly in a way South America or even the United States wasn't. We were always pretty certain that once we emigrated it would be for good, although we thought that we probably would like to return to Germany for visits once in a while after we got established.

We had a not too inaccurate idea of the regions and major cities in Canada at that time. Still, the size of the land, the tremendous distances that you covered when travelling, was something neither Ali or I had ever really imagined. At first it was just overwhelming. But that was partly what attracted us. One area that we really didn't know very much about was what the people [the society] were like here. . . .

It's hard to put all those feelings and experiences of coming to a new country into words. On the one hand it wasn't all that strange, apart from not knowing the language. Basically, after all, we were all part of the modern world. The feeling of strangeness really only came later, after we left Toronto and were both on the bum so to speak. And Western Canada really was a lot different than the east, at least at that time. Still, we weren't fully prepared for what we found and experienced over the first few years.

The main problems were straight forward enough, just trying to earn a living, learning the language, and getting to know the ropes. What we found the most strange was the pretty free and easy attitude to what you could get away with in some things and the tremendous provincialness in other areas. For example, Ali was once stopped by the police on a Toronto beach for wearing a topless swim suit. Ali, mind you, not me. That was in the first year we were there and we couldn't believe it. On the other hand, in a lot of places you could just go out into the woods and make yourself a cabin and squat there. That was just as unbelievable. In many ways Canada, of that period, turned out to be much more colonial than we expected. . . . There was another feeling we had too. The feeling that nobody, not the government nor any group nor even most people you knew seemed to care very much about what happened to you. Although that feeling may have been because we came just as the depression was starting and we were greenhorns to boot. . . .

What I think I really missed the most, and was most astounded not to find, was a lack of social (i.e. cultural) facilities here in Canada available to ordinary people. Of course there were plenty of people here, and in Berlin, as everywhere who never did anything except visit their families, talk about their work and children, and go to their local pubs. But in my day, in Berlin, as in the other big cities of the world, there had developed all sorts of ways for ordinary people to have as full a round of plays and lectures and what not, as they wanted. Museums were next to free, tickets to opera and theatre were very cheap if you didn't mind poor seats. There were zoos. There were all sorts of well stocked public and loan libraries around. There was very little of that here. And that really did shock me. . . .

Of course, every time you said anything that compared Canada or some conditions here unfavorably with conditions elsewhere, or even compared it to what could be, nobody wanted to listen. Always somebody would say, "If you don't like it here, why don't you go back to where you came from," or something like that. That was almost like a catechism for some people. As if that were an answer to anything. As if things were so perfect here or any place else, that they couldn't stand a lot of improvement.

A Mennonite Family in the Depression

ARTHUR KROEGER

> *Arthur Kroeger, later a prominent public servant, was the son of a Russian Mennonite family who settled in Alberta in the mid-1920s. In 1930 father Heinrich, mother Helena, and the children moved to land owned by Davey Jones, an eccentric and affectionate bachelor. Arthur was born two years later, as the Depression deepened.*

I was born in the farmhouse on Davey's place in September 1932. My mother was forty-six. At the time, births in hospital were the exception rather than the rule. The road system was primitive, few rural residents had cars, and there was no medicare to cover the costs of doctors and hospitals. In the area, perhaps half a dozen women regularly served as midwives. Two of them, Mrs. Holmen and Mrs. Cross, attended when I was born. When my mother's labour pains began, most of the children were at school and my brother Peter, age four, was taken to a neighbour's. He recalls that when he was brought back some hours later, I was covered with a former flour sack and being spoon-fed sugar and water by Mrs. Holmen. My father was pleased and excited. That afternoon, when Helen, Anne, and George came home from school, they were surprised to find a new baby in the house. They had not known that their mother was pregnant. In the days that followed, I inherited the small cradle that my father had made for Peter some four years before.

In December 1932 my father made the following entry in his notebook: "Received for Christmas from D. Jones $7.00." This was a very substantial sum, and Davey was by no means well off. His generosity expressed his compassion for an indigent immigrant family with a new baby.

Even with the additional money that Nick and Henry were able to earn in the early 1930s, food for the family was sometimes in short supply. One of my earliest recollections is eating boiled wheat for supper, which our family did quite often at the time. Sometimes a meal would be made of beet peels. Or my parents would roast rye kernels as a substitute for coffee. On one occasion when there was no food in the house, our mother walked into town—a distance of two miles—and returned with a large box of apple peels and cores. A shipment of relief supplies in the form of a carload of apples had arrived by rail in Naco. The apples had been badly bruised and so had to be processed at once. Mother asked for and was given the residual peels and cores, which she boiled when she got them home. For the next two days the family lived on applesauce.

Sometimes privation could be compounded by human action. Anne recalls taking a sandwich of lard on bread to school for her lunch one day when she was perhaps eight years old. A local farm boy knocked the sandwich off her desk and then, as a joke, stomped on it with his boots.

One night the same farm boy and some of his young friends gathered outside our house at Davey's and made threatening shouts about "foreigners." For our parents, it brought back terrifying memories of what they had experienced during the Russian civil war. They drew the blinds and huddled inside, waiting for the intruders to leave. The next day Mother went to the secretary of the municipality, Jim Norton, to talk to him about the incident. It did not recur. Our family was always treated with kindness and compassion by the community leaders.

Although a substantial number of Mennonite families were settled in the area during the 1920s, they never established their own church. One factor was the distance between the farms where the various families lived; another was the fact that after a few years a number of the Mennonites moved to other parts of the province to seek a more rewarding life than was offered by farming in the Palliser Triangle. Those who remained held their religious services in each other's homes, with leadership from someone who had been a church elder in Russia. Once a year they would hold a Bible conference, and at Christmas they held special services at which they sang traditional Mennonite hymns. They also came to participate in the services at the other local churches. My father's notebook records he attended a religious service at the home of an English neighbour, Jack Thornton. There is also an entry from 1935 about "the English Minister" coming to visit the family.

Although many Canadians of Anglo-Saxon origin had very reserved attitudes towards "foreigners" (i.e., immigrants from Europe, and particularly the Slavic countries), the Mennonites were generally well accepted. When the first families arrived in the area, the Consort *Enterprise* carried the following editorial on May 7, 1925:

> The Mennonites are a class of people who have suffered much privation and abuse on account of their religious and other beliefs; they are absolutely honest, steady, and working people. . . . While they have little money, they deal and live entirely within their means.

Nevertheless, the Mennonites generally kept to themselves during their early years and concentrated their efforts on making a living in their new country, something that did not prove easy. Becoming integrated into society and its various organizations was for the future. The local businesses, social groups, and political organizations were solely in the hands of people of British descent; there is no record of "ethnics" playing a role in any of them during the early years.

In the files of the Consort *Enterprise*, a Mennonite name appeared for the first time when Irene Epp won a prize in the 1934 school festival—some nine years after the first Mennonite families arrived in the area. The following year, Anne Kroeger was cited as having won a prize for recitation.

However, the files of the *Enterprise* also record a striking instance of how the community could reach out to their new neighbours. On June 26, 1930, it reported, "The service of Sunday, 22nd was given by the Mennonite choir and their Minister, Mr. George Harder." Local residents remarked on what good singers the Mennonites were.

Some Mennonite families who came to Canada were determined from the outset to become Canadian, and the parents insisted that their children learn and speak English. The majority of parents, however, sought to preserve the language and culture they had known in Russia. The Kroeger family fell into this category, and in the early years we spoke only the Low German language at home, so that when Helen and Anne began school in 1929 they knew scarcely a word of English. We three younger sons had an easier time of it because our older siblings, notwithstanding their parents' concerns, increasingly brought English into the household.

Like many Mennonites who came to Canada from the colonies in Russia, my father felt an irreparable sense of loss all his life. To a considerable extent, he lived in the past. He worked hard, but the world in which he lived was not his world and he viewed it in a detached way. On June 8, 1933, Heinrich received a letter from his younger brother, Abram, who had remained in the U.S.S.R. and had reproached Heinrich for leaving. Its message was in stark contrast to the cheerful letter the family had received from my mother's sister, Susanna Rempel, in 1928. Abram wrote:

Today I received a letter from [sister] Maria, which was full of tears and grief. I sent her some money. We are not doing well ourselves. We both work, I in the office, my wife in the bureau. There is a lack of food. The summer was practically rainless, hence a crop failure. . . . Elsa, our only daughter was buried in 1930. We are very sad. Hermann attends school the second year and does very well. We often regret the fact that we did not follow you in 1926. . . . Give me a detailed account of your way of life. We think of dying.

Father kept this letter to the end of his life, and from time to time referred to it in conversation with us. He did so in tones of resignation, wishing that what it said was not so, wishing that he could have regained the life he had known before the war.

Deporting the Bolsheviks, 1932

THE GLOBE

> *During the Depression, the sick and the suspicious were jettisoned from the country by the thousands. Immigrants with left-wing sympathies were particularly vulnerable to deportation, which pleased the Toronto* Globe's *editorial board.*

A remarkable fuss is being made about the deportation of a group of Reds, who admittedly are not at home in this country, do not like its ways and traditions, and whose main object in life is to change them by revolutionary action. The agitation contrasts strikingly with the comparative silence over the deportation in the past year or two of thousands of people, mostly British, whose only crime in most cases was that they could not find employment or that they were sick. Members of Parliament are asking anxious questions of the Government, lawyers are keeping the wires hot, newspapers are printing "sob stuff" in the pretense that something unfair and inhuman is being done. Compared with this, the protest was feeble which accompanied the actions of the Government in sending home British people who committed no offense, who came here with no other object than to improve their condition of life and become happy citizens of a fortunate Dominion.

In 1931 there were 6,582 deportations, 4,248 to the British Isles. If clamor proportionate to that over the Communists had been raised in all these cases, the country would have heard of little else during the year. Have Communists such a hold in Canada that they can command so much more attention in supposedly influential quarters?

The Provinces and the Federal Government responsible for removal of the Reds are taking logical steps. The only regrettable feature is that action has been delayed so long, permitting the revolutionary organizations to profit from the discontent over unemployment. Bolshevism and its exponents have no claim to consideration from the patriotic people of Canada. Ample warning has been given by the conviction of eight leaders that communistic doctrines are illegal. Those who continue to defy the law in the face of this have no right to expect sympathy. If the Government chooses the deportation remedy, it is strange that the Reds and their sympathizers seek grounds for objections. Their theories and activities are based on the declaration that Canada is not good enough for them. The country from which they came may suit better. It is altogether reasonable to give them a chance to try it.

In any event the Dominion has enough troubles without permitting Bolshevism to intensify them, which is all it can or will do. If Major-Gen. MacBrien [commissioner of the RCMP] was correctly quoted when he made a speech in Toronto some weeks ago, unemployment would be notably reduced if the country were freed of Communists. Their number must be larger than is usually suspected, and every one of them spells trouble in manifold ways. Deportation should be continued with all the speed possible as long as there is an alien Communist remaining.

While the Natives Starve

ROBERT JACKSON

There was precious little relief available for the needy during the Depression. In a letter to Prime Minister R.B. Bennett, citizen Robert Jackson complained that foreigners got more help than the "natives." Charlotte Whitton, the leading social reformer of her day, made a similar charge in an official report to Bennett, complaining about "foreigners on relief" and their "language differences, their tendency to segregate, their corporate loyalties, their susceptibility to seditious propaganda, their known proclivity to hoard money, and the consequent difficulty in ascertaining their actual need of relief." If, however, recent immigrants asked for government assistance, they were labelled as destitute and became liable for deportation. Deportation, indeed, was a method of reducing the list of those who were on welfare, such as it was in the 1930s.

Montreal 10-22-34
To his Excellency: The Premier

Dear Sir.

Well I just left the releif office where I saw a Chinaman that couldnt read or write english or french apply for releif, that been in the Country since 1928. on previous occasion I saw Chines, Negros, and Greeks get releif checks, on July 2nd 1934 I applied for releif, but I havent realized any yet; altho my Grandfather and Grandmother settled here around 1835 my Father Mother and myself were born here, and I am destitute. Feed, Clothe and House the foreign, while the natives starve and freeze is the slogan of our local politicians.

Robert Jackson

Sadness

ANTHONY (TONEK) SLEZINA

A Moravian Slovak, Anthony Slezina came to Canada in 1927. He at first went to British Columbia, near the Alberta border, working as a miner, in the lumber industry, and on the railway. He was then a farmhand for three years, buying his own place in 1935. His wife and son did not join him until 1937.

I spent the first two years on the farm all on my own. Alone, like a plank in the fence I was. I did not even have anybody in the surrounding neighbourhood. And when, after a while, I got a dog to keep me company, he ran away. He could not stand the loneliness either. As a matter of fact, it was over two years. It was almost two years and a half that I was all on my own. But time was not the main concern.

When one is away from one's family nearly eight years, one month more or less does not make much difference. What was involved was not so much the time. Rather, it was what one was doing during that time, how one felt, how one was taking it all.

When I was saying that the three years I spent working for the various farmers flew like water, I must say that the two and a half years on my own farm were just the opposite. They seemed to me endless and I was telling myself that eternity itself could not be that long. It was because I was so alone that all possible doubts began to press hard on me. The immigrant's sadness descended upon me.

It was true, I continued all that time with my everyday work, I did not slacken. On the contrary, I worked harder. But the sadness was getting so heavy that if it were not for my family having arrived just then I do not think that I would have stood it on my own much longer. Perhaps I would not have stood it for that year. It was simply beginning to get unbearable.

It was not that the doubts were all that numerous. But it was that they concerned the basic thing, my existence here and my family over there and at that time there was very little left of my determination to stay here.

The fact that one had to manage the work all by oneself, that one didn't have anyone who would help dispel one's doubts, that there was so little leisure, almost none, that afflicted all of us here. The starting farmer was no exception. But with him all this reached greater intensity.

One could have worked any place—in the mine, on the railroad or for a farmer—and one could have done all kinds of work. But one was never as miserable as the farmer. Never! One did not have so much hard work, such loneliness and sadness, not so many pressing doubts, perhaps. And even when the worst came to the worst, one had a little bit of free time, one had someone to talk to, someone to cheer one up. And even if one did not have all that at the place one was at, one could have packed up and left for some other place, other job. A starting farmer did not have this possibility. Once he bought his own farm, he could not leave it for good. He was chained to it.

Well, he could have gone away for a while, to do his bit of shopping in town, or to settle some matters. Sometime he even had to go

away. That was in case he was working at the same time for some
other farmer. But, aside from that, he could not move from his farm at
all. Well, that is if he wanted to make something out of his farm after
a while, if he was taking his farming seriously.

Concerning Mr. Cohen, 1937

W.L.M. KING

*The prime minister took a nightly walk from his home, Laurier
House, in the company of his beloved dog, Pat. This is what he
encountered on a cold Ottawa February evening in 1937.*

Monday night I decided to take a little walk and encountered, on
Wilbrod Street, a number of women who turned off to other streets
and left an old man struggling along on the sidewalk by himself. I
was afraid Pat and I would knock him over, so I turned back to see if
he was all right. He said he was, and we walked down together. Then
I spoke of the day being cold and sidewalks slippery. He said he had
had a fall. I said I hoped he was all right. He said he was. I asked him
then if he would not take my cane. He said no, he was all right. I
however took him by the arm and walked along, trying to find out,
as a matter of curiosity, who he was. He first told me he was 78; then as
we got along, that he lived in a house just beyond one of the old
houses done over in Sandy Hill district. As we got near the house, he
told me that it was his own, that he had bought it and given it to his
daughter. I asked him his name, and he said it was [Charles] Cohen.
That he had a furniture and clothing business on Rideau and Bank
Streets; that he had three sons and daughter, and had divided all he
possessed, among them. He was now living with his daughter. He said
he had paid $35,000 for the house. When we got opposite the house,
I walked with him to the steps. . . .

Before parting, I told him who I was, and shook hands with him.
He smiled in a most benevolent and surprised sort of way; then
removed his glasses so that he could have a good look, shook hands
again, and went up the stairs.

The whole thing was like a little play in itself. What was so apparent was that this old man had come from Russia, probably as a beggar peasant. He had gone on pursuing his ideal of work and saving, and had now been able before death to amass a fortune, acquired a large property in the centre of the City, and end his life by leaving his sons established, particularly as gentlemen, and his daughter with a house. He, himself, quite satisfied to leave the world possessing nothing, having, meanwhile, gained more than he could have dreamt of.

In my mind, I could not help thinking of the added feature which undoubtedly he will tell his children, of how the Prime Minister of the country had offered him his cane, walked with him arm in arm, and had shaken hands with him, taking him to his own door, speaking of him as neighbour, etc., all of which is illustrative of the opportunity of Canada as contrasted with the peasant life as it has been in Russia for generations. The only unfortunate part of the whole story is that the Jews having acquired foothold of Sandy Hill, it will not be long before this part of Ottawa will become more or less possessed by them. I should not be surprised if, some time later, Laurier House was left as about the only residence not occupied by Jews in this part of the City.

Am I Less Canadian?

ESTHER THOMPSON

> *Born in Norway, Esther Thompson worked for the Department of Agriculture in the province of Manitoba. She gave this reminiscence of her immigrant experience in an address to a women's club.*

I came to Canada at the age of 10. I had been brought up in an atmosphere where we regarded many things with simple reverence. There was much about us to delight in and wonder at. I knew little of scorn and nothing of being scorned.

I had been in Canada but a few months when I heard a neighbor speaking about some laborers. He referred to them as Dagos and

Bohunks. The names were strange to me but I realized that the persons spoken of were offensive and to be avoided.

Later, after being in Canada five years, when I went to the nearby village to write an examination, I heard the lady at whose house I stayed, discuss with other ladies, "Maids." It seemed that these ladies felt towards their maids (who were foreign, two of whom were Scandinavian) as the neighbor had felt towards the laborers. I gradually learned that certain people were not like other people and that they were "foreigners." These and other impressions I gathered about the foreigners shocked me and even grieved me. It seemed that one ought to apologize for being a foreigner or conceal it, but that I never did nor even thought of doing, yet the attitude of people around me had its influence on my relationship with my parents and on my attitude to the country from which I had come.

I was at the difficult age when I doubted even my parents and wished to have my own way. The natural difficulties which my parents had to contend with were multiplied and complicated by the attitude of people around me. My mother and father, nearly 50, were not learning the language. Being lonely, often very lonely, they spoke of the old home, the beauty of the land and the life of the people. I was beginning to learn the language and to get a little contact with the new land. While [I was] still a foreigner, my father and mother were "more foreign" and there was no regard around me for "the foreigner." My parents discovered my indifference and tried by various means to remove the indifference and foster regard and affection for that which they treasured. They failed, and I became more silent and aloof.

I left college. Later, while at the Saskatchewan University, I came under two influences which recalled me. I lived in the house of a woman who was very interested in Scandinavian literature, who surrounded me with an atmosphere of interest and regard. I was asked by the University Women's Club to give a paper on Scandinavia. What I had known about Scandinavia I had forgotten. The contacts I might have cultivated I had lost. I had many evenings to myself and nine months in which to prepare the paper. I started to explore. I quiver now with a kind of intoxication when I recall my discoveries. I shall only mention a few. I found Ibsen again. I had heard of him as far back as I could remember; I had heard his plays and poems read aloud; I had memorized his poems at school, but unconsciously I had classified him with "the foreigners." I now learned that he was a really great man whose books were read by thinking people all over the world. Then I found Bjornson again. I had known him much better than Ibsen, but had forgotten about him. I learned that he was a great Norwegian who fostered, with all his fine gifts, the spirit which made Norway demand independence and obtain it in 1905. I continued my search in Denmark, Sweden and Norway, and discovered, without mentioning names, painters, sculptors, musicians, poets, playwrights, novelists, scientists, scholars and statesmen. I also discovered schools, museums, theatres and laws. When I found people like Sigrid Undset of Norway, Selma Lagerloff and Zorn of Sweden, and Brandes of Denmark, I was so distracted with joy that I could not sit still; I had to get up and walk—perhaps run.

These experiences had a marked influence on my relationship with my parents, and that which they treasured. I found a new point of contact with my father. I asked him about movements, periods and persons. I asked my mother to tell again the charming legends and myths I had heard as a child, and to talk to me about customs, costumes, tapestries, embroideries, and even dishes. My parents must have noted the change and secretly rejoiced to find that they still had contact with their daughter in this strange land where, through no fault of their own, they will never feel quite at home, where their roots will always be bare and on the top of the soil.

The discoveries I made influenced my attitude to myself. I had not apologized for being a Norwegian nor had I concealed it, but I was gradually forgetting that I was. I was about to lose my inheritance, to neglect to claim it. And this was my only gift to Canada, the best I could ever give to the land which had adopted me. I now began to dig around my roots, and the digging was like developing the impression on a negative.

Am I less Canadian, less loyal to Canada, because I remember with affection the country from which I came? Does the English language mean less to me because I speak another and read Norwegian classics in the original? Regard fosters regard. *What I feel for what is Scandinavian is an exact measure of my feeling for what is Canadian.*

Joining Up, 1938

GUS GARBER

> *During the 1938 Munich Crisis, with Hitler threatening his native Czechoslovakia, Vladimir Hortig thought the best thing to do was to join up for the war to come, as described by Gus Garber in the* Montreal Herald.

Vladimir Hortig, 41-year-old taxi driver, is a good Canadian. As a matter of fact, he's probably a better Canadian than many of us because he was scoutmaster here for five years, a member of St. John's Ambulance Brigade, a voluntary blood transfusion group and Toc.-H. [Talbot House, a service organization founded in the First World War].

Vladimir, who since his naturalization as a Canadian a number of years ago, calls himself James V. Hortig, was born at Maly Ujest in northern Czechoslovakia, but a stone's throw from the German border.

"I'm waiting for a recruit office to open and you can bet my name will top the list," he said in his fluent English. He also speaks excellent French, German and Czechish. "The best thing for us Czechs to do is join the Canadian militia."

"Fellow Subjects of a Beloved Ruler"

IMPERIAL ORDER DAUGHTERS OF THE EMPIRE

> *The IODE specialized in the Canadianization of immigrants, which they interpreted to mean indoctrination into "the privileges and duties of British citizenship."*

Official ceremonies of welcome to newly-naturalized citizens of Canada were inaugurated some years ago by the Imperial Order Daughters of the Empire, and these are held at different times throughout each year in the different Provinces, the object being to impress upon New Canadians of foreign birth the privileges and duties of British citizenship and to welcome them as fellow subjects of a beloved ruler.

This gesture by the Daughters of the Empire has brought a new meaning to Naturalization by adding friendly interest to what was formerly a legal status. The ceremonies are usually held in a civic building and are attended by civic officials and by Regents of Chapters of the Order, and brief addresses are made. Standard bearers of the Order are also present carrying the British Flag, that symbol of international honour, national liberty and individual freedom. On these occasions, greeting cards are presented to the new citizens by representatives of the Order, which read as per attached: (they are mounted for presentation on stiff cardboard). The thousands of new citizens to Canada who have received the cards are most appreciative of them, and in many cases they are framed and hung on the walls of their homes.

In addition to the ceremony of welcome and the presentation of greeting cards, the Daughters of the Empire give practical aid to them when necessary, and do everything possible to make them contented in their new environment. In one of the Provinces the Chapters of the Order award several scholarships each year for the training of school teachers in Canadianization work in districts which are largely peopled by the foreign-born. In another Province, the work of the Daughters of the Empire has been so highly regarded by the newcomers that a number of them applied for membership in the Order, and a Chapter has been organized which is composed entirely of New Canadian women.

Before the tide of immigration had dwindled by national necessity to its present condition, members of the Order met the immigrants who arrived in Canada at the different ports and helped them over the difficulties of arrival and of further travel to inland points. Since the decline of immigration, more time and effort has been expended by the Order on the education and general well-being of the foreign-born who have become citizens of the Dominion.

In their work of Immigration and Canadianization, the Daughters of the Empire have expended thousands of dollars, but the real value of their efforts cannot be estimated in figures, and is a patriotic work that is rewarding to everyone concerned. When the Greeting

Cards are presented to the new British subjects, they are reminded that while their Naturalization papers entitle them to citizenship in the Dominion of Canada, true citizenship belongs in their own hearts. They are also assured that the wish of the Order is that their new status in a British country may bring happiness to them and that they may become advocates of peace at home and abroad.

The St. Louis, *1939*

GEORGE M. WRONG ET AL.

A distinguished group of Canadians, led by historian G.M. Wrong, appealed by telegram to the prime minister to afford sanctuary to the 907 Jewish refugees aboard the ship the St. Louis. *The government refused, and the* St. Louis *became a tragic symbol of racial intolerance and lost opportunity. Historians Irving Abella and Harold Troper comment, "Of the more than 800,000 Jews seeking refuge from the Third Reich in the years from 1933 to 1939, Canada found room within her borders for approximately 4000. In a world which was decidedly inhospitable to refugees, Canada was no exception. Yet, even by the standard of the time, Canada stood virtually alone in the niggardliness of her contribution."*

Toronto Ont June 7, 1939
Right Hon W.L. McKenzie King P.C.
Premier of Canada Niagara Falls.

As a mark of gratitude to almighty God for the pleasure and gratification which has been vouchsafed the Canadian people through the visit their Gracious Majesties King George and Queen Elizabeth and as evidence of the true christian charity of the people of this most fortunate and blessed country we the undersigned as christian citizens of Canada respectfully suggest that under the powers vested in you as Premier of our country you forthwith offer to the 907 homeless exiles on board the Hamburg American ship Stlouis Sanctuary in Canada.

George M. Wrong
Elizabeth Wrong
B K Sandwell
Nellie L Rowell
Malcolm W. Wallace
May Wallace
Robert Falconer K.C., M.G.
Lady Falconer
Robert J. Renison, Bishop
Constance E Hamilton
Joseph Shaw-Wood
Ruth McLachlan Franke MD
Andrew F. Brewen
M I Brewin
(Rev) R J Irwin
F Erichsen Brown K.C.
Isabella R Erichsen Brown
M Cartwright
G Brock Chisholm MD
Gwethalyn Graham
(Rev) John Frank
Patricia Frank
Kathleen Russel
H P Plumptre MA
J Lovell Murray DD
Ella M Murray
(Rev) Walter Corrie Almack
Annie Georgina Almack
Ellsworth Flavelle
Muriel Flavelle
(Rev) Norman A McMurray
Grace E McMurray
Fred W Routley
(Rev) E Harold Toye
Leonore Toye
Robert S Rayson DD
Peter Bryce DD

Vera McIntosh Bell
(Rev) L M Sommerville
(Rev) Gordon Hern
Isabelle R Dale

War and the Enemy Within

ROYAL CANADIAN MOUNTED POLICE

> *The RCMP's Security Bulletin for October 23, 1939, barely six weeks after the outbreak of Canada's Second World War, ended with an admonition about the "enemy within," including immigrants from central European countries, such as Austria. The government soon interned 800 Germans and German Canadians, as well as outlawing fascist organizations and ethnic publications and groupings on the left of the political spectrum.*

Educational Campaign For "Better Canadians"

It is our opinion that a National Educational Campaign might be undertaken to point out the benefits of democracy and responsible government in order to offset the insidious and poisonous teachings spreading throughout our social structure. This campaign should be extended not only to the English-speaking Canadians but to those of foreign extraction, such as Ukrainians, Austrians and those from other central European countries, where recent events have been the means of dividing their opinions and leaving them in a state of mind which makes them easy prey to subversive propaganda.

In these weekly bulletins we hope to be allowed to advance further suggestions and perhaps elaborate definite schemes that may prove helpful in the strengthening of our civil security menaced by the "enemy within."

Things Turn Nasty

KARL BUTZER

Karl Butzer, who became one of North America's most celebrated academics, emigrated from England early in the Second World War. Although his father detested the Nazis, Karl was a German immigrant at a time when Canada was fighting Hitler's Germany.

Things turned nasty in the fall of 1941. I was being called names in second grade, and then a gang of more than a dozen boys jumped me on my way back from school. I wasn't really physically hurt but was humiliated and terrified. I told the principal, and he scolded them in his office the next day. When the boys filed back into class, the young teacher, Mrs. Brawley, asked if they had gotten the "strap." They replied no, and then she said, "Good. You didn't deserve it." That gave them the license to do what they wanted, and it became a year of terror. I became afraid to go out on the playground during the breaks, and after school I was stalked by a gang of boys who regularly followed me home to line up in front of the house, shouting, "Heil Hitler!" My grades plummeted, and I slipped from third in a class of twenty to second or third last: every month we shifted class seats according to rank, the best performers sitting up front. I was regularly sitting in the last row now and began to lose my sense of self-esteem. I became ashamed of my origins.

In the summer of 1942, my parents felt they had to get me into new surroundings. So we spent some weeks at a sort of vacation motel near Lachute. It was a relief, and we met a group of empathetic people who were really nice to me. They were bilingual French Canadians, and I recognized that they were different. My parents noticed that too, and later that summer we went to a small French hotel in Fourteen-Island Lake, in the Laurentian Mountains near Shawbridge (now named Provost). The owners, the St. Pierres, were farm people and had five bilingual children. They became my first friends in the New World.

That fall my parents kept me out of school, and I went to Mrs. Shaw, the retired principal of my school, for home tutoring. Totally isolated now, I really felt ostracized and finally told Mother that I wanted to go back to school, even if the kids beat me up. I did, and although I was still afraid to go out on the playground, the third grade teacher had her class under control, and there were no more incidents, despite the overt hostility of most of the boys.

When she thought she was alone, Mother cried a lot. She explained that Aachen had been heavily bombed, and she was afraid that her own mother had been hurt. She might never see her again. My father was also in bad spirits. Later, I learned that he had deliberately switched from designing machines to sales. When he had started working for the war effort, he was helping save England from German attack. Now the mills were grinding out aluminum to build planes that killed civilians in German cities. He just couldn't handle that, as a matter of conscience.

In the summers of 1943 and 1944 we rented a summer cottage in Fourteen-Island Lake, and I began to experience life as a child should. I played with the smaller St. Pierre boys and worked with the bigger ones on the farm. I learned how to cut and bale hay, milk cows, and fork manure. I learned to dance to the jukebox tune of "Stardust" at the Dew-Drop Inn with thirteen-year old Cécile, blonde and adorable to a nine-year old boy. I also learned to speak French. Our family became insiders in the little French Canadian community of five families. We were told about Mr. Dujardin, who always watched the door, that he was on the run for evading conscription. Once he jumped out of the back window of the Dew-Drop Inn as the police came in the front door. As French Canadians, they told us, they didn't want to fight England's war, so we were not "the enemy." They tended to see us as friends, perhaps as fellow underdogs. Our friendship with the St. Pierres lasted for life. The oldest boy, Raymond, later went to work in Montreal, and Father sometimes had lunch with him when they worked in the same district. The two of them remained in periodic correspondence until my father's death. Ironically the St. Pierres were bicultural too, as I comprehended later. Their grandmother had been a vivacious Irishwoman.

In fourth grade a school inspector came into every class once a month. After rustling through some papers behind the teacher's desk, he would ask about the children's ethnicity. All the "English" children had to stand up, and so forth. Finally he would ask, "Are there any foreigners?" Now I had to stand up in the aisle. "What are you?" he would ask. "German," I had to say. Every month the same routine, with the same effect. The other children were reminded, and the hostility, bullying, and name-calling flared up again. I remember wondering, with growing anger, why he had to do this even though he already knew the facts.

There is another incident, one of only a few that I have recounted to others, that is very applicable. When a pencil or an eraser went "missing" in class, the teacher promptly came down to search through my desk and that of Paul Laberge, the only French Canadian in the class. But eventually it turned out that Charlie Benson had the item. That happened not once but several times—the teacher predictably pounced on the desks of the only two minority students, but the stolen trinket was always in Charlie's. This was a classic reflex— you're not one of us; therefore you must look dishonest and disreputable; and so you're the obvious suspect. That is probably why police selectively stop or pick up African American motorists for "suspicious behavior."

Whenever I was in Montreal I had nightmares about children beating me up, and my mother started taking me to a chiropractor. He was French Canadian, and he was very kind. I enjoyed the visits and the manipulations and felt that they really calmed my jangled nerves. We began to use only French-speaking professionals; it made such a difference. Some of them were unfriendly, but it wasn't directed at us. The English-speaking Jesuits no longer came over, leaving my mother wondering why. Instead three German Jesuits, who had been in Canada when the war broke out, started visiting. One of them, who was a dreadful bore, tried talking to me in German on his first visit. I understood perfectly but couldn't find the words to respond. It made me aware that I was always answering my parents in English, and that now irritated me so much that I began to try to speak in German again.

It had become evident to all of us that we were socially isolated except for a very small circle of German, Jewish, and French Canadian friends. Something important happened after the Normandy invasion in 1944. Father began listening closely to the radio when he was home; this was so unusual that Mother had to explain why he was on edge. After all those years of wishing for an Allied victory, the impending destruction of Germany was quite another matter for him. It was a two-edged sword, and I immediately understood. Having been told for as long as I could remember that the Nazis must be defeated, it gave me a palpable sense of relief to discover that my father was also tortured by the contradictions of loving Germany while also hoping for victory over Nazi Germany. Yes, it was all right to feel for Germany. No matter how bad it was, it was my country. My ethnicity had become clear to me.

Unionizing Galt Malleable, 1943

GARABED PALVETZIAN

> *Armenian immigrants gravitated to the iron foundries of southern Ontario, taking up residence in the streets around firms such as the Galt Malleable Iron Company. During the Second World War, Garabed Palvetzian, a moulder by craft, was a leader in the successful fight to bring the United Steelworkers of America-CIO Local 2899 to Galt Malleable. His actions came at a price.*

The foreman, timekeeper and superintendent were like dictators. The foreman and timekeeper were corrupt. Went to moulders' homes to drink. Men couldn't open their mouths. Boss gave you a job. It's ten cents a mould but if you didn't buy him a bottle, he would give you five cents. It was during the war. We were trying to get the union [the CIO]. . . . Sixty-five men signed. The next day at the plant, my job was gone. A huge job in its place. I had to pour twenty-two hundred pounds of hot iron in the morning and twenty-two hundred pounds of hot iron in the afternoon. And that was in addition to all the preparation. I asked the foreman for help. He refused. I asked to work close to the fire. He refused. It was inhumanly heavy work. The foreman marked six cents a mould on my card. That was not fair. All that iron! All that heavy work! A hundred moulds for six dollars! . . . The foreman said it was office orders. I went to the superintendent. . . . He said, "you better give us seven days notice." I said, "you give me notice." He wrote on my card that I was being dismissed because I was not used to working in the malleable!

A Dutch War Bride

OLGA RAINS

Olga (Trestorff) Rains recalls the Canadian liberation of Holland, and some of its repercussions.

January 1945, Haarlem, Holland

Watching through my bedroom window.

The sky, covered with Canadian, British and American bombers, a sight I will never forget. The sound was very heavy, they were loaded with bombs on their way to Germany. I was very ill with the disease diphteria, for which there was no medicine. The electricity had been cut off, water was down to a trickle and we had no fuel to keep warm. Food was very scarce and we were slowly starving to death, not knowing where our next meal would be coming from. The nazis had stolen everything we had, including our dog. They were desperate as they knew that they were on the losing end of the war. I lived in the last province to be liberated and that winter was the coldest we had for many years.

Since 1940 when the nazi's invaded our country, they tried to break our spirits with harassment. All we had left was our dignity and our willpower to not give in to their demands. Thousands and thousands of Dutch people died of cold, diseases and starvation that last winter of WW II.

Thanks to God I was still alive.

Then the Canadians came and liberated us. They found us in terrible shape, emaciated and barely alive. For two weeks on end we ate crackers and lard, to bring our stomachs back to normal. The first month after the liberation, I was still too weak to do anything. In the first week in June 1945 I met Lloyd, my husband, one of the Canadian liberators. It was love at first sight, three weeks later we became engaged and on December 24, 1945 we were married with the permission of the Canadian Army in the beautiful old city hall in Haarlem. Lloyd went back to Canada in January 1946 and I followed him in August 1946.

On August 8, 1946, the long awaited telegram arrived, saying I was to leave Rotterdam with the Lady Rodney to England, from there we sailed with the S.S. Mauretania to Halifax. I found the trip across the ocean very exciting, despite the fact that I did have some seasickness. I shared a cabin with another Dutch War Bride and two English brides who each had a small baby. The Dutch brides helped the English take care of their babies. There was a bathroom in our cabin, which was a luxury we all enjoyed.

The food served in the dining room was delicious, the crusty buns, bacon and eggs, oranges. Tears came into our eyes the first time we saw all this. The staff and the Red Cross ladies were very helpful and understanding to all the brides. Of course some of them must have thought; "You brides stole our Canadian men!" In the evening we would mix with some of the dignitary's like the Bishop of Canterbury and General Montgomery; they enjoyed talking to the War Brides and vice versa. There were movies and live music in the evening for everyone to enjoy.

We were all so glad when Canada came into sight and could hardly wait to get off the boat and be on our way. We arrived at PIER 21. For some brides the husbands were waiting, but for others it was different. We were told to check the bulletin board in the big hall. There were messages for the brides. One of the brides on this boat got the brush off from her husband. He had changed his mind and told her to go back to England.

Each bride was escorted off the boat by a soldier who brought us to a huge building. There we had to hurry up and wait in line. Our papers were checked and again we were escorted to the train. My destination was Sault Ste Marie, Ontario, a three day train ride with a stopover in Montreal and Sudbury. There Lloyd was waiting for me on the station. He looked so nice in his civy clothes. I was wearing a huge hat, a good friend had given me; he didn't like it one bit. I took it off and never wore it again. The ladies in Canada didn't wear those fashionable hats yet. Canada was somewhat behind in fashion at that time. In Sudbury I bought my first high-heeled shoes and ate my first banana split. Lloyd bought me a gold watch to replace the one a German soldier had stolen from me.

I couldn't believe all the food I saw in the stores and I wondered why Lloyd didn't buy me any bananas. I didn't want to ask. My first dinner in Canada was a hot pork sandwich. I had never eaten gravy on bread, but I really liked it. The next day we were off to Sault Ste Marie by bus. It was a rough ride and the roads left something to be desired in those days. I wasn't used to all those hills, coming from a flat country. I thought that ride would never end. We made a few stops along the way and when we stopped in Blind River I met for the first time an Indian lady; she made me a delicious egg salad sandwich.

The country side was beautiful. I never seen so many trees in my life, more trees and more rocks. What impressed me most were the high clotheslines, the big cars and the wooden houses.

Upon arrival in the Soo, as they called it, my in-laws were waiting for us. They accepted me as I was and I did the same. We all seemed to realize that we came from different worlds. I was one of the very few brides who did not have to live with my in-laws. Lloyd had rented an upstairs in a home; we had running water hot or cold. The bathroom was inside with flush toilet and bathtub, we had to share with family downstairs. I cooked on an electric stove and had my own kitchen. Compared to other War Brides I knew, I lived in luxury.

The first winter was very hard on me. I was sick most of the time; I was pregnant. The temperature dropped to 40 below zero and when I walked outside, I felt that everything on me was frozen. I had never seen so much snow; it kept piling up, I couldn't believe it.

When Spring came around I felt a lot better and in July 1947 we had a healthy baby boy. When he was six weeks old we moved to Southern Ontario, to Hamilton, where we lived for twenty years. . . .

In 1980 when Lloyd and I came back to Holland for the first time, we were confronted with meeting the War Children. These are the babies that were left behind by the Canadian soldiers. These "babies," now in their fifties were and are still looking for their Canadian fathers. Now seventeen years later, we have been able to help many of them find that missing link, I have written three books on this project which we call ROOTS. The Dutch TV Network has made an eight hour drama series about the War Children, their father and mothers. This project has become our lives work now and is a hobby which we hope we will be able to do for many years to come. Last week we had the pleasure to be knighted by Queen Beatrix of the Netherlands and I received a beautiful medal for our work with the War Children.

In 1992 Lloyd and I decided to leave Canada and move to Holland. The winters are milder here, the distances are shorter and as we are getting older we feel that this is an asset. The family comes to visit us often and we also visit them in Canada. As a War Bride I have enjoyed the privilege of having lived in Canada, and am still a proud Canadian.

Democratic Living

IGOR GOUZENKO

> *A cipher clerk at the Soviet Embassy in Ottawa, Igor Gouzenko had doubts about his work as a Russian spy. These doubts were reinforced and magnified by an encounter with a fruit dealer who had come from Lithuania. Gouzenko defected in September 1945, bringing with him Soviet secrets. The Kellock-Taschereau Royal Commission concluded that there had been widespread Soviet espionage in Canada and that Igor Gouzenko had "rendered a great public service to the people of this country, and has thereby placed Canada in his debt."*

For the first time, this spying on Canadians was beginning to make me feel uncomfortable. The arrival of Anna, the subsequent birth of my son, Andrei, and the supreme contentment of our home at 511 Somerset Street, had altered my outlook. Candidly, everything about this democratic living seemed good. I had been in Canada long enough to appreciate that the free elections were really free, that the press was really free, that the worker was not only free to speak but to strike.

Near my home was a fruit store and the old fellow who owned the shop had unconsciously become a profound influence on my judgment. He was of Lithuanian descent and absolutely unschooled; too simple, I appreciated, to be skilled in lying propaganda. Aside from the wonders of his oranges, peaches, pears and bananas, I was frequently awed by his remarks. To one direct question on a forthcoming election, he replied loudly:

"No damn chance I vote for Liberals this time—not last time either, not this time sure!"

Such a statement made while his country was at war and the political party mentioned was in power, left me completely astounded. Later when he told me of suing the City of Ottawa for some alleged infringement of his little property, I was even more impressed. This old fruit dealer, an immigrant who had come to Canada some fifteen years ago, showed no fear whatsoever of secret agents. As a matter of fact, he knew nothing about me, not even my name. Yet he spoke freely and emphatically as no native of Moscow would ever dare to speak. And he spoke surrounded by fruit riches Moscow people hadn't tasted in years.

These are the people, I thought, against whom the Communist Party world domination schemes are now aimed. The very influences which I so deeply admired, as exemplified in the old fruit dealer, were to be destroyed in the process of conquest. There was imbedded in my deepest mind a seed of doubt that I would have hastened to deny. But it was there all the time, I know now.

Nobody We Knew: Sachiko's Story

R.L. GABRIELLE NISHIGUCHI

As part of her extensive research into the post-Second World War deportation of Japanese Canadians to Japan, historian and archivist R.L. Gabrielle Nishiguchi interviewed Sachiko Nakamura (née Ohata) and tells Sachiko's story here.

Between May 31 and December 24, 1946, 3,964 persons of Japanese ancestry—66 percent of whom were Canadian by birth or naturalization—were transported to Japan under a federal government deportation program. Not one of these immigrants and their mostly Canadian-born children had been charged with a crime or act of treason. Yet the Canadian bureaucracy had endeavoured throughout World War II to cobble together a scheme that in their own words would "reduce the numbers" of what some considered a "troublesome" community of immigrants. Theirs were the faces of visibly different foreigners, with unpronounceable surnames. They were nobody we knew.

The shoddy treatment began in December 1941, after the Japanese Imperial fleet attacked the American naval base at Pearl Harbor, Hawaii. First, the federal government caved in to panic and pressure for the removal from the west coast of a perceived warren of potential spies and saboteurs. For the duration of the war, Japanese Canadians were to eke out a hard existence in abandoned mining shanties in the British Columbia wilderness; on B.C., Alberta, and Ontario road camps; or on prairie sugar beet farms. Then, in January 1943, through an executive order-in-council, their property was liquidated to provide maintenance for dislocated families. Finally, throughout the spring and summer of 1945, federal bureaucrats put into motion an efficient plan for removing thousands of the sickest, poorest, and most vulnerable Japanese Canadians from Canada by offering them money to go to war-devastated Japan. The Royal Canadian Mounted Police supervised a nation-wide survey of every man and woman of Japanese ancestry over the age of sixteen.

For a calculation of the human cost of this bureaucratic zeal and legislative legerdemain, we turn to a single story—Sachiko Ohata's story, told mostly in her own words. She was born in Mission Hospital in Ruskin, British Columbia, on January 11, 1935. Her father, Yoshito, worked in a local sawmill; her mother, Shigeko, supplemented the family income by picking strawberries. It was a carefree childhood. Sachiko remembers: "We lived in a big bunkhouse. There was lots of room. We had a big chestnut tree. In the fall, I got up early in the morning to look for the first chestnuts on the ground. There was a small river near our home. On special days, Dad would take the whole family fishing."

However, Yoshito's aging parents begged him to come home to take up his responsibilities as their eldest son. He dutifully returned, only to realize that he and his wife had been away from Japan too long. He was "too Canadian," and his wife was perceived as being "too free." They waited until the birth of the eighth child, a son named Takashi, before coming back to Canada in 1937. Yoshito's mother and father found it impossible to forgive their son for this glaring break with tradition, and he was all but disowned.

Back in British Columbia, Yoshito was worried that his children would not be able to make a good living in that province. Both he and his wife were naturalized Canadians and had struggled to make ends meet during the Depression, battling both hard economic times and local prejudice. He made a difficult decision—to send his five oldest children, all born in Canada, to live with family in Hiroshima, so they would be able to find work in Japan. The three daughters—Yoshiko, Chizuko, and "Terry"—and two sons—"Mas" and Eiji—were not welcome at the Ohatas' farm; they were sent instead sent to live with Shigeko's family, the Kumagawas.

In June 1941, Yoshiko, the oldest daughter, died suddenly. Beset by worries and grief, Yoshito and his wife became anxious to bring their surviving children back to Canada. They finally scraped together enough money and sent four tickets to the Kumagawas in Hiroshima. Grandmother Kumagawa put all four children on the train bound for Yokohama. They were to set sail aboard the *Hikawa Maru*, which was due to dock in Vancouver harbour on October 31, 1941. Shigeko met the ship. One by one passengers disembarked. Sachiko recalled: "Mom waited until the last person came off the ship. My brothers and sisters were not on board. For the first time, I saw my mom cry." For some unknown reason, the children had not been allowed onto the ship. They had returned to Hiroshima, but Grandmother Kumagawa did not have enough money for another train trip. Then the war broke out. The four oldest Ohata children were trapped in Hiroshima.

Sachiko was six years old. On Christmas Day, 1941, just weeks after Pearl Harbor, she received her first and only doll. "In those days the dolls' eyes rolled [up and down]. I was kind of a tomboy and I poked them. I broke her eyes. I was embarrassed and hid her in the attic. Sometime in the New Year, Dad was taken away to a road camp, maybe Hope-Princeton, B.C. When my mother, brothers, and I left for Hastings Park [the Vancouver evacuation centre], I thought we were just going somewhere with my mother. I left my doll in the attic. There were no dolls in the camp, no dolls in Japan. I never owned another doll after that."

During the fall of 1942, the Ohatas moved first into a tent and later into a wooden house in Popoff, British Columbia. "There were seventy-two houses in all at Popoff. We were in house number 68 in the last row. Behind us was a small stream and railway tracks." In January of 1943, Shigeko Ohata gave birth to her ninth and last child, a daughter, "Tammy," whose birth accentuated the absence of her four oldest children. Throughout the war, the Ohatas never knew anything at all about their children in Japan. Sachiko recalls: "Every day Mom put rice on our little household altar. Every day she prayed that my brothers and sisters were safe. She worked hard making *udon* [Japanese flat noodles], which she sold to make money to bring the children to Canada after the war." One of Sachiko's happiest memories was, as a nine-year-old, volunteering to be "Miss Canada" in a school concert at the Popoff relocation camp.

Between May and September 1945, the government demanded that every person of Japanese ancestry indicate on a form whether they would relocate east of the Rocky Mountains or go to Japan. Japanese Canadians who chose Japan were promised generous financial assistance. No assurances were given that persons of Japanese ancestry who chose to stay in Canada would be allowed to return to their former lives along the B.C. coast, or that any of the prohibitions against their buying land or applying for trading and fishing licences would be lifted.

The Ohata family was wracked with guilt and indecision. "My mom and dad waited until the last possible minute before signing that form. They didn't want to go to Japan—especially mother. None of us wanted to go to Japan. That's what really hurts. They set a date, didn't they? A certain date that you had to sign. We didn't want to go to Japan." But without assurances that Yoshito would be able to earn a decent living east of the Rockies, how could they save enough money to bring any of the children back to Canada? Would discrimination be even worse than it had been before the war? Federal money was being offered for them to leave Canada. None was offered to help them find their children and bring them home. Their oldest child in Canada was not even thirteen years and was not able to help support the family. Sachiko remembers: "I saw my parents fight. My dad threw a *chawan* [Japanese rice bowl] filled with rice across the room. He told my mother we had to go back to his home in Hiroshima. We had no choice."

After Yoshito signed the deportation form, Shigeko wrote a letter to a friend saying, "Even if I die, I must find my children." Sachiko did not want to go to Japan, but when she complained, Shigeko told her, "It's a nice place. You'll have your brothers and sisters. You won't have to do any chores. You do all the work now. In Japan, your older sisters will do it for you." Sachiko's mother continued to save whatever she could from her noodle money, and when she knew that they were going to leave Canada, she bought cloth to make clothes for the children she had not seen in nearly ten years. She also wanted a final photograph of her four children in Canada. She sewed special dresses for Sachiko and "Tammy" and the boys were put in their Sunday best for this event.

Deportation day arrived in the fall of 1946. The Ohatas were put on a train and taken to Vancouver. "I remember the train passed through Midway, B.C. From the window, I saw my uncle waving goodbye to us. My mother kept telling me that we were going to a better place." Sachiko, eleven and a half years old, remembers waiting to get on the ship and playfully stepping out of line. "An RCMP man got really upset and told me to get back in line."

Sachiko's mother was ill for the entire voyage. "She was throwing up every day. When we landed in Japan, October 1946, they took us to a big hall. We all slept together on *tatami* [straw] mats. I don't want to talk about the food. All I'll say is that I remember they gave us rice full of worms. The worms were stretched out, maybe a half inch long, cooked." Hiroshima station was "just a plank, everywhere was flat, drab and burned out." They took the local train to Kabe Station and walked for forty-five minutes to the Ohata family home. When they arrived, they were hungry and exhausted. Yoshito's uncle brought them small bowls containing rice balls mixed with barley. The rice was full of bugs that had a peculiar smell but they had no choice but to eat it, bugs and all, Sachiko recalls.

The war had only exacerbated Yoshito's parents resentment about their son's pre-war return to Canada. To make matters worse, he had brought back more mouths to feed. Shigeko begged her husband to find them another place to live. The children who had been stranded in Japan during the war were now teenagers. They poured out story after story about how they had survived the war. Eiji, now sixteen, had seen the mushroom cloud over Hiroshima city in August 1945. Temples and schools had been set up as hospitals. Eiji, then fourteen, had been forced to carry the burnt corpses of those who had died in temporary shelters to large pits dug in the ground.

Sometime in February of 1947, Shigeko caught a cold that turned into pleurisy. Yoshito took anything they had brought from Canada, including the material that Shigeko had planned to use to make clothes for her stranded children, and traded it on the black market for fresh fruit. Sachiko's mother died in June. The children who had been stranded in Japan were devastated that the mother they had waited so long to see again was gone. They felt guilty that they had aired their frustrations to her, and at times, they openly resented the children who had been with her during the war. All the children tried hard to suppress their anger about their life in Japan.

Sachiko was miserable. She battled fungus in her toenails from working barefoot in the rice fields, and head lice. She was tired of being bullied because of her difficulty with the Japanese language. Since she was a year older than her classmates—she had been put back a year—Sachiko was a head taller than everyone and stood out even more because her only coat had been sewn by her mother from bright red Canadian cloth. She remembers yelling at her dad, "I wish you had died and mom had lived." Whenever the children would explode, Yoshito would only say: "Just blame it on me." He never spoke about his wife again, but faithfully went up the mountain to the little marker he had made for her. When she was dying, her body was so full of water that she couldn't drink anything. "He would always go up the mountain to give her water." "Here's the water you always wanted," he would say to her. He never remarried.

By virtue of the executive orders under which the Ohatas left Canada in October 1946, Yoshito had lost his Canadian nationality and was barred from ever re-establishing himself in Canada on a permanent basis. While he couldn't return, he knew how much his children longed to go back there. He asked Shigeko's brother, living in Midway, British Columbia, for help. Yoshito now watched as one by one his children left him to return to the land of their birth.

In July 1956, it was finally Sachiko's turn. "Mas," who was already in Canada, had saved enough money to send her an airplane ticket. Her father told her, "You are leaving your home for good—it's like you are going away to be married. We must have a party and invite our friends and relatives." Sachiko, now twenty-one years old, was sad to leave, but she was happy to be going home. "I had a tiny vanity case and kept packing and unpacking it. I also had a small apple box. I had so few belongings. I really wanted to go to Canada. At my party, I started singing 'O Canada.' I remembered all the words." On the plane home, she recalls that "I didn't know how to eat in the Canadian way." It had been ten years since she had lived in Canada. "I watched this girl that was eating next to me and did whatever she did."

In 1966, Yoshito came to Canada to visit Sachiko. He loved his stay and was reminded of all the things he missed about Canada, but because of the terms of the deportation order he had to return to Japan. He remained in Japan and died of a stroke in 1975—in exile, dreaming of the rich trout streams of British Columbia.

There is a postscript to Sachiko's story. "When I turned sixty-five, I had to apply for my Old Age Pension. Everything was in order. The pension lady said to me: 'I need proof that you went to Japan after the war.' I was so angry. I said you should have that proof. I did not want to go to Japan. You people decided that we had to go. I was just a little girl. I had to go with my parents." Recalling that day, Sachiko whispers, "I don't like rejection, maybe because I was hurt so many times. Canada rejected me, that's what it is, I think. To get back to Canada, we did it all ourselves, didn't we? Doesn't that mean that we really loved Canada?"

We need to preserve Sachiko's story, so that the next time we encounter those known only to us by ethnicity, religion, or race, we will be less tolerant of our own surprising inhumanity. We will remember Sachiko. Now she is someone we know.

Travelling West, 1947

ROBINA EVELYN LEE

> *Glaswegian Robina Lee met her Royal Canadian Navy husband-to-be during the Second World War. They married in 1947. She reached Canada on the ocean liner* Aquitania *in October and headed west, as related in this excited letter to her parents. The war brides were celebrities, watched over by the Red Cross and considered by the government not immigrants, but fully fledged Canadian citizens from the start.*

Canadian National Railway
Manitoba
29th October, 1947

Dear Mom and Dad,

I'm on the last lap of my journey now, and am scheduled to reach Vancouver at 9:20 a.m. on Friday the 31st October.

The "Aquitania" reached Halifax on Sunday at 1 a.m., over a day late, due to the bad weather. In fact, from the accounts in the newspapers here, it's the worst crossing she's ever experienced. Sunday morning was pretty hectic as everybody had to pass through the Immigration authorities who came on board, so you can guess that would take some time when there were over 2,000 passengers. However, I was lucky, as Canadian citizens and Canadian war brides were called first and I was off the ship by 2 P.M. The Red Cross were there to meet us, and made a very welcome cup of tea while we were waiting for our train. I got through the Customs all right—they didn't even open any of my luggage, though lots of other people weren't so lucky, and I tipped a Redcap to put my suitcase on the right train for me. I wanted to make sure it did get on the train, and seeing is believing! I didn't much care for the journey from Halifax to Montreal as all the Canadian War Brides were travelling together in two special cars on the train so I had to part with some of the friends I made on the ship. There were 65 of us, including children, and the noise was terrific.

Rather a tragic thing happened during the night though. One of the girls had her five-months old baby sleeping in her bunk with her, and about 2 a.m. she woke up and found that it had suffocated in the pillow. We had two Red Cross nurses travelling with us from Halifax to Montreal, and they were informed right away, but the baby was dead. The train stopped for a couple of hours and the mother had to be taken off as there'll have to be an inquest. Wasn't that terrible?

We stopped at a little place called Mont Joli on Monday forenoon, and were allowed off the train for 20 minutes. It was typically French, even the newspapers and magazines were all written in French. Still it was good to get a breath of fresh air. By lunchtime we were at Quebec and saw the Chateau de Frontenac. It was certainly a wonderful sight.

I thought the food aboard ship was good but, honestly, the meals on the train are just about perfection. In fact, they look so beautiful when they're put down in front of you that it seems a crime to have to break them up with a fork. For breakfast to-day, I had half a grape-fruit with a maraschino cherry in the middle, two fried eggs, toast, marmalade and coffee. The coffee is served with plenty of sugar and a whole jug of real cream. For lunch, I had Green Pea Soup, Braised Beef with Creamed Carrots and Potatoes, Lettuce Hearts with French Dressing, Strawberry Ice Cream and Spongecake, and coffee. I was sitting have a cigarette afterwards when the waiter came up and asked if I'd like something else. I thought he was kidding, and said, "How much more can you get with a dollar meal ticket?" He said as long as I sat at his table I could have anything I wanted, whether my meal ticket covered it or not, and he immediately dashed off and brought me another helping of Ice Cream. There's nothing like getting in good with the waiter!

The Red Cross gave us two kinds of meal tickets—one priced at 45 cents, and one at a dollar. Breakfast is 45 cents, lunch is a dollar, and for dinner we have to give up 1$45¢, so you could imagine the meals would be quite expensive if you had to pay your own. However, the Chief Steward in the Dining Car must feel sorry for me or something, because sometimes he only takes a dollar ticket from me at night, & for breakfast he rarely takes one from me at all, and he always says to the waiter, "Let her have anything she wants."

Well, anyway, we got in to Montreal Central Station at 7.30p.m. on Monday and the Red Cross were meeting us again, to see to our

luggage and put on the right trains. Montreal Station is really beautiful, isn't it—I wish I could have seen around a bit more but my connection left at 8.30p.m., so there wasn't time.

Now that I'm on this train, I have no more changing to do, thank
goodness. The rest of the war brides have gone their different ways
so I just feel like an ordinary passenger now I'm on my own. I have
an upper berth, and, strangely enough, haven't fallen down the lad-
der yet! However, there's still time!

From Montreal to Winnipeg, the scenery seemed to consist of
nothing but trees. You could hardly imagine how there could be a
housing shortage in Canada when there's so much timber around.

We got into Winnipeg this morning at 10.20a.m. and the train
halted for an hour. Another girl and I went for a short walk along
one of the main streets. There are some beautiful cars, Johnny would
revel in them I'm sure—Studebakers, Packards, Chryslers, etc. It's
been a beautiful day too, as warm as can be, and I don't think I've
ever seen a bluer sky. It's such a brilliant blue, it almost hurts your
eyes to look at it. The streets in Winnipeg are very wide and there are
some lovely buildings. When we got back to the Station, I sent off a
cable to Al, and then we went into a Restaurant for a cup of coffee
and a ham sandwich. I was just finishing mine when I heard a voice
booming through the loudspeaker in the Station, calling for Mrs.
Lee, and when I got up to the train, I found a man from the Red
Cross just checking up that I was all right. They certainly have a
marvellous organization.

Since we left Winnipeg, the country has flattened out into prairie.
There are no more trees, only vast stretches of land with here and
there an occasional homestead. We're still in the province of Manitoba, but to-morrow should be in Saskatchewan—after that comes
Alberta, the Rockies, & then Vancouver.

The trains are really very comfortable and you don't notice the
length of the journeys. It's amazing how quickly the days go in. Every
15 minutes or so, a man comes along selling coffee, sandwiches, coco-
cola, chocolate, candies, salted peanuts, apples, oranges, grapes, and
so on. As a matter of fact, I've just finished having a coco-cola.

Well, I guess I'll close for now, & finish this letter to-morrow.
It's pretty difficult trying to write in these trains as they're much

bumpier than the ones back home. They stop and start a lot too, and you just get about jolted from one end of the car to the other. Cherio for now.

Thursday, 30th

Well, another night is over and we've passed Edmonton, Alberta, and should be nearing the Rockies in about half an hour. We had about an hour's stop at Edmonton at 8.20a.m., and, gosh, was it ever cold there! There was snow on the ground and very heavy frost. Since we left there, though, we strike due south and it's beginning to get warm again. The sun is still shining and everything looks really beautiful. I was up at 5 o'clock this morning and saw dawn breaking as I was having breakfast.

Most of the people I've met have now dropped off at intermediate stations and, as a matter of fact, so many passengers got off at Edmonton, that they took away about four coaches and I had to move up to another car. The girl who slept in the bunk under mine on the "Aquitania" is still with me though she's in the next car. However we pay each other visits and go in to meals together. Her name, by the way, is Ita (pronounced Eye-ta) and she's Irish. She's a very nice girl, very pretty too, and is just coming back to Vancouver after spending a six month's holiday with her parents. Her husband will be waiting for her at Vancouver too, so we're both going to be busy to-night trying to make ourselves look fairly presentable before getting in to-morrow morning.

After two weeks continuous travelling, you do feel a bit of a wreck, and there's nothing more ruinous to one's peace of mind than to fall asleep and know one's tailoring is going all to pieces! It's a good thing that my travels will be over soon because all my clothes are getting crumpled, my hair could do with a good wash, and, generally speaking, I'm beginning to feel dishevelled a little more than somewhat! A few more days like this one and Al probably wouldn't even recognize me—I'd have to tie one of these Red Cross labels around my neck or something.

GEOGRAPHICAL NOTE:—We've just crossed the Athabaska River and are approaching the first of the Rockies. All the lower parts are densely wooded and, here and there, you can see lakes with the sun beating down on them and making the ripples look like diamonds. The train seems to be going round in circles now and every so often you can see the engine way up ahead as it twists and turns. There's no getting away from the fact that the scenery is beautiful—I only wish you were here to share it with me.

We've slowed down considerably now, as we seem to be climbing steadily.

I've certainly met all sorts of people on this trip—some marvellous fun, some crashing bores, a couple of would-be smart guys, some very nice girls, and one, who got off at Edmonton, couldn't read or write. She's English too, believe it or not, but I don't suppose it matters much whether she's educated or not, as she's married to a French-Canadian lumberjack and, from his photograph, he doesn't look as if he could read or write either! She used to amuse me though. Her favourite expression was, "They don't tell nobody nothink!"

I think I'll finish this letter off here and will write you again whenever I reach Vancouver. It's really painful trying to keep a pencil in your hand with the train swaying from side to side so much.

In the meantime, give my love to Margaret, John, Patricia, Betty & Johnny, and Norma if you see her.

Lots of love to you both,
Evelyn
xxxxxxxx

Refugee Doctors Need Not Apply

A.D. KELLY

> *A.D. Kelly was the assistant secretary of the Canadian Medical Association, arguing in a 1947 submission to the government in Ottawa that refugee physicians ought not, for the good of international life, to be admitted to Canada. His reasoning was ingenious, if disingenuous.*

Let it not be said that the Canadian Medical Association is uncharitable or unkindly in its thinking towards these professional brethren who find themselves in such a sorry plight. But it is incomprehensible to me that the Government of Canada will so disregard its international obligations that refugee physicians will be admitted to Canada, when all indications point to the wisdom of settling them in the needy areas of the globe. It must, therefore, be a very narrow humanitarian viewpoint which will suggest that refugee physicians should be brought to Canada when their services are so urgently needed elsewhere.

Our Remnant of a Family

MOSES ZNAIMER

The parents of entrepreneur Moses Znaimer were the Displaced Persons—the DPs—of a war that almost destroyed them and their people.

We arrived in Canada in May of 1948: Father, Mother and me. That's all that was left. We were post war (WWII) refugees from a "Displaced Persons" camp outside a town called Kastle in Germany. Just getting to that DP camp had been a saga involving two frightened Jewish kids, barely out of their teens, on the run from the Nazis, each the survivor of a substantial family, who had been thrown together by the fortunes of war, and had me in the middle of it all.

It is difficult to be sure whether what we think of as our earliest memories are actual memories, or stories we were told when very young. Perhaps a picture of such a story forms in the imagination of a child and, over time, takes on the detail and gravitas of memory. As is the case with many Canadians today, my earliest memories—whether stories told to me long ago or images that are truly remembered—have to do with the passage from a troubled place to a place of refuge.

I live and work in and out of Toronto, a city that has become, to an exciting degree, a city of immigrants. When I step out of the ChumCityBuilding and walk along Queen Street West, I'm forever amazed at just how wonderfully diverse T.O.

has become. But how many of those passers-by, I also wonder, are visited by stressful memories of uncertain journeys, anticipation, fear? People born and raised here can barely be aware of how many of their fellow citizens carry with them echoes of tragic events and places that seem all but impossible within our experience, here, in the "Peaceable Kingdom."

That's why I'm so proud of the strength my parents showed in completing the journey from that shattered old world to the promise of this new one. During that journey, how many times did Chaja and Aron swallow what must have been overwhelming dread, and press on? How many times did they look at their infant son and wonder what on earth the future could possibly hold for him? For them? I often think that one of our great strengths is the simple courage that so many now-quiet, now-ordinary citizens showed in just getting here.

My mother, Chaja, was Polish and my father, Aron, was born in Kuldiga, Latvia, where his family was in the shoe business. He escaped on a borrowed bicycle minutes after hearing the Nazis were invading. It was June 22, 1941. Chaja was born in Dubienka, and spent her teenage years in Lodz, where the family owned a stocking factory. Despite Chaja's "bourgeois" background, when the Russians occupied, because of her education, she got work in a munitions factory and was evacuated to the Soviet Union as the Germans advanced. By the time she got together with Aron, she had acquired a Komsommol (Communist Youth) card, an indispensable entrée to jobs and rations, and had done a stint in a Kolkhoz (collective farm). She escaped with the help of an older man who fancied her. She then escaped from him too and, ever the confident one, approached Aron on a boat leaving Markstadt, when she heard him humming a familiar Yiddish tune.

Thus they began an epic journey of survival, moving constantly, east and south, marrying, and having their first child, Moses, moi, in Kulab, Tajikistan, one of the Central Asian Union Republics of the former USSR. Aron had foresight. He always knew when it was time to leave, and at each stop they left behind young colleagues they would never see again. Chaja was shrewd and had a magical way of making friends.

At that time Aron worked in a granary and found himself framed for giving short measure. It turned out someone had tampered with the scales. It was wartime and the penalty was death. He was arrested and interrogated by the dreaded NKVD (secret police). Chaja, all of 4'10" and ninety pounds, bullied her way into a meeting with the prosecutor's wife. This connection and the gift of Aron's only valuable possession, a St. Moritz pen, secured his release and bought them enough time to finger the real culprit.

Because Aron had the foresight to use Chaja's surname, Epelzweig, instead of his own, the family was able to get out of the USSR when Polish nationals were repatriated after the war. Poland remained relatively porous and relatively easy to get out of until the Iron Curtain was finally, firmly brought down in 47/48. So it was that a midnight rowboat across Berlin's Spree Canal brought us into the Western Zone. After a stay in Hesse-Lichtenau, that DP camp in the American Sector of Occupied Germany, the three of us managed to emigrate to Canada. We steamed into Halifax harbour aboard a converted troop ship, the SS Marina Falcon. From there we went by train to Montreal, Quebec, where Aron had found two living relatives, our sponsors—"Auntie" Lina and her son Gershon Goldberg. So, that's where, seven years later, in 1955, I was "naturalized" as a Canadian citizen. I've always liked that word naturalized, as if life before had been somehow unnatural, which, of course, it had been.

I have two strong recollections from the period before we got to Canada. One relates to food, the other to drink—not surprising perhaps, given it was wartime. Both, I have no doubt, are actual experiences. I don't just remember them. I can, in fact, still taste them. In the first, I'm lying in my cot, and mother gives me a piece of bread. It's a warm crust that's been rubbed all over with garlic and baked with bits of the garlic pushed inside. Nothing could be simpler. I start to cry because it's so good. Quite an odd thing. Was I hungry? Was I sick? I can't recall.

In the second, some soldiers come by the Camp Mess and offer me a drink. It is cold and dark and sweet and effervescent; and I love it! When I get back to our barracks, I tell my parents about it, but they have no idea what it could be. In the following days and weeks I keep after them to get me that taste again. Was it dark beer? Was it kvass (a Russian drink made from black bread)? Was it strong and sweet iced tea? None of these! Only when we were finally settled in Montreal, and I tasted my first store-bought Coke did I realize what that treat had been. Even more wondrous was that something so scarce and unknown in that camp, was, in my new world, available in every cooler, in every drugstore and corner store in town, for five, then seven, cents.

It's at this point—our arrival at that DP Camp in the American Zone of Occupied Germany—that memory for me starts to accumulate into something certain. This is where I begin to have my own stories; and one of the most vivid has to do with some munitions that a couple of playmates and I found in a stream near the camp.

Towards the end of the war, piles of ammo, big machine gun bullets and larger shells had been dumped in that stream. A retreating Army, I imagine. We amuse ourselves by fishing them out and trying to set them off. An adult comes upon us just as I raise a howitzer-type cartridge in my hand, poised to smash its base on a rock. He lets out a wild holler and starts to run toward me, gesticulating wildly. I drop it and take off. He follows. He chases me into a nearby abandoned building. In retrospect, I'm sure he was only concerned for our well-being, but at the time his determination frightened me. I get away by jumping out of the second floor of that bombed out building. It's quite a leap, and I wake up the next day with a serious hernia as a result.

This is bad news. Our longed-for immigration to Canada depends on passing our medicals. So, prior to my physical, I am literally tied down to keep me from jumping about, and on-board ship and later on shore, the hernia is suppressed with a truss. My condition was never discovered by the authorities, but even years later, mom still half-expected Immigration to come through the door and say, "hey, wait a minute . . ."

Of that two week Passage to Canada on that converted troop ship, I remember a stormy Atlantic, my parents down below, deathly seasick, and me on my own, hanging out with the sailors, including the very first Black man I'd ever seen in my life. I remember the vast sheds where we new arrivals are slowly processed; then another long train trip; and, finally, Montreal. Immediately, I am sent to a hospital for my hernia. Suddenly, cut off from the Yiddish, German, Russian, Polish, Latvian, Hebrew and God knows what else was flying around my milieu, I come out, two weeks later, with a functional command of English and quite a few colourful words of French.

Aron's first job in Canada was as a presser, and Chaja began work in a bakery. We settled into a 3rd floor walk-up on St. Urbain Street; Libby and Sam, my sister and brother, were born; Chaja continued to work. Aron was reunited with his sister Becky who had managed to escape to Northern Rhodesia. Of that generation, she was the only surviving sibling on both sides.

Eventually Aron was able to start a small shoe store, but his heart wasn't in business. Every spare moment his head was in a book; he could savour a newspaper all day. Although Saturday was the busiest day of the retail week, he would be happiest if there were few customers so that he could sit in the back listening to Live at the Metropolitan Opera.

Chaja became a waitress; at least that was her title. She essentially ran a successful steak house for a Damon Runyan character whose clientele included Jimmy the Book and Obie the Butcher. In addition to serving, she did the ordering, bookkeeping, and played mother-confessor to a staff worthy of a soap opera. She was always grateful to be working, never dreaming she was exploited, though we were convinced she was. Chaja never got over the loss of her entire family. It was a black hole she didn't let us into, and we barely know the names of all the Epelzweigs. However, she built a new extended family, "the Kollezshankes," a group of immigrant women who were like sisters until the day she died.

Our parents lived for their children, working endless hours at jobs they did not love. They gave us a great education, independence, and a love of learning and Jewish culture. They made education easy for us, but for them it was a reward for long years of struggle. After seven years of night school, Aron earned a BA in Jewish Studies from Concordia University. He was 72. It was his proudest achievement. After retiring, Chaja studied for two years and received a diploma in Gerontology from College Marie-Victorin. As usual, she made close friendships with people from different backgrounds including an Anglican priest who became a regular at our Passover Seders.

Aron and Chaja were devoted to each other. While caring for Aron in his final illness, Chaja ignored her own health. Aron died in February 1992; Chaja in November 1993. They did not live to see what would have been their greatest joy—the birth of their grandchildren, to my brother Sam and his partner Lesley Stalker. Leith Aron was born three weeks after Chaja passed away. His sister, little Chaya, arrived in May 1997.

> For a child, being "stateless" and on the run is not all bad. You see the world, you pick up languages, you hear different musics and eat different foods. You begin to understand the richness of the world and the joys to be had from being open to all kinds of peoples and cultures.
>
> Even before starting grade school I'd already lived through aspects of a World War and taken a hazardous trip around the globe. These experiences left me a cocky little kid with a strong sense of self. It was a different story for my parents. For all their remarkable qualities, the capacity for happiness had been irretrievably killed in them. A certain gloom settled over everything. We were survivors; and one aspect of being a survivor is learning to keep your head down. I was not brought up to go out and conquer the world. I was brought up to be grateful that we weren't being killed in the streets or sent to the ovens; above all, I was not to make trouble. Though I was a dutiful son and respected my parents enormously, it was a lesson I never learned . . .

All immigrants feel that they are the last ones. I know I did. They think they're on the bottom of the totem pole that leads to success and respect in Canadian life and everyone else is ahead of them in power and privilege. Of course it's not true. The inflow is perpetual and yesterday's refugees are tomorrow's establishment, or at least their kids are.

Still, I identify with all newcomers and have my fingers crossed for every one of them. I've lived their drama of struggling with a new language, and absorbing a new culture while trying to hang on to old traditions. But hard work and zeal for self-improvement actually do bring results in this blessed part of the world. Our little remnant of a family found in Canada a haven of tolerance in a land of opportunity and I'm sure they will too.

"White Man's Thinking," 1949

A.L. JOLLIFFE

> *Canada's director of immigration in the 1940s as he had been in the 1930s, A.L. Jolliffe argued much as officials had since early in the century. Blacks could not adapt to the Canadian climate, and Canadians would not accept them.*

Generally speaking, coloured people, in the present state of the white man's thinking, are not a tangible community asset, and as a result, are more or less ostracized. They do not assimilate readily and pretty much vegetate at a low standard of living. Many cannot adapt themselves to our climatic conditions. To broaden the regulations would immediately bring about a large influx of coloured immigrants. Quite realistically, this would be, in my opinion, an act of misguided generosity.

The German Parish

LUCY AMBERG

> *Lucy Amberg was a German-speaker from Romania whose sister had emigrated to Canada in 1938, believing "that she was coming to a land with plentiful opportunities, like everyone used to think." Lucy followed in 1948 and the next year arrived in Toronto, where her first and lasting connection was with St.*

Patrick's Church on McCaul Street, which had been built for Irish Catholics but had become by the late 1920s the church for German Catholics in downtown Toronto.

To me St. Patrick will always be my home. I was active there as a teenager, and as a married women. We had picnics, outings, our monthly communion breakfasts, we raised money for Japanese missions. The reason why I felt so close to St. Patrick is that when I arrived in Germany, I happened to be in a part of Germany that was completely Lutheran-Protestant, whereas in Romania we were very strict Catholics. Living in Germany, I felt very much uprooted from a Catholic upbringing at home in Romania. Living in Germany without a church, I felt immediately at home when I found German people of the same faith. It was only here that I realized how many religions existed, and I realized that there were other religions, because back at home in our town in Romania, everybody was Catholic. Being young, we hadn't traveled much, so when I came to Canada I hung on to St. Patrick. I was married there, and after we got married we kept going there, we came bowling every Wednesday night. When the children were young we didn't go bowling for a few years, because we didn't want to leave them with baby sitters, but a few years ago we came back. We are going to church and see a lot of familiar faces. And as we are going there for supper and dances, there are never enough seats, because people still come, even the very old and middle aged and the young. I am extremely happy that even my youngest child is going there.

Dearest Nia, 1950

WILLIAM AZZI

With his parents and two of his sisters, William Azzi immigrated to Canada in 1950 from a small village in the Emilian-Tuscan Apennines of Italy. After landing at Pier 21 in Halifax, the family took the train to Vancouver, where his aunt Rachele had settled years earlier. Another sister, Nia, and two brothers remained behind in Italy. As a youth, Azzi was active in boxing and soccer; he took the nickname "Willie," after one of his heroes, Italian-American boxer Willie Pep (born Guglielmo Papaleo). Azzi went on to become a high school accounting teacher, but remained active in sports as a soccer reporter for Vancouver's Italian newspaper L'Eco d'Italia *(which his family owned for several years) and as a coach, taking several teams to the provincial or national soccer championships. Twelve-year-old Willie wrote his first letter home to Italy in August 1950. His sisters added postscripts.*

Vancouver
21-8-50

Dearest Nia and dearest brothers:

Finally, I have decided to write you. Today we received Gianni's letter which he sent by regular mail with all the pictures. Earlier we had received two other letters on the first of which I learned that Luci got her first tooth. Too bad that she decided to grow one now, I would have loved having been there. Dear little Luci I so wish I could see you!

I should tell you something about the trip but I will send you a diary by regular mail. By now you know that the trip went reasonably well. On the ship, however, after Gibraltar we experienced some not so nice moments. Everyone, or nearly everyone, was sea sick. Some were vomiting on one side and some on the other side. Renato and Gianni would have enjoyed it a lot.

Tina and I slept together in a little bunk on the side of the window. One night we woke up soaked in salt water. Courageously, Tina then tried to shut the window but another wave hit her squarely. Mom was a little afraid, Lea was sea sick and the Vulcania was dancing. Things went a little better afterwards, but the window always remained closed and the appetite diminished a lot.

On the train, on the other hand, we almost starved, only sandwiches and coffee and milk. Now let's talk about other things. I remembered that in the middle of that school book with the red cover, that is on Gianni's desk, I left my wallet with 150 lire and a membership card with "Societa Sportiva Meazza" written on it. Dear Nia, with the 150 lire buy some candies for Ronny and Luci. You can give the wallet to Gianni if he wants it, if not you can send it to me at a later date. Give the membership card to Pupo, but don't wait till the end of summer. The time has come, dear Gianni, that I sold the soccer boots, that you gave me as a gift, for 500 lire. I didn't tell you before because I was afraid that you would take the 500 lire from me. I still don't know who won the Tour de France. I hope that Arrigo will write me and tell me the result and that he will also send me other sporting news with perhaps some newspapers.

I'm glad that Ronny remembers me once in a while and that he liked my little organ. I also often think of him and Serena. I wonder when I'll see my little nephew and nieces again! That ship and that train sure put on a lot of kilometres!

We are all well and I hope that the same applies to you.

Zia Rachele and zio Carrari are very good and kind. They would like us to always be happy and festive. Dad has already started to work. He comes home very tired. Give my wishes and kisses to all the relatives. Tell zio Ercole that soon I will write him too. A special wish and kiss for zia Emma. To all of you many, many affectionate hugs and kisses from your brother Willie.

Wishes, kisses, and hugs from me too. Lea

Mom wanted to send her wishes too, but she's in the middle of ironing. Next time she will write too and we will all cheer loudly and at length. Kisses to all and many wonderful things. It's raining here too. Tina

A Migrant Chain

FORTUNATO RAO

A chain of migrants and migrant tradition linked Italy's Calabria to Canada.

Oh, you would be surprised what a chain of people linked Canada to Calabria. I sponsored my sister and brother, who are seven or eight years younger than me, in 1957, and my mother in 1959. In 1959 we bought this house here. This is the first house and this is the only house, which I'd never change with any other in the world. I sponsored an uncle and other people too. I sponsored a good number, I would say. Where I was not able to sponsor them, I found some employers to sponsor them. They had a trade and they came in.

A lot of people were sponsored because Canada was in need of people like bricklayers. Sam Sorbara sponsored God knows how many people. We heard he received twenty-five dollars for his trouble to arrange the immigration in a legal way. He also arranged mortgages for immigrants and had real estate connections, and made money in this too.

Some people came on contract with the Canadian government. In San Giorgio people found out about these contracts from travel agents who advertised them. Then they had to go to the Canadian consulate in Rome to make the arrangements. People on contract with the government came to clear the bush, or for the mines in Timmins, or to work in the West. But for one reason or another they didn't like it. Some were not ready for the environment. If they came in the winter they weren't suitably dressed; they came only with light clothing. They served six months or a year and then they went to the city and sponsored other people.

There were Italians here before the war who could sponsor you. Even if you did not have relatives in Canada before the war you could, we would say, "catch up Italian style." Let's say I am Rao and you are Sturino but we're not relatives. We say that from San Giorgio, my mother and your mother are relatives on the women's side. In other words, they connect first cousins, second cousins. So even if they were not cousins, we claimed it through the women's side. That way we had everything planned when we went up to the consulate and they asked us who called us from Canada. We said, "My cousin." If the consul asked any questions in Rome we would reply, oh yes, my mother and his [the sponsor's in Canada] were two sisters, and we are first cousins. Everything was fabricated about us being cousins. We didn't need any affidavit. There were lots of people in Canada from San Giorgio: Rao, Ferraro, Fazari, Macri, Sorbara. All of the surnames were here. Everybody started coming. When they did not have their own sponsors, they went out of the circle [of kinship] creating the relationship. We used to say we were related through the mothers when the names were not the same. This was done who knows how many thousands of times in Italy and they never figured it out in the 1950s and 1960s.

San Giorgio has people in every city of Italy. We have people in Germany, France and Switzerland. We have people in, you name it. We have people in every country of Europe including Russia. From San Giorgio we have a large number people in every country in South America, all over the U.S., Canada and Australia, you name it. Everywhere you find San Giorgesi and they went there for only one thing, to work. The people have emigrated all the time from San Giorgio since the world was created.

Before the war there were many San Giorgesi here in Canada. I remember Giorgio Consiglio. He was living south of College Street on Clinton Street. One day we went to see him and he was retired at that point. I asked him how long he had been here and he said twenty-five years. I looked at my cousin and said, "Jesus, he had roots here, eh!" I shook my head. And now I have been here nearly fifty years. That fellow, he came here before the war. Others, too, like Sam Sorbara, whose son is Gregory. There is Raffaele Macri with a number of his brothers who came before the war, to Toronto, around 1920. We have a lot of people in Hamilton who came before the war. In Guelph, we had people from a hundred years ago who emigrated from San Giorgio. They were the first in Ontario going back to the last part of the 1800s.

Time to Adjust

LILLIAN SULTEANU

> *Lillian Sulteanu immigrated to Canada from Roumania via Israel. Arriving in Montreal in 1951, she quickly acquired a university education, overcoming barriers of culture and language.*

It must have been about three or four months after we arrived that our bell rang for the first time. The only people we knew were those who collected the rent once a month. We were so alone, we had no one here and we went into a panic. We had been the first ones of the family to come to Canada, and there was always the fear that remains with you when you come from a police state or Communist country. We thought it was the police coming for us and were afraid to open the door. It took us a while to get rid of the fright whenever the bell rang.

There were a lot of things to which we had to adjust. Some of them were embarrassing. I remember one situation when my mother called up the Irish janitor when the bathtub was blocked and we couldn't use it. He came upstairs, and although my mother had gone to night school a few times, she couldn't speak English too well. Her French was much better. She didn't know the word for "wash" in English and used the French translation. "My daughter wants to make 'lave'" (laver), as she tried to explain that what I wanted was to use the bath to wash myself. It sounded as if she was offering me to him, and the man looked at my mother and me as if both of us were crazy. I can laugh about it now, but it was very embarrassing then.

We stayed there for two years, and it was like a hotel for visiting family. My mother and father each had sisters and there was a cousin as well who came and stayed with us until they could find an apartment of their own. In those two years we were never without roomers.

My cousin, who came from New York, told my parents that no matter what, I should go back to school and finish my education because I would have no chance at any kind of future without one. In Roumania I had finished ninth grade. I had been going to a kind of technical school for construction in preparation for architectural training. This was part of the Russian system where you had a choice between high school and technical school. However, I was not aware that choosing this would disqualify me from entering university. I would simply become a technician and even though I had taken advanced mathematics, calculus and physics, I would not be considered good enough to go to university.

Suddenly the opportunity was there for me to start again, even if I was older than the other students. I didn't realize how the entire cultural scene, the difference in being an immigrant, would affect me. I enrolled at Montreal High School on University Street and was the only one in class living downtown. Because of the location I had no friends near me to visit. Another barrier was the language. In Roumania, the second language had been French, and once the Communists took over it became Russian. Although the students at school tried to be nice to me and talk to me, all I knew were about twenty or thirty words in English. We didn't know that there were organizations like Jewish Immigrant Aid Services that could have helped us to integrate. I had two friends, both immigrants, one from Poland and the other from Roumania. The latter worked as a mother's helper and would translate for me. So if anyone asked me a question, it would go through her. We were both in the same class, and to this day we are still friends.

But the differences between the Canadian children and the few immigrants were very noticeable and at times for us, very painful. When there were class parties, we weren't invited. We didn't belong. I think back and I know why. It wasn't only the language. I know I looked odd. I wore socks, not stockings, because in Roumania and Israel, too, you only wear stockings after you get married. As for lipstick, forget it. European kids weren't allowed to wear it until they married. There was no question about it—I did look different. I couldn't make myself look like everyone else. I was used to the old country code of dress and even if I wanted to change, I didn't have the money to keep up with the other girls. It takes time to adapt.

Another problem was that I had to study in a room where there were usually five or six people sleeping. I needed a light to see what I was doing and I had be very quiet so as not to disturb them. With my meagre vocabulary I was required to study Shakespeare and learn entire sections by heart. I couldn't understand ordinary, modern English and here I had to learn Elizabethan English from memory. There were no special classes for teen-aged immigrants like me who were dropped into the school system. But there were night classes at Montreal High School for adults, and at night I would go to those with my mother. But they weren't much use to me. The students were learning "How do you do?" and "How are you?" and I was trying to understand Shakespeare. I listened to the radio and that helped. I read with a dictionary in one hand and when I did my homework, I had to look up every single word. It took ages and I had no help.

Then someone referred me to a woman who was teaching at home as a volunteer. She had children and couldn't get out. It took me two hours to get to her house and she gave me one hour a week. Again that wasn't much good. I had to work very hard, but I think my teachers appreciated the work I was putting in. I won a scholarship the first year. We had to pay something like five or six dollars a month for school, and with the scholarship it didn't cost anything. However, when I finished high school, I was the recipient of another scholarship for $200 to go to university. This was in 1953, and I decided to go at night so I could work during the day. What was so unbelievable for me was that I had passed the English tests so well. I don't think I was given anything I didn't deserve, but what amazed me was that there were Canadian children who failed. I took the same tests they did, and I hadn't been getting any after-school help. I didn't think I had any special ability and my memory wasn't that marvellous, but what I did have was a lot of will power. Because of the experiences I had been through, I appreciated learning more than people born here. An education is something you can take with you; no one can take it away from you. To this day I have not been able to get enough of learning.

"Keeping My Faith"

TARA SINGH BAINS

> *Tara Singh Bains was one of the first South Asian immigrants allowed into Canada under a quota system agreed on among Commonwealth countries in 1951. He discovered that the pressures to compromise his Sikh faith and practices came from within his own family.*

My niece, my sister's eldest, was living in her own home in Ladner, south of Vancouver, where her husband farmed a big chunk of land with frontage on the Fraser River. My five nephews all lived with my sister. The oldest was only five or six years younger than myself, and the youngest was a child of eight. They were all Canadian-born. The older ones were from my sister's deceased husband and the younger from her second husband, but they were all living together as one family without distinction.

These nephews thought that if I shaved, I could make better progress in Canada. Gradually they brought up the subject of my hair and beard, and then more and more, and it was very painful to me. They talked about Indian culture, how backward it was and so on, without thinking that I could be well informed about cultures and affairs around the world. In fact they were generally well behind me. They came to acknowledge that, but all their talk was aimed at inducing and seducing me to shave. They wished me to change my outer form, which was my God-given form. Quite a few times I reminded them, "Look here, fellows, faith is faith. I don't feel inferior being an Indian or being a Sikh, and I never thought it would be my own people who would hate my hair. No white man has done that to me so far."

In the beginning these discussions were friendly. Then they became more combative. They frustrated me so much that at one point I told my brother-in-law, with tears in my eyes, "I did not know that my hair would be an obstacle, and I am greatly grieved." He must have admonished them, and their tone became less aggressive, but the discussions continued. One evening I was reading the paper on the chesterfield, and my brother-in-law and sister were preparing to go out to see a cinema show in a movie-house. My sister said, "We would be glad to take you, but they don't allow turbaned people in." That remark hit me hard because it showed what she was thinking. I didn't want to see a cinema picture. The thought had not entered my mind. And there probably would have been no problem if I had gone. I never heard anyone else say that turbaned people could not go.

That was the first indication that my sister agreed with my nephews, and I understood then why she had never tried to intercept their remarks. When I went with the family to parties with friends and relatives, then somehow the question of my hair would be taken up by our hosts. I found it hard to stay in the house when this subject kept coming up. I wanted to get away from it without causing any disturbance. About twenty-five or thirty yards from the house, adjoining the barn, they had a bunkhouse for their employees. It had a good vacant room on the side facing the main house, so I spoke to my brother-in-law and sister. "I enjoy my early morning prayer when I sing it loudly. I can't do that in the house because the children are sleeping. Let me move into that room in the bunkhouse." That was my excuse, and it was a truthful one, so they fixed up that room, and I moved into it.

From then on I was spared a lot of those discussions because at break times, after eating, I could go into that room to rest or read something. The Chinaman in the other room was an experienced person but knew just enough English to get along. I could still feel the force of their campaign to get me to shave. Communications were restrained, and that weighed heavily on my mind. If I had not been as well educated as I was, I could not have resisted as I did. All the time I was bothered by the thought that I was a source of displeasure to my elder sister and benefactor. This began to affect my health. My mind kept going back and forth: "If I do submit, would I be the same again, or could I recuperate from my weakness?" Finally, my human wit conquered my faith.

One evening, at supper break, as I was washing my hands and face in the laundry room in the house, Mac Singh came in from his farm. He was my sister's eldest son, an intelligent, hard-working person who later married a Dutch girl and eventually became land commissioner for Surrey. At that time he was renting a farm of his own but living at home. All of a sudden I said to him, "How about if I cut my hair? It should be a matter of pleasure to you people." I stayed back to let him break the news to everyone inside. Then all the restrained behaviour disappeared. All was happiness. I told my sister and brother-in-law that I wanted two large, good-quality photographs, one before and one after I shaved. My brother-in-law asked why, and I told him that I wanted to keep them on my bedside table to remind myself what I was and what I had become. He understood from that that I had not made a willing choice. But my sister was so happy she went out to the bunkhouse for the first time in weeks and made up my bed and changed the sheets.

The next day I wrote a letter to Piara Singh, my younger brother, who was working as a machinist for Indian Railways at Bina Junction in central India on the Great India Peninsula Railway. When I left India, Piara Singh saw me off at Delhi and said, "I would like to see my brother come back in the same form." At that time I believed it would be easy to keep my Sikh form, and the opposition of my relatives in Canada came totally out of the blue. In my letter I told Piara Singh how I had been defeated for the time being but that I would recover. A wound may leave a scar, but it will heal. I could go clean-shaven while it was necessary, but I could regain my Sikh form.

The postal services in those days were very efficient. A reply would come from India within a fortnight or, at the most, sixteen or seventeen days. Generally my wife and I exchanged two letters a month. With the help of Almighty, my brother-in-law was slow to arrange for my photograph, so I had not cut my hair or shaved when a touching reply came from Piara Singh. He promised to pay my return airfare if things did not turn around, even if he had to sell his wife's jewelry. I got the letter at noon during lunch break, and after taking my lunch I went to my room and read it. It troubled me so much that I started to weep aloud. I tried to keep my voice low, but my tears were flowing, and I lay on my bed, determined to keep my faith, and decided that I would leave the house right away if it had to be.

My sister's third eldest son, Udham Singh Gill, or Jack, as he was called, came to my door. My nephews and I were nearly the same age, so they called me by my name. He said, "Tara, let us go. Time is up." He saw my wet face and said, "What happened? Is there any sad news in the letter?" I said, "Now listen, Udham, I am going to bury this matter once and for all. Would you be kind enough to go into the house and tell them if this matter is raised again, no matter how slightly, I will leave and that person will be my opponent totally." Of course he did what I asked, and from then on things started to stabilize. Better days followed. My form was accepted in the family, and although outside the family from time to time people would ask how long I could carry on, I felt no pressure.

The Shadow of Leaving

HELMUT WALTER OTT

The pain of separation was experienced twice by a young Austrian who came to Canada in 1952 and left five years later—but only briefly.

Leaving Austria, and my home town of Graz, was not easy. Even now, the memories surrounding separation bring with them feelings of sadness. As a child I was very close to my grandparents and close to my friends. I had completed the first three grades in the *Nibelungenvolksschule* and felt very much at home in my neighbourhood. Though our parents forbade us to go there, among the fascinating play areas I remember were the piles of rubble and numerous bombed out buildings left after the war. As children, we used to play cops and robbers in those bunkers because they provided great hiding places. The countryside around Graz was lovely. In the summer our grandparents frequently took us to the surrounding woods to pick mushrooms; in the fall, we searched for chestnuts. I was very close to my grandparents. My brother and I were their only grandchildren as my mother was their only child. In a nutshell, I had close friends, a home, and a sense of belonging. Life felt totally complete for me, perfect and happy. The thought of leaving Graz was a jolting intrusion which I put out of my mind for as long as I could.

Nevertheless, as the departure date crept closer final farewells with acquaintances increased, as did promises never to forget one another. The shadow of leaving eventually fell across all our daily activities. In the last few days we visited my grandparents daily. I can still see them watching from their second storey window, waiting to see my brother and me getting off the street car. We liked to visit Oma and Opa. But those final days were sad. Opa and Oma seemed quiet and downcast. They would look at us with an empty stare for long periods of time. Eventually their eyes would brim with tears and Oma would repeat, "Why must you go *so* far away? Stay here. Things will soon get better. Stay home; otherwise we are all alone."

My brother and I tried to lighten the situation. We reassured them we would only be gone for a little while.

My father had written encouraging letters from Canada. His clinching argument in each letter was the promise that when we came to Montreal my brother and I would find a room filled with all the toys imaginable. This promise, more than anything, fuelled us with a desire and determination to come to Canada at all costs.

When the moment of departure finally came, my grandparents and mother wept openly. I felt a lump in my throat saying goodbye. My brother and I tried not to cry. Suitcases in hand, the three of us took leave of Oma and Opa's apartment. We must have been a sorry sight with those big suitcases as we descended the staircase to the street and waited for a streetcar going to the train station. Opa and Oma said they did not want to come and see us off because it would be unbearable for them. From the street, my brother, my mother and I waved a last good bye to the tearful faces in the second storey window and then boarded the streetcar to the train station. Surprisingly, the first people we saw . . . there were Oma and Opa. They had taken a taxi in order to see us one final time. It was already late afternoon and before long, after another round of tearful goodbyes, we felt the train's forward motion. As it picked up speed we continued to look and wave from the open window. My final memory is grandfather standing close beside grandmother, waving a white handkerchief: two receding figures in a dimming light. The train turned a corner and they were gone. . . .

Within a few days [in Montreal], the novelty and excitement wore off. I was ready to go back home. I now wanted to tell my friends and grandparents what I had just seen. Here reality set in. We *had* to stay in this place. I felt stranded and started yearning to see my grandparents and friends. We became very homesick. Tears and recriminations often arose within the family. "Why did my parents have to do this?," "Wasn't it selfish?," "Why can't we go back home?" Stretches of days would pass when my parents would not speak to each other nor my brother and I to them. We sulked. We pouted. We grumbled. We hurt each other with our words and our silences.

Squabbles were resolved only to be renewed. Various diversions to cure homesickness were attempted. With other immigrants we

went to beaches along the St. Lawrence River. But they were homesick too. We kept sightseeing. Somehow this simply heightened our
alienation. The social life around us did not touch us; its reality
seemed unreachable. We did not fit in. Our culture was different, our
language was different, the foods we ate were different. On the one
hand, I think we wanted to belong; on the other we really could not
because it was too soon. We did not know then that personal adjustment takes a long time. "Fitting in" also means giving something up
about oneself. It was still too early for us to give up anything. We
were not yet ready. So we remained outsiders. "We are Austrians and
not Canadians," we said.

Besides, there was no way for us to return home. My parents had
enough money to come to Montreal, but not to return. So we had
to hold on, to persevere while my parents saved what money they
could. (How often I heard the word "persevere" in those days!) My
mother, who had completed her professional school diploma in
Graz, found work first as a hot dog wrapper at Hygrade Meats, and
subsequently in a small business gluing vinyl to the outside of boxes
for record playing machines. I suspect my parents earned very little
and after weekly bills were paid I doubt there was much money left
over. But at least we had the hope that we would go back as soon as
we could, instead of having to wait for five years.

During those first few weeks my brother and I were afraid to
leave the apartment on our own. We watched for hours the flow of
traffic from our first floor window overlooking St. Hubert Street.
We learned the names of automobiles and made up games like
counting how many Nashes, DeSotos or Chevrolets passed within
a given time, or from how far away we could tell the car's make. In
time, we also discussed the kind of car each of us would own once we
grew up. He wanted a Cadillac. I liked Oldsmobiles. . . .

For my brother and me, Canada gradually started to feel like
home. We made friends, we learned English and could now speak it
without difficulty. As with other Quebec boys, the hockey players of
the Montreal Canadiens became our idols. In small measures we forgot more and more of the written German language and the Austrian
culture. There was no one except my parents with whom to practice
the language, and even their German showed increasing sprinkles of

English idioms and vocabulary. Changes were slowly taking place in ourselves. It was even alright to put one's feet onto the coffee table at home. We left Montreal two years after we arrived; not to go home but to take up residence in the Eastern Townships of Quebec. This was a new environment much closer to nature and to small town friendships than Montreal. There I spent three exceedingly happy years and made congenial Canadian friends.

The first five years in Canada passed quickly. My parents debated whether or not to return to Graz as planned. By then, my brother and I certainly did *not* want to go back. Our grandparents were already a somewhat distant memory having been supplanted by new-found friends. My parents themselves were unsure, but eventually they decided that we should return. My mother especially wanted to see her parents again. So in November of 1958, (I was 14 years old) my mother, my brother and I returned to Austria. My father stayed behind. He planned to work in Canada for at least another year before returning.

We took leave of our Canadian friends and travelled again by boat, this time from Montreal to Le Havre, and from there by train via Paris to Graz. Our homecoming provided us with a rude shock. The Graz to which we returned was a foreign city. It was so different from how I remembered it. Ironically, now that I was back, I felt I did not belong. My grandparents and former friends, although very kind and encouraging, seemed distant to me. The relatives felt more like strangers. All of them had grown older and no longer looked as I remembered them. My childhood friends had not put their lives on hold either awaiting my return; some I had difficulty recognizing; others I did not even remember. They had all carried on with their lives by forming new friendship circles to which I did not belong. What's more, I had difficulty speaking to them because expressing myself in the German language was difficult; it felt unnatural. Graz had also changed visually. The ruins in which I used to play six years before had disappeared. Unfamiliar new buildings stood in their places. New automobiles and mopeds raced about where I remembered only bicycles, old trucks, and horse-drawn carts.

My brother and I had to attend school. It lasted only two days. Our manners were all wrong. We offended teachers by not standing up when they addressed us. We intended no disrespect. However, we had not made such formal behaviour habitual in Canada and kept forgetting to stand up. I felt freakish as other boys made fun of my manners (or lack thereof) and ridiculed my broken German. The experience was so devastating my brother and I hated it and refused to return to the school. Both of us stubbornly clung to our demand to return to Canada. Homesickness had taken hold once again but this time in the other direction—we sought the community we left behind in the Eastern Townships of Quebec. All the pleading, all the promises, all the begging and convincing by my relatives fell on deaf ears. My brother and I sobbed at the thought of staying in Graz; we vehemently argued our own view and rebutted every other. We were stubborn and unrelenting in our insistence to leave. Seven weeks later our mother and the relatives gave in. It was decided we would return to Canada. Ironically enough, my grandparents made it possible for us to buy the tickets. From their savings they paid for the tickets with which we left them again. Not until I became an adult did I understand how deeply they must have cared for us to give up their own happiness for ours.

Sense of Continuity

HARTLEY JANSSEN

> *In 1953 Hartley Janssen emigrated from Holland at the age of ten with his parents, a seven-year-old sister, and a brother who was not quite two years old. He wrote this reminiscence fifty years later.*

My paternal grandfather was a career soldier in the Dutch army. He spent most of both world wars in prison camps. In the First World War, when he was serving as a spotter, his plane was shot down over enemy territory. These experiences left him embittered. My grandmother nursed him back to health and stayed with him until his death from emphysema in 1964. My grandmother was active in the International Red Cross both before and after the war. She also received commendations from General Eisenhower and the British government for providing a safe house for airmen in their attempts to return to England.

On the recommendation of his father, my father volunteered for active peacetime duty in order to have a choice of service and reduce his conscription time from two years to one. As it happened, hostilities broke out and he remained in the armed forces until Holland was overrun. He then went into the underground for the remainder of the war. He was caught once but released by a sympathetic colonel, who had just lost a son similar in age to my father. In 1942 my father married the daughter of a prominent doctor. My mother, unlike my father who was an only child, had three siblings, including two big teenage brothers. The family hid two Jewish sisters for most of the war. With food severely rationed, my grandparents suffered from malnutrition and some of the associated illnesses.

I was born in 1943 and have no memories of the war. After the war, my father rejoined Royal Dutch Shell ("stolen" by the British during the war, according to my mother). He was then recruited by his former commanding officer to join Berini, an Italian motorized bicycle manufacturer. Some years later a reorganization left both of them out of a job. Not long after, father's friend contacted him once more and advised that Volkswagen was hiring to establish a presence in overseas markets. My father went to Germany for interviews and was taken on. It takes a man with a pragmatic view of the world to work for people whom not that long ago he had fought actively against. Volkswagen had offered my father the choice of Belgium, South Africa, and Canada. Our parents chose Canada because they believed it would give their children greater economic opportunity, and in particular less competition in access to higher learning. In addition, some years before, my mother's brother had emigrated to Cambridge, Ontario, at age eighteen. I still marvel at the decision of my parents to leave the familiarity of their home country. It was especially hard to leave their parents behind. It was also difficult for those left behind, especially my maternal grandmother. I missed one set of grandparents who always spoiled me, but not the maternal grandparents because grandfather was rather severe and didn't suffer fools (me) gladly.

In 1953 our family of five emigrated from Holland. I was ten, my sister seven, and my brother one and a half years old. My father had already taken up his new job to help start up Volkswagen Canada. I had been a voracious reader and had read cowboy and Indian novels, so I assumed Canada to be a wild and forested land. Imagine my disappointment as we approached the airport in Toronto. However, I was delighted to see so many television aerials; there were still only a few very rich people in Holland who had TVs. We moved temporarily into rental accommodations, a modest bungalow in a middle-class neighbourhood in North York, while our house was being prepared. As the export of foreign exchange from Holland was severely limited after the First World War, my father had purchased a prefabricated house in Holland and had it shipped to Thornhill.

As a ten-year-old, the promise of a new country far outweighed the loss of weekly visits with grandparents. I was excited by the prospect of moving to a place where I could indulge in my passion for the outdoors, particularly for fishing. It was only later that I understood how fundamentally our lives were changed. Our expectation of a less competitive environment in both education and work was by and large fulfilled. I liked the Canadian school system, once I could handle the language, and did not really have to work very hard until graduate school. I had not been doing terribly well in school in Holland and had not liked the teachers. My father's lack of post-secondary education had meant he would have had to struggle most of his life to earn a decent living in Holland. Within a dozen years of emigrating, he was offered the position of president of Volkswagen America. He turned it down because he would have to move the family to New York and the move would probably have led to American citizenship, two unattractive prospects, according to my parents.

As we arrived in the month of May, my sister and I went to a nearby public school. I was placed in grade three. Because I had no English-language skills and the teacher did not know what to do with me, I was directed to write out the times tables from 1 times 1 to 12 times 12. I already knew them by heart up to 10 times 15. I tried to indicate that I also knew some algebra, but to no avail—perhaps the teacher had never seen algebra. As a break from writing times tables,

I was allowed to copy a grade one reader ". . . see Dick run, see Jane run, see Dick and Jane run. . . ." Against my mother's advice, I wore a new watch, given to me by my paternal grandfather, to school. I took it off to wash my hands, left it behind, and upon returning to the washroom some time later found it gone. Using sign language, I managed to communicate my problem. However, the watch was never returned. I was very disappointed at the dishonesty of my fellow pupils.

Not knowing the English language was initially frustrating because I could not communicate with other kids, teachers, and storekeepers. My parents both spoke English, although they still had to master idioms. Mother once sent me to the store to buy a "flask" of milk. During my first summer holidays, playing with neighbourhood kids, I started to speak some English. My sister learned much faster than I, as she seemed unafraid of making mistakes.

In the fall we moved into our new home and I started at a new school. I wore shorts to school the first winter, as was the practice in Holland, but my mother was eventually compelled to purchase some long pants. I think it may have been because of peer pressure more than the biting cold. I recall being called "foreigner" by one of my classmates. I didn't know what it meant, but was determined to throttle him. It was the only incident I can recall when I was considered different from Canadian-born boys. I was judged too big to be in grade three, so was moved to grade four, a full year behind where I would have been in Holland. The teacher, Mrs. McGillavrey, helped me to adjust and provided remedial reading classes, which were attended by other kids also needing assistance. Soon I no longer needed reading help and successfully made it to grade five and even managed to come second in a school spelling bee contest. About this time, I realized I had started to dream in English and concluded I was now fluent in my adopted language. At Christmas I was moved into grade six and had now made up the earlier time lost. I also started playing hockey, first as goalie for the school team (using my mother's bolt-on figure skates) and later on defence for a community-based league in Richmond Hill. My parents were later approached by the Chicago Blackhawk organization with an offer of a place on a major junior hockey team. However, the thought of my living away from home and the reduced emphasis on education scuttled the plan.

At home we were encouraged by our parents to speak English. They did not join any Dutch social organizations, nor did they seek out other Dutch immigrants. They believed in integrating with Canadian society as soon as possible. We kept a number of traditions, though, including the exchange of gifts on Christmas Eve and the lighting of real candles on the Christmas tree. Our parents attended church and decided the United Church most closely followed the teachings of the Dutch Reform Church. I don't think my parents were particularly religious, but felt strongly that we should be exposed to the teachings of the bible as part of our moral upbringing. When we received our naturalization papers, I remember we were all quite proud. Prior to this event, I once gave my parents a scare by joining the cadets in high school. They feared that, as a Dutch citizen, I could have been stripped of my Dutch citizenship and been a person without a country because I had joined the armed forces of a foreign land.

I had developed a close friendship with about five classmates, and we often played tackle football in the fall and road hockey in the spring after school and on weekends. These friendships endured into grade twelve, when my father was transferred to Vancouver and I entered university. By now I considered myself a Canadian and rarely thought about what life might have been like had we remained in Holland. I had even had my name Canadianized: I was named Hubertus Anna Nicolaas Janssen at birth; the diminutive of Hubertus is "Huib," invariably mispronounced by Canadians as "Herb" or "Hoyb" or some other variation. Therefore my parents asked an English couple to suggest a name beginning with "H" that was not too common, and henceforth I was known as "Hartley."

Over the years I have visited Holland in order to maintain contact with relatives. On these visits I was always left with the feeling that there were too many people and cars and too little space. Competition for jobs was also keen, and life in general seemed more difficult in Holland than in Canada. I don't think I could return to Holland and feel comfortable. And yet my roots are there. An amateur historian has traced my maternal ancestors to the Dutch admiral Tromp, who sailed up the Thames in the seventeenth century with a broom up the mast to demonstrate that he had "swept" the seven seas of the British navy. On the paternal side, I am related to the Duke of Alvarez, who was sent to subjugate the Dutch during Spanish rule. I wear a ring with the Alvarez family crest, normally handed from eldest son to eldest son. These ancestors provide a link and a sense of continuity for me. However, I think of myself as a Canadian who happened to have been born elsewhere. Canada embraced me and it is my home.

A Rhodesian in the Army

MICHAEL PILLAR

> *In July of 1955, Mike Pillar resigned from the Rhodesian military and with his wife, Joan, and their two young sons began a long journey to join his father, who had come to Ottawa a few years before.*

Somewhere south of Montreal, a Canadian customs and immigration officer boarded the train to check credentials. He impressed me as being a friendly type who displayed an interest in where we came from. Of course, he eventually got around to asking us the important question dealing with the purpose of our trip. I told him that I hoped to continue in the military. This resulted in a more serious direction to the inquiry. What, he wanted to know, would I do if the Canadian Army did not accept me? I replied that I would seek employment elsewhere and added that we would be staying with my parents. At this, he agreed to allow us to proceed and stamped our passports accordingly. His parting caution, however, was that his department would be monitoring the situation. The message was quite clear— get a job or be prepared for a return journey to Rhodesia. In retrospect, he was doing his job as required and I, in turn, should have better planned our immigration!

A few days after our arrival, my parents and their younger children left on vacation and we had the run of their house for two weeks. I wasted no time in visiting the recruiting station. After numerous tests and interviews, I was informed that—despite having performed below par in those tests calling for a knowledge of things Canadian—I had been granted a short service (temporary) commission and was told to report to the 1st Battalion, the Canadian Guards in Camp Petawawa in two weeks' time. I used the interim period to search for a car. A dealer in Toronto was offering a brand-new Ford Tudor for $1,900 so I jumped on the first bus I could catch. To say that I was delighted with my first North American-type vehicle would be an understatement. This youthful enthusiasm came to an abrupt end, however, when I got behind the wheel and found myself driving, for the first time, on the "wrong" side of the road in a big city. More by good luck than good judgment and despite the occasional foray into the left lane, I managed to make it back to Ottawa unscathed.

What were the biggest changes I noticed as a newcomer to this country? Perhaps surprisingly, for someone coming from central Africa, I was most shocked by the heat and humidity of the Ottawa summer. Of course, an even greater revelation awaited me in the form of an Ontario winter—but more of that later. Certainly, shopping in supermarkets was a novel experience, as was the abundance of ice cream and frozen foods of all types. Air conditioning was something new. I also was aware of a marked change in the brand of English spoken. This was something of a challenge, and I quickly learned not to ask for a "joint" in the meat department or to request that the service station attendant check under the "bonnet"! After being used to driving on the strip roads in Rhodesia, I found the highways to be a delight. Having played cricket, rugby, and field hockey all my life, I found the North American equivalents somewhat bewildering. Perhaps most noticeable was the attitude of the average Canadian. With few exceptions, I found them to be more relaxed, helpful, and friendly than were most Rhodesians.

I have an idea that the commanding officer of my new unit didn't know what to do with this somewhat older lieutenant who spoke with a strange accent, knew nothing of the Canadian Army way of doing things, and had arrived without a uniform! His problem was quickly solved when Army Headquarters chose me to attend a twelve-week Young Officers' Course at the Infantry School in Camp Borden. While I got along reasonably well with my one hundred plus fellow

students I was, not surprisingly, subjected to some good-natured rib-
bing. A group of them, for example, decided that Pillar should get
some skates and join in a pick-up game of hockey. I have no doubt
that they anticipated an evening of entertainment watching this
newcomer fall around on the ice. What I had not told them was that
I had roller skated as a kid and played field hockey at school and in
the Rhodesian Army and, to the apparent disappointment of the
onlookers, took to the new environment with comparative ease.

Civil Defence, 1955

TASS GRUNDEL

> *Because of squabbles over financial responsibility at all three
> levels of government, the lack of clear instructions to the public,
> and the increasing power of nuclear weapons, civil defence was
> viewed by most Canadians as a waste of time. Recent immi-
> grants from Europe felt quite differently, as their community
> newspapers attested. They had witnessed the way in which civil
> defence could save lives in England and Germany, and thus
> were vigorous proponents of General F.F. Worthington's federal
> civil defence agency. An enterprising German immigrant, Tass
> Grundel, addressed this letter to Worthington in November of 1955.*

Dear Sir:

The Metropolitan and the Provincial CD authorities suggested that I
communicate direct with your office. I got in touch with the local
CD authorities in regards to the following matter:

The importance of the CD is getting bigger every day mainly out of
2 reasons:

1. The steady flow of immigrants is enlarging the communities
   and so the targets: large cities.
2. The increasing war-potential of the Soviet-Union is a danger,
   which can't be overlooked. The present friendliness of the

THE LAND NEWLY FOUND

Soviet-leaders is making wide circles of the population lax and desinterrested [sic] in CD-work. Not being prepared can mean death to 100,000 people and more.

My suggestion is: Activating of New-Canadians. Most of the European Immigrants know by own experience what an air-raid is like. Many of them would be glad to help the CD in her work here for 2 reasons.

1. own experience taught them, that unpreparedness could mean death + destruction
2. to proof [sic] that they are loyal to Canada and willing to carry certain responsibilities.

Who am I—and what I would like to do

I am an immigrant myself. I came from Germany nearly 5 years ago and hope to become Canadian citizen next year. My 2 children are Toronto-born.

In Germany . . .

I worked as a reporter, detective, interpreter and investigator (British Army), Administration—Officer (U.S. State Dept.) Editor, Publisher, and Radio-Commentator.

In Canada . . .

I was holding positions as Canada—Chief Correspondent (News Agency), delegate intern, Red Cross Conference, Real Estate Agent, Business Mngr. And—to get a better knowledge about Toronto—as an Taxi-Driver.

I faithfully believe that I could be a very valueable help to you and your work. If you would decide to accept my program you'll never feel sorry that you did it. With your acceptance, you give the new Canadians proof, that they are not secondary citizen, that they are really wanted. Give *them* the opportunity to proof, what they are willing to be:

Good Citizens, the Canadians of Tomorrow, within the framework of Civil Defence.

"You Chose Canada"

IRENE BROWN

> *Irene Brown's emigration from England was planned and sponsored by her uncle. She was to come in 1957, but when the Suez Crisis of the previous year erupted, he insisted that "you'd better get over here fast, before another war happens and then you can't come at all."*

I was a little homesick at first. In fact, we were both very homesick for 2 years. And it's funny, because when we went for our interview at—we went to Liverpool, to Canada House there, for our medicals and interviews and one of the things that the man said to us was, you'll find that you're homesick for 2 years. It just about lasts that long. So, stick it out that long, because after that you'll find you're just fine. But he was absolutely right. He also made a very interesting comment, which I really—really comes back to me when I read the paper these days, because there are so many letters from people saying that we should be so nice to the new immigrants and, you know, that we should do this for them, that for them. Nowadays, it's almost a business of falling over backwards to fit everybody into what—give them what they want. And this fellow said to my husband and I, one thing I should warn you. When you get to Canada, always remember that you're going there, because you choose to. They're not asking you to. So, he said to my husband, when you go to work, don't ever turn around and say to the fellows you're working with, oh, we do that much better in England. And I thought, yes, that's wise advice, and I don't think my husband ever did, you know. I think he took that to heart, because he said, after all, you have to admit that that's the way they do it in Canada. They're entitled to. And you have to fall in with what they do. It's not the other way around. And I agreed with that and so did Ed and I think we both tried to work along with that and fit into Canada, rather than expecting Canada to fit in with us, which—don't you feel that's fair? I do, too, and I did then. And I think I always would. We had asked to come here, just as this gentleman said we had.

From the Kremlin to Cornflakes

JÁNOS MÁTÉ

The Hungarian Revolution brought 30,000 refugees to Canada, among them János Máté, who remembers a Canadian train and a Kellogg's Cornflakes box, welcoming him in his own language.

Had it not been for Adolph Hitler and Josef Stalin, my older brother Gabor and I may never have had the opportunity to crunch on Kellogg's Cornflakes in our childhood. Such gratification would most likely have been delayed by some thirty-five years until the collapse of the Berlin Wall and the Soviet Bloc in 1989. But then the lives of people are so often shaped and scripted not by their own design but by the consequences of external events, and the convergence of historical processes with the ambitions of the so-called men of history. So it was for our mid-European Jewish family in nineteenth- and twentieth-century Hungary and Czechoslovakia.

The lives of our parents and grandparents were, more often than not, a series of adaptations to the shifting sands of history . . . the ravages of wars, political upheavals, redrawn borders, regime changes, and opportunistic swings in governmental policies on the legal status and civil rights of ethnic minorities, especially those of the Jews.

On November 23, 1956, when the Communist regime in Hungary was still in a state of disarray because of a month-old and tenacious armed uprising against Soviet dominance by the population, our family crossed the border between Hungary and Austria. We became refugees. This was not an easy decision for our parents. Father was then forty-six years old, and mother thirty-seven. With two young sons, a couple of suitcases in hand, and with virtually zero financial resources, they left behind whatever security they had—their apartment, furniture, and other worldly possessions; all their friends and few remaining family members; father's employment. Without any guarantees about the future, they faced the unknown. Up to 150,000 people made the same monumental decision to flee Hungary during that time. The immediate impetus to leave came from relatives in West Germany who phoned to say "What are you waiting for?" but the actual decision to leave was many years in the making. An added incentive came from the anti-Semitic slogans that began to appear on the walls throughout the city, and an acquaintance saying to Father that "while he was a good Jew, other Jews could go to hell."

Leaving Hungary was a constant factor in our parents' plans following the Second World War and the tragedies that befell our family during the Hungarian Holocaust. However, when the opportunity to flee presented itself, despite her abhorrence for Hungarians whom she held responsible for the death of her parents during the war, Mother was reluctant to leave. She feared for her family. Father was more determined. They consulted my brother and me. We looked at one another and with boyish exuberance and a sense of excitement at the promise of an adventure and without full comprehension of all the implications, we enthusiastically embraced the idea of emigrating.

Our mother, Judith Lowi, was born in Kassa, Hungary, in 1919, into an orthodox yet modern, intellectual, European-cultured Jewish upper-middle-class family. As a result of the Treaty of Trianon at the conclusion of the First World War, the northeastern part of Hungary was ceded to the newly formed state of Czechoslovakia. Consequently, by the time she was two, without ever having moved, our mother was no longer living in Kassa, Hungary, but in the city of Kosicze. She was a Czechoslovak citizen.

When Mother was a small child, each year on her birthday thousands of people celebrated on the streets of Kassa. Only when she was a little older did she learn that in reality these parades were in honour of Tomas Masaryk, the beloved president and founder of the Czechoslovak Republic, whose birthday happened be on the very same day. Following the Munich Pact between British prime minister Neville Chamberlain and Adolph Hitler and the dissection of Czechoslovakia, Kosicze once again reverted to Hungary, just before the outbreak of the Second World War.

Our father was born in 1910, in Budapest, Hungary, into a poor

Yiddish-speaking family. His parents migrated to Budapest from a small town in Galicia, Poland, at the turn of the century. They fled Galicia, which at the time was a province of the Austro-Hungarian Empire, to overcome severe economic hardships that resulted from formal restrictions on Jews, as well as to escape anti-Semitism and anti-Jewish riots that swept the region in the late 1890s. Though born in Budapest as Andor Meltzer (and as his papers stated, also known as Andor Feldman), our father's Hungarian citizenship, as well as his family name, remained ambiguous because of the refusal of the Hungarian authorities to recognize the validity of his parents' marital status. In accordance with Polish custom, his parents only had a Jewish wedding and therefore had no civil marriage certificate that would be recognized by the Hungarian state. Consequently, our father had to bear both his father's and mother's family name.

In 1941, the government of Admiral Horthy, the regent of Hungary, in a move to further appease Adolph Hitler, enacted its third set of anti-Jewish laws that were aimed at progressively stripping Jews of their basic civil rights, ownership of property, and participation in normal day-to-day life of the country. Included in the 1941 Jewish laws were measures to deport to Galicia all Jews of Polish descent that could not prove their Hungarian citizenship. Our father fell into this category. To avoid deportation, he went into hiding and, for nearly nine months until his Hungarian citizenship was secured through legal means, he slept each night in different hiking lodges in the nearby mountains of Buda. Most of the 18,000 Jews who were deported to Galicia during that time were massacred by the German SS and their Hungarian and Ukrainian cohorts.

In 1942, along with 60,000 other Jewish men, our father was conscripted into the Forced Labour Battalions of the Hungarian Army. From 1942 till the end of the war in 1945, he dug trenches, built bridges and fortifications, and hulled timber throughout the Hungarian countryside. Over 50 percent of the men in the Jewish Forced Labour Battalions perished. Our mother moved to Budapest from Kosicze in 1942. Our parents were married on March 2, 1943, in the town of Tecso, near where father's labour brigade was temporarily stationed. Father was granted four hours' leave by the lieutenant of the brigade to attend his wedding. The lieutenant told him that

"Jews don't need more than half an hour for their wedding ceremony, so that will give you another three and a half hours to be with your bride."

On March 19, 1944, Hitler invaded his ally, Hungary, to prevent the country from switching sides in the war. Within weeks the full-scale deportation of Hungarian Jewry to Auschwitz began. The Jews from the provinces, including Slovakia and Kosicze, were taken first. Mother's parents, Dr. Joseph and Anna Lowi, and her sister, Dr. Marta Lowi, were transported on cargo trains to Auschwitz from Kosicze on June 3. Her parents were immediately murdered in the gas chambers. Nearly 550,000 Jews were deported from Hungary within a period of a few months, and over 300,000 of them perished in the camps. Another 250,000 died through forced labour, starvation, massacres, and death marches. Mother, together with my older brother Gabor, who was then less than a year old, survived those months in the Budapest ghetto and then in a Swiss government-sponsored safe house for Jews.

After the devastation of the war, life resumed. I was born in 1946, and along with the other babies born immediately after the war was considered to be part of a generation of hope and renewal. Father rebuilt his small furniture manufacturing shop, which had been bombed during the British and American assaults against the Germans in the city. A few years later the Stalinist Communist government of Matyas Rakosi, in an absurd drive against the so-called petit-bourgeoisie, taxed his shop, with its grand workforce of eight people, out of existence. Father went to work for a painting cooperative. One time, with a desire to move the family to the newly formed state of Israel, Father went to apply for a passport. The deputy minister in charge was a friendly Jewish acquaintance of his from the Jewish Forced Labour Battalion. The deputy minister said, "Sorry, Andor. I cannot permit you to leave Hungary. We need good people like you to build a new society."

The ideologically driven absurdities of the system abounded. All the news was managed. People learned to read and exist between the lines. But we children, we believed. We believed in the idealism, in the promise. My brother and I attended an all-boys' school. As all other children, we became Young Pioneers and wore the school uniform of white shirt with a red kerchief. With great enthusiasm, we attended May Day Parades. We learned about the brave Soviet armed forces that liberated Hungary from Nazism and we cheered for them in the movies. We learned about the great accomplishments of Communism and the decadence of Capitalism and jazz and swing. The newsreels repeatedly heralded the wonderful achievements of the system under wise leadership. Happy peasants working the fields with brand-new combines. Smiling young factory workers churning out mountains of goods, well ahead of the Five Year Plan. And we believed.

One day in school, when I was in grade two, we were discussing candles. The teacher asked if any of us had ever lit a candle. I offered that we lit candles during Chanukah. The next day our parents were gently advised by the principal to tell their children not to talk openly about matters with a religious connotation. The government had cadres of political educators going door to door and from neighbourhood to neighbourhood. One Sunday Father opened the door to one such educator who came to tell our parents about the wonders of the system. After half an hour's conversation with Father, he began to bare his soul and in the midst of tears shared his litany of complaints against the regime. Father consoled him: "There, there, comrade, things are not all that bad."

On Friday, March 6, 1953, we awoke to funeral music. Funeral music on the radio, blaring out of loudspeakers on the streets, continuously playing in the halls of the school. Iosif Vissarionovich Dhugashvili, known to us as Uncle Stalin, had died. That night, after a day of eulogies at school, and more funeral music on the streets, I began to cry. Alarmed, my parents asked, "What is the matter? Why are you sad?" and in between sobs I blurted out, much to my parents' incredulity, "Because Uncle Stalin has died."

The system and I survived Stalin's passing. On Wednesday, November 25, of the same year, the legendary Hungarian soccer team made history by defeating England 6–3 at old Wembley Stadium in London, and thus broke England's ninety-year unbeaten streak on home soil. The significance of this occasion rivalled or even surpassed that of Stalin's death. The entire country stood still as the game was broadcast on the radio in all the halls of government, hospitals, factories, and on the streets. The country was united. The victorious team was wildly celebrated. Soccer reigned as the second officially sanctioned religion of the country after Communism.

Our family was not religious. We were Jewish culturally and historically, but with the exception of the High Holidays, rarely did our parents go to synagogue. Nevertheless, we identified ourselves, and we were seen by our neighbourhood friends, as Jews. We therefore were different. Hunting for eggs and sprinkling girls with perfume at Easter, as much as I loved the idea, was not part of our culture. Neither was Christmas. We were different, we felt different, and consequently, as a child I sometimes felt ashamed and self-rejecting. Only occasionally did we experience overt anti-Semitism. It took the form of being called a "dirty Jew" and fights after school. On one occasion, in the spring of 1956, my brother and I were ambushed by a group of our neighbourhood friends. They spat out racial epithets as they punched us a few times.

On the eve of the revolution, Tuesday, October 23, 1956, my brother and I were playing outside our apartment block. One of the other boys came to us with great excitement to tell us that university students and workers were demonstrating downtown. When we informed our parents about the demonstrations, we asked Father if we would have to go to school the next day. "Of course," he replied. Early next morning, Father got ready to go to work. As he left our building, the caretaker said to him, "Where are you going?" "Why, to work," he replied. "To work . . . haven't you heard," said the caretaker, "there is a revolution." We spent the next three weeks mostly indoors. We slept in the inside storage room of the apartment, our parents fearing that stray bullets might hit our windows that faced the street. We saw some men in small bands running with guns, and a couple of bullets did hit our building. Mother baked bread.

We weren't allowed to tell anyone about our plans to emigrate. The night before we left Budapest, we were permitted to say goodbye to our closest friends. That night our parents' best friends slept over. As my brother and I took a bath in our wood-fire-heated bathtub, we had some fear of the unknown. We promised each other that no matter what happened, we would stay together.

On the morning of November 23, we took a train from Budapest to the border town, Sopron. The train was jammed with would-be refugees, all of whom were pretending to be going on holidays in the countryside. Upon arrival in Sopron, Father went searching for a guide who, for a handsome fee, could take us across the border at night. Our guide was a peasant who put us up in his barn for a night and a day along with three other families. The following evening, after dark, we started to cross the border toward Austria. It had been raining for many days and the ground was soggy with ankle-deep mud. Our mother, whose walk was hindered by muscular dystrophy, kept falling. Mud had filled her boots and rubbed the skin off the back of her ankles.

The occasional search flares lit up the night. Our greatest concern was being intercepted by Hungarian border patrols. We did encounter one patrol with a German shepherd. Our guide immediately vanished into the dark. Father took off his watch, took out whatever cash he had, and handed it to the two soldiers. They apologetically accepted the bribe, pointed us in the right direction toward Austria, and departed. Immediately afterward, our guide reappeared. We never knew whether the whole encounter was a setup. We proceeded into the darkness ahead until the faint beams of several vehicle headlights appeared. The jeeps belonged to the International Red Cross and the Austrian Border Police. We had arrived.

We were immediately taken to a small Austrian town and housed in a school gymnasium. The Red Cross provided us with oranges and chocolate. Oranges were a rare delicacy in Hungary, and receiving them confirmed for my brother and me that it was good to be a refugee. The next two weeks we spent in makeshift shelters in Vienna and Germany and then proceeded by train to Munich to temporarily stay with our father's sister's family. Along the way, at each train station, hundreds of Austrians and Germans greeted us with care packages . . . clothing, food, toiletries.

Our parents' first intention was for us to go to Israel. After many hours of deliberations, however, the decision was made to apply for visas to Canada. It was thought that, at our parents' age, it would be easier for them to start all over again in Canada than in Israel. The decision was reinforced by the Canadian government's open-door policy toward Hungarian refugees, which included all-expenses-paid voyages to designated destinations in Canada. Nearly 40,000 Hungarian refugees came to Canada during the ensuing months.

We boarded the 20,000-ton ocean liner the *Arosa Sun* in Bremmerhaven on January 24, 1957. The ship picked up more passengers in Le Havre and Southampton and, after a stormy ten-day voyage across the Atlantic, arrived at Pier 21 in Halifax on February 4. Most of us were seasick during the entire passage.

We met other Hungarian Jewish families and their children on the boat. As we settled in Canada, some of them became part of the lasting extended circle of friends for our parents and for my brother and me. For our parents those friendships were crucial as they faced the challenges of survival in the new land.

Fifty years later, the manager of research at Pier 21 Canada's Immigration Museum was miraculously able to produce the ship's registry of the *Arosa Sun* from our voyage. Among the names of all the crew and passengers are the names of my parents and my brother and me . . . the earliest official record of us having immigrated to Canada.

On February 5, we got on a train that was to take us to Vancouver, a city that to our parents seemed like the end of the world. The Canadian government had a policy of populating the west with new immigrants. Our parents knew very little about Vancouver and were much more inclined to settle in Toronto or Montreal. However, the government insinuated that those who chose not to proceed to Vancouver might not receive any further governmental assistance, so the choice was effectively made for us.

As we boarded the train, each Hungarian refugee was greeted not only with care packages from the Canadian Red Cross, but also by a representative of the Kellogg's Cornflakes company. We were each handed several little boxes of cornflakes. We had never seen cornflakes before. On each box was taped a little note in verse form, written in Hungarian. The note said: "God brought you to Canada" (or "Welcome to Canada"), "A country of excellent products," "We would like to introduce to you one of Canada's outstanding products—Kellogg's Cornflakes." Over the next couple of days on the train, we made several futile attempts at eating the dry tasteless flakes that crumbled in your mouth. Eventually we learned to add milk and sugar. To this day, fifty years later, many of those refugees, including me, still have an emotional attachment, a product loyalty, to Kellogg's Cornflakes, their first taste of Canadian culture.

We arrived on the West Coast on February 10 after a six-day train ride across the vast snow-laden prairies. We were first housed in a military base in Abbotsford. From the base each night we could see searchlights in the distance. Little did we know that those lights were not for aerial defence, but for a car dealership in Vancouver. After about ten days at the military base, the Hungarian Jewish refugees were bussed to Vancouver and were generously hosted by Jewish families. We were hosted by a well-to-do family that lived in a sprawling house, overlooking the waterfront, near the campus of the University of British Columbia. Our first impressions of life in Canada were thus very favourable.

A few weeks later, we moved into an eastside triplex along with five other Hungarian families. The children from the house attended New Canadian English classes in a nearby school and became forever indebted to our patient and creative teacher, Miss Stanley. Our parents meanwhile did whatever they could to carve out a living. Mother took in boarders, Hungarian single men. Father's first job was sweeping the elevator shaft of an office building. He then got a job painting the offices of the same building at night. Near the end of his life, he recalled that he was so proud when, after his first week of work, he could take home $20 to his wife feeling confident that he would be able to support his family.

In Budapest our parents and their friends always gathered for New Year's Eve celebrations. In the midst of good food and joviality, they listened to special variety programs on Hungarian State Radio. On New Year's Eve 1958, our first in Canada, our family got together with some of our Hungarian Jewish friends for a party. When I saw my parents dancing, I cautioned them, "Dancing is okay, but no babies." Nine months later, my mother gave birth to her third son, George. He was the first Canadian citizen in our family. Within our circle of friends, several of the other Hungarian families that arrived in Canada around the same time also had babies. The new arrivals were planting their Canadian roots.

In Hungary we had often felt marginalized for being Jewish. In Canada we were sometimes marginalized for being immigrants.

Instead of "dirty Jew," the slur became "you dirty DP" (displaced person). One time I was attacked by a group of Italian kids, who in their Italian accent yelled, "You dirty DP, why you no go back where you come from." There were several other similar incidents resulting in fist fights. Being an adolescent is never easy. However, the normal challenges of adolescence are greatly compounded by the hurdles that immigrants face. For years I felt very self-conscious of my accent. Only when someone said to me, "Having an accent means that you have a more interesting background" did I begin to accept that it was all right to speak the way I spoke. For years, I felt like a cultural alien.

Father and Mother never took their Canadian citizenship for granted. Once they became citizens (May 22, 1962), they never missed voting in an election. From the first day that we arrived in Vancouver Father had one mantra: "I have never felt so free in my whole life." He often reminded his sons that he was fifty-two years old when he had the opportunity to cast his very first free ballot.

Father also greatly appreciated the quality of the drinking water that came out of the tap in Vancouver and the city's fresh air. He would ritually hold up a glass of water, gaze at it in wonderment, and then take a deep breath.

Our parents worked hard all their lives. They never became wealthy, but they provided for their three sons and took great satisfaction in seeing them live productive lives. Father especially took pleasure in announcing to the world that all his three sons married "Canadian girls." For him this was the very proof that the decision to flee Hungary was the right one. But the greatest pleasure for our parents was taking delight in their eight grandchildren, their symbol for the continuity of life and hope in the future.

I left Europe as János Máté and arrived in Halifax as John Mate. As a ten-year-old, I willingly relinquished the name I knew all my life in favour of the promise of easier assimilation. But I was never a "John." That is a very English name, and it always felt foreign to me. The day after our mother died on November 5, 2001, in the midst of my grief, I let go of my immigrant name, John, and returned to the earliest sounds of my childhood, to the name that Mother gave me, János. I was no longer an immigrant.

Beyond Civilization

STEVE ZABAN

Steve Zaban arrived in Canada from Communist Hungary in 1956 with a pregnant wife and five dollars in his pocket. He was a grateful refugee, but he found 1950s Winnipeg a long cultural way from home, as he recalls in this interview with Rebecca Sampson. Over the years, building on his original profession as an engineer, he established a company, Secutron, that manufactured and installed alarm systems. One of his firm's major contracts was for the airport in Budapest.

Landing in Canada almost fifty years ago was a shocking experience. It was like going back two or three hundred years in history, especially in Winnipeg—not a theatre, not an opera house, no sport events on Sunday. Could not have a glass of wine in the restaurants and on and on. I was as ignorant about Canada as most Americans but I knew there were lots of forest and log cabins. I would not go to the U.S.A., Australia and New Zealand were too far, and I did not want to stay in Europe—seen too many armed conflicts. Besides, Canada had no flag (a plus in my book). Canada was also a great melting pot. After 10 P.M. only your friends would knock on your door.

Such Hardworking People

FRANCA IACOVETTA

A child of a post-Second World War Italian immigrant household began her history of Italian immigrants in post-war Toronto with memories of her parents, "such hardworking people."

I grew up in the 1950s and 1960s in a crowded southern Italian immigrant household in an ethnic neighbourhood in downtown Toronto. Some of my earliest and most vivid recollections are of the evenings when my parents would come home from work. My mother used to arrive first, following a day's shift in the industrial laundry where she repaired tablecloths, hotel sheets, and towels. Having spent the day under Nonna's watchful eyes—my grandmother spent much of her adult life in Canada helping to raise her children's children—my brothers and I would rush Ma at the door, begging to be allowed to play outside until Papa came home. In summertime the answer was usually yes, because my father, a bricklayer (and, later, a subcontractor), would not be home until dark. Soon after my mother's arrival, the other women of the household came home: my aunt, who lived upstairs with my uncle, cousin, and grandparents; and then "the lady downstairs," whose family rented the basement flat. It was not until Papa arrived and emerged from the basement shower that Ma, having tended to my baby sister, served supper. Afterwards, we children were sent to bed. I shared my bedroom—the main-floor living room—with two younger brothers and the family TV set. My parents slept in the dining room, and two older brothers occupied a third-floor attic room. At night, I would listen in on my parents' conversations. I can still hear the adults gathered around the kitchen table, endlessly discussing how to get jobs, the daily grind at work, and the struggle to get ahead. Amid the talk was the constant refrain: "*siamo lavoratori forte*" ["we are such hardworking people"]. It is a refrain that in the years between 1946 and 1965 was also heard on the lips of sympathetic outsiders who marvelled at the remarkable capacity the Italians had for hard work.

Doubtless, thousands of women and men of my generation—the Canadian-born children of the postwar immigrants who left the rural towns and villages of southern Italy for a better future here—have heard their parents describe themselves as hardworking people. Most of us grew up acutely conscious of our immigrant heritage, and we were inundated with countless stories of the hardships our elders endured as newcomers. To be sure, we felt a sense of genuine pride in their accomplishments, even if we, as children, did not always appear to appreciate fully the sacrifices they had made on our behalf. As their children, we also understood, if only instinctively, that while decades later our immigrant parents could reflect positively, even nostalgically, on early life in Canada, the years of settlement and adjustment had been challenging indeed. The late 1940s, the 1950s, and early 1960s were a time when . . . our parents, as newcomers to this land, performed the dangerous or low-paying jobs that others shunned, spoke little English, and sometimes found themselves the victims of abuse. At the same time, they proved immensely resourceful, exhibiting a tremendous capacity for hard work and a talent for enjoying life, and each other's company, even in adversity.

L'ancrer fermement au Québec

YOHANNA LOUCHEUR

> *Forty years after his emigration from France, a daughter retold her father's story and could not help but add her own commentary. The text makes reference to icons of French culture, like Joe Dassin, the Franco-American singer whose music was enormously popular at the time.*

Tous les sifflets de train, toutes les sirènes de bateaux . . .

Le premier contact de mon père avec le sol canadien fut pour le moins . . . frappant. En "maudit Français" typique, mal préparé aux rigueurs de nos (bientôt *ses*) quelques arpents de neige, il débarquait à Montréal le 9 janvier 1966, quelques jours avant son 23e anniversaire, par un −15° qui parût inhumain à l'enfant du pays basque (mais qui était en fait, il l'apprendrait très vite, assez doux pour un mois de janvier). Malheureusement, ses souliers se révélèrent de piètres accessoires sur la glace qui l'attendait à la descente d'avion, lui offrant dès son arrivée, Jean-Paul II avant l'heure, son premier contact très intime avec le sol de Montréal.

Ce vol plané était l'aboutissement de longs efforts pour se rendre à . . . New York. J'ai souvent taquiné mon père en disant qu'il n'était visiblement pas très doué pour déchiffrer les cartes géographiques— passer par Montréal pour aller à New York? Témoin aussi les errances de mon enfance sur la route des vacances et d'Old Orchard; les passants à qui nous finissions par le persuader de demander des indications ignorant où se trouvait "Holhorcharde," ou leurs explications étant offertes dans une langue qui lui était incompréhensible, malgré trois mois passés à Londres à sa sortie de l'école hôtelière.

Pourtant non, ce n'était pas une carence géographique, mais bien une stratégie . . .

Rentré de Londres avec le goût du voyage et la ferme intention de voir l'Amérique (comme le ferait bientôt Joe Dassin sur toutes les radios), il demande à faire son service militaire dans la marine. Pas de bol, on l'envoie chez les parachutistes! Mais le rêve de travailler *sur le France*, paquebot mythique, et de suivre les nombreux Basques émigrés en Californie, persiste. Après 16 mois de service militaire, le retour au civil et aux boulots saisonniers, dans des conditions souvent difficiles et sans grandes perspectives d'avenir, le pousse à entamer les démarches d'émigration vers les États-unis.

L'agence de voyage qui distribue les formulaires lui recommande d'aller d'abord à Montréal, pour apprendre l'anglais—rappelons-nous qu'il s'agit ultimement d'aller à New York. De plus, l'agence vante les mesures canadiennes pour encourager l'émigration des gens qui ont une formation professionnelle (mon père est chef, ma mère esthéticienne, les perspectives sont bonnes). Soit! Donc formulaire canadien, puis entrevue à Bordeaux, et après une attente de 6 mois c'est le départ, avec le manteau "d'hiver" emprunté au père—et bien sûr les fameux souliers. Il faut pour l'instant laisser derrière les 2 filles, qui les rejoindront plus tard: je serai la première née à Montréal.

Débarqués avec $31 en poche, il faut payer l'hôtel rue Guy, $20 pour la semaine, puis le repas du soir, environ $6 . . . Les économies fondent vite! Le lendemain, trajet à pied (toujours avec les fameux souliers, quelle épopée!) jusqu'aux bureaux d'Immigration Canada rue Dorchester, où on remet aux nouveaux arrivants un peu d'argent et des noms d'employeurs potentiels. Une visite au Ruby Foo n'est pas convaincante (un chef français dans une cuisine chinoise, vous n'y pensez pas?!). De toute façon, le grand hôtel Queen Elizabeth l'engage très vite, après un examen pour confirmer ses qualifications; il commence dimanche, exactement une semaine après son arrivée.

Mais le démon du voyage le reprend vite—et n'oublions pas qu'il faut apprendre l'anglais. Il se joint donc au Canadien National, à bord des trains qui vont vers l'Ouest—il ira ainsi jusqu'à Winnipeg. Mais ni le trajet (assez monotone, il faut bien le dire) ni le travail (scrambled eggs, fried eggs, boiled eggs, sunny side up!) ne le captivent et il revient vite au Queen Elizabeth, auquel s'ajoutent rapidement d'autres boulots—restaurants du Vieux Montréal, enseignement. Tout ça pour louer un appartement avenue des Pins, premier d'une longue série de déménagements et, surtout, acheter pour $200 sa première voiture américaine—une Oldsmobile 59 rouge (oui, avec des ailerons), qui sera malheureusement volée quelques temps après. Ses histoires de voitures, de déménagements ou de chiens, feraient en soi un roman.

Les premières vacances en France, en 1968, ne lui font pas regretter son départ, au contraire. Et puis la vie, le travail, l'entreprise (plus de chefs pour lui casser les pieds!), les fermes finiront par l'ancrer fermement au Québec; les sirènes new-yorkaises ont définitivement perdu leur attrait. Étonnamment, aucun ami ne suivra ses traces, mais son frère le rejoindra quelques années plus tard, attiré à son tour par l'Amérique.

Et Joe Dassin incarnera en 1970 le rêve américain des jeunes Français impatients de voir d'autres horizons:
"Tous les sifflets de train, toutes les sirènes de bateaux
M'ont chanté cent fois la chanson de l'Eldorado
De l'Amérique"

Le Canada, c'est aussi l'Amérique, non?

Aussie Youth

VALERIE JACOBS

Australian youth was on the move in the 1960s and Canada was often a port of call.

When I arrived in Canada from Australia as a young woman in 1967, I planned to stay for about a year before moving on to the U.K. and Europe and working my way back to Australia through the Middle East and Asia. I was part of the "young itinerant Aussie on the move" contingent with which the world is so familiar. A variety of things has kept me here, most of them men.

When I first came to Canada, I could vote as a citizen of a member of the Commonwealth. This privilege was removed (I'm not sure when) but the government gave all members of the Commonwealth a five-year grace period when we could continue to vote without becoming Canadian citizens. But then the crunch came, and I had to make a decision. At the time, Australia would not allow me to hold dual citizenship, although Canada would. In order to become a Canadian citizen, I had to give up my Australian citizenship, and this was a very difficult decision. However, not being able to vote in the country in which I was living, and was likely to continue living, was not something I could easily contemplate either. It was ironic in a way, as voting in Australia is compulsory, and I used to contemplate refusing to vote just because I didn't like the idea of being forced to do so.

So I took out my Canadian citizenship and over the years have tried to turn myself from an Australian into a Canadian. No easy task because Australians tend to be blunt and not worry much about being politically correct, which is not the Canadian way. However, over the years I have become a passionate proponent of CBC Radio, peacekeeping, maple syrup, wilderness canoe trips, bears, and the Canadian ability to compromise in pursuit of a peaceful solution to a problem, although I still haven't entirely got the hang of always being polite and politically correct no matter the provocation. I find that I and my fellow immigrant friends are much fiercer in protecting the Canadian way of life than my somewhat more laissez-faire Canadian-born friends, including my Canadian-born husband.

The process of deciding to become a Canadian citizen made me understand how much one sacrifices taking on a country and culture not one's own, and I did it from the perspective of replacing one culture with another very similar, including the same language (although there are those who would argue that point). I am full of admiration for those who make the leap from very different cultures and languages to take on the Canadian way of life. I am not sure I would have had the courage.

"A Racist Country"

REVEREND HAROLD JACKMAN

Reverend Jackman, a minister in the British Methodist Church, was born in Trinidad in 1922 and came to Montreal at the age

*of forty-five. He threw himself into black community activities
there and subsequently in Toronto as a leader in the Universal
African Improvement Association. In this interview from the
late 1970s with Diana Braithwaite, he recalled an unhappy
Quebec experience.*

My nephew was living in Montreal, and he invited me down there to
become the assistant pastor of the Bible Pentecostal church, and that
is why I went to Montreal. But then, I stayed in Montreal for two
years and a half, and I didn't like the rabid nationalism. As a result of
this, I decided to move to Ontario. But one of the things that struck
me was that, in Quebec there were no Black policemen, there were
no Black drivers, and I found racialism in Quebec very, very prevalent. It was bad, when you were Black, it was worse when you didn't
speak French. Two things went against you in Quebec.

They tried to force me and told me I must speak French; I said, I
don't have to do anything. I'm not against learning to speak French,
but when somebody tells me that I have to do something and they
don't pay me to do it, I don't do it; because I feel that I'm free to do
what I want or not to do. Canada was a racist country. Going on the
bus and on the subways, the white people if you sat down, they never
came and sat down by you.

After the Prague Spring

IVAN AND MARTA STRAZNICKY

*In 1968, Communism loosened its grip on Czechoslovakia. The
Prague Spring made everything seem possible, but the Soviet
Union quickly closed down the experiment and people like the
Straznickys saw a Russian soldier on every corner and knew
that their brief freedom was over.*

Ivan: I would have emigrated from communist Czechoslovakia ten
years earlier at least if I could have, but before 1968 the border was
sealed—there were fences, watch-towers, mines, dogs—you name
it—and you couldn't go. When the Soviets came, I began thinking

immediately about leaving the country. It didn't make sense for me to stay because I would be persecuted again. There were some things said during Prague Spring that some people remembered—you know revenge was to be expected.

Emigrating from the country was the only solution. I knew that my kids would not be able to go to the university, if for no other reason than because we were churchgoers. I am not a religious fanatic, but going to church is important to me and I was not prepared to give that up.

I knew that the children would suffer because of that. I had a reasonably good job, good income. My standing there as a professional was much higher than it was in Canada after we moved, but we were beginning to talk about emigration.

Marta: Ivan started to talk about our emigration. It was the beginning of September 1968. I said "No way," because I was really afraid—scared to death to leave my nicely furnished apartment. Ivan gave me reasons why we should leave. And I gave him my reasons why we should stay home.

Ivan: There were many families in which the man would emigrate first, leaving the wife behind, expecting to bring the wife and children later. And there were married couples who left children behind with grandparents. I felt very strongly that I would not leave without the whole family in one group. This was one of the questions posed to me at the Canadian embassy in Paris, when I was interviewed for my landed immigrant status. I thought the family must go together. To me, if I could not persuade my wife that we should leave, then we would not have a good chance of starting anew. Of course, everybody knew that it would be a hard life at the outset. We certainly didn't come here to have it better economically. That was not a consideration at that time.

Marta: We told the children we were going to France for recreation.

Ivan: I had a pen-pal for seventeen years. We had never met. Her name is Odette, and she is French.

Before the Prague Spring, you simply couldn't go abroad if the Communist party did not allow you to. After the Prague Spring, anybody could go. And certainly, shortly after the invasion, the Czechoslovakian authorities would let anybody go if you had a piece of paper that said somebody was going to pay for your stay abroad. There was no convertibility between the currencies, so even though by 1968 we had enough money in Czechoslovakian currency, it was no use to us abroad. So I just wrote my pen-pal that she had to invite us, and she did. We were still afraid to put all of our children in our passport applications. We made two trips. The second time, we emigrated. The first time we went just to persuade my wife that life would be better in the West than it is in the communist regime.

Marta: We were invited to go to France at the beginning of December for one week or ten days and we went there with three children. Two children were staying with my mother.

Ivan: We were undecided as to whether we wanted to emigrate to New Zealand, Australia, or Canada. I didn't want to go to their embassies in Prague because I knew, obviously, that they must be under surveillance already, so I wanted to go to Paris to visit the embassies there and then see what would happen.

Marta: It was very hard for me to leave. You are attached to even material things plus, of course, family, parents, surroundings, and everything. I felt miserable at that time because I did not know English and I was pregnant.

Ivan: I don't think that you should have the impression that we left the country without a consensus. There was consensus. Before I left for work in the morning, we would discuss it and decide that we were going, but by the afternoon, my wife, being pregnant, got tired and had different thoughts, and we were not going. The next morning we were going and the next afternoon we weren't going. It went on like this for some time. One afternoon when, again, we were not going, I asked her if she knew what she wanted. She said that she did not, and I said that if she did not, then I did. We were going, and she said "Okay." And we went.

Marta: He decided and I just followed him. I could not decide on my own. It was a struggle every day because I thought it was the biggest decision of my whole life. When he decided and I said okay, it was easier for me. I was relieved because he knew English. I knew he was going to do something about our well-being. I trusted him and it was easier.

Ivan: We flew to Paris. I was making a very good income because I had a good knowledge of the classification of American patents. I made good extra money with my expertise, so it was no problem for us to buy tickets to Paris as long as you were purchasing them in Czechoslovakia.

I organized the first trip as a sightseeing tour for her to see life in the West. I was hoping that when she saw that you don't have to stand in a line-up at the butcher's every day, that you can go to the market and they have fish if you want it, and if you wanted to buy a kilo of butter, it is there to buy. I was hoping that she would agree that we were going.

Marta: It was absolutely terrific in France. I liked it very much. When we came home from Prague by train to the city of Olomouc, it was absolutely dark, and at every corner there was a Soviet soldier. I said to myself that I was going to leave. It was like the Middle Ages, like a nightmare. Comparing those two countries, France and Czechoslovakia, worked for me, but unfortunately, just for a couple of days. Then I settled into my routine. Staying with our friend was more like being tourists than refugees. We didn't really know what it would be like to be an immigrant or a refugee there. It was not going to be easy. And again I said, "No," to him because I thought it would be hard, very hard with those small children. I couldn't provide more money for the family. I knew that. It was as if my hands were tied, and maybe that's why I was afraid to go. I knew I could not work, that somebody must be with the children. It would all be on him.

Ivan: We visited the three embassies and chose Canada strictly on superficial things. We chose Canada because of the way we were treated at the embassy. With the Australians and New Zealanders, you had the impression that they thought you might be allowed to come to that country. But in the Canadian embassy, there were no reservations—"Of course, come over. No problem. Welcome."

Going North

STEPHEN EATON HUME

Stephen Eaton Hume is an author who teaches English at the University of Victoria in British Columbia. His Texas grandfather, a lawyer, lived in Eagle Pass, a small town on the Mexican border. His other grandfather was Cyrus Eaton, the American industrialist who was born in Pugwash, Nova Scotia, and moved to the United States to make his fortune. Eaton would make Pugwash famous by giving its name to a series of international conferences he sponsored that won the 1995 Nobel Peace Prize. Here Hume talks about living in Texas, going to military academy, getting arrested at the Pentagon and going to jail, and making a pilgrimage to see his grandfather in Nova Scotia. He recounts a privileged upbringing, yet he also draws a vivid illustration of racism and violence in America. Hume eventually goes north, reversing the direction his grandfather took some seventy years before.

It was cold in Hartford, Connecticut. The sun wasn't going to come up for another few hours. I was walking across the Trinity College campus to the car that was taking me and other students to the Pentagon. It was October 21, 1967.

On my way to the car I saw a friend of mine—he was on his way to play a hockey game against another New England school. He carried hockey gear and walked with goalie pads on his legs. We stopped and talked. We didn't see each other that often, but we were close because we had once fought a bunch of "townies," kids our own age from Hartford. My friend was a ruthless scrapper. He could punch like a professional boxer. I could fight, too. I had learned how to brawl in southern Maryland, where I had grown up on a tobacco farm. An extended family of black people lived on the farm too, working the crops and taking care of the animals. The family's ancestors had lived on the farm all the way back to the days of slavery and the Revolutionary War.

My parents travelled a lot. When they did, they left me in the care of this family. Naturally, I played and fought with their children. We used to fistfight to see who would be left standing or who would cry "uncle." Around this time my father sent me to a military academy, ostensibly to knock some sense into me, but also to groom me for the Marines. Sometimes the white boys at the military academy would taunt me and call me a "nigger lover" and then the fists would fly. Southern Maryland was south of the Mason-Dixon Line, and racism and segregation were the ugly facts of life.

My friend asked me where I was going. I told him, and I wished him luck with his hockey game. I didn't feel like the typical war protester depicted in the press. I didn't belong to any political organization. I was a loner. To use the words of Ralph Ellison in *Invisible Man*, "I was nobody but myself."

The professor who was driving us to Washington, the author Stephen Minot, had served in the Army Air Corps in the Second World War, and like many other teachers and spiritual leaders in 1967, he believed that Vietnam was not a true war of self-defence like the Second World War, but a war of aggression. He was my draft counsellor, which meant in my case that he was advising me on how to immigrate to Canada. It was against the law in America to counsel young people to resist the military draft. I had been to Nova Scotia, where my maternal grandfather lived, but I had never been to any other Canadian provinces or territories.

My grandfather, Cyrus Eaton, was a financier and philanthropist who believed the Vietnam War was madness. Born in Pugwash, a small village in Nova Scotia, he went to work for John D. Rockefeller as a young man, became an American citizen, and made his fortune in steel and railroads. For years he had used his house in Pugwash as a meeting place for scientists and thinkers to promote peace among nations. He counted Bertrand Russell, Fidel Castro, and Soviet premier Nikita Khrushchev as his friends. During the Cold War, he advocated nuclear disarmament. To my parents' horror, he won the Lenin Peace Prize in 1960, when America was still reeling from the effects of the Communist witch-hunts of Senator Joseph McCarthy. The award embarrassed my father, who was campaigning to run in the Democratic primary for governor of Maryland. He lost the 1962 primary election, but made a strong showing on an anti-slot machine, anti-racketeering platform. I divided my summers between Cyrus's waterfront estate in Upper Blandford, where I canoed and sailed, and my paternal grandparents' home in Eagle Pass, Texas, a small, two-storey house with lime trees in the yard, just a few minutes from the Rio Grande and the Mexican border.

I was born in Dallas in 1947. My Texas grandmother, Lupita, was born in Monclova, Mexico. I spoke Spanish at an early age. My Mexican nanny avoided the American movies at the Aztec Theater in Eagle Pass. Instead, she took me across the bridge into Mexico to a smaller cinema that showed emotionally charged, Spanish-language films about fateful duels and star-crossed lovers. My grandfather, a criminal lawyer, took me jackrabbit hunting in the desert at night. We chased the animals from the back of a speeding truck. You had to shoot clean and straight. If you didn't, the rabbits would yell like humans when they were wounded—this haunted me. When the truck stopped, and the engine was off, you could hear coyotes.

The major left-wing group on American campuses in the 1960s was the Students for a Democratic Society. I wasn't a member, but I had belonged to the National Rifle Association, an outfit with a deep American heritage that supported the war and advocated the right to bear arms. I was a sharpshooter and loved to hunt.

My godfather was Admiral Frank Jack Fletcher, a Medal of Honor winner who played a key role in the first American naval victories of the Second World War. When I was a boy he gave me a Japanese officer's sake bowl that had been recovered from the Battle of the Coral Sea, and twelve sterling-silver mint julep cups, one each year, until my twelfth birthday. The cups, traditional gifts in the South, were named for the drink they often contained: bourbon, sugar, shaved ice, and fresh mint. I stopped seeing Frank Jack when our families drifted apart.

In the two years after I graduated from boarding school in 1965, something changed to make me turn against the State. Was it boxing champ Muhammad Ali, who had refused to be drafted into the military? Was it talking to my grandfather Eaton? Was it Dante's *Commedia*? Homer? John Donne's tolling bell? Was it anti-war movies like Kubrick's *Paths of Glory*? Was it *Dr. Strangelove*? Bob Dylan's "Masters

of War"? Was it reading *The Autobiography of Malcolm X*? Was it
Gandhi? CBS News? Jesus? Buddha? Whatever the turning point, I
saw that crimes were being committed against humanity and that the
war was corrupt. I wasn't going to follow orders, blindly pushing—
or polishing—the buttons of the government's war machine.

I thought by going to the Pentagon that October morning I
could help stop the war. I did not know that tens of thousands of
other people would be converging in the same place that day.

When we got to Washington, D.C., we joined the huge crowds
that were flowing toward the Lincoln Memorial and the Pentagon
on the Virginia side of the Potomac. Soon after we reached the fields
and parking lots surrounding the Pentagon, people began to run and
shout for help. Tear gas drifted across the fields. I saw a woman with
a stroller chased down and clubbed by a military policeman. I lost
contact with my group. Companies of armed soldiers thundered
across the tarmac. In the chaos I heard a rumour that the poet Allen
Ginsberg and The Fugs, an avant-garde rock group, were trying to
levitate the Pentagon and exorcize it of demons. People were scattering and trying to protect themselves. We were like the pigs on the
farm that ran squealing helplessly around the corral before they were
slaughtered. It was Goya's "Saturn Devouring His Son." It was all brutality, confusion, alarms. Into the gaping jaws of America we went.

I should mention that my father was a submariner in the Second
World War. He won the Bronze Star in 1944 on the USS *Jallao* for saving his crew and sinking an attacking Japanese ship. (I didn't know
about the Bronze Star until twenty years after he died, in 1992, when
I sent away to the Navy Department for his citations.) When the war
ended, he worked as a JAG (Judge Advocate General) lawyer at the
Pentagon. I used to visit him in his office and crawl under the desks
and make his pretty secretaries scream. After the Pentagon, my father
was stationed at Pearl Harbor. Hawaii—Punahou School (where I
didn't have to wear shoes), three-finger poi, the Night-Blooming
Cereus in our yard. I used to hang out at Pearl and imagine myself
shooting back at the Japanese planes on December 7, 1941. My father
managed the SubPac baseball team. I went to almost all the games
and sat in the dugout with the players, cussing up a storm and gag-
ging the first time I tried to chew tobacco.

In 1967, at the time of the Pentagon march, my parents were divorced. My father was living in Texas. My mother was living in the Georgetown section of Washington, D.C. I couldn't forget that my dad had brought the war home with him. He was a drunk. He drank Old Crow bourbon from a water glass. But he had a gift—he could play the violin, especially 1920s jazz tunes of Joe Venuti. He was so consumed by rage the gift was almost dead. When we lived on the farm a show used to come on TV every week—"Victory at Sea." It was a documentary about the exploits of the U.S. Navy in the Second World War. He would leave the room when the TV showed the enemy dropping depth charges on submarines. When I was a teenager I ran away from home and lived by myself in Ocean City, Maryland, after he picked up a shotgun and tried to shoot me when he was drunk. He survived the war, but the war killed his soul.

The last time I saw my father was the summer of 1963, when I was sixteen. I had a phone call that he was dying. I took a bus from Annapolis to our farm, where I found him drunk and comatose in bed. I phoned the family doctor, who came over and signed papers that temporarily committed my father to a sanitarium in Baltimore. The doctor asked me to sign the papers too, though I was underage. One of the black men on the farm, Melvin, who had been my father's bodyguard during the gubernatorial campaign, drove my father and me to the sanitarium in my father's Cadillac. I was in the back, with my father lying across my lap. When we got there, two orderlies carried my father inside. I went to the administrator's office. He was nervous and offered me hard candy from a bowl, but I refused. I asked to see my father. When I found his room, he was in a fetal position, naked, on a bare mattress. I said goodbye and walked out and did not look back.

Back to the march. A rope, about waist-high, was in front of me. Soldiers and U.S. Marshals stood on the other side, and an armed man said, "Do not cross this line." No one was going to tell me not to cross any line. So I did. Then I got down on my knees, as if in prayer, and the moment I did there was a deluge of clubs and fists, and I was upside down, and I was pulled along the ground and then it stopped. I looked up. A black man in an MP (military policeman) helmet had his face next to mine, and he said, "You okay?" I nodded yes. He pulled me to my feet and someone put my hands behind my back and handcuffed me and put me in the back of a van. I was driven to a waiting area where a bus with wire mesh on the windows transported me to the federal prison in Lorton, Virginia.

We were fingerprinted, processed, and housed in a huge dormitory with a latrine. The arrested included Noam Chomsky, the linguist from the Massachusetts Institute of Technology, and John Dellinger, the patriot and civil rights worker who had organized the march. Dellinger was an old hand at civil disobedience and had driven an ambulance during the Spanish Civil War. It was Dellinger who said there were two kinds of Vietnam veterans—those who fought against the war and those who fought in it. Two years later, in 1969, he and six other defendants known as the Chicago Seven were tried for criminal conspiracy and inciting to riot at the 1968 Democratic National Convention. The prison dormitory was crawling with intellectuals and thinkers. I didn't know what was going to happen to us. That night I lay down on my cot and tried to sleep. A couple of cots over, some men were arguing about the revolution and the military-industrial complex. I told them to shut up. I was dog tired.

The next morning I woke hungry and stinking of sweat. I waited in line to go to mess hall. The novelist Norman Mailer was standing next to me. His shirt and suit were dirty. He was built like a bull. "What do you think we're having for breakfast?" he asked me. "I don't know," I said, "but I hope it's good." "Me, too," he said. "I'm hungry."

I had coffee, cornflakes, and a leftover square of vanilla cake. I returned to the dormitory. Later that day, in alphabetical order, we were sent to another section of the prison and appeared in makeshift courtrooms before U.S. commissioners to be judged and sentenced. I was given the choice of five days in the prison or a fine with a suspended five-day sentence. If I opted for the suspended sentence I had to sign a paper promising not to return to the Pentagon for six months. Behind me people were shouting, "Don't sign anything!" I didn't have any money—the fine was around $25 or $30. I did not want to stay in jail. I noticed at breakfast that some of the regular prison population looked like they ate skinny college kids with long blond hair. A young professor in my group offered to pay my fine. (I got his address and a few weeks later paid him back the money.) Tuli Kupferberg, one of the Fugs, was in my group. He was older than me and had long hair and a beard. He told the judge he would take the five days.

I returned to Trinity College.

The next year, on April 4, 1968, Martin Luther King Jr. was assassinated in Memphis. Bobby Kennedy was assassinated in Los Angeles two months later, on June 6. The dogs of war had come to America. That summer I took the ferry from Bar Harbor, Maine, to Nova Scotia and talked to my grandfather at his estate. His reading during those few days consisted mostly of *The Wall Street Journal* and the philosopher David Hume, whom he could quote. As usual, he did not drink alcohol and took boiled mineral water with his meals. We talked about the war, but we also talked about the sport of rowing, and poetry, and the science of geology, and the formation of the earth. The house was quiet—there were no TVs. When I was younger, I had to sleep in a tent—it was part of outdoor learning for the Eaton grandchildren. This time, I slept in an upstairs bedroom with a fireplace—the rooms had fires because the house had no central heating. When I woke in the morning I lay there in the dark and listened to the crackling pinewood, and thought. When he was roughly my age, my grandfather had gone south. Now I was about to go north.

In June 1969, a few days after my graduation from Trinity, I piled clothes and books into an old VW and drove from Hartford, Connecticut, to Niagara Falls, New York, the honeymooner's paradise. I checked into a motel and kept an eye out for the FBI. I didn't want to be arrested before I could cross into Canada.

The next morning, I drove to the border. I announced to the startled Canadian officials: "I want to become a Canadian." I took a written test to see if I qualified to be a landed immigrant and I passed.

I drove into Canada and headed for Toronto.

I had been accepted at the University of Toronto's graduate school. The English curriculum at Trinity was based on the work of Northrop Frye, who taught at Toronto. He would be one of my professors.

But when I got to the university, the housing office was not open. So I drove to another motel. Motel living obviously suited me. The motel was near Scarborough Bluffs. I stood on the bluffs and looked out at Lake Ontario.

Then I had a strange thought. I thought of Roger Harley.

Harley was a Canadian who taught at my Episcopalian boarding school. There were some good things about the school—it got me away from the violence of my home, for one thing. For another, I was introduced to the writings of Buddhist and Christian mystics. Still, the school was operated on the demerit system and was tougher than the military academy I had gone to. Boys had to do chores every morning before class. Our beds were inspected, the chores were inspected, haircuts were inspected. Any infraction—for example, lateness or blasphemy—meant demerits. We had chapel every morning before class—there was also Holy Communion at 6 a.m.—and a two-hour study hall at night after dinner. The food was usually like chow from a county jail—watery eggs, watery soups, oatmeal that was so cold you had to slice it from the bowl. Classes were held six days a week but only half a day on Saturday. On campus was a small, ivy-covered building with Army cars parked out front. Personnel from a nearby military base apparently used the building.

The toughest master at the boarding school was Harley. Everyone said he had been in the Canadian army, but no one really knew. The Canadian army? What was that? Harley—we called teachers "masters"—wore a fierce scowl. He smiled only when he gave demerits. You had to work off accumulated demerits in your free time, on something called a work squad. I spent a lot of time on work squads. Harley once made me work off my demerits by walking laps around a field in the cold rain with a log on my shoulders. He carried what looked like an officer's baton, and he had a nasty habit of shouting in your face. But he had another side. I had taken an advanced English seminar with him and he had taught me Yevgeny Yevtushenko's poem "Babi Yar," in Russian and English, about the brutal Nazi massacre of Jews near Kiev in the Second World War. ("I seem to be Anne Frank," Yevtushenko wrote, "transparent as a branch in April.") One day two of my friends took red paint and wrote "Go Home Canuck" on the side of Harley's car. I helped them find the can of paint in the boiler room. At the last minute I decided not to join in the prank. Soon, everyone was talking—did you see Harley's car? The entire school was called to assembly. The boys who had done the deed were commanded to come forward—the school had an honour code, and boys were supposed to admit their faults, though in reality the system was nothing more than a snitch culture. My buddies dutifully came forward, confessed their crime, and were punished.

Months later, Harley seemed to have a nervous breakdown. I watched him fall apart. He began to cry and to talk about time and space and eternity. He developed an obsession with lamps, which he would turn repeatedly on and off. Some of the students were happy for his misfortune and laughed at him. Then one day he was gone.

I hadn't thought of Roger Harley in years. The irony of "Go Home Canuck" struck me with the force of a beautiful idea. It was as if, in the past, I had been given a message about the future. I thought of Harley and all the sound and fury of growing up, and it made me laugh. I looked out at the water. Lake Ontario was enormous! It stretched before me like an ocean. The next day I checked out of the motel and drove to Toronto. I found a one-room apartment on Markham Street, near College Street, a few minutes by streetcar from the university. All around me on Markham Street immigrants from Italy and Portugal were going about their daily business, tending their gardens, talking, and laughing. Sometimes, at night, especially in the hot Toronto summer, I wished I were back on the farm, or in Eagle Pass. I missed the Rio Grande and the sight of families washing their cars in the shallows of the big river. I missed the smell of mesquite in the desert. But the Eagle Pass I knew, and the southern Maryland I knew, didn't exist any more. I was home.

From the Old to the New Canada

ANDREW FAIZ

> *Andrew Faiz was born in Pakistan, coming to Canada at the age of ten with his parents. His biggest culture shock came later.*

It wasn't something that my parents really wanted to do, but it was something they felt forced to do in many ways. All of our family . . . well, a lot of my parents' friends [had] been leaving Pakistan in the mid-sixties, and they would say to my parents: "Why don't you leave this country?" And my father particularly always said: "Why would I ever leave? I've got a great job. I've got history, culture, community, family, property. Why would I ever leave?"

And then in the late '60s, something happened that made my father re-think his position, and he began to work towards immigration. And the thing that happened was that he didn't get a promotion that he had been counting on for a very long time, and there's a back-story to this. We are Christians, and therefore represent something like three percent—or less than three percent—of the population of Pakistan. And as a Christian, my father was denied a promotion that he had expected, felt the promise of, for many years. He was, in many ways, a self-taught man, and had worked . . . he was a senior vice president with Pakistan Airlines. He always expected he would be one of the senior executives, if not the president of the company in due time.

When we arrived in Canada, we moved after a short while after staying with some friends. We moved to a neighbourhood that, in many ways, has become my obsession. A neighbourhood called Flemingdon Park, and Flemingdon is today a very multi-ethnic, multi-cultural neighbourhood. In the early '70s, when we first moved into it, it was just beginning to turn into this multi-ethnic neigh-bourhood. It had previously been sort of a middle-class, WASP-y neighbourhood, but a lot of the WASPs and the middle-class were moving out, but immigrants like myself were moving in.

In Canada, we suddenly land in this neighbourhood, which is incredibly multi-ethnic, and it was a very radical shift. But, again, I was just a boy. I was only ten years of age, and my siblings were eight and six at the time, so we just sort of absorbed that, and it wasn't such a big deal. In many ways, the biggest cultural shock of my life was not coming from Pakistan to Canada. It was when I was eighteen, going from the multi-cultural world of Flemingdon Park, and the schools and the environment there, to a very white-washed world of Victoria College at the University of Toronto. That was my huge cultural shock, because I suddenly went from this new Canada—this futuris-tic Canada, Flemingdon—to this old, ancient Canada of Victoria College.

"I Was Quite Afraid," 1970

GODWIN ENI

> *Dr. Godwin Eni, an Ibo of Nigeria, fled his country during the turmoil of the Nigeria-Biafra Civil War. When he arrived in Montreal and saw military tanks at Mirabel airport, he imagined that he might be getting more of the same in Canada, then in the midst of a crisis of its own. He went on, as one of only two Africans in Saskatoon at the time, to complete graduate studies at the university hospital there, while experiencing his first prairie winter. He has lived and worked as an African Canadian in a number of cities and provinces.*

I was completing my studies at the university during the war, and Ibos were being killed in the streets, and war was declared against the members of the Ibo tribe in eastern Nigeria. And eastern Nigeria seceded and called itself Biafra. So during the war, it was a very traumatic experience for Ibos who were living outside of Ibo land. I was unable to return to eastern Nigeria, and many Ibo professors and students had to find a way to save themselves, so we escaped into the bush, and lived in the bush for a very long time.

. . . Shortly before we arrived in Montreal, I was told . . . I mean, the pilot announced that there was a riot, and that the British Trade Commissioner by the name of James Cross has been kidnapped, and that there were soldiers at the airport trying to prevent some separatist groups from leaving the country. I was traumatized by this news because I thought Canada was a . . . Canada was a peaceful, quiet, neutral country. I was surprised to hear about this, so I was quite afraid. I thought there was a war going on in Canada. In fact, I wished I could go back to Nigeria and be killed in Nigeria, than to be killed in Canada, because I didn't know anyone, and I didn't have any relatives, or any acquaintances. So when I arrived at Mirabel—I believe it was Mirabel airport then, international airport—I refused to leave the airport, because when I looked out through the window outside, I saw a military tank rolling across! And I was quite afraid.

I summoned the courage to get into a taxi, and I told the taxi to take me to the nearest hotel. He took me to a hotel, which was a short distance, I believe. I had only fifty pounds in my pocket, so I gave it to the taxi driver, and I asked him to keep the change, because I didn't know about Canadian money or the value of fifty pounds. I was only too anxious to get into a building where I can protect myself.

"Frightened Faces"

MILLY CHARON

> The grandparents of Zaven Degirmen were survivors of the Armenian genocide during the First World War, when the Turks slaughtered more than three and a half million Armenians. Fifty-five years later, he, his mother, and older brother arrived in Montreal, ostensibly as tourists. They were in fact refugees from the oppressive Turkish military regime. Here Degirmen is interviewed by Milly Charon, a steadfast activist for immigrant rights and the author of two fine books of immigration reminiscences.

When he had lived in Canada a number of years, and after he had received his citizenship in 1978, Zaven's future wife, whom he had known as a child in Turkey, came on a visit. She was able to come as a tourist in 1980, but the rules in force at the time stated that she had to apply for landed immigrant status outside Canada. Even if she married in Canada, she would still have to leave the country to apply. Zaven took her to Longueuil Immigration Centre to fill out her application.

"The official asked all kinds of absurd questions, which, of course, she couldn't answer because she didn't speak English or French. I had to translate.

"'Why did you come here?' she asked her.

"I answered that she had come to visit and we had just gotten married.

"'Couldn't you have found someone already here to marry?' came the question.

"I looked at the official, a woman, and laughed. 'Well, you weren't available at the time.'

"She didn't laugh. She looked like ice.

"This kept going on and on, over and over, and then came medical difficulties. Blood samples were required, and they took blood six times. They told me that any person who has been here for three months and has non-immigrant status has to pass a medical examination.

"However, someone at the lab mixed up the blood samples, and suddenly I received a call from Immigration, saying that my wife was to go to the Royal Victoria Hospital immediately. Why? I asked. They had found syphilis. I should tell you that this is the greatest possible insult there is to a person from my country, especially a woman. It is a terrible condemnation. I couldn't even tell my wife what I had been told. I said it was some kind of virus whose name I didn't know in Turkish.

"The doctor at the hospital laughed uproariously. My wife was still a virgin. How could they make such a stupid mistake? So we went back and everything was straightened out, but it took such a long time. We had to go back every three months or so. I would have to get permission from my boss to take my wife to Immigration, until finally in exasperation I said to the woman officer: 'Listen, lady, it takes only a week for people to get to the moon, and we've been coming here for two years now.'

"Her answer was: 'In order to get to the moon, they worked twenty years to make it possible.'

"When my wife's sister came to visit us some time later, she was held at Dorval Airport by Immigration officials. My wife and I went to pick her up, but she had had some difficulty with her airline connection in Europe and had missed her plane. Instead of coming directly to Montreal, she had been rerouted via Chicago.

"An Immigration officer called my wife and me into the office, and when I told him the woman he was holding was my sister-in-law, he looked at me slyly and said: 'Are you going to find somebody for her, so she'll stay here?'

"I just looked at him, but I had the gut-feeling that he couldn't do anything to me because by then I was a Canadian citizen. If he were to get nasty, I would give as good as I got. So I smiled and asked, 'Do you know anybody here who would like to marry her?'

"He looked at her again and asked, 'Are these both sisters?'

"'Yes, they are.'

"'They don't look alike.'

"I held up my hand. 'Do my fingers look alike?'

"'No,' he admitted. 'You're very quick.'

"'I'm also a Canadian.' He got even.

"'Give me your identification,' he demanded.

"I had to prove the woman with me was my wife, that I was a citizen, but what infuriated me was that he had no right to ask for *my* identification papers. I wasn't travelling; my sister-in-law was. I said I didn't have any papers with me, and, indeed, I didn't. However, what frightened me about the system was that he took my name, went next door and returned, saying . . . 'You entered Canada on September 2, 1970 . . . you got married on this and this date . . . your wife was accepted on this date' . . . he droned on, and he had everything about us down on paper. I was thinking, shockingly enough, that Big Brother was watching. Everyone's life is on file. Who would have thought we were coming to a police state?

"But you don't know how good it felt for the first time in my life to be able to talk back to government officials, to the authorities. That's what Canadian citizenship did for me. I could fight back, and it made me feel like a human being and not an animal cowering inside myself."

A period of enlightenment was beginning for Zaven. He started noticing things and hearing remarks that he had ignored or shrugged off before. Only, this time, he didn't turn away in frustration. He began to speak up. He advised new immigrants on how to integrate more quickly and more easily. He explained that they should get involved with French and English-speaking Canadians and not isolate themselves sitting at home, feeling sorry about everything. "Get active," he told them. "It's your duty to learn languages and communicate."

"This inability to communicate and the resulting isolation are the two main reasons why immigrants suffer from depression. I still have it periodically, to this day. Do you know that to be able to talk to a girl, other than an Armenian, was a big triumph for me when I first arrived in Canada? I couldn't even pronounce names like Ruth and Claudette. I know of many people who left Canada, and returned to their own countries because they couldn't take the loneliness here—the lack of communication—and were unable to get into any kind of business. Most of the people I knew were merchants, and the red tape of permits, leases, licenses, and other papers intimidated them so much that they were afraid to even make the attempt to sort it out. Some even believed that if they screamed at their kids or smacked them, the kids would pick up the phone, call the police and have them jailed."

Zaven also discovered that prejudice and racism existed, and were difficult to combat. He felt he had been insulted many times. He heard "*Maudit immigrant*" at work or "*Deporté*" and "*Tiens, un autre deporté . . .*" in French and English. The language was different, but the meaning was always the same. When he had first heard remarks about DPs, he hadn't reacted. In Turkey his minority group had been called "heathens" for centuries. So he figured that if Turks could name-call, so could Canadians. However, one incident on Bay Street in Toronto shook him up.

"There were three cars in three lanes, two of them heading in one direction, and the third in the opposite direction. Beside me on my left was a Sikh driver in a turban, and diagonally was a Caucasian, all of us stopped and waiting for the red light to change. The white guy rolled his window down and spat in the Sikh's direction as we went by when the light changed to green. Something clicked in my head. What is this, I asked myself? It's like the racial tension in the Southern United States between the blacks and whites. It can't be happening in Canada. I couldn't take it. I was so upset, I left the city the same day. This kind of treatment of any minority has to be stopped. The public must be educated, and it has to start early, in the schools. I have seen so much of it in Turkey. Is there any difference here?

"Canadians whose parents or grandparents once were immigrants must learn to understand what newcomers are enduring, even if it means going back to their roots to find out. Every immigrant who comes here contributes something—either by paying taxes, or opening a store or other business, or employing fellow Canadians, or having children. There appears to be a lack of communication between immigrants and established Canadians. And politicians seem to forget we exist, except at election time when ethnics are wooed for their votes. Politicians show up, make all kinds of promises to the minority groups and when the election is over, the orators go back to Parliament Hill or the National Assembly, and forget the minorities completely.

"I remember some member of former Premier Lévesque's Cabinet coming to an Armenian organization and donating some money in memory of the Armenian genocide, in order to get votes. He didn't give a damn what happened to the Armenians then or now, and if he had been asked where the country was located, he wouldn't have been able to answer. Immigrants, unfortunately, fall for this brown-nosing, because they don't know any better. They know little or nothing about the voting process, yet they make heroes out of politicians who come offering gifts at election time. Immigrants are so happy to be noticed by someone important that they don't see the reason for the sudden visits.

"And this is what I try to explain to new immigrants. I tell them to read papers, listen to the radio, watch TV and not to just one side. I feel that newcomers should learn the political systems in Canada and how to choose candidates, how to vote. Immigrants must be represented in municipal, provincial and federal affairs. They should get involved with other minority groups. Often ethnics will be loyal to representatives of their own backgrounds, voting for them even if they aren't capable politicians. Newcomers feel comfortable with their own. An ethnic representative will understand their problems."

Zaven would like to see some changes in the way people are treated at Immigration centres. In his capacity as a registered interpreter, he realized that many who translate are not accurate in explaining questions or answers. Often the real meaning is lost in the translation.

"For example, when I was at the Immigration centre with my sister-in-law, I explained the situation and my role in it. The officer ordered me out of the office, saying he needed a real interpreter, because I was talking with my emotions as a relative. I could understand that, but I noticed that when I tried to say something which the official interpreter relayed to the officer, it came out as something else, and not what I had really said.

"When I translate for immigrants, I always repeat everything to make sure it hasn't changed through one stage of relay. There is a great difference in the questions: 'Why did you come to Canada?' and 'Why did you choose Canada?' If my mother hadn't chosen Canada I wouldn't have come here. I know of others who chose it, too, but are waiting for years to get a definite 'yes' or 'no' to their plea for political asylum. I could talk at length about refugees waiting for such a long time to be accepted or turned away—living with the fear one finds on Death Row—execution next day, next month or next year. It's like dying slowly, and not knowing when it will happen. The indecision is agonizing."

Through the Wire Fence

LORI WEBER

Lori Weber, a Montreal teacher and author of young adult novels, grew up not knowing quite what to make of her German heritage. Cultural depictions of Germans and a trip to her father's hometown only added to the confusion.

Part German, part Irish/English mix, but Canadian. Is this the best place to start? Isn't the street that I grew up on more important? There, in the Park Extension area of Montreal, we were a patchwork quilt of origins: French, Irish, Greek, Italian, Swedish, Japanese, Chinese, Dutch. Each flat had its own particular flavour, its own particular smells. Our Japanese friends were looked after by their ancient grandmother, who was as shrivelled as an apple doll and who allowed us to do whatever we wanted. It was in their flat that all the kids gathered to colour on the walls. When they came out in the evening with bowls of noodles, we said, and we truly believed, that they were eating fried worms. In the corner of her eye the grandmother had a stye that looked like an upside-down volcano.

All these things somehow or other signified Japanese to me: the crayoned walls, the worm-noodles, and the stye. The Swedish girls across the street wore white starched shirts, even on weekends, and their blond hair was always neatly combed. They sang in a choir that had made a radio commercial that we all envied, yet they weren't allowed to slide down the two-storey bannister because it would stain their underwear. These characteristics I associated with being Swedish: neat, fastidious, stern.

In school all my friends are Greek: Rita, Roula, and Elli. They all have dark brown hair and eyes, but I am dirty-blond and my eyes are green. Their mothers make them do housework and they scream down to their children from galleries, unabashed, "*Ella tho, hligora.*" Their grandmothers live with them and are always clad in black, their grey buns pulled tightly back. They sit statue-like on park benches, shoving over-ripe bananas into the mouths of their tiny grandchildren. Around their necks some wear bright blue evil eyes that dangle when the grandmothers bend over to pick dandelions in the fields beside L'Acadie. By the time I am ten I know more Greek than French. When we are just two we speak English, but when they outnumber me they switch to Greek.

In grade four a flood of tears overwhelms me, and my teacher, Miss Goldbaum, takes me outside. I confess the source of my misery: I can't always understand what my friends are saying. I feel small, defenceless, terribly hurt, and left out. She summons them and we hold a conference where she makes me tell each of them how their exclusion makes me feel. They are stunned, apologetic. They didn't realize. They assumed I understood. They promise not to do it again, but they do. Repeatedly, for years. The desire to speak their first language when they are together is too strong. To compensate, they make me an honorary Greek. They bring me braided cookies brushed with egg yolk, and when plans are being made for the Greek Easter parade they take me along for a costume fitting.

We are in the Edward VII schoolyard on Jeanne Mance. In one of the upper flats across the street my grandmother's two eccentric sisters live. One has a history of spontaneous nudity and the other plays the piano and was once engaged to an Indian from Caughnawaga (now Kahnawaké). I always pictured him in a skirt with a feather band around his head, carrying a tomahawk. The family, scandalized, broke up the liaison. These aunts are proof to me that not all English people are uptight and proper. They are aberrations, family sore spots. We do not visit them often.

We form a long line of girls, waiting to be measured. The sample costume hangs on the fence, which is made of thousands of wire diamonds linked together. It is lovely, a blue skirt and a white shirt, the colours of the Greek flag. I feel conspicuous, silly. But mostly I am envious of the connection that runs through the veins of the long line of girls, that seeps gracefully and historically into their tongues. The woman who measures me is compassionate. She switches to my tongue. She is amused. I know that she knows I am not one of them. I am an imposter, but she measures me anyway. I lift my arms and she wraps the tape around my flat chest. It is then that I start to cry. I cannot go through with it. Beyond the costume is the whole ritual I will have to partake in, the candlelight parade, the songs whose words I will not be able to sing. (The following year a Catholic friend takes me to her choir and I have the same reaction. The hymn rolls awkwardly over my tongue. I have to force it between my lips. It is as foreign to me as Greek.) I run from the schoolyard in tears and hop on the next 80 bus that will take me under the two tunnels home, deprived and solitary.

My parents seem to me to have no identifiable culture. They are atheists who listen to Bob Dylan, decorate the living-room wall with a poster of Che Guevara, and put up a plastic tree at Christmas. I know that my father was born in Germany, but this doesn't seem to make much difference to our family. He doesn't eat German food, or wear lederhosen, or even drink beer out of tall steins. In fact, I know very little about his German past. When anyone asks me what I am (which is a question everyone in Park Extension asks), I say, "Canadian, but my father is German." According to my father, Germans make the best immigrants because they blend in, assimilate. Later I come to think of it more as camouflage, a desire to remain incognito, to erase the past.

I don't know what being German means exactly, but I know from an early age that German is something to be ashamed of. ("You're

Germish," the kids tease.) That is why it contains the word "germ."
That is why Miss Goldbaum made me and Werner and Achim stand
on our desks one day. She was teaching us about the war. She made
us stand because she wanted everyone to know that just because we
were German they shouldn't think we were in any way responsible
for the horrors she was about to describe. We were innocent. We
hadn't been born yet. Ironically, in that instant, something is born in
me, an awareness that being German means something different
from being Greek or Chinese or Swedish. It carries more weight, or
at least the weight is different. It means being something that one has
to apologize for, to be embarrassed of even. It's a lesson I will learn
many more times. When I'm nineteen and applying to live in a house
in Toronto, one of the tenants stamps out of the room and declares
that if I am accepted he will be forced to take his showers at the U of
T, given that the house has a gas stove in the kitchen. These words
sting, as do the words, "Yuck, my least favourite people" (said with
scrunched-up face) when I point out an available Master's student to
a friend who is looking for love.

The worst part of these attacks is that there is no available defence.
What do you say to the Jewish man who doesn't want to share his
living space with a German? And what to retort to the friend who is
repulsed by my suggestion, in particular once I'd learned that her own
mother was a survivor of Auschwitz? This Germanness is a curse; it is
a deep wart that no solvent can lift from the body. As an antidote, I
think of the beauty of the country itself—the Alps, the Black Forest,
Bavarian castles, the charming cobblestone towns—but I knew nothing of these as a child.

Later, as I grow, I will begin to cling to more solid knowledge,
family facts that get divulged slowly, painfully. My father's father
worked bringing relief to German families during the war, often
travelling from town to town in the south. He wasn't sympathetic to
the Nazi cause. My own father, always a rebel, once stole the German
flag instead of the opposing team's during war games with the Hitler
Youth that he was obliged to join. For this, his father was beaten.
Then there is the arm, the severed arm of my grandfather, that somehow was taken as punishment for something. The how, why, and
when of the episode have never been divulged, and probably never

will be, but how my mind latches onto the image of this severed arm. It is proof that my father's family were not Nazi supporters. Supporters don't lose arms, they gain medals, favour. I believe that the arm allows me to, in part, share in the victim status, or at least lay claim to a minimal amount of victim status. The day I am refused tenancy in the house in Toronto I think that if only I had that arm I could hold it up like a trophy: V for victory and V for victim. This is why the defence of such attacks is so difficult. I am connected to the side that did the victimizing, and, as such, any defence of this side is unacceptable, unthinkable even.

Yes, that fated day in grade four Miss Goldbaum, a teacher I adored and who had helped heal the wounds of my exclusion from the Greek circle, introduces me to the concept of guilt and shame. Although she is careful to point out to the class that we were born in Canada and are far too young to have been involved in the war (this is 1970), she forgets that our fathers (and Werner's and Achim's mothers) were born there, and that they were alive during the war. I never again look at my father in the same light. His crooked hands, which he caught in one of the machines he repairs for a living, are no longer symbols of the daily sacrifice he makes for his family. They resemble the swastika that Miss Goldbaum held up. They are twisted the exact same way. When he is in the shed doing "things," I can no longer imagine him fixing ordinary household items, like bikes and chairs. He is experimenting, destroying, cooking up evil concoctions. When he is stern, which all fathers sometimes are, he is being more than stern. He is showing his true genetic colours (a sentiment that Margaret Thatcher, beehive and all, would agree with: "They will do it again, it is in the blood"). I wonder if Werner and Achim look at their fathers this way too now, but I can't ask them because they disappeared soon after the stand-on-the-desk episode. They obviously told, but I was too ashamed to ever utter a word.

All these feelings about German I take with me to the German House on Cremazie, when my father and mother decide that, at the age of ten, I should become German. Finally, a tiny voice inside me declares, I am to have a culture. Yet I approach the experience warily, for many reasons. For one, I am not used to being the same as anyone else. I am more used to being different, to looking in, to listening in, to standing like a sore thumb in the wrong line-ups. The idea that I am being asked to become part of a group intimidates me, as it will continue to do even now. I am terrified. I try my best to take the German lessons seriously, and sing my young heart out during music break ("*Laterne, Laterne, Sonne, Mond, und Sterne*"), but I feel false, fake.

When I learn that Germans capitalize the German forms of you (*Du* and *Sie*) and not the I (*ich*), I immediately think that this is proof of goodness, of respect for others. I am too aware of trying to stack my deck, to undo the only impressions of Germanness I have gained until now. *Hogan's Heroes* is the most popular sitcom of the day. For half an hour every week people everywhere laugh at the stupid Germans (even my father loves the show). The villains in all our favourite Saturday morning cartoons sound just like my father and are obviously German. At *Bedknobs and Broomsticks* I cringe and cry in the dark. The villains, once again, are replicas of my father. In fact, as a child I had a hard time seeing my father as an individual, a separate and real person; he was a symbol, one that was replicated in so many negative ways.

At the German House I also have to learn to do proper German dancing, where a boy holds your hand and puts his other hand around your waist. The girls sit at tables and wait to be asked. When a boy finally does ask me, I realize I don't know the steps. I am clumsy. I am totally self-conscious twirling into these predetermined steps that are not mine. He tries to twirl me and I break like wood. He pushes me away and mutters some disbelief at my ineptitude. My parents sit behind me, waiting, I feel, for me to suddenly become German, as though the steps to the dance were somehow lying dormant in my genes, waiting to be released. I return to the table, awkward, heavy. I have failed. I refuse to go back. My father is angry, disappointed. I feel his anger is unfair because until that day he had never tried to teach me anything at all about his culture. Not a word. My mother didn't speak German either, so it was a completely foreign language. Greek was more familiar. "*Then thello naertho sto horo,*" I'm not going to the dance, I tell my friends.

I never again attempt to become German. I try to forget the whole issue, and for the most part do this until we take a trip to my father's hometown when I am eleven. It may be easy to block out the war in Canada, but in Europe this is impossible. The fact of the war screams out to me from every nook and cranny of the old town. It is in the sawed-off limbs of the old men who hobble on canes and crutches, in the bags of goitre that old women carry under their chins from years of drinking tainted water. It is in the cracked-toothed castle that sits like a decrepit crown on the top of the hill at the centre of town. Green army trucks pump their way continually through the narrow-veined streets, the soldiers in the back calling out in a variety of languages, mostly French, Italian, and English. It is in the sadness of my father's eyes when he looks at his mother, and it is written in the deep lines on her face and the million wrinkles of her hands that seem immune to the flames that burst beneath them when she lights the old stove. But mostly it is in the deep hole that lies in the ground under the root cellar, hidden by a camouflaging heap of potatoes. It was there that my father and his brother hid their sister from soldiers. As an eleven-year-old I couldn't imagine why she would need to be hid, but later I understood that rape was common. Even later yet I discovered that this aunt of mine was really my father's half-sister and that her real father was Jewish, the most potent reason for hiding her.

It is during that visit too that I am able to add a dimension to my father that makes him less of a cut-out stock character. I pad his Germanness with curves and angles. I learn of the time he walked himself to the hospital (*krankenhaus*—sickhouse), doubled over with the pain of a nearly ruptured appendix. I learn of the betrayal he felt when his parents sent him far out into the country to pick potatoes, knowing full well that his life was in danger. I learn that my father and his brother cannot look each other in the eyes and reminisce without crying. I learn, that year, to be a little less ashamed of being German. I learn that the war, any war, is not just team A versus team B, but a million shades of A's and B's, shades that might save me, tuck me inside their shadows and hide me. But I don't get over (and never will) the discomfort that being of German descent elicits.

One last memory strikes me. The family that lived next door to my father's was so kind to us when we visited. The mother, who was my grandmother's age, baked us special cookies and gave me a fistful of mad money (*Spielgeld*). The old father, without telling anyone, put up a swing in my grandmother's backyard, attached to a high branch of one of her sturdy trees. That afternoon he pushed me on it, obviously thrilled to watch my happiness as I pumped myself higher and higher towards the orange-tiled roof of my father's home. That night my father told us that that couple were the chief informants in their town: true, one hundred per cent Nazi sympathizers. The next day my mother looked the swing over carefully, as though she thought he might have cut gashes into it, and was just waiting for me to fall, break my neck, and die. Then she wanted to take it down and give it back, but my father refused to let her do this. It would have been rude. The neighbour had given it in kindness. The war had ended twenty-five years ago.

As for me, I continued to use the swing, but never again as freely as on the first day. I never again swung so high. The episode filled me with questions. How could my father have lived beside such people? What relationship did his family have with them? How could an evil man benevolently build a swing? What if I had been related to them, instead? How could anyone really know anyone? How could I look at this person and smile in a friendly fashion unless I was totally able to disconnect him from his history? Could such a manoeuvre be done?

These are the questions that run through my mind the day we leave my father's hometown. Across from me on the train my father is crying, sobbing, the tears running over his crooked fingers, down his palm, soaking the cuff of his shirt. Outside, on the platform, my old grandmother runs beside the train under our window. She is waving a white handkerchief, as though she is surrendering.

And then suddenly we are back in Canada, a place with so little history, a place where people are always in the process of remaking themselves, redefining who they are. A place of newness, or improvisation. I see it everywhere in my neighbourhood, this blending, this criss-crossing of culture. And it is what I gravitate towards: the mix, the blend, the anomalies, the hybrids.

The first thing I do when I get home is call Elli. She asks me about my trip to Germany. I tell her I had fun, but I don't tell her about the man next door, or the root cellar, or the way my father cried. She asks if I brought her anything, but I didn't. It is not a souvenir type of place. When she went to Greece the year before she brought me back a plastic Acropolis paperweight. What would be the German equivalent? No, the most salient parts of my trip and the impressions left on me are destined to remain private, relegated to a back corner of my mind, as concealed as the root cellar, but just as deep.

Elli cannot wait for me to meet their new boarder, Costa, who doesn't speak a word of English and arrived a few days ago from Athens. He is exotic, incomprehensible, and when Elli's mother isn't home he tries to fondle our little breasts. I take comfort in his difference, preferring, as I will for the rest of my life, the aspects of him that I can't know, will never know or relate to. My upbringing in Park Extension has left me with that—a preference for difference over similarity, a discomfort with belonging (since belonging was never an option). It is a legacy that leads at times to a sense of isolation, but at others to complete connectedness with everything and everyone, since one can always be an observer.

The fact of having a German heritage is one that most of the time means very little. My father was right. Our family did blend in with the mainstream far more than the families of any of my ethnic friends. We don't have any equivalent to the large Italian wedding, the Passover Seder, or the Sunday afternoon picnics of the Filipino community in the park across the street from my old apartment. I used to watch them with that familiar mixture of awe, envy, and relief. They would number at least one hundred, ranging in age from ancient to newborn, the families all mixing and blending together, brought there by the ties of their blood and the meat sizzling on the barbecues. Such ethnic identification is completely foreign to me. The ability to be so at one with my background would also be completely impossible, given the complexity of feelings that being of German heritage has always caused.

Just nights ago at a potluck dinner a woman told a story of a despicable woman who had recently become a decent man's girlfriend. Through her whole discourse she referred to the woman as "that German." Nobody at all who was listening seemed to recognize this as a racist comment, except for me. The amazing thing was that the teller of the story is an enlightened and well-educated young woman who works for refugee organizations in Montreal. She is well known for her tireless crusades to aid the downtrodden and needy. Yet she could say "that German" with impunity, in a way that I've heard the word German used a hundred times before. It would have been unthinkable for her to pepper her story with "that Italian" or "that Chinese" or "that Mexican." But "that German" is seen as acceptable because of what German still represents.

Such derogatory utterances don't even sound wrong or jarring to the ear, unless one is German, I'm sure. Funny that when she was telling the story my mind drifted back to the beautiful blue and white costume for the Greek Easter parade that I never did get to wear. I could see it hanging on the wire fence, as though it had been waiting all this time for someone to claim it. At that moment, I would have gladly crawled into it, to camouflage myself and take on a new identity. I wondered what it would be like to be able to lay claim to a heritage that one could be one hundred per cent proud of, that was above reproach. This, of course, is probably just an idyllic fantasy. Perhaps all people are embarrassed by some part of their culture, and perhaps everyone has a parallel image of that blue dress, a symbol of otherness that they sometimes wish they could easily adopt.

That night, at the potluck, I never did point her racism out to her, and if it happens a hundred times more I probably never will. I will always, in some ways, be the ten-year-old child standing on a desk, completely immobile and burning with shame, listening to the adored teacher tell stories that are difficult to hear.

"Alone in a New Land"

NEIL BISSOONDATH

> *The deliberately parcelled out cultural, racial, and religious divisions of York University in the early 1970s made newcomer Neil Bissoondath uncomfortable. He became one of the leading critics of a Canadian multiculturalism then coming into vogue.*

The cafeteria in Central Square was large and brashly lit. It was institutional, utilitarian, a place for *feeding* oneself rather than enjoying a meal. The sounds of trays and cutlery roughly handled clanged from among the busyness of students grabbing a bite between classes. Off to one side, others too harried to pause for long fed quarters to the coffee machines.

I was new to the country, the city, and the university, still foundering around in the unfamiliarity of my surroundings.

The cafeteria seemed a benign atmosphere, friendly in an impersonal way. Inserting oneself here, into the midst of the controlled chaos, would not be difficult. As the eye got used to it, though, other aspects emerged, and it eventually became clear that the apparent chaos was in fact subtly ordered.

A map could be drawn of the cafeteria, with sections coloured in to denote defined areas. To mark out, for instance, the table at which always buzzed quiet Cantonese conversation; or the tables over in one corner from which rose the unsubtle fervour of West Indian accents; or the table more subtly framed by yarmulkes and books decorated with the Star of David. And there were others.

To approach any of these tables was to intrude on a clannish exclusivity. It was to challenge the unofficially designated territory of tables parcelled out so that each group, whether racially or culturally or religiously defined, could enjoy its little enclave protected by unspoken prerogatives.

This idea of sticking with your own was reinforced by various student organizations, many of them financially assisted by the university. Controversy arose at one point when an application for membership in the Black Students' Federation was received from a student—in fact, a staff member of the campus newspaper—whose skin colour seemed to disqualify him. The question arose: did one have to be black to belong to the Black Students' Federation? Was not a commitment to the issues raised by the association enough to justify belonging? Just how relevant was skin colour? The final decision was to admit him—on the grounds not that race was irrelevant but that, as an organization financially assisted by the university, it had to respect York's regulations prohibiting discrimination on the grounds of race and colour.

I did not belong to the federation, but the resolution was pleasing anyway, even though there was a tincture of discomfort at the way in which it had come about: through technicality, not through the application of principle.

Another moment remains with me. One day a Jewish friend with whom I was going to have coffee insisted that I accompany him to the Jewish Students' Federation lounge. As he fixed us each a coffee he said in a voice clearly intended for others in the room that I should feel free to help myself from the coffee-maker at any time. And then he added in strained tones that the lounge, provided by the university, was open to everyone: I was to ignore anyone who tried to stop me. It was in this way that he sought to make me part of unsuspected internecine tensions—while publicly declaring his own position.

The issues made me wary: I neither joined the Black Students' Federation nor revisited the Jewish Students' Federation lounge. I learned, instead, to keep my distance from the tables that would have welcomed me not as an individual but as an individual of a certain skin colour, with a certain accent, the tables that would have welcomed me not for *who* I was and for what I could do, but for *what* I was and what I represented. I had not come here, I decided, in order to join a ghetto.

Segregated tables, notions of belonging, invitations to parties that would offer ephemeral visions of "home": alone in a new land, I faced inevitable questions. Questions about my past and my present, about the land left behind and the land newly found, about the nature of this society and my place in it. At eighteen, about to embark on a new life, I felt that these were weighty issues.

For many at those tables, though, these were questions of no great import. Their voices were almost aggressive in dismissing any discomfort that they might have experienced by flaunting the only government policy that seemed to cause no resentment: Canada as a multicultural land. Officially. Legally. Here, they insisted, you did not have to change. Here you could—indeed, it was your obligation to—remain what you were. None of this American melting-pot nonsense, none of this remaking yourself to fit your new circumstances: you did not have to adjust to the society, the society was obliged to accommodate itself to you.

An attractive proposal, then, a policy that excused much and required little effort. It was a picture of immigration at its most comfortable.

And yet I found myself not easily seduced.

The problem was that I had come in search of a new life and a new way of looking at the world. I had no desire simply to transport here life as I had known it: this seemed to me particularly onerous baggage with which to burden one's shoulders. Beyond this, though, the very act of emigration had already changed me. I was no longer the person I had been when I boarded the flight in Trinidad bound for Toronto: I had brought to the aircraft not the attitudes of the tourist but those of someone embarking on an adventure that would forever change his life. This alone was a kind of psychological revolution.

Multiculturalism, as perceived by those at whom it was most explicitly aimed, left me with a certain measure of discomfort.

The Junta's Victims, 1973

FARLEY MOWAT

A prominent author urged the Canadian foreign minister to open the country to the victims of the Chilean military regime that took power on September 11, 1973. The next year, the government's policy changed, and more than 12,000 Chileans entered Canada from 1974 to 1978. By the end of the 1980s, that number had doubled.

I have been observing with mounting distress and anger the actions of the Government of my country in regard to the junta coup in Chile.

By now it is completely and absolutely obvious to any thinking person in this country that we have, either deliberately or through the activities of an exceptionally incompetent Ambassador in Chile, publicly committed ourselves to the support of what is obviously a militantly right-wing organization in Chile. Furthermore, we have clearly turned our backs upon the cries for help from a very large number of Chileans who are being savagely persecuted by the new junta. It would appear, from all the evidence which is available to us, that your department, while it has been happy in the past to welcome political refugees from such countries as Hungary and Czechoslovakia, is resolutely determined to refuse the same humanitarian opportunities to refugees from Fascist countries.

I wish to go on record with you as being outraged by the attitudes of your department in this regard. I hope you will find it in your heart to immediately open Canadian immigration doors to the victims of the Chilean junta. It would be very pleasant indeed if Canada not only acted correctly in this matter, but demonstrated rather more clearly than it has done in the past, that we are not simply echoes of the American State Department's attitudes toward free and democratic governments in the South American continent.

Escaping Chile

GABRIELA ENRIQUEZ

> Gabriela Enriquez was one of the Chilean refugees who came to Canada after the overthrow of the government of Salvador Allende by General Augusto Pinochet. Her husband was a Communist professor in Santiago who hid from the authorities and eventually found his way to the Canadian Embassy and then to Canada.

One day I received information that Canada would allow the wives and children to come, too, and that we should get passports. My father knew some people and I got my passport very fast.

It was very uncertain. We didn't know what to do. I didn't know what was going to happen to my husband, and the situation in Chile was getting worse and worse. People were disappearing. People were killed. Some of our best friends were killed, and the situation was getting really uncertain. I didn't know what the future was for me.

The children felt terrible, their father was gone, and there was a curfew and you couldn't go outside. Besides, you didn't trust many people because you didn't know who people were. In our case, many of our friends were gone. You would talk to some people and overhear stories that something had happened with this one, something happened to that one, somebody was killed. You just live in fear. You don't know what is going to happen.

When I was informed that we were going to leave the country, I was happy and unhappy. I didn't want to leave my family, my father, mother, brother. I felt as though I wasn't deciding for myself. Somebody else was deciding for me what I should do, that I should leave the country. But I also wanted to be secure with my children and my family. Finally we left the country. That was on 10 January 1974. A military aircraft came from Canada, a big plane. We all left on the same plane.

We had to go inside the embassy. Some people were screaming at us and some people were saying goodbye. They took us on buses to the airport. We were only allowed to bring two pieces of luggage. In the end, we brought mostly toys that were important to the kids. It was very difficult. I didn't know what to take. I didn't know what was important in the house. I didn't know what was going to happen with the whole house, my car, the furniture, all the photos we had, ornaments. And they said we could only take two pieces of luggage—from our whole way of life!

When we were on the plane, they told us that we were not going to Montreal, we were going to Toronto. I knew very little about Canada at that time. I knew there were two languages—French and English. Because my husband spoke English, he thought that maybe Toronto would be the place for us. I also knew it was very cold, but I never knew it was as cold as it was. It never crossed my mind.

January is summer in Chile, and I was dressed for summer. I put on another pair of socks. I thought maybe double socks would be good, and two sweaters would be good. What a surprise! When we arrived in Canada, it was terrible. Never in my life have I felt cold like that. Besides, I didn't have the right shoes because when I was leaving, I didn't think about any other kinds of shoes—boots. I had tried to get better winter clothing for my kids, but I was thinking about the Chilean winter, not the Canadian winter. We arrived on 11 January at six in the morning.

When we left Chile, we were escorted by the military and police. We couldn't say goodbye to our family. We left Chile via Mexico.

The Mexican government didn't allow us to exit the plane in Mexico. They refuelled the plane with us inside, and only allowed us to open the door for the kids because it was hot inside—very, very hot.

Afterwards we flew to Toronto. When we arrived, they took us all into a big room and made us wait for a medical exam. There were some doctors to see if we were all in good health. Then they took us to our hotel and gave us some food. They took us to this place called Ontario Welcome House. At that time it was very close to Harbourfront. We got some clothing and they gave us some other stuff, too.

We lived at the hotel for a while. The government was paying for the hotel. They said that we could stay at the hotel a maximum of two months. We stayed two months. There were some Chilean students living in Toronto who helped us, and some other Canadians who were very much involved with Chile and helped the whole group. They tried to place everybody. For us, it was difficult because we had three kids.

In the whole group, there were not many people who spoke English. I would say only two or three, and my husband was the only one who could speak English well. He was always needed to translate, to go to the doctor because someone got sick, and to take people different places. That's why we stayed in the hotel—because he was helping others move out of the hotel. That's why the people in charge told us not to worry—they knew he didn't have time to look for his own place and they needed him as an interpreter. We were left at the hotel and for us, it was something so different.

It was January; it was so cold. We didn't know the city and were always wondering about our family in Chile. We didn't have much communication with them. The newspaper didn't print much about what was going on in Chile. We felt very separated. These Canadian groups were very nice to us—there was a sense of solidarity, but when we walked in the street, we found the people cold. Even the way people lived was different from us. Immediately, we felt we were in a very different place from our home.

Finally, we moved to a flat on the west side of the city. We rented the second floor from a Portuguese family. The parents didn't speak English, but their kids spoke English.

You had to get used to a new kind of life, living in a flat, and sharing the house with other people who were very different from us. They played music that was not our music, and were very loud. They cooked different foods and the smells were completely different.

We collected some furniture, plates, things that we needed for the house. My husband was always thinking that we were going to leave soon, that the military was not going to last very long, and that we were going to return to Chile in two months, three months, no more than six months. You always have that in mind, but I said that I couldn't live with that. I have to build my nest for the security of the kids. We had to do something.

There was a school nearby, and we sent the kids to school. We went to meetings for the Chileans. We thought the government was going to fall and didn't think we would be here permanently. They were giving English language classes to the men. They didn't want to give classes to women, especially to women married with kids. We had to fight to get people to give us the opportunity to have ESL classes.

I thought it was very important to learn English. In the Portuguese family, the lady didn't speak English, the father spoke only broken English, and the kids spoke only English. I could understand when the lady spoke to the kids in Portuguese because Portuguese is very similar to Spanish. She told them not to speak to her in English because she couldn't understand. I could picture myself with the same problem. I thought, if I don't understand this language, this is what is going to happen to me. We were a very close family and I didn't want to see myself in this situation. This poor woman was screaming, "I don't understand you." That's why we met with other women and we made some noise, and finally the government gave us the opportunity to go to the ESL classes.

We all came as refugees. When we were all in the embassy in Chile, we were interviewed by Canadian immigration. They started the papers in Santiago and after a while, many people received their landed immigrant papers. I believe there were two who never received their landed immigrant papers. One was a person who had to leave for Spain, and the other was my husband. He never received his papers as a landed immigrant. One day I went to immigration to ask for an extension of our minister's permit. We all had minister's permits to stay in the country. I saw my husband's file. His file had a lot of things written on it—TOP SECRET—maybe because he was a member of the Communist party. I don't know the reason. Until the day he died here in Canada, he never received the landed immigrant papers. I only received the papers two years after his death.

Belisario was healthy when he came to this country, but he got leukaemia in 1975, after a year in Canada. He had had a very bad cold and went to the hospital, where they found he had leukaemia. In January 1976, he passed away at Mount Sinai Hospital. He lived with acute leukaemia for two months.

We were left without him in a new country, almost two years after we arrived. We were not allowed to go back to Chile: his name was on a list of those forbidden to return. . . .

Always With You, 1978

RAMESH MEHTA

> *Ramesh Mehta, at thirty-five years old, wrote a series of letters to his wife, Hansa, and children, Bina and Krishan, while he was living in Toronto and looking for work to enable the settlement of his family in Canada. At the time of this 1978 letter to his family in London, England,, he was living with his brother and sister-in-law (Kakubhai and bhabi), his mother (Ba), and one other brother (Tinubhai). Ramesh left Nairobi, Kenya, in 1970, when it became difficult for many Asians to renew work permits. He found a job at Canadian Tire, where he has worked for more than twenty-five years. The exodus of thousands of Asian families to England and Canada coincided with African decolonization and the process of economic Africanization.*

My Sweet Darling Hansa,

Perhaps I will receive a letter from you to-morrow. Well, this is just to say hello to you guys.

I miss you my darling. I feel hopeless and lonely. As it is I can't call you here because the situation is not in our favour and I don't think it is fair to Kakubhai and bhabi to be burden on them. Things are getting bad day by day. I haven't lost my confidence. It's only time I ask. Please you too keep patience and calm. Please promise me that you will not lose your confidence. Cheer up. This is not the end of the world. It wasn't the end of the Roman Empire when it was ruling England and England ruling the world and now depression ruling the world. Remember there is a broad day light after a long dark night. May be this is a good experience for us. I call it "A BLESSINGS IN DISGUISE." Now I have my eyes wide open. This is to say in this world there is you, me, Bina and Krishan. We are going to look after ourselves and NOBODY ELSE. *AGREE*? Come on now be happy and feel sure of yourself.

How is Krishan doing? Did you register him with a doctor for his injections? Please get his injections for defence against polio, smallpox, wooping cough, diptheria, diarrhea and so on. Well, do your best. Please look after Bina and don't allow her to be lonely and miss me. Give her father's and mother's love. See that she is happy at school and take one advice from me for the three of you:

Do exercise, eat properly, rest plenty, always think high and bright and please do not—I repeat DO NOT worry at all. Come what may! And say to yourself "I am not going to be deterred by anything. I am going to be firm and strong."

Let me not get carried away. I am sure you are mature and responsible and you know what you are doing. Please take this from me "I AM ALWAYS WITH YOU" in body and soul. I love you darling.

Hey! 15th of this month is your birthday. Many many congratulations from me with plenty of love and kisses. May God keep my darling always happy. I wish I was there to kiss you Darling. I will be sending you a card and please buy those saris and other things from the Sudan store. I will give you surprise for your birthday when I see you. That's a promise.

Let me write to you about Canada. Well first of all Spring is just round the corner and snow is melting now. Things are brightening up. There is going to be a flower show. Lovely roses and other flowers are going to be on the show. Politically Canada is going to have elections in 78 (expecting in early spring). On the election platform topics like unemployment, inflation and economy are the main issues.

Would you believe me? Inspite of all the problems to-day in Canada Canada is a wonderful place to live. Living standard is 2nd best in the whole wide world. 1st being Switzerland. North America is super—we have colour TV, big automobiles, luxurious houses and thick carpets and above all clear blue sky and panoramic sunset—beautiful with nice colours. In this country there is plenty of food. There is no doubt or question about this.

Ba is okay. Tinubhai is looking for a job too. But he has no luck either so far. Everybody is fine at this end.

With plenty of love and kisses my darling I am yours and only yours. Please look after kids. Pass my regards to everyone over there. We are one.

The Vietnamese Boat People

PHAM THÊ TRUNG

> After the end of the Vietnam War in 1974, thousands of refugees escaped the country by boat. Pham Thê Trung's boat was ten metres long and four metres wide, jammed with more than twenty frightened souls for the five-day voyage to Thailand. They almost didn't make it through the brutal weather, the Communist patrols, and the pirates.

I had no freedom. In 1979, my family was still in Saigon and I lived by myself. I was single. I decided to escape in 1975, but I didn't have a chance to escape because I had to work to survive. As I wanted to live by myself, it was hard, so I had to get along with the government, who gave me a job. I had to work with them for three years, but I am an artist and I want to do it my way—in freedom. If you don't have freedom, you cannot create things. That's the reason I decided to escape. . . .

When I was in Vietnam, I decided that when I go to another country, I would choose Canada. I like Canada because of the kindness of the people, and the country can support and help lots of countries around the world. I like Canada because they don't get involved with lots of war or politics. People are kind, they give help to people who want to develop. That's the reason, and I was curious. Canada is at the top of North America. I was curious, I wanted to travel. Maybe in the future, I could get a passport and go to the United States or Europe. I feel in that way it's very good and very fine for me.

I escaped. It was not like going on holidays. You go on this kind of trip to escape. I had to be careful to avoid accidents. Pirates came and you have to take care of yourself, but when everything was quiet, my soul needed to rest. When I looked at people dying in the ocean or something else I saw, I thought [I] should record it and keep it in my mind, so when I have a chance to write, I can tell the story, or I can paint it, or I can do my art through my experience. So I was really careful to watch everything around me, to record everything.

When I arrived at the refugee camp, I started to do something. Every day I took paper to sketch. I wanted to keep it like a diary, so I went around the camp and painted and drew every day. I made about fifty drawings and sketches by ink and water-colour. People organized an exhibit for my art and they came and enjoyed it and some people bought. This was at the camp, but the Vietnamese did not buy. The people who worked at the camp came—people from the United States and Europe and Canadian people. They came over to help people. They bought my paintings. I was happy because they wanted to help me and I had something for them.

If people were interested in my work, I would sketch their portrait for them as a souvenir. There were lots of people from the churches, Catholic and Protestant. I met lots of young people who were volunteers. They said they wanted to help. I had the chance to speak and learn English there. I made one or two friends there. One was from England, one was from Holland, and one was Canadian.

I met a minister of the Mennonite church in Canada. He used to work in the refugee camp, but now he is in Winnipeg. He is a very kind man. I remember he took me to get permission from the Thai camp security and he sponsored me for one day to travel to Bangkok, so I could enjoy freedom for one day. He took me by taxi and showed me the museum. He showed me the royal murals and the temples—

beautiful. That was one day for me in Bangkok, and then I came back to the camp.

Some people there knew English and they could teach or you could learn some geography of the country where you were going—Canada's geography, population, religion, culture, how many people live there, the provinces. That's how you have to do it. You have to be ready to learn it and go to one of the countries you choose.

I was surprised when I was first directed to Montreal. I have only one relative in Canada. He is my cousin, a pharmacist. I got in touch with him by mail. I told the embassy officer that the only place I have relatives is in Saskatoon, Saskatchewan. I thought I would go to live close to him in Saskatchewan, but I was surprised when I was sent to Montreal.

They can send people everywhere. Some people go to Edmonton, Vancouver, Halifax, Toronto, everywhere. When they interviewed me again, they asked me if I wanted to live in Ontario. I said I don't care, I am happy with this land that I chose. You send me to Toronto, anywhere, I don't know. They asked me about my occupation. I said I work as an artist, so I can go somewhere suited to me. They said okay and sent me to Stratford, Ontario. He said Stratford might be good for me. I don't know how. I came over here. Stratford is the name of the village where Shakespeare was born in England. That is a very beautiful place—romantic. I came here to live—very nice.

I had an older brother who lived in Japan. I didn't want to write a letter directly to Vietnam. At that time, the communists were very serious. If there were any problems with the politics, it could still involve my family in Vietnam, so I wrote letters to my brother in Japan, and he wrote to Vietnam. From Japan to Vietnam would be okay, but not from Canada or the United States. I used to do that.

I was government sponsored. In Stratford the first year, some people came to help and they rented the apartment. The government helped to show me how to live, what the apartment looked like, everything in the town.

We rested about one month. We had government applications for OHIP, social insurance numbers, everything for a landed immigrant. Then in the summertime, in June, there were ESL classes, English as a second language. We went there until Christmas, six months.

I still worked. I started to work with ink drawings, and I made some artwork to show at the gallery in Stratford. That was two months after I arrived in Stratford. I brought about fifty sketches from the refugee camp, and I showed them to the community at Stratford.

At that time, it was the Stratford Festival. The local church I attended helped me to arrange a show there and frame my work. And maybe I could sell. They appreciated my work. Lots of people came to buy. They helped me make a better life. I don't make lots of money. At that time, I had about $400 or $500, so I was happy. That was a lot of money for me at that time. I connected with some people in town and they wanted to have something special, so I painted some things in their house. I painted some portraits and made some money.

After I finished school there a year later, I wanted to go work in a bigger city, so I connected with some of my friends in Toronto. The Vietnamese community in Toronto is bigger now and I wanted to join the Vietnamese community, so I left Stratford.

When I first arrived in Montreal and Stratford, I was surprised a little bit, but not very much because in Saigon I used to learn art and I read lots of western books about art or geography, or *Reader's Digest*. I knew what Canada, the United States, and France looked like. I could imagine. The buildings are higher, and there are more cars, traffic, lots of traffic here, the highway is busy. The country is different. Life is faster, and you travel, and you have to follow the law and everything. At that time, I didn't go very far, but I saw everything. I feel very comfortable.

The first winter, it was really cold. You can see the snow you dreamed of, you can see how Christmas is. In Saigon, if you are Christian, you go to church, but you cannot enjoy Christmas like in Canada. They don't like religion to get involved with the communist politics.

In Saigon, many churches were closed, but some small churches are still open illegally. There were about fifty or one hundred people meeting. If the village or town communist officer says you are not allowed to organize a meeting, you have to go away. When you get permission, you could have a Christmas celebration.

In Canada, I find that every community is very proud of its culture. In Canada, they welcome all. You can wear your own costumes. In Vietnam, if you work for the government, you can only wear one uniform, all in one colour. Also, you have to eat the same food as the others. That's the way you have it. You line up to get food every day. But here you are free, you work hard, you get some money, you save money, you can buy a house. If you don't have lots of money, you still get enough food.

We Portuguese Came to Canada

DOMINGOS MARQUES AND JOÃO MEDEIROS

In the mid-1950s, farm and railroad workers from Portugal began to come in considerable numbers—more than 17,000 in the decade. The Portuguese celebrated their twenty-fifth anniversary in Canada in 1980.

So we Portuguese came to Canada. It's a fact of history and every day our impact on this country grows. Our story began 25 years ago with the landing of the first immigrants at Halifax, followed shortly by their wives and families. We were full of enthusiasm when we entered the new country, putting our trust in Customs officials and Immigration officers—for we knew no-one. We had nothing to give but our labour. However, we did make friends with other immigrants on the journey over, and many group photographs witness this. We promised, of course, to keep in touch with each other. Who knew when we might need help? And soon some found they did, for we were all separated from each other, and sent to work on farms or railroads. For the most part the first immigrants were completely isolated, not only by the fact of the absence of family and friends, but even more so because of their lack of French or English. They had no employment security either. Life was certainly very tough. But who ever told us that immigration was going to be easy?

We were not surprised at having to work hard or put off by the loneliness of our lives. And we *were* lonely, even to tears sometimes. We realized that we had to go through all this to get out of the vicious cycle of life in our home country. So new immigrants kept on arriving. We wrote home asking our brothers, nephews and friends to come and join us. Small plots of land at home were sold, family houses were mortgaged to pay for the journey. And we got a visa for Canada. Sometimes we could only get a tourist visa. But we got here. It seemed to us the only thing to do.

Many had had illusions before they left Portugal. They had wonderful dreams of getting rich quickly, and even in Canada, while they were sweating during the day, would dream nostalgically of returning home with a purse full of money. Then they would build a house with a back garden where they would plant their own vegetables—or they would buy a building in some village or city. They would be free and independent at last. Their children would never have to labour to earn a living as they had had to do. But the dream began to fade away after some years, and in the end ceased altogether. There were many of us who packed our bags ready to go back and live in Portugal again, but when we arrived home everything seemed to have changed. Our calculations were all wrong. Besides, our children had no desire to leave Canada, they had grown roots which went deep down. And if we hoped to be really independent in our home country, then we needed more money. Prices had risen, workers were demanding higher wages. We could never obtain the comfort of which we had dreamed. Even the employers and officials in Portugal didn't treat us with the same concern as those in Canada. There were many reasons why we decided to come back after all. Bowing to reality, we returned, and saw life as it really was. There were no more dreams now. We had to get a job at once, go to the Supermarket on Friday night, pay up the arrears on our mortgage, make certain we had U.I.C. [unemployment] benefits and so on.

Still, after 25 years, we are not really free. We are bound to our homes, to our children and to the Canadian way of living. The chains that bind us are our businesses, our jobs, our right to a pension, even the friends we have made in Canada. Many of our children were born here, as the maternity wards in all the hospitals testify. The schools are filled with Portuguese students, and the telephone directory with names of Portuguese residents. The gravestones in some cemeteries bear Portuguese inscriptions.

For many of the Portuguese now living in Canada, Portugal is just a memory of a happy holiday on the beach, a plane flight, a sunny climate. However some nostalgia remains, so many of us put up on our walls a painting to remind us of "home," a house or some flowering trees perhaps.

But we are not just a number of individuals in Canada who happen to be Portuguese. We are conscious of communities, either small communities clustering around a church or club, or large communities like those in Toronto and Montreal. Some families of Portuguese origin are now moving to the suburbs of the cities. We have entered the commercial world, we have aligned ourselves with one political party or another, as we have learned how to distinguish between different interests and different classes. In the past there was a time when the Portuguese were something like icebergs floating in the middle of a multitude of other immigrant groups. We had no voice in our new country. Although we had been very articulate in Portugal we grew dumb when we came to Canada, not finding words to express our thoughts either in French or English. So we became dependent on others who were more privileged than ourselves who acted as our spokesmen without receiving our votes.

Now things are starting to be different. Winds of change are blowing. We have learned that we must understand what people are saying, and we must learn to express ourselves in French or English. We have studied a new language at school and don't have to keep silent any longer. We can say "yes" when we mean yes, and "no" when we mean no. We are prepared to make demands, to ask questions, to protest if need be. The iceberg is melting in the ocean which, for 25 years, was unaware of its existence. Even though our command of English is not perfect yet, we are able to make our voices heard at the work place, in the field of education, and even in public debate. This country is daily becoming "our" country, so we don't intend to sit by passively and in silence, or to isolate ourselves from everyone else. We are demanding the same rights in making political decisions.

We are proud of all we have achieved by our labour. If anyone looks at the big buildings downtown in any of our great cities, or at the express-ways, they can see what Portuguese immigrants have helped to construct. We have left evidence of our work in offices, forests, mines and factories. The very earth bears witness to our blood and sweat. We are well aware of what we have contributed to build up this country, even though we don't hope to see our praises inscribed in marble.

We are confident of the future. We have never been afraid of struggle or conflict. And so we offer our hands to all fellow-Canadians, of whatever race, creed or colour, who with us want to build up a state in which justice, freedom and unity are not mere catchwords but a living reality.

"More Sri Lankan"

SIVA SEGARAN

> *The Sri Lankan Tamil community numbered almost 70,000 at the time of this interview with fifty-one-year-old Siva Segaran, who escaped the communal violence of his country in 1985. He had found employment as a settlement worker at the Tamil Eelam Society of Canada. His ties to Sri Lanka remained strong, and he hoped, as many immigrants do, to return home one day.*

As long as I am in the Tamil Eelam Society, I would have to be more of a Sri Lankan than a Canadian. And Canada encourages people to practise their own religion and culture here. There is a multicultural ministry, and they give funds to different communities to maintain whatever they had in their own country. So when they encourage it, naturally we should make the best use of it.

The Canadian government is trying to eradicate racism in this country. They are conducting seminars and spending a lot of money to eradicate racism, but in my work experience, I have observed racism frequently. The only advantage is that if you can prove it, they will be charged. You can even fight it in a court of law. This is a free country. You have every right to fight it out in the courts. That is a thing to be praised.

On the whole, I am happy that I brought my children to a good country where I can give them the best education. My two eldest children came here when they were about twelve and thirteen years of age, so they remember the life they lived in Sri Lanka and India, but I can see a little difference in the youngest one.

We attend almost all cultural activities and mix with the Tamil community regularly. Whenever we go to our relatives' house, we take our children, so they know what we like. They never displease us. They are obedient and they like the way of life we live. The youngest one would like to speak in English all the time because she can express herself better in English than in Tamil. We always speak to our friends in Tamil. My children have no problem understanding.

When she left Sri Lanka, the youngest one was about two years old. She doesn't know much about our relatives. When we went back to Sri Lanka last year, I think it was the first time she saw my mother and other people. She left early so she couldn't remember most of her relations. But now she is old enough to remember them, so she really enjoys it. In fact, they wanted us to stay for several days. They all had a nice time with their cousins, my wife's sister's sons. We had a happy time there. Because my youngest daughter spent most of her life in Canada, returning to Sri Lanka was a very strange experience for her, but when she saw her cousins whom she hadn't seen for about five or six years, she behaved just like everybody else.

Even if the political situation gets better in Sri Lanka, I wouldn't go back immediately. My eldest daughter is in university and my son will also be going next year. I just can't spoil their lives or their future plans. They have to finish their studies first, so I have to think about migrating to Sri Lanka or anywhere else at a later date.

I would like to go back to Sri Lanka or India after I am sixty-five. For an old man, Canada is not the place to live. The weather is not suitable for old people. You can walk freely and safely in tropical countries, but not in Canada.

All my relatives are in Sri Lanka except for one brother living in Canada and two brothers living in Switzerland. When I move back to Sri Lanka, my children will have to decide whether to live with us or stay in Canada. I would not mind if they stayed in Canada as long as they maintain their culture and they don't forget the way of life Tamils lead in Sri Lanka. Deciding who to marry is a thing we have to decide later on. Even if it is my children's choice, if we like the people they choose, it is okay, but we would not like them to marry outside the community.

Canada is a good country. In Sri Lanka, we don't enjoy the language rights we enjoy in Canada. Here people have a good understanding. So, for anybody who wants to come and who wants advice from me about migrating to Canada, I always say it is good in Canada.

"Send Them Back!" 1987

MACLEAN'S

> *An immigrant Canadian complained about the refugee claims of 174 East Indians who arrived in Canada in July 1987 aboard the freighter* Amelie. *He was joined in his protests by Canadians from coast to coast, although,* Maclean's *magazine reported, many disagreed.*

Vancouver lawyer Luke van der Horst calls himself a "common Canadian" who complains about things he does not like—but seldom does anything about them. But when van der Horst heard that 174 East Indians had landed in Nova Scotia claiming refugee status in Canada, his habitual passivity quickly changed. He and a group of friends paid $2,500 to place ads in two newspapers, calling for tougher enforcement of immigration laws. Van der Horst, 49, who came to Canada from Holland in 1952, said last week that his group wanted to make sure that members of Parliament knew their feelings. He added, "We felt as Canadians that we were being duped and taken advantage of."

Although many disagree with van der Horst, his views were echoed across the country as increasing numbers of Canadians voiced anger at the East Indians' arrival—and confusion about the immigration rules that allowed them to stay.

In Halifax, dozens of motorists driving past Stadacona naval base on Gottingen Street, where the mainly Sikh migrants were detained, slowed their cars and shouted angry slogans. Exclaimed one driver: "Send them back!"

In Montreal, when CJAD radio hotline host Joe Cannon asked his audience for calls on the subject of their choice, 80 per cent wanted to talk about the Sikhs. Said Cannon: "Most of the callers wanted the refugees to go home. They didn't like the rules being broken—and they didn't like Canada being laughed at."

In Toronto, riding offices of MPs were flooded with calls from constituents protesting the East Indians' arrival. Liberal John Nunziata said that he had received about 50 calls—many from people who had immigrated to Canada through normal channels or who had relatives waiting to be admitted to the country. Said Nunziata: "The mood out there is rather ugly."

And in Vancouver, a group called Citizens for Foreign Aid Reform gathered 2,700 signatures on a petition calling for tighter immigration laws. Conservative MP Mary Collins said that her office received nearly 1,000 calls, letters or petitions. The message, according to Collins: "They feel it's unfair that people can get in who appear not to be legitimate refugees." Those sentiments were sure to deepen as the debate continued over how Canada should treat those seeking refuge within its borders.

Safety and Survival, 1990

ENRIQUE ROBERT

> *An El Salvadorian lawyer, proud, sophisticated, and well-educated, learned life all over again in Toronto.*

I arrived in Canada on a very cold morning of 1990. January 19, 1990. It was not planned like that, but that was also my birthday—my thirty-fourth birthday to be exact. We had left our homeland El Salvador a week earlier, as my life and the life of my loved ones were threatened by the death squad, and the army in El Salvador. The Canadian government offered me shelter, but because of the state of the war at that time we didn't have a plane to leave on. The airport was off-limits to us. So we crossed the border into the neighbouring country, Guatemala, and from there the Canadian government literally took charge and helped us with visas and put us on a plane from Guatemala to Miami, and Miami to Toronto.

The arrival, as stressful as it was, also relieved some of the pressure of the fear for our safety. Traveling with me was another family and my three children, and they were very little. My youngest son was five, my daughter was six and my eldest son was eight. We landed in a refugee shelter on Jarvis St. in Toronto, and we lived there for a couple of months. Then we moved to an apartment and life in Toronto began.

Safety was not an issue anymore, but to survive, to learn the language, employment, food . . . all that. Even the weather, as I have said in the past, the cold weather for someone who comes from El Salvador that is summer thirteen of the twelve months of the year, was not easy to handle. But we did have some help. We did have friends that supported us and gave us shelter. I went to school to learn English as a Second Language like any other seven year old kid goes to learn their ABCs—singing "now I know my ABCs . . ." and stuff like that. Anyhow, the story of learning English is no different than anyone in Canada, except that I was already thirty-four and had three children. One of my most important issues was not to become dependent on my own children. One of the phenomena that many immigrants suffer here is that we learn the language slower than our own kids, and we start depending on them to translate for us. So I didn't want to do that, because I was aware and it was clear that my children needed my support. It was a challenge to learn.

My first earned money was shoveling the snow a block away from the rooming house where I was living. From that time, fourteen or fifteen years ago, I have done a lot. I'm an attorney by training with a Masters degree in criminology and labour law, with a specialization in human rights. I clearly do not practice law, but I became a community activist, a community development worker. I work in housing for people with no house. I work in shelters for the homeless. I became not only a Canadian and a Torontonian, but I became an activist of my new country and my new reality.

My Beliefs and the RCMP

BALTEJ SINGH DHILLON

Sponsored by his brother who lived in British Columbia, Baltej Singh Dhillon entered Canada on compassionate grounds after

his father died in Malyasia. He wanted a career in the RCMP,
but was unwilling to remove his Sikh turban and beard. After
the regulations changed, he entered the force in August 1990.

After high school I made the decision that I would pursue a career in
Law and in preparation attended Kwantlen College. While at Kwantlen, I had the opportunity to volunteer for the Surrey RCMP and
helped start the Block Watch program in Surrey.

This volunteer position turned into a summer job and gave me an
opportunity to work closely with RCMP officers. One officer in particular—Greg Nixon—became my mentor. He impressed me with
his dedication to duty and his genuine concern for the community
that he policed. With his guidance and support I made a decision to
pursue a career in law enforcement.

I applied to the RCMP and was informed by the recruiting officer
that although he was going to take my application, at present there
was no policy in place that would accommodate the turban and my
beard. He asked if I would be willing to remove my turban and shave
my beard; I advised that I would not and that to compromise my
faith would be to compromise everything I believed in and I couldn't
and wouldn't do that.

I then waited for approximately 10 months while the Solicitor
General at the time deliberated on the recommendations made by
the Commissioner of the RCMP to accept the Turban into the uniform of the RCMP.

During this time, opponents of this change and those who were
looking for an excuse to voice their racist beliefs came to the fore-
front and a storm of controversy surrounding this issue began to take
shape across the country. I made a conscious decision that I would
take advantage of the media attention and use it to educate my fellow Canadians about my beliefs, my faith, my choice.

A Cold Paradise

A SOMALIAN

A twenty-six-year-old man describes his flight from civil war in Somalia to a sister in Ottawa.

She sent me money to buy a ticket to Canada. That is how I got here. My first impression of Canada was that this was a magnificent, beautiful, and suspiciously calm country, a secure place, where I could walk at any time of the day and sleep without being afraid. I felt myself to be in a paradise—although, I have to admit, a cold paradise.

I was astonished to realize the magnitude of freedom that exists in Canada. I read newspapers every day and I receive enormous pleasure from reading different opinions, different discussions, even seeing caricatures of famous Canadian political leaders. I did not know such a thing was possible. There was not a single hint of such freedom in Somalia. Our leading newspaper, *October Star*, is a sort of diary of the speeches of our leader.

Another thing which made an even a greater impression on me was the existence of rule by law. I do not know how to say it in English properly—I was amazed that every citizen obeyed the law. In Somalia there is just one law, that of the stronger. This is the only ruling law in my country. But what has captured my heart and mind is the peace and the tranquillity of this country. I am not sure that Canadians really realize the incredible conditions they live in. There is no bigger good than to live in peace and to have the luxury to make plans for the future. To have the feeling that you are indeed a human being and not an animal.

Although, not everything is idyllic. In Ottawa there are about 10,000 refugees from Somalia. It would not be an exaggeration to say that there is a certain attitude taken toward them. The main stereotype is that they are on welfare, have no English, and are Muslim. However, I know three languages. I was an university student. I am well educated. I have a certain respect for who I am and what I can do. I want to live a normal life, to be a part of Canadian society, not to be treated as an alien, as an outsider. And I am sure that I can make it. I feel confident that I will succeed.

I have to admit that for a couple of months I felt quite down, quite depressed. I did not know anybody in Ottawa. I stayed home and watched television and I read newspapers. I did not have any focus. None. But this was just a two-month period. I think that the general stereotype towards Somalis hurt me deeply. The fact that I am from Somalia does not necessary mean that I live on welfare, on taxpayer's money, and am lazy.

I began to work in a grocery store. Seven days a week; for thirteen months I did not have a single day off. I worked hard. I built up respect in my colleagues. I saved some money. I applied and I managed to sponsor my fiancée. She came three months ago. Now we both work full time in the same grocery store. We feel happy. We have money, we can afford to save money. Well, I know it is not that much but the main thing is that we work. We do not receive welfare.

The Best Multiethnic State

A SARAJEVAN

A Bosnian refugee from thirty months in the combustible city of Sarajevo, besieged as the parts of the former Yugoslavia warred with one another, found Canada an oasis of calm and comity.

Canada is a like a huge park, nice, calm, and secure. However, I still have the desire to run at the intersections. I still keep looking for a bottle of water in the bathroom while I brush my teeth because for almost thirty months I was used to not having running water, and I have to keep matches in my pocket, just in case electricity shuts down. These are just reminders from a strange and difficult period of my life, which I will be happy to put aside.

I am looking forward to the future. I do not want to look to the past. Despite this, I know that I cannot erase my Bosnian roots. I really don't know if Bosnia can be again the same multiethnic state. But right now I am happy to live in Canada—I think this is the best multiethnic state. And to give to my children the chance to grow up in such an environment.

An Encounter with ESL

KARISHMA KAPIL

From the vantage point of adulthood, Karishma Kapil recalls herself as a bemused girl of ten, the daughter of Indian parents from Zambia, meeting a patronizing teacher on her first day at a Canadian school. It was soon clear that there would be no need of English as a Second Language (ESL) lessons.

"Hello," he said in a big booming voice. "After reviewing her records I think we will place her in Grade 5 and she will have to attend ESL which is . . ."

"ESL?" My mother frowned. "What do you mean ESL? English is her first language. She was in Grade 6 in Zambia, so why not put her in Grade 6 here?"

"Well, our education standards in Canada are higher than what you may have had in Africa. I don't think she'll be able to cope with Grade 6 here. ESL will help her integrate properly in an English-speaking society," said the principal. He seemed a little uncomfortable with the look my mother was giving him.

My mother left the office in a huff, and the principal led me to my new classroom. The label on the door said Grade 6. He walked over to the teacher and they started to talk. The teacher had a pained look on his face. "COME ON IN," he said. The teacher also had a big loud voice.

"Attention class," he said. I thought, why isn't his voice loud when he speaks to them? "We have a new addition to our classroom. She has come all the way from Africa and is going to be joining us for the rest of the year." Africa? Why was he saying Africa? Africa is a continent, not a country. "Please make her feel comfortable. She may not speak English very well, but be patient. English is not everyone's first language." Why did he say I did not speak English well? I sat down at my new desk and prepared for my first day at school. My new teacher resumed his lesson in fractions. How come he did not ask me my name?

A loud bell rang and everyone started to line up at the door. I guessed we were going outside. I really wished I did not have to go. It was so cold. "Look, the refugee does not even have a winter jacket!" I put my head down and pretended not to have heard. I felt like shouting that I had a name and that I was not a refugee. The teacher opened the door and everyone shoved their way out. Within a few minutes I could not feel my nose anymore. My toes started to hurt and I started shuffling my feet to stop them from hurting.

A second bell rang and all the kids that were playing in the playground started to run back to the classroom. Once inside, the teacher moved to the front of the class and smiled at me.

"CAN ... YOU ... COME ... TO ... THE ... FRONT ... OF ... THE ... CLASS ... AND ... TELL ... US ... ABOUT ... YOURSELF?" Why was everyone talking to me like that? I wasn't deaf. He was beginning to make me feel stupid when he spoke so slowly. I walked to the front of the class.

"H.... hi." My mouth was frozen. My jaw did not want to move. I was still too cold from standing outside. Everyone started laughing. The teacher got that same pained look he had before.

"Okay class, that's enough. We should not make fun of people who come from other countries and cannot speak English. She'll learn. We're going to send her to ESL and hopefully by the end of this year she will be able to communicate with us." It wasn't fair. He didn't give me a chance to try again.

When I walked into the ESL class there was not a single student there. The teacher looked up and seemed happy to see me. "Hello. I've been waiting for you," she said. "Okay, honey, what's your name?"

"Karishma."

"You understood my question, Karishma!" She looked very surprised.

"Yes."

"So please tell me about yourself."

I started to tell her that today was my second day in Toronto. I told her everything about my family, myself, my old school and how, today, after school, I was going to go shopping to buy some winter clothes. My new ESL teacher did not say anything to me. She got up and walked out of the classroom. I was left sitting there staring after her wondering what I had said that made her leave. After a long time, she returned; her face was all red. She seemed angry.

"Come along, honey. You're going back to Mr. Herrick's class, you don't need mine. He is going to give you some tests the rest of the students have already taken. If you do well, you'll stay. If you don't, they'll put you in Grade 5. Do you understand?"

I nodded my head, and got up from my chair. I guessed I would be staying in Mr. Herrick's class after all because if he tested me on things he was teaching in class earlier in the day I'd do fine. I had already learned all that at my old school.

An Inventory of Belonging

KEN WIWA

Writer Ken Wiwa reviews his complex exercise in a construction of identity, a process in which Canada was crucial, after his father was put to death by the Nigerian military regime.

I remember the first time I came to Canada. It was in April 1995 and I was wandering around a cavernous building at Toronto Airport clutching my Nigerian passport. Preying on my mind were the endless hours I'd always had to wait in long lines of foreigners whenever I entered Britain. But here in the muffled and shiny greyness of the customs and immigration hall at Lester Pearson were six or seven lines of people waiting to have their passports inspected. I scanned the room, looking for a sign to point me in the direction where non-Canadians were meant to line up for interrogation by some humourless official but all I could see were indeterminate groups of people, a United Nations of accents, colours and fashions. Where are foreigners supposed to go, I asked? The question was invariably met with raised eyebrows, bemused shrugs and vague pointing. I gave up, joining the longest line out of habit.

Fast forwarding through my memories I come to a beach in the South of France. It is October 6th 1998 and I am about to make a decision that will change my life. I am strolling along a sandy beach on a lukewarm evening. The waves are rolling in off the Cote d'Azur and I am gazing out over the sea and thinking that somewhere out there, somewhere on the horizon is Africa. Even though my country is out there I am not in a nostalgic mood. My thoughts are focused instead on the future. As I walk along the deserted beach the impulsive instincts that periodically intervene in my life kick in and almost before I know it I have decided that I am going to live in Canada.

I was 10 years old when my father decided to send me to school in England. When I took my seat in the aircraft at Lagos airport in Nigeria, I had no idea that I was swapping the security of an idyllic African childhood for the uncertainties of adolescence in Europe. I had no idea that I would spend the next twenty years trying, unconsciously, to get away from Nigeria. Or that when I would eventually make an accommodation with my father, my fatherland and my country, I would be living in Canada.

Which is where I am now. In a house in Toronto, delving through my memories, trying to find some rhyme and reason, a line of logic through the erratic sequence of events that brought me here.

Most immigrants have a straightforward enough reason for leaving home—religious or political persecution or the lure of a better life or opportunity abroad. Push and pull factors as I learned at school. But my story refuses to fit into such neat categories. Although there are elements of the push and pull factors in my experience, I didn't exactly come here in search of better opportunities nor was I fleeing from political persecution. Whenever I am asked "Why Canada?", I usually sigh and reply enigmatically that all roads led to Canada.

Between leaving Nigeria in 1978 and the decision on a beach in France 20 years later is a circuitous and internal journey of self-discovery.

Let's rewind the video of my life back to April 1999. I am in London. It is six months after I made the decision on the beach in Cannes. I am moving to Canada in four weeks' time. In my mind's eye I can see myself watching my son sleeping. Somewhere in the corridors of my memory, I hear a television documentary on the lions of the Serengeti.

When the cubs are old enough to fend for themselves, the familiar tone of the disembodied narrator is explaining, its parents will chase them away and into the wild where the young lions will roam until they are ready to settle down and establish a pride of their own. When they are ready to die, a lion will trek for miles across the parched Serengeti to the exact spot where it was born.

Hearing those words in my mind's ear triggers an old, recurring anxiety; my father sent me abroad so that I would return home one day to apply my expensively trained mind to the problems facing our people. But here I am in Canada, as far away from Africa as he could possibly have hoped. And this after all the financial and emotional expense of my education, after my father has been murdered for trying to protect the idea and sanctity of our home and community. A familiar pang of guilt stabs at my conscience. As the feelings of betrayal well up, I find myself reflecting on those lions on the Serengeti. Whenever I feel the past gnawing at my conscience, I try to pacify my guilt with the thought that we are all lions on the Serengeti. Because all of us, at some point in our lives, have to leave home to establish our pride, to find a place of our own. Which when you think it through means that a lion never dies in the same place as its progeny.

I can see a blue jay skipping in and out of the branches of the big pine trees that landscape the view from in here. Every now and again the pines ruffle furtively as a squirrel darts in and out of the branches while I always keep half an eye out for the racoon that often startles me each time I catch sight of the morose expression on its face. But as much as I would love to glean some poetic insight from the scene outside, I already know that the story is in here, hidden in the belongings scattered around my study.

I knew the minute I set eyes on this room that I wanted to live in this house. It is a small room, maybe 10 foot by six, in an annex of my bedroom. I say "I knew" but it was as much an unconscious as a conscious decision. So many of the choices we make in life are informed by our past and I strongly suspect that my decision to live in this particular house was probably decided years ago when I used to spend my summer holidays loitering in my father's study in an annex of his bedroom in Nigeria. I would scan the shelves of his library, plucking out any book that caught my epileptic fancy, dipping in and out of its pages, reading indiscriminately; Swift, Shakespeare, Dickens and Sir Arthur Conan Doyle. Flitting from Soyinka to Senghor between Achebe and Pepper Clarke, I would search for something to help while away the holiday until it was time to return to school in England.

I don't even have to look to confirm that some of the books on the shelves in here are familiar; I too have accumulated a library of books by Chinua Achebe, by Wole Soyinka and by John Pepper Clarke. I also have two books by the grand old man of African letters, the former Senegalese poet, soldier, priest and president, Leopold Sedar Senghor. Monsieur Senghor was my father's ideal of a Renaissance man, *l'homme engagé* as Ken Saro-Wiwa liked to envisage himself. I've never actually read Senghor but I bought his books anyway. I am conscious that this room is something of a shrine to my father, an unconscious need to belong, to establish a connection with him and with home.

Was it fate or accident that compelled me to reconstruct my father's house in here? Who knows? Of course there are as many, probably more differences than similarities in the books on our shelves. I don't, for instance, share my father's passion for classic English literature. Shakespeare and Dickens have never captured my imagination as they did my father's. He was an Anglophile, a passion he developed as a schoolboy at his secondary school in Southern Nigeria. This love of things English has been bred into my family's genes; my great grandfather started it—he was the one who brought English missionaries to our village. I suspect it was the reason why his son, my grandfather, Jim Wiwa, has an English name. Papa later worked for the English trading conglomerate UAC (United African Company) as a translator but my father was the first one in my family to receive a formal English education. Through a government scholarship he went "abroad" to Umuahia, a town 125 kilometres from home where he was one of a handful of Ogoni students. It was at Umuahia that Ken Saro-Wiwa fell in love with all things English. Modelled on an English boarding school, Umuahia was run by expatriate teachers in the colonial service. By the time Ken Saro-Wiwa's first son was ready for secondary school, Nigeria had long since been independent from the British and the school system we inherited from our former masters had been abused by the ruinous politics of Nigeria. Which was why my father sent me to school in England.

I arrived in England on a bitterly, bitterly cold day in January 1978, and I spent the next 20 years trying to acclimatise. Although I was schooled in England, my life was divided between Africa and Europe and I floated between two worlds, charting the course that had been mapped out by my father's love of all things English and his fierce commitment to our home. If it was probably inevitable that I would reject Africa if only as a declaration of my independence from my father's politics, England, to a certain extent, also forced my hand.

England is an island, proud of its imperial history but the English are always fearful that foreigners will swamp its culture. So every immigrant is encouraged, overtly and covertly, to assimilate—to become one of us. It is a tradition and philosophy that the Anglo-Saxon has perfected during 1,000 years of conquest and assimilation. The strategy has served them so well that English is now the world's international language. A language whose original dictionary has been swamped by an influx of words and phrases annexed from other languages. Ralph Waldo Emerson once observed that "the English language is the sea which receives tributaries from every region under heaven." So like many other immigrants of an impressionable age, I was swept up into the English channel.

Twenty years in England moulded my identity. My accent, my values, my worldview—so much about me became anglicised. It wasn't until I was 26 years old that I began to question my emerging identity.

Up until then there had always been this vague, unexplored, uncomfortable and unspeakable feeling of shame, of betrayal that I identified more with European values than African ones. And so when my father's involvement in politics in Nigeria demanded that I repay the faith he had invested in me, I obliged him as any dutiful son would but I was aware that my involvement in my father's politics would have long-term consequences for my identity. The deeper I was drawn into his world the more resentful I became that so many of my choices in life had been motivated by a desire to escape his influence rather than what I actually wanted for myself. After he was murdered in November 1995, those feelings intensified. I was torn between my now politicised identity as Ken Saro-Wiwa's son and the apolitical, anglicised identity I had hidden behind in England. I was hovering between a country I had tried to leave behind and now wanted to forget and a country that was trying to shoehorn me into an identity that no longer fitted me. By the time I was 29 I had no idea who I was or what I wanted to be. I had no clear concept of where home was or to whom or to what I owed my allegiance. I was rootless, deracinated and adrift in the world.

In September 1997 I determined to resolve, once and for all, the dilemmas and competing claims on my identity.

I flew to Toronto to see an old friend. I'd known Mark Johnston from the time when we worked together on the campaign to try to save my father's life. Mark had returned to Toronto after my father was murdered, and when I confided to him that I was thinking of writing a book he put me in touch with Alberto Manguel.

When I returned to London, I dashed off a couple of chapters and sent them to Alberto. He was living in London at the time where he had edited an issue of *Index on Censorship* magazine featuring one of my father's short stories.

"Would you like me to be gentle or tough?" Alberto asked after reading my sample chapters.

"Be tough," I braved.

"Well, this is bullshit," he duly obliged. "When I hear you talk about your father," Alberto explained, "it makes the hairs on the back of my neck stand on end. These chapters don't do that for me," he said, thumbing the manuscript with a fastidious frown on his face.

I went away and had another go, writing and rewriting, trying to pour my anxieties onto the page. I went back to Alberto and he pointedly put the manuscript aside and patiently listened to me describing my dilemmas again. When I finished, he leaned back in his chair and stroked his beard.

"Hmm," he purred. "You haven't found your voice," he mused in his gentle lilting accent.

He suggested I write a letter to my dead father, and I left to look for my voice. In a sense life is all about this struggle to find a distinctive voice to call our own. In our voices you hear your influences; your parents, your role models, your community. My problem, in September 1997, was that I just couldn't decide what my authentic voice sounded like. Was I a Nigerian who had been educated in England? Or an Englishman who was born in Nigeria? Was it the middle-class accent and values I had picked up at my boarding schools or was it the Nigerian accent and values that spoke up instinctively when I was in the company of my African friends and family? What was my default accent?

I experimented, trying out my different voices, switching identities, chopping and changing, torturing and confusing the poor manuscript. During yet another anguished confession, Alberto wondered if I liked living in England. I told him I had nothing against the place but I was concerned that in England I was fixed as Ken Saro-Wiwa's son and people now had preconceptions of who I was or ought to be. And once you are pigeonholed in England it is a tough place to try to convince anyone that you have anything else to offer and I didn't particularly relish the prospect of spending the rest of my life being introduced as Ken Saro-Wiwa's son—especially as I was now a father myself.

Alberto wanted to know if I'd ever considered moving to Canada. I replied that I'd always had a soft spot for Canadians especially after the way Canadian writers and the Canadian government had adopted and spoken out in support of my father. I might have even explained that I'd once had a drunken premonition that I would one day live in Canada during my first visit to Canada in 1995 when I attended a PEN benefit in honour of my father. But when Alberto suggested that I should consider moving to Canada, that the government has a visa program that encourages writers and artists to come and work in Canada, I recoiled from the idea. I couldn't imagine upping sticks to a country I barely knew. But over the course of the next year the idea grew on me. The more I struggled to find my voice, the more I came to appreciate that a change of scene might help. So I began to reconsider. Especially as I kept running into Canada's growing literary profile. And the more I heard that this was due to Canada's openness to writers from all over the world, the more attractive the Canadian option became.

Which is what I was discussing with Mark Johnston on that beach in Cannes in October 1998.

In my mind's eye I am back there again and I can hear the waves washing up against the beach, the swish of the sea, rather like the sound of the wind rustling through the trees outside my window. Mark is once again explaining that Canada is proud of its reputation as a country where writers are encouraged to come to find their voice without losing their identity. He is saying something about a mosaic but I am staring out over the ocean towards Africa. I hear his pitch but I'm not sold on the idea. Not just yet. He says something about a UN statistic that he always brings up to impress me about his country. I would normally dismiss Canada right there but then impulsiveness grips me and within six months I will be living in Canada.

I sometimes wonder as I am staring out of the window here, at the U-turns, chance meetings, reckless gambles and inspired decisions on which our lives turn. Do we actually actively make choices or are we passive ciphers of the choices that fate imposes on us? Suppose I hadn't been on that beach in Cannes, with Africa so close and yet so far? Was it really some unconscious, paradoxical desire to return to Africa that sent me on this grand detour? Because of course the irony is that when I am in this room I actually feel closer to home, to Africa than I have ever done since I left.

When I look around the mess in here, the jumble of books, newspapers, passports, compact discs and photographs, I see a pattern in the rug. I see the outline of my face, I hear the sound of a voice, barely audible like the whisper of a faint voice carried on the wind. Take, for instance, the books on my shelves—they are not arranged in any particular order but I know, instinctively, where to find every title. There is a method to its madness because those books didn't get where they are by accident. I remember why I bought each book, why and when I placed them at some seemingly random place on the shelves.

When I was leaving England I had to prune my library. I had far too many books and I decided to leave behind the ones that had helped to construct the identity I was no longer comfortable in. I spent hours trying to decide which books to take and which to leave behind and yet I still ended up shipping a hundred titles over. Books are deceptively heavy and cost me far more than I could afford but I brought them anyway because I was moving to a place that encourages you to bring your past with you. You get a pretty hefty baggage allowance when you come to Canada.

I am scanning some of the titles on my shelves now. I see Rushdie's *Midnight's Children*, Rian Malan's *My Traitors Heart*, Octavio Paz's *The Labyrinth of Solitude*, V.S. Naipaul's *Enigma of Arrival*, James Joyce's *Ulysses*. There's Elias Canetti's *Auto Da Fe* and my favourite "uncles" Ralph Ellison: *Invisible Man*, Michael Ondaatje: *Running in the Family*, John Edgar Wideman: *Fatheralong* and Vargas Llosa's *The Storyteller*. Then there are more recent acquisitions like Pico Iyer's *The Global Soul*, Dionne Brand's *At the Full* and *Change of the Moon*, Don Gillmor's *The Desire of Every Living Thing*. Even the books that have been added since I arrived in Canada have a recurring theme: the quest for personal identity against the foreground of politics and the recurring echoes of history.

There are two books in here though that I always carry around with me wherever I travel. These two books contain a log of all the journeys I have made since 1995. My passports record some of the places I travelled on my father's behalf: to New Zealand; Canada and the U.S. There are many places like Germany, Austria, France, Belgium, Ireland where I didn't need a visa in my passport but I went to all these places in an effort save his life. Even after he was killed I carried on travelling, trying to understand what his life and death would mean to me. I went to Burma, to South Africa, back to Canada again and finally to Nigeria to bury him last year. I still travel a lot—sometimes on his behalf but increasingly on mine. Wherever I roam these days all roads lead back to Canada.

My passports also tell a different but connected story. In my Nigerian passport I am declared as Kenule Bornale Saro-Wiwa. In my British passport I am listed as Saro Kenule Bornale Wiwa. The official who issued my Nigerian passport last year informed me somewhat gleefully that he had to use the name that was on my previous Nigerian passport. So even though I had changed my name legally by deed poll in 1993, the Ken Saro-Wiwa name lives on in

Nigeria. I will soon be eligible for Canadian citizenship and I toy with the notion of reclaiming the name if I were to apply for a Canadian passport. It's only a fleeting thought though because the short answer to the question, why Canada? is that I came here to find out who Ken Wiwa is.

Canada, as it promised, has given me the space to reinvent or at least to discover myself and I now have a very clear sense of who this Ken Wiwa is and to whom and what he owes his allegiance. That said, I am also aware that deep down there will always be a Ken Saro-Wiwa in me.

I often shrink from the realisation that so much of my writing is self-centred but I also suffer from the delusion that my experience reflects a wider, universal, or at least, Canadian concern. The world is shrinking, people moving around so much, mingling, intermarrying, changing so quickly that we keep being told that we now live in a world without frontiers, in a global village. But I sometimes wonder in this brave new world whether it won't be more important than ever to root ourselves in something, to somewhere. We still need to fix our values in a coherent system of beliefs, to believe in something, an idea, a community of shared aspirations perhaps. We have to lay down a default identity that we turn to and cling to in times of stress and confusion and bewildering change. As James Baldwin once surmised, too much identity is a bad thing but too little can also be a problem. I imagine that's why the only shelf in my library that displays any semblance of order is the one devoted to my father's books and letters. Because my father roots me, reminds me of the place I came from. He is my default template, the clay that I mould in my own image. And so now that I have defined him, quantified his values and made sense of the questions he once posed to my sense of self, I can now look for my own answers. And when I am in here I feel reassured that he is close at hand, that I can reach over and re-read his words, look between the lines, talk to him and engage in a debate with him. When I am in here, I am in my father's study, I am also back in Africa. I am in Canada. I am at home.

There is a folder on the shelf of my father's books and in that folder is a letter he sent me from his detention cell. That letter contains the most important words my father ever wrote:

I don't mind you growing your children outside . . . you should use the advantages which your British experience has offered you to promote your African/Ogoniness. . . .

Those words have become my mission statement in life. They define and sustain me in my quest to fulfil my obligations to myself, my family, my father and my community. If Ken Saro-Wiwa had known how things would turn out for his first son, he probably would have substituted Canadian for British experience in that letter because it is from in here, in Canada, that I have found the space to express myself and promote my home.

Two Sides of the Globe, 1995

DENISE CHONG

During Citizenship Week in 1995, Denise Chong ruminated on her Chinese heritage and her Canadian inheritance.

South China at the turn of the century became the spout of the tea pot that was China. It poured out middle class peasants like my grandfather, who couldn't earn a living at home. He left behind a wife and child. My grandfather was 36 when exclusion came. Lonely and living a penurious existence, he worked at a sawmill on the mud flats of the Fraser River, where the Chinese were third on the pay scale behind "Whites" and "Hindus." With the door to Chinese immigration slammed shut, men like him didn't dare even go home for a visit, for fear Canada might bar their re-entry. With neither savings enough to go home for good, nor the means once in China to put rice in the mouths of his wife and child there, my grandfather wondered when, if ever, he could return to the bosom of a family. He decided to purchase a concubine, a second wife, to join him in Canada.

The concubine, at age 17, got into Canada on a lie. She got around the exclusion law in the only way possible: she presented the authorities with a Canadian birth certificate. It had belonged to a woman born in Ladner, British Columbia, and a middleman sold it to my grandfather at many times the price of the old head tax. Some years later, the concubine and my grandfather went back to China with their two Vancouver-born daughters. They lived for a time under the same roof as my grandfather's first wife. The concubine became pregnant. Eight months into her pregnancy, she decided to brave the long sea voyage back so that her third child could be born in Canada. [The] false Canadian birth certificate would get her in [again]. Accompanied by only my grandfather, she left China. Three days after the boat docked, on the second floor of a tenement on a back alley in Vancouver's Chinatown, she gave birth to my mother.

Canada remained inhospitable. Yet my grandparents *chose* to keep Canada in their future. Both gambled a heritage and family ties to take what they thought were better odds in the lottery of life. The gratitude owed them can perhaps best be expressed by my mother's brother in China—the son of my grandfather and his first wife. In the late 1980s, my mother and I found the family left behind. My uncle pressed a letter into my mother's hand on the last night of our visit. It read, in part, "As parents, who would not be concerned about the future of his or her children? I hope to get my children out of China to take root in Canada. Then, the roots of the tree will grow downwards and the leaves will be luxuriant. We will be fortunate, the children will be fortunate and our children's children will be fortunate. The family will be glorious and future generations will have a good foundation. . . ."

My own sense, four generations on, of being Canadian is one of belonging. I belong to a family. I belong to a community of values. I didn't get to choose my ancestors, but I can try to leave the world a better place for the generations that follow. The life I lead begins before and lingers after my time.

The past holds some moral authority over us. Rather than forget it, we must acknowledge that we have one, and learn the lessons of it. We have to be vigilant about looking past the stereotypes and seeing the contrasting truths. It means understanding that someone's grandfather didn't change the family name from French to English to forsake his heritage, but to make it easier to find a job. It means lifting the charge against the early Chinese of having no family values by seeing how the laws and history cleaved their families in two. It means going to the Legion and looking at a Sikh and seeing the veteran as well as the turban.

If we don't, we won't see that the layers of injustice cut deep. It happened in my own family. My grandfather couldn't afford a concubine. To repay the cost of my grandmother's false papers and passage to Canada, he indentured her as a tea house waitress. In the bachelor societies of the Chinatowns of their day, a *kay toi neu* was seen as one and the same as a prostitute—both were there to woo men to spend money. My grandmother would spend the rest of her lifetime trying to climb up from that bottom rung of society. I, too, condemned my *Popo*, until I learned what she had been fighting against all her life.

Despite the luck of my mother's birth, discrimination continued to cast a long shadow over her growing-up years. Her parents separated. In neither of their lifetimes would either find work outside Chinatown. My mother knew too well the path to the pawn shop where she accompanied her mother to translate as she bargained her jewelry to pay her gambling debts. The wall on my mother's side of the bed at the rooming house was wallpapered with academic certificates. My mother wanted to become a doctor. She didn't know that it would be years after her time before the faculty of medicine at the University of British Columbia would admit its first Chinese student. Despite the narrow confines of her life, the opportunity of education gave my mother a chance to dream.

Eventually, exclusion against Chinese immigration was lifted and other barriers of discrimination began to fall. My mother's generation was the last to grow up in Chinatown. Gradually, the Chinese became part of the larger society. In 1947, my mother no longer had to call herself Chinese. With exclusion lifted, and the new citizenship act that Canada brought in that same year, for the first time in her life my mother could call herself Canadian.

My parents walked out from the shadow of the past. They were determined to raise their five children as Canadians. In our own growing-up years in Prince George, my mother wanted us to be as robust as our playmates; she enriched the milk in our glasses with extra cream. My parents wanted us to take to heart the Canadian pastimes. They bought us skis to share among us. Every winter they bought us new used skates. There was a piano upstairs on which we learned to play *O Canada* for school assemblies. There was a hockey net in the basement so my brothers could practice for the pond.

My parents wanted us to understand that we were part of Canada's future. They instilled the importance of an education. They encouraged us to believe that individuals could make a difference. I remember when Mr. and Mrs. Diefenbaker came to Prince George. I remember when a dashing Pierre Trudeau made his first visit. My parents made sure we were turned out to greet every visiting dignitary. My grandparents, in their time, were barred from government jobs. I, their granddaughter, would come to work as senior economic advisor to Prime Minister Pierre Trudeau. . . .

My family story is about one family living on two sides of the globe, in a village in China and in the Chinatowns of the west coast of Canada. I knew I had to understand my grandparents' difficult and tangled decision to leave China for an unknown land. I had to understand the cultural baggage they brought, in order to see what they shed along the way and what they preserved. I had to see what they created anew as they acquired western sensibilities.

I also had to open the windows on the old Chinatowns in Canada. I had first to chip away at the layers of paint that stuck them shut, so intent had the former inhabitants been on shutting out inquiry. Some wondered why I'd want to write the story of my grandfather, who came a peasant and lived out his days alone in a rooming house. And why my grandmother, who lived by the wages and wits that came with being a *kay toi neu*? I see no honor lost in laying down the truth of their lives. It re-visits the once harsh verdict I myself had.

The same holds true for other leaves of the Canadian album. Often, the only ones whose memory is preserved are those who either prayed or worked hard, or both. But others are just as real, if not more so, with their strengths and weaknesses, triumphs and foibles. My story happens to take place in dingy rooming houses, alleyways and mah jong parlors in decaying Chinatowns. The backdrop of others may be the church basement, the union hall, school or hockey rink, or even the front porch. These stories, like mine, serve to illuminate Canada's social history. . . .

My grandfather's act of immigration to the new world and the determination of my grandmother, the girl who first came here as a *kay toi neu*, to chance the journey from China back to Canada so that my mother could be born here, will stand as a gift to all future generations of my family. Knowing they came hoping for a better life makes it easy to love both them and this country.

In the late 1980s, I would find myself in China, on a two-year stint living in Peking and working as a writer. In a letter to my mother in Prince George, I confessed that, despite the predictions of friends back in Canada, I was finding it difficult to feel any "Chineseness." My mother wrote back: "You're Canadian, not Chinese. Stop trying to feel anything." She was right. I stopped such contrivances. I was Canadian; it was that which embodied the values of my life.

Lessons in Patience

LAYLA SHARIF

Layla Sharif is an Afghan-born Canadian who left her homeland to escape the civil war. Immigrants are always at a disadvantage, she points out, not least in searching for work that matches their credentials.

Chances are you immigrated to Canada. If not you, then your parents or grandparents did. Immigrants built this nation because Canada has always welcomed those who want a better future, and because it has always required newcomers to maintain population levels and stimulate the economy. Most Canadians believe that everyone has the right to seek out and enjoy a life free from oppression and hardship and to find a better life for their families.

I immigrated to Canada from Afghanistan almost 14 years ago. It was not an easy trip and definitely not easy times. I came to Canada without my ten-year-old son and my husband and it took me almost three years and three months to sponsor and get them here, and we were finally reunited (actually I can give the exact days and hours but now that it's over, that doesn't matter any more). When I first came to Canada it was in the month of January. It was a cold and gloomy day. Dirty snow was everywhere BUT I was happy to have made it to Canada. My brother-in-law met me at the airport. On the way to his home, he kept on pointing out places and mentioning their names. I was so tired and at the same time too excited to hear what he was actually saying. The following day I wanted to start working right away. I did not know that you needed a SIN and work permit before you could actually work. That was my first lesson in being patient. Later I would use this to keep me focused on getting my family here as soon as possible. So believe me I know how difficult it is to be without your loved ones in a strange, new land. But for the sake of saving our lives we had to go through this.

Before I came to Canada I had only lived in my homeland the first 5 years of my life and returned when I was 10 or 11 for only one year. We left again and only returned when I finished my university. I have been fortunate to have travelled around the world with my father who was an ambassador of Afghanistan to Germany, Turkey, Pakistan, Japan, Russia and many other countries. I finished my high school in Japan, got my MA in Ukraine, former Soviet Union. I can speak almost 4 languages and I worked for the United Nations almost 6 years in Afghanistan.

But when I came to Canada and started to look for a job, like many other people, I was told that I have an impressive resume but did not have Canadian experience. Once I remember I was interviewed by a supervisor for a well-known company in Toronto. She talked to me for almost an hour; she was so impressed with my resume and background. But as she was wrapping up the interview she politely said that I have such a wonderful and impressive resume but unfortunately she cannot offer this job to me as I might have difficulties working since I don't have Canadian experience. So after six months and after mailing many, many resumes and going to many, many interviews, I finally found a job in an advertising agency. It was a good job, nice co-workers but not challenging enough for me and not in my field of study. I left it when they were downsizing the company and luckily at this time my husband's sponsorship application was almost done and they finally arrived in Canada. It was the most wonderful time of my life. I thought I was reborn and enjoyed every single day. The first thing you do, as you all know, is get your paperwork done—apply for OHIP, get SIN card, visit employment centers, get your resume done, etc. So that is how we spent our first several months. Yes, we also went sightseeing. I think I saw more of Toronto then when I was here before them.

Having my family here now it was time to find another job and by this time we had our baby daughter. So I started looking for a job that was near my place and had different shift work hours. My husband was studying English at this time. Since I had worked in my school library before, I wanted to see if could find a job at the public library. I applied and the following day they called me for an interview. I had to pass some written tests and finally was hired to work at the branch very close to home. This was a good job and I enjoyed it very much. I met people and I was [tested] almost every day—people would ask me about new books and if I had read it—what was my opinion etc. I had to recommend reading materials to clients of all ages, issue membership cards, explain the rules and regulations and so on. My knowledge of languages was very useful as I could speak to them in their language and explain to them, sometimes do translation for the head branch manager.

Because of my knowledge of languages I was asked once by a friend to come with her to see her MP and translate her concern to his staff. From then on I was asked to come and translate for others as well. I was finally offered a part-time job in the MP's office.

I have now been working full time for a Member of Parliament as his office manager for almost 6 years. Although the job is also not in my field of study, I have developed, over the course of the years, an excellent understanding of Canadian government, and the immigration system in particular. It has allowed me to meet new faces, analyze and think differently and be able to help others with immigration problems.

My husband's and my family—like all middle class families— were highly educated, honoured and wealthy. My husband was a university professor in Afghanistan. He was very well known in many circles but coming to Canada he lost that status. I come from a well-known family but once you are an immigrant none of that matters or is of interest to Canada. You have to start all over again.

Immigrants are always lost, always searching, struggling to improve, to understand. It takes them years to get back on their own two feet again.

Smugglers' Slaves, 2001

TOM FENNELL, WITH SHENG XUE

Maclean's *magazine exposes the tortured life of the illegal immigrant.*

The glare of a lightbulb dangling from the ceiling of his decrepit basement room casts a harsh light on the young illegal's life. A beetle scurries from under a mattress on the floor beneath a grimy window. Three shirts lie by a battered suitcase; a few Chinese-language magazines are piled in the corner. "Here they are," says Yong, a tall 21-year-old from the Chinese province of Fujian, pulling a small photo album from under the mattress. The pictures take him back to a happier time. In one, his mother straddles a motor scooter, in another, his father stands smiling in the sunshine. Yong longs to be with them, but it is an impossible dream. Last year, he paid $65,000 to be smuggled into Canada, via a route that took him to Burma and finally to Toronto, where he expected life to be much easier. Instead, to pay off the debt, he now works 12 gruelling hours a day butchering chickens in a Chinese-owned slaughterhouse. "I miss them so much," he sighs, gazing at the pictures of his family. "It is very hard."

Not far from Yong's, in a garment factory on the second floor of a century-old warehouse in Toronto's Chinatown, Ah-Zhen, 23, slumps at her sewing machine and breaks into tears. Like Yong, she works hard—night and day trying to raise enough money to pay back the smugglers who brought her to the promised land. They are not alone: over the past 10 years, almost 15,000 Chinese have entered Canada illegally and, after launching refugee claims, are now working for less than minimum wage on farms or in restaurants and factories. Lacking identification to open a bank account, they stuff their meagre earnings under their mattresses, only to hand a large part over to often-shady immigration consultants and lawyers working on their refugee claims—a process that can take years to complete. "I just wish I could make some money and go home," says Ah-Zhen, as she pulls another piece of black cloth from a bin beside her and tries again to feed the fabric under the needle. "My family got into deep debt because of me. Now we owe a lot of money to the smugglers and others. I dare not go back."

Those who have—sent back by the Canadian government for entering Canada illegally—face stiff fines and prison sentences. But despite the risks, and the hard life that usually awaits them here, the migrants keep coming, undaunted by the smugglers who will control their existence for years under threat of violence—making them, for all intents and purposes, little more than slaves. Since January, 1996, alone, nearly 7,000 Chinese have declared refugee status in Canada—most of them from Fujian province, which is on the east coast of China just north of Hong Kong, and whose people, desperate to escape poverty in an area where the average yearly income is about $2,000, have historically tended to go abroad to seek their fortune.

The great majority of them, like Yong and Ah-Zhen, entered the country illegally, arriving by plane in Vancouver or Toronto with fake documents. But others have come by more dangerous means. In 1999, nearly 600 people from Fujian arrived off the coast of British Columbia in four rusting ships. Hoping to slow the illegal flood, Canadian immigration officials clamped down; of the 600, 67 remain in custody pending refugee hearings, 272 were imprisoned and sent back to China after their refugee claims were dismissed, and 191 were released pending refugee hearings (of those, 149 have disappeared into the Fujianese community and warrants have been issued for their arrest). But the tough response has had little effect. According to Immigration Canada estimates, almost 2,000 Chinese will still enter the country this year as refugees—most of them illegally.

Immigration Minister Elinor Caplan visited Fujian last year to encourage the Chinese to clamp down on the smugglers. But according to a report published last week by the Canadian Security Intelligence Service, Canada can expect even more illegals to enter the country over the next five years. The report says that as the Chinese economy slows during that period, a growing number of unemployed people will try to buy their way into Canada. While Caplan did not comment on the CSIS report, she said the government hopes to introduce changes to the Immigration Act next year that could slow the flow of bogus refugees by allowing immigration officials to more easily detain people they believe are hiding their true identities. "It will contain important clarifications for the grounds for detention," said Caplan. "It also streamlines the process to be faster while remaining fair."

According to Det. Jim Fisher, Asian crime co-ordinator with the Vancouver police, snakeheads—as the smugglers are called—now charge as much as $100,000 to supply fake passports and visas and to arrange the passage to Canada. The demand is great. Wu, a lanky 31-year-old Fujianese who entered Canada illegally in 1999 at Toronto's Pearson International Airport, remembers the overwhelming response a smuggler received when he visited the city of Tianjin in southern Fujian. "They stormed the snakehead's home," says Wu, who currently works as a minimum-wage labourer on a Chinese construction gang in Toronto and asked that his full name not be used. "'Let me go—put me in a group,' they asked. No one put a gun to their heads."

Ottawa's crackdown has had one effect—it has forced smugglers to be far more cautious moving the Fujianese into Canada. Many illegals are now stranded in safe houses in Europe and South America, waiting to be moved to Canada. Ah-Zeng, 25, a waiter in a seafood restaurant sandwiched between two bars in Toronto's Chinatown, was fortunate: he arrived in 1998, with fake documents indicating he was the nephew of a Chinese man already living in Canada, and experienced few delays in his passage from Beijing. His brother has not been as lucky—Ah-Zeng, who is now a landed immigrant, says he has been detained in a safe house in Mexico City for almost a year. "He called me collect in October to say he hopes to be here soon," says Ah-Zeng, finally able to take an early-morning break after nearly

14 hours on his feet. Pulling a cigarette package from the pocket of his wrinkled white shirt, he adds: "I told him to go back to China, but he is desperate to come to Canada."

Desperation has its limits. Both smugglers and potential migrants now consider an ocean crossing too risky—and with good reason. Enforcers working for the snakeheads often accompany their human cargo and fear being caught at sea by authorities. But there are greater dangers. A number of Chinese illegals currently in Canada told *Maclean's* that, in 1999, a fifth boat crammed with people was also on its way towards British Columbia and sank, killing hundreds. Within the close-knit Fujianese community, some are now grieving for lost relatives and friends. "People saw 600 arrive in Canada," says Wu. "No one could see the others—who would never arrive."

A Muslim After September 11, 2001

SUHAIL ABUALSAMEED

For newly arrived Jordanian Suhail Abualsameed, the September 11, 2001, terrorist attacks on New York and Washington suddenly changed everything.

When I first did my immigration process and came to Canada, it wasn't much of a story of why I did come to Canada, and I didn't really realize what was my calling, if I might call it [that]. It was more or less a change of scenery, you know? I had the chance to come here and I thought, "What the hell? I have a lot to experience and see of the world, so why not?"

But . . . just a few months after I arrived here, 9/11 happened, and me being an Arab, a Muslim, was faced by a new reality. I suddenly understood where I am in this world and how I am perceived by other people. Although I never really identified as a Muslim, for example, I'm definitely not a religious person, I was forced to be seen and see myself as a Muslim. I had to reconsider my identity. The identity of being an immigrant, being a person of colour, being an Arab, being a Muslim, came to light. And that affected probably all of my processes from that day on, and what's happening in my life in Canada, because I by nature, like many Arabs, am a political person. And because of the work I do here, working with newcomer and immigrant queer youth, it got me into a scene where the politics play a large role in our life. I became more and more political, and more and more involved with the community and with the politics of being Arab, of being Muslim, and being queer at the same time. Suddenly I became the token of a queer Muslim, an Arab, and an immigrant—all of them together, two of them together, combined, separate—and started being invited to speak in public about it. Because of that, that I am being pushed in a way—unintentional, intentional, willing, and not being conscious about it. Being pushed to a direction where I am in the centre of politics that affect my community. I became involved very closely with the queer Muslim community, running support groups and organizing political forums and social activism.

Through that, through my work with Supporting Our Youth running the newcomer and immigrant youth program, doors started to open to me. Getting involved with Passages to Canada [a program run by Toronto's Dominion Institute], through that got me a new forum to go and speak to a much wider audience, and outside my community. I've been called a few times to talk about Canadian identity, which was funny that I am the immigrant that has been here for only four years. I've been invited to talk about Canadian identity, and how being an immigrant, being a Muslim, being a queer person, all that fits into the concept of identity. Being somebody who has been working in the community, and probably been more involved in the community than many of the native Canadians—native in the sense of people who were born and have lived here all of their lives. [I] obtained my concept of citizenship before I [got] my legal status of citizenship. I became Canadian, in many senses, although I don't identify as one. I became very integrated with this culture, and with the society in a much shorter period than many others.

All Mixed Up

ANDREW CHUNG

Andrew Chung, the child of a Chinese father and a "petite, blond, white woman from the foggy coast of Newfoundland," tells of his mixed-up life in an increasingly multi-ethnic, multiracial society.

There was a time when I couldn't eat Chinese food. Rice, sure, rice was okay. I'd been eating it ever since I could remember. I have pictures as a toddler slumped over in my high chair, sound asleep, with rice sticking to my face. My family still calls me "rice baby," as I prefer rice to potatoes, for instance, even with Christmas turkey dinner.

But real Chinese food was a different story. I'm not talking about the westernized Chinese fare like the pineapple chicken balls. I mean the real chow mein. When, in the city, we would go to a restaurant for dim sum, the gooey spare ribs, the slippery pork rolls, the meat-filled buns, the clammy chicken feet, and the watery congee with the thousand-year-old eggs would cross our table, I would sit, arms folded, as various astonishing animal parts rolled by, dazzling the eyes of the other patrons, horrifying my vanilla palate. And all I would eat would be . . . rice. I would make my parents take me to Mr. Submarine after the meal. Once, my father tricked me into eating pig stomach soup. I wondered aloud what the rubbery meat was in the delectable broth. But he didn't tell me until I had gobbled it all up. I was furious. The reality, however, is that I never gave the ribs, rolls, buns, or feet a chance. My gut instinct was this was not my kind of food. None of my friends from school ate this stuff. I didn't have it in me to be different.

These days, more than a decade later, I do. Have the spirit to be different, that is. It's just that this Canadian society I live in won't let me. Paradoxically, it won't let me be the same, either, leaving me in a kind of identity vacuum. Leaving me feeling like I don't truly belong. This happens even as we trumpet the richness of multiculturalism, and as we live in an increasingly multi-ethnic, multiracial society—

even as that reality is, quite unwittingly, spinning a legacy of mixed-race people like myself.

My father, a robust man with midnight-black hair and a strong jaw, is Chinese. He grew up in Hong Kong. A physician, he came to Canada for post-graduate training, where he met my mother, a petite, blond white woman from the foggy coast of Newfoundland. Of all places, they settled in Fairview, a tiny outcropping of 3,000 in northwest Alberta. It's a beautiful place, where the vistas are far and wide and flowing with canola and wheat, dotted with maple-lined coulees and carved with ancient hills. And it's far and different from any place they ever knew.

I am a half-breed, or a double-breed, depending on how you look at it. People like me have been historically called many things: mulatto, métis, halfie, two-toned, or less nicely, mule, malblanchi, mongrel. Some people make up labels for themselves. For a time, golf hero Tiger Woods called himself "cablinasian," an amalgam of Caucasian, black, Indian, and Asian. My own preferred neologism is "chewfie." I don't look Chinese. I've been called Spanish, Greek, Italian, Lebanese, or, as an Israeli friend once put it, "just plain white." Friends have said only my eyes, with their folded upper lids, appear remotely Chinese, upon close inspection.

According to my mother, my parents never experienced racism in Fairview, probably because my father held such a prominent, respected position in the community. Nor did they in Newfoundland, where they met. Where my mother grew up, there were no visible minorities. The only tensions, if any, were between Catholics and Protestants, worn-away vestiges of the Irish homeland. So my father was viewed with awe, rather than skepticism or racism. As my mother says, "He had two eyes, two arms, two feet, a nose and a mouth. He was just born in a different place." Still, I am sometimes astounded at my parents' audacity. When my parents were married it was 1968, one year after Virginia dropped its anti-miscegenation statute. Today, black men are still accused of selling out if they date white women. White men are guilty of orientalism for dating Asians, who are, if you buy the stereotype, docile, submissive, quiet. But my parents and those like them were at the cusp of a new racial era, one that is only today bearing its colourful fruit. There are more mixed marriages and common-law unions than ever in Canada; ergo, more mixed-race children than ever.

Like so many other mixed kids in this country, I grew up in an overwhelmingly white society. But I was never considered white. My brother and sister endured more racism in Fairview than did I. They both appear more Asian. But even I heard my share of name-calling. "Chink" was one. "Ching, Chang, Chung," like a taunting door chime, was another. Sometimes, as a child, and even as an adolescent, I regretted the fact that my family was different from those of my peers, all of whom were white. All kids hope and pray their parents don't say or do something embarrassing in front of their friends. But my sense of dread spawned from the race and culture of my father. I was sometimes embarrassed that he didn't speak perfect, unaccented English. I felt resentment over his Chinese features! I grew up feeling like my Asian side was not as valuable as my white. Tragically, I typically felt gratified when people would say I didn't look Chinese.

Insofar as I was never white, I was never Chinese, either. As a ten-year-old child on a visit to Hong Kong, I remember the humiliation and loneliness I felt, and my parents probably felt, as I cried and cried in the middle of a renowned restaurant. Like most Chinese eateries, it was frenetic, jam-packed, and loud, infused with the intoxicating aromas of dou-si, ginger, oyster, soya, and heated oil. Nobody was eating demurely. That's normal. Chinese people slurp and chomp and often eat with their mouths open. And meals are very communal. At a giant round table of dozens of relatives I hardly knew, some of them were picking unidentifiable food from various platters with *their* chopsticks covered in *their* saliva and placing the bits on *my* plate. As they gestured for me to eat, I became more and more anxious. I couldn't tell them to stop. I didn't know how. I couldn't eat. I didn't know what it was. I became desperate. And the tears started to pour. My relatives looked shocked, but more to the point, saddened. Here was a child who hardly looked Chinese, could speak not a word of Chinese, knew nothing of his family pedigree or broader Chinese history, and couldn't even eat the food. Here was a child who certainly didn't befit his surname.

As I got older, those resentments turned into disconnection. I felt utterly bereft of a Chinese heritage. Not looking the part, too, has made for some absurd encounters. Such as the one at Shoppers Drug Mart, where the blond clerk narrowed her eyebrows and brazenly queried, "Are you sure you're Mr. Chung?" Or at Blockbuster Video, where the clerk—Filipina, I think—was genuinely amused at my Chinese surname. "You don't look like, a, you know . . ." she ventured, a half-smirk etched along her jaw. These experiences have led to signature stage fright. When I sign a credit card slip, for instance, I experience a small paroxysm of panic, fearing the clerk will not believe I am the man who is signing the name on the card.

The clerk at a video game shop in the belly of Toronto's Eaton Centre once eyeballed me up and down suspiciously, causing a cold sweat to break out along my spine. Riled, I messed up my autograph. She demanded picture identification. I obliged, mostly to prove that I was not a criminal. The only thing I was guilty of, in fact, was being of mixed race. The ultimate irony is that such questioning also happened to me at a Benetton store, the clothier famous for its edgy multi-ethnic ads that asked the world to be colour-blind. Does this mean that mixed-up people like me can't even be comfortable in a retail outlet after which our generation is sometimes named?

This kind of identity skepticism is not a daily occurrence. But it has happened enough to colour almost every new encounter, to create an expectation for it. "What are you anyway? What's your background? Where are you from?" Whatever the question's permutation, it comes from friends, acquaintances, at work, in bars, clubs, on the subway. Ironically, it happens most often at checkout counter, the "blindness" of capitalism, its apotheosis of money exchange above all else, notwithstanding. Is this an innocent interaction? According to one of my friends, whose father is an Iraqi-Arab-Jew and whose mother is a British Caucasian, people pose the question because, simply, they're curious. With fair skin, deep brown eyes, and mahogany hair, she gets asked all the time. Scrutinized without mirth, it could be argued that there is something very menacing about it. After all, the very existence of questions proves that the answers matter. And this exchange, whether benign or not, makes a distinction between, and implies a difference among, the one asking and the one answering. It is, exactly, the process of "othering."

At the base of this process is the message that, when it comes to larger society, we are not included, like the batteries in an unpopular toy. My Arab-Caucasian friend concedes that when people question her about her background, they are acting as if they have the right to that personal information, something not automatically accorded in reverse. "My mother never had to think about whether she was black. She was," writes journalist and author Malcolm Gladwell, who is half-black, half-white and grew up in southern Ontario. "I have to think about it, and turn the issue over in my mind, and gaze in the mirror and wonder, as I was so memorably asked, *what* I am."

People still feel, today, they should know someone's background, that in a world becoming more and more complicated, they want neat and clean categories. This dynamic exacerbates a deeply personal and disconcerting symptom of non-belonging for mixed-race people in Canada, which begins in early childhood: that though they are spawned from two races, they feel they belong to neither. How is this possible, when Canada prides itself on multiculturalism, a policy made popular by Prime Minister Pierre Trudeau and championed by governments ever since? The celebrated idea behind the policy made Canada a place where nations of the world have set up satellites. And those nations are encouraged to remain as nations.

In this way, attachment to an ethnic "community"—real or imagined—is, at the very least, a possibility. For instance, my black Caribbean friends tell me that no matter where they go, they can "always find family." That means they always feel closer to home among other Caribbean people, and if not, other black people. There is a natural, unspoken, and unconditional kinship. For mixed-race people, time and time again, the practical result is that such a possibility is unavailable. An established "community" does not exist. No constituency is "natural." There is no "home."

For those who do not neatly fit in to one in the family of nations, there is trouble. Some might hypothesize a mixed-race person has the auspicious ability to claim part of multiple nations rather than just one, as in the census, for instance. But real-life experience proves the opposite: instead of fortifying a sense of identity, being mixed dilutes it. I can say I am Asian and Caucasian. But I don't feel I am either. I can say I am Canadian, but the "pure" nations within Canada don't recognize me.

My natural reaction is to try to fit in, at all costs. If neither side quite believes it, my knee-jerk inclination is to try harder. It's why I didn't cause a serious stir in the video game shop, didn't explain to the ignorant clerk my hydra-headed racial roots or the changing philosophical ideas of mixed race. Or why I said nothing when I was in a taxi recently in Toronto and we had to cut through Chinatown. "These fucking Chinese!" the Caucasian cabbie screamed. "Not one of them can drive!" He was clearly unaware of the "Chinese" in his midst.

For many of us, it thus becomes a cycle of self-questioning and self-hatred, confusion and a Durkheim-worthy sense of rootlessness. We can try, as citizenship demands, to take comfort in the civic rule of law and our constitution as our source of belonging. But in a state of immigrants where nations are so clearly defined—more than 200 of them—it feels unreal. We can try to imagine our community. But that's unreal as well. Where's mixed-race Barbie or G.I. Joe? Where are the sitcoms or films about mixed-race people and their experiences? Sure, there are stories about mixed relationships, going back to Shakespeare's *Othello*. To this day, however, mixed relationships are still viewed as a novelty. The constant surprise and confusion on the part of so many upon encountering someone of mixed race provide evidence that we cannot get beyond the baseness of race in Canada. Our multicultural policy, too, has made the idea of ethnic kinship perhaps more important than it otherwise would be.

I have never been the same as everyone else: never truly accepted as white, never truly as Asian. In a country that supposedly celebrates difference, I have never been allowed to be different, either, for the very same reason: I've never truly been accepted as someone who is neither white nor Asian. Therein lies the frustrating, discomfiting paradox that is the life of a mixed-race person in Canada. Official multiculturalism, unfortunately, does not imply mixed culturalism.

While multiculturalism in Canada hasn't done much for mixed-race people, it would not be hard to change this. In my view, the decades-old policy of official multiculturalism in Canada is an outmoded concept that needs renovation. It does not yet recognize the emerging reality of mixed-race citizens. Quite apart from encouraging the successful cultural retention of the state's many nations, multiculturalism must now be flexible enough to accommodate the blurring of boundaries. At the very least, just as the government recognizes the individual races and ethnic groups in the country, it must make an effort to recognize, even market, those who fall in between.

As I mature, the very notion of *difference*, of being different, is becoming a source of pride. I feel proud that my mother is white, my father Asian. I feel proud of the way I look; that, sometimes, I am considered a mystery. And it's possible to look to the future with a hint of optimism. There are more and more organizations that deal with the reality of mixed race. There are campus interracial support groups, especially in the United States. And the Internet, while far from fostering a nation, is at least a proto-organizer, implying that we are not alone. And as the numbers of mixed-race people continue to grow, as Canada's census indicates, the mixed-race voice will only grow louder. The beginnings, one might say, of belonging.

We Children of Immigrants, 2003

MADELEINE THIEN

The author daughter of Malaysian-Canadian immigrants moved from Canada to Holland, herself taking on the perspective of the emigrant.

As I write this, I am sitting in a small flat in the village of Scharnegoutum, in the province of Fryslân, in the rural north of the Netherlands. My fiancé, a Dutch citizen, and I, the daughter of Malaysian-Canadian immigrants, moved to Holland last year. At the age of 29, it was my first experience of emigration, enacted almost 30 years after my parents immigrated to Canada in 1974.

Here, in the rural north, the lingua franca is not Dutch but Frisian, a surviving but distant relative of old English. A year of living here and I can speak passable Dutch, but to live in a language that is not your own is difficult, lonely and very humbling. When I think of Vancouver, I remember how it feels to be at home in a place, to be among the landmarks of childhood that are engraved in my memory, that will not be replaced by another country.

My mother was 30 years old, and had two children, when she emigrated to Canada. She had grown up in Kowloon, Hong Kong, not far from the gambling dens and neon lights of Mong Kok district. She went to school in Australia, where she met my father. They settled in East Malaysia, lived there for a few years, and then decided to throw chance to the wind and immigrate to Canada. It is too late now to ask her what she hoped to find in Canada, though I think that most children of immigrants instinctively know the answer to that question. It's written upon our childhoods, and is played out in the present existence that my siblings and I are now living.

To say that my mother hoped to find a better life is to fall back on a cliché that still holds true. In the 28 years that she lived in Canada, my mother returned to Hong Kong only twice: once, when I was a child, and once, to celebrate her father's 80th birthday. My mother did not like Hong Kong. She loved the expanse of Canada, the beauty of Vancouver and the surrounding islands, the landscapes marked by the footprints of glaciers. "When you are famous," she used to say, "you can buy me a little house on the Sunshine Coast."

For the last decade of her life, she worked as a purchasing manager for Canfor Corp., and travelled extensively to the lumber mills of the province. I will always remember the incongruity of my mother, a petite, laughing Chinese woman, who, for her work, always carried a construction hardhat in the trunk of her car. She died in Prince George last year, a world away from the geography of Hong Kong.

A few months ago, my fiancé and I went into a souvenir shop in Leeuwarden, the capital of Fryslân. We fell into a discussion with the shop owner about immigration, race, and national identity. My fiancé, who had lived in Canada for eight years, was describing, with enthusiasm, the multicultural city of Vancouver. The shop owner frowned and shook his head. "The foreigners in Canada," he said, "will never dream in Canadian."

There is a saying in Dutch: Never do you forget the language in which your mother loved you. For me, that language is English. Like many new immigrants, my parents raised my siblings and me to speak and think in the language of the new home. My mother watched in quiet curiosity as I hoarded books from the library. Like my sister's daughter, who is now 11, I read at the breakfast table, in the car, on the bus, even while walking. She must have been certain that I dreamed in English because it was the only language that I had, and the one in which she had loved me.

In Leeuwarden that day, I told the shop owner, *Maar ik droom in Canadese* [But, I dream in Canadian], but he didn't really believe me, and I didn't have the language to explain how this could be.

When my parents arrived in Canada in 1974, neither one had ever set foot in this country before. One of my mother's sisters was already settled here, and so there was family to welcome them. I was born just a few months later, an automatic Canadian, the only one in my family who never required immigration papers.

I can't speak for all immigrants, but it seems to me that in our family there was a hope that was never explicitly stated. And I think that hope was to be regarded as being deserving of their new citizenship, of being considered equal, not by themselves, but in the eyes of those around them.

My mother fretted over her English, something that surprises me still because it was near perfect. My sister and I were enrolled in Chinese language classes, Chinese calligraphy, dance and painting, in addition to piano, ballet, acrobatics, swimming and tap dancing. We performed in Chinese New Year festivals and in parades; I was a toy soldier in a National Ballet production of *The Nutcracker*. My mother believed that all the opportunities of the world were here, and all we had to do was open our hands and grasp them.

Living in the rural Netherlands this past year has been difficult. On the streets, I am regularly confronted by racial slurs, something that I have not experienced in Canada since I was a child. In social life, such is the state of my Dutch that personal and complex conversations are difficult. I express myself with the vocabulary of a child, and, as a result, am sometimes treated as one. In my head, I reassure myself that I am more than I appear to be on the surface. I hold onto the person I know I am, as I was in another country, another time.

I wish that I could confide in my mother because I know, with certainty that she would understand. In the end, we only want to be free to live our lives as we choose. Immigration is part of a conversation that is necessary in our increasingly globalized world: Who has the right to seek a better life? And how does one enact that right?

In his book, *The Warrior's Honour*, Michael Ignatieff writes about the construction of national identity, and of a nation's abiding myths. He writes toward the hope of individuals coming awake, "to come to yourself, to force a separation between what the tribe told you to be and what you truly were."

When I say that my mother dreamed in Canadian, it is part of an expression of hope in the potential of the Canadian Charter of Rights and Freedoms, and in the individual human rights and obligations that this document entails. The Charter does not express the society that we have, in my opinion, but the society we glimpse, and that we each create in our day-to-day choices, and in the actions we take within our communities. Where a true multicultural society exists in Canada, it exists in the choices and consciousness of the people, to see minor difference for what it is, and to know that the rights we hold are equal.

For as long as I can remember, my mother would finish her day job, and then go to teach business courses in the community colleges. She helped to start a support group for new immigrants. She seemed to move effortlessly through myriad circles of Canadian society. It was not effortless, of course. My mother looked at the opportunities, the gains and losses available to her, and she chose. Such choosing brought both heartbreak and joy to her life. In doing so, she claimed a place in the old Canada, and helped to bring about the new. . . .

We children of immigrants often seek to return to the country that our parents have left behind. I have made my own wanderings through Malaysia, through Hong Kong and China. We know there is something to be recovered, we want to open what our parents have closed, we are ever curious. I make these journeys not because I hold onto the belief that there is another place and culture in which I might be more at home, but because I place my trust in empathy, in what Michael Ignatieff describes as the possibility that "human understanding is capable of transcending the bell jars of separate identities."

I want to understand. I hope that by understanding, I too will be able to choose wisely.

In the end, the old question remains. What is a good life, and how do we seek it? In this time and place, the act of immigration, as well as our attitude towards immigration, is one way of trying to answer that question. In the course of her life, I think that my mother found the answer in Canada. I follow after, carrying the same question.

Giving Up on Canada

MARINA JIMENEZ

A star immigrant gives up on Canada.

With great reluctance, Umesh Yalavarthy, a physician from southern India, is giving up on the Canadian dream. He and his wife moved to Toronto 2 1/2 years ago. Young, educated and fluent in English, they were ideal immigrants, according to Canada's recruitment plan.

His wife, a chemist, qualified under the point system that seeks to bring professionals to Canada. She sponsored her husband, a recent graduate in family medicine, who expected he would obtain his medical licence here without a problem. Dr. Yalavarthy, 27, knew Canada had a dire shortage of doctors and was in particular need of family physicians in rural areas. He was prepared to go anywhere.

He passed the Medical Council of Canada evaluating exams. However, three years later, he still couldn't obtain a residency position to repeat the training he had just finished in Hyderabad. There were more than 2,000 foreign-trained doctors vying for just 200 spots.

Turns out, the elusive residency post was much more attainable south of the border. This spring, Dr. Yalavarthy will leave the multicultural milieu of Toronto for Chattanooga, Tenn., a city less than one-tenth Toronto's size and in the southern Appalachian Mountains, where hardly any foreigners live. He will become a resident in internal medicine at a hospital there.

"I really love Toronto, and if they ever let me practise here I'll be happy to come back. Our dream was not to emigrate to Tennessee. It was to emigrate to Canada. We have lots of friends here," said Dr. Yalavarthy, whose wife and newborn daughter will join him in a few months. "But in Canada they doubt our credentials. I think that is unfair. I was one of the top students in my college. In the U.S., if you score well on the exams, you can get a residency to repeat your training."

My Two Countries

MARGARET WENTE

> *Born in the United States, Margaret Wente, a columnist for the* Toronto Globe and Mail, *contemplates her mixed identity and compares her two countries.*

You can always tell when you've crossed the border into America. Every little airport has at least one heavily armed man in combat uniform, ready to protect the homeland. Those big weapons, prominently displayed, always give me a jolt. They remind me that I'm in a country that's still at war.

Last week, I flew down to North Carolina to spend a few days on vacation with the American half of my family. Tobacco made North Carolina rich, and now high tech and research are making it richer. It is not like any place in Canada at all, except perhaps Alberta. Everywhere you go, there are fireworks for sale, along with great southern barbecue. The supermarkets are stocked with aisles and aisles of fabulous, cheap California wine.

"Don't put magazines in your suitcase if you don't want it opened," warned my American sister, Carrie. She works as a baggage inspector at O'Hare, searching checked luggage that looks suspicious. Her job didn't exist before 9/11. Now she's protecting the homeland, too. She explained that, on the X-ray machines, magazines look like plastic explosives that have melted slightly at the edges. She's never found any explosives, but she tells amusing stories about the amazing array of sex toys that people carry around.

My family and I don't talk much about politics, which is just as well. I am probably more politically conservative than any of them.

My dad thinks George Bush is the worst president of all time. Whenever he e-mails me, he always signs off: "George Bush is an asshole. Love, Pops." He wishes he could move to Canada.

My other American sister, Carol, is busy raising four young kids and doesn't have much time to worry about politics. She's more concerned about bad influences on TV, and tries to make sure her kids watch programs that have a moral point. She recently joined a local Baptist church, and has been born again.

One of my Canadian nieces came to North Carolina, too. Her boyfriend didn't come because he's boycotting America on principle.

Because I'm a Canadian of American descent, this time of year, between July 1 and 4, always reminds me of my mixed identity. Like most people whose lives have straddled the border, my feelings about my two countries are also mixed. There are many things I admire about the United States. Despite its sins and missteps, I think it is the greatest force for good the world has ever known. There's also plenty about Canada that drives me nuts, starting with our national sanctimony complex. Clifford Krauss, who reports on Canada for *The New York Times*, is dead-on when be describes Canada as a dictatorship of virtue.

And yet, I've never felt happier to live here.

In the U.S., 40 states have passed laws banning same-sex marriage. In Virginia, where my dad lives, same-sex partners are barred from basic pension rights and can't even help make medical decisions for their loved ones. Here, in Canada, they can get married. Canadians are thoroughly fed up with this story by now. But it made headlines around the world, and the fact of it still astonishes me. It makes me proud for us. And even though some people are troubled by same-sex marriage and others are bitterly opposed, it's worth remembering that gay couples in Canada had already achieved a legal and moral status they have almost nowhere in America.

In the U.S., more than 20 states are looking for ways to sneak creationism back into the curriculum. In Canada, radical educators are looking for ways to sneak phonics back into the curriculum.

In the U.S., the abortion wars are still raging, and an activist Supreme Court might repeal Roe v. Wade. In Canada, Henry Morgentaler got an honorary degree from a major university, and an activist

Supreme Court has opened the door to sweeping health-care reform.

The U.S. is on a tear of fiscal recklessness that will haunt it for a generation. Canada probably will be counting its surpluses for years to come.

The U.S. is piling up future pension and medicare entitlements it can't possibly meet. Canada has the best-financed public pension plan in the world.

The U.S. has a growing oil-supply problem. We're up to our wazoo in oil.

The U.S. is the most hated and feared country in the world. When you're the world's only superpower, it goes with the territory. Nobody hates Canada because nobody cares about Canada one way or another. We don't count for much in the world, but, in some ways, that's a good thing. Nations that don't count for much are less likely to need men with weapons guarding every little airport.

Don't bother getting smug about all this. If you feel the urge, just remind yourself about the embarrassment that is Ottawa. Much of our good fortune came our way by luck, not design, and I often think we're rich despite ourselves. We have the immense good luck to share the continent with the wealthiest, most successful and most benign (yes, benign) empire in the history of the world. We were so inconsequential that they never bothered to try to take us over after 1814. They never even bothered to extract levies for defending us. We're like the obscure junior cousins of a fabulously powerful family. We get to share the wealth, but not the headaches, and they supply the protection. And we get the luxury of griping about how they screw things up. What could be better?

America is like family to me. Our lives are inextricably entwined in complicated ways. I love them, and sometimes they drive me nuts. They're wonderful to visit, but I wouldn't want to live with them any more.

When I flew back to Toronto from the U.S., I was careful not to pack my magazines. When I arrived, there were no men with guns. The signs above the customs officials said, "Welcome to Canada/ Bienvenue à Canada." I was happy to be home.

Brazilian and Canadian

ADRIANA RIO BRANCO NABUCO DE GOUVÊA

Adriana de Gouvêa felt not between two places, but in both places—imperfectly so.

I suspect that among the millions of immigrants living in Canada today, I am the only one who can claim that she came to Canada because of box jellyfish. If it wasn't for box jellyfish, I would not be a Canadian citizen today.

Nine years ago my friend Flávia and I were planning a holiday trip to Australia. Our goal was to spend the bulk of our time on the coast. Having only recently acquired a scuba-diving licence, I was looking forward to exploring the underwater paradise of the Great Barrier Reef. When sharing our plans with a friend, we found out that our trip would fall in the middle of box jellyfish season in Australia. Consider the following description of the effects of a box jellyfish sting: "You have virtually no chance of surviving the venomous sting, unless treated immediately. The pain is so excruciating and overwhelming that you would most likely go into shock and drown before reaching the shore." We had no second thoughts about changing our itinerary. With Australia ruled out, Bali was the chosen destination.

What does all this have to do with immigrating to Canada? In Bali I met and fell in love with a Canadian, whom I ended up marrying two and a half years later. It was to be with him that I left my native country of Brazil to live in Canada. I suppose I could say that I came to Canada because I fell in love with a Canadian, but if it wasn't for box jellyfish. . . .

I didn't think much before deciding to move to Canada. A hopeless romantic, I concluded that since I had found my soul mate, the natural thing to do after almost two years of a long-distance relationship involving countless miles of international travel—we managed to meet almost every month—was to move to Canada. I had no specific expectations of what my life would be like in Canada, except that Ross and I would "live happily ever after." That was enough for me; I didn't really worry about the details.

So on October 12, 1998, at age twenty-seven, I left my country, my job, my family, and my friends and got on a plane to move to Ottawa. The days that preceded my departure were not easy. It was one goodbye after the other, one harder than the last; each time I felt that a piece of me was being torn away. The impulsiveness of my decision and my complete absence of rationality were finally catching up with me. I had lived abroad before, had travelled around the world, had spent long periods away from Brazil and from family and friends, but for the first time there was a sense of permanency that I had never felt. I wasn't *travelling* to a foreign country, I was *moving* to one, and that only hit me on the eve of my departure.

I have always thought of the world as a small place and never felt the need to be anchored to my native country. I was born and raised in Brazil, but had the opportunity to live in the United States for a couple of years, in Japan for a few months, and to travel to countries in Latin America, Europe, and Asia. I enjoyed being in different places, learning new languages, and meeting people from different cultures.

Whether the impetus to travel the world was a result of "nature" or "nurture," I don't know; both pointed me in that direction. There are several cosmopolitan people in my family. My great-grandmother was the daughter of a Polish woman and Russian man who immigrated to Argentina, where she was born. She was educated in Germany, and later married a Brazilian diplomat. Her daughter—my grandmother—spent her childhood hopping around the world, moving around as her father got assigned to Brazilian consulates and embassies in different countries. She must have liked the itinerant life, since she married a Brazilian diplomat, my grandfather. As a consequence, my father grew up all over South America, Africa, and Europe and can speak five languages. On my mother's side of the family there is also plenty of cultural melange: my maternal grandmother, for instance, grew up in France and, even though her parents were Brazilian, she could not really speak Portuguese until she was eighteen, when they moved to Brazil. With a family history full of stories such as these, and being the result of a genetic fruit salad—I can say that I am of Portuguese, Russian, Polish, Belgian, Amerindian, and Scottish blood, just taking into consideration the ancestors that have been captured in existing family trees—no wonder I've always felt somewhat of a cosmopolitan myself.

When I moved to Canada, I knew very little about the country. The school curriculum in Brazil does not pay much attention to Canada, and neither does the Brazilian media. As I was getting ready to leave Brazil, a friend gave me a little book, *Canada: A Country to Discover*, which he had picked up at the local Canadian consulate. As I flipped through the pages of the book, I learned about "the land," "the regions," "the people," "the government," "the economy," "the culture," and "Canada and the world." I read about bilingualism, multiculturalism, internationalism, and all the other Canadian "isms" (with the exception of "separatism"). What a great place to live, I thought. As a history buff, I had also decided to purchase a book on Canadian history to avoid looking too ignorant in my new environment.

As soon as I settled down, I began to plan my new life. I enrolled in university and, in spite of doubting my ability to succeed given the fact that I would have to study in my second language, things went well. Living in a city as culturally diverse as Ottawa, I certainly did not feel like a fish out of water. In my daily life, everywhere I went, I encountered immigrants from all corners of the world. From the beginning it became clear to me that there were many different ways to be Canadian and to be considered one.

Language turned out to be my strongest weapon in the process of adapting to my Canadian life. If it wasn't for my language skills, I wouldn't have been able to adapt with relative ease, understanding what others were saying, making myself understood, being able to watch TV, read the paper, study, and work. I started to learn English when I was seven years old. By the time I was ten I could understand my parents when they spoke in English to say things that they didn't want the kids to understand. I managed to keep this a secret for a while, but was eventually caught. By the time I moved to Ottawa, I could speak English fluently and could read and write in English as well as I could in my native language. I dream and think in both languages, and when I stub my toe it's 50-50 on which language the obscenity that I utter will be in.

The problem, however, is that although I am proficient in both languages, I am not 100 percent natural in either of them. In English, I speak with an accent and there are always times when I can't find the appropriate word or expression. When I'm nervous, all of a sudden I start speaking awkwardly and with a heavier accent. Because in Canada I hardly ever have the opportunity to speak Portuguese, I ended up losing some of the naturalness when speaking my native language. It is very disconcerting when I talk to my Brazilian friends and family on the phone and I can't find the right words to express myself or choose words that sound unnatural. Sometimes I even end up having to insert English words in the middle of a Portuguese sentence. How ironic is this: I'm unlearning my mother tongue.

Getting used to living in Canada was much easier than getting used to living without Brazil. As soon as I settled down in Ottawa, I began to realize that I was getting attached to symbols of Brazilian identity that had never before been too important to me. As a student of public history, I've read and written about "imagined communities" and "invented traditions" at the collective level; it seems to me that I am doing the same at the individual level. Each time I go back to Brazil to visit, I search for little bits of Brazil that I can bring back to Canada with me: books, photographs, decorative objects, CDs, spices, and as many kilos of Brazilian coffee as I can fit in my baggage.

In Canada, I began to listen to Brazilian popular music more than ever before, to read profusely on Brazilian history, decorate my house with Brazilian folk art, and watch the daily hour of Brazilian television programming on the multicultural channel. I also began to get curious about my family history. Collecting family trees, old photographs, and history books on my ancestors, I felt that I was holding on to my identity. Even though I was comfortable and felt at home in my Canadian environment, to feel rooted I needed to be surrounded by these symbols of "Brazilianess." If I didn't have these symbols, I'd be lost.

Removed from my "natural habitat," I began to reflect on what makes me a Brazilian. Why is it that, for instance, even though I don't particularly care about soccer, during the World Cup I put on my Brazil soccer jersey (and make my husband put on his) and turn into a hysterical soccer fan. I find myself acting as a "typical Brazilian," getting nervous, jumping on the couch, excited, yelling at the television set, and feeling that the outcome of the games really matters to me. For someone who is completely oblivious to any other sporting modality or event, this is a strange phenomenon. What I like about the World Cup craze is the feeling of unity, and knowing that every Brazilian (this is not an exaggeration) will be watching the games, feeling proud together if we win, feeling heartbroken if we lose. Even when I'm alone at home I still act crazy when watching World Cup games. I feel genuinely Brazilian.

If the soccer instinct comes naturally, other things don't. One day I accompanied a Brazilian friend, who also lives in Ottawa, to the rehearsal of a music group called Samba Ottawa, composed of Canadians and Brazilians who share their love for the traditional percussion-based Afro-Brazilian rhythm. Someone handed me a maraca, and I joined in enthusiastically, feeling more Brazilian than ever. An hour into the event, my head started to hurt, and it suddenly dawned on me that I had never been particularly fond of samba. The next hour dragged on as I realized how silly it was for me to try to "act Brazilian" when this particular aspect of Brazilian culture had never really been a part of my life.

For someone who has immigrated alone, as I have, the most difficult part of moving to a new country is to leave family and friends behind. In my second year in Canada, I got a phone call from my brother telling me that my father had just found out that he had cancer and was going to have surgery in three days; it was a high-risk procedure and there was a chance that he would not survive (thankfully, he did). And here I was, thousands of miles away, in shock and feeling helpless. Even though this was the busiest travel season of the year—just before Christmas—a kind travel agent was able to get me on a flight the next day. I was fortunate to be able to afford the ticket and couldn't help wondering how difficult it would be for immigrants who leave their families behind and don't have the means to go back when they want to or need to. I also couldn't help wondering about the many future occasions when I would want or need to be by my family's side; would I always be able to go?

Through the seven years I've been living in Canada, I've missed countless weddings, christenings, birthdays, and holiday celebrations with my Brazilian family and friends. Today is my grandmother's eighty-ninth birthday. As I am writing this, I know that my whole family is with her; my mother, sister, brothers, uncles, aunts, cousins, and the rest of my very large family are all gathered at my grandmother's place, eating, drinking, catching up, gossiping, and laughing. At times like this I ask myself how much longer I can go on missing these family moments that were always so important to me, even though there were times when I took them for granted. When I spoke to my grandmother on the phone earlier today, she told me that I would have to be there next year when she celebrates her ninetieth birthday. I didn't tell her this, but I don't know if I will be able to.

I now see Brazil with different eyes (Canadian eyes?). When visiting my native city of Rio de Janeiro, I notice things that I have never paid attention to before; there is a sense of novelty, of awe. I never get tired of staring at the ocean, admiring the lush vegetation, and observing the different faces and behaviours. All these things that were always there when I was growing up seem new and exciting to me now; they look "exotic." When I am in Rio I feel both at home and as a tourist. I don't try to make sense of this; I just accept the paradox.

Canada has been good to me. I've been accepted as an immigrant and later as a citizen with relative ease. I've been able to study, work in the fields that I have chosen, and always felt respected and welcome. Never did anyone question my right to do anything that any other Canadian—born in Canada or otherwise—has the right to do.

I officially became a Canadian citizen in 2004, in a ceremony led by Immigration Judge Susanne Pinel, who is best known as children's entertainer "Marie-Soleil." This was not my first encounter with "Marie-Soleil"; two years earlier, she was the keynote speaker at my graduation from teacher's college and shook my hand after I received my diploma. Because Canada respects the right to dual citizenship, I was allowed to remain Brazilian as I became Canadian. The citizenship ceremony was friendly and informal—very Canadian. Judge "Marie-Soleil" invited the children to join her on stage and gave them little Canadian flags to wave while we all sang "O Canada." By then, I could sing the anthem in English and French and did so very proudly. I got goosebumps, got teary and all. I had sung the anthem many times before, but that was the first time I did it as a Canadian. It meant something to me. For the first time I felt Canadian . . . Brazilian and Canadian.

My Disjointed Life

TOU CHU DOU LYNHIAVU

How fortunate Tou Chu Dou Lynhiavu was to have found Canada, but how full of mixed emotions—thankfulness, yes, but also with indelible memories of Laos's tragic history and the ambivalent welcome of his adopted country.

I can only and sporadically remember fleeting episodes of my childhood and my youth. Nevertheless, they remain vivid in my mind, moments frozen in time, despite space and time. They are not a series of fading picturesque paintings or photos hanging on the wall. They are an integral part of my existence. Back in Laos, my parents had a decent life. Born a Hmong (an ethnic minority in Laos), I was fortunate enough to learn my mother tongue, Laotian, French, and Thai. During my most formative years, my father was never really around. War and duty always took him away from the family home.

In 1975, Lane Xang (the Land of the Million Elephants and White Parasol, the historical name of Laos) died with the abolition of the 600-year-old Laotian monarchy. All the familiar institutions disappeared over night. The Pathet Lao communist regime took over. Most Laotians who worked for and defended the monarchical regime tried to escape. Many crossed the Mekong River to Thailand. Others walked through the jungle. In their journey, the Laotians themselves created their own trails, filled with blood, deaths, sweat, tears, and bitterness. Those trails were littered with torn clothes and precious personal and family belongings. Many made it to safety. Some did not. A few lucky individuals managed to bury their loved ones hastily in shallow graves. Others were simply left behind, barely covered with leaves. Those who drowned simply returned to nature.

I left Laos in 1979 and became a refugee. I stayed in Thailand for a full year while my parents and my siblings were still in Laos. It was a lonely time. In the refugee camp, I played soccer nearly every day and all day. I had never thought that the additional soccer skills and techniques I learned a quarter of a century ago would later prove useful when my wife volunteered me as a soccer coach for the Gloucester and Cumberland Soccer Associations in Ottawa. Coaching soccer gives me an opportunity to play with my children and to see them, along with those of others, grow up. I am very happy that their childhood and innocence have not been brutally stolen.

My parents in Laos were full of fears and uncertainties, but prayed that my two uncles who were sent to "re-education" camps would be released soon. Staying, they hoped, would indicate their loyalty to the new political masters and would shorten the imprisonment of my uncles. Days turned into months. Months turned into years. They never came back. Survivors of these camps told my family years after we had settled in Canada how my uncles died. My uncle Ly Cheu died of ill treatment and malnutrition. He was forced to eat grass and shrubs while being subjected to a daily routine of hard physical labour. My uncle Lyteck, too, endured torture. The Pathet Lao slashed his skeleton body, rubbed salt and pepper onto his wounds, bound his hands together behind his back, tied a rope around his neck, as if he was an untamed beast, and put him out in the field, under an unforgiving sun for three days and three chilling nights. Deprived of food and water and despite a beaten body, he refused to die. In the end, the Pathet Lao had to murder him. They also imprisoned my father. Beaten several times and buried right up to the neck for several days, he barely survived the abuse and torture. In 1980, my family joined me in Thailand.

I came to Canada with my parents, six brothers, and two sisters the next year. Never had it crossed my mind that I would become a Canadian. When the Boeing 747 took off from Bangkok, it was a hot and humid day, with a temperature in the mid-30 degrees Celsius. We were looking forward to our journey. We had some knowledge of Canada, in part because Canada had participated in a peacekeeping operation in Laos for nearly twenty years. But I do not have any clear recollection whether we, as refugees, had any pamphlets or books about Canada. All we cared about was that we were coming to another country, a new land, a country far away on the other side of the globe, a land where warfare, persecution, and oppression would probably never touch us again. We left behind friends and familiar surroundings, languages, cultures, geography, and ancestral grounds. Nearly twenty-four hours later, we entered the Canadian airspace. Much later on, I reimbursed the Canadian government for the plane ticket that brought me to Canada. The government wanted me to repay $75 per month. I could only afford $20. In the end, the government accepted my proposal. It took me a few years to pay it off, but I did it.

We arrived in Montreal in early March or April. As we landed, snow still covered the ground. It was bright and sunny, but very cold and windy. Shortly after the airplane door opened, I realized why we had been given these huge, heavy, and hooded clothes. Up to that point, we only had some idea about snow. Some years earlier, family members had been to Canada. I remembered seeing photos of them with a white landscape in the background.

From the airport in Montreal, we were driven to a nearby military base. We stayed there for about a week. Then we flew to Bagotville in a small plane. We were met by a sponsor and a Laotian man and were driven to Mistassini, Lac St-Jean. When we arrived at the house of one of our sponsors, we were served supper and soup. Unaccustomed and tired, we hardly ate. It took us months to develop an appreciation for some of the foods. A while later, Dr. Khamlay Mounivong, a professor at the university in Chicoutimi and a childhood friend of my father, paid us a visit. He brought along some rice. We were extremely happy to see a familiar face and greatly appreciated his generosity. After all these years, I still have not fully developed a taste for many of the "western" dishes in Canada.

We stayed in Mistassini for about a year. We were very happy to discover that there were already some Laotian, Cambodian, and Vietnamese families there. Friendships developed. The sponsors and the teachers gave us a hand in filling out all the necessary papers for health care and other services and benefits. School was not a pleasant experience for me. I was not familiar with the local accents and idioms. Verbally, I struggled. My mind wandered. At times, I fought against boredom and against falling asleep. Because I was not proficient with the local particularities, some of our sponsors thought I was incapable of being anything but a mechanic: they did not need to have long conversations.

A lack of suitable employment opportunities in Mistassini led us to Chatham, Ontario. Most of my siblings were still young. Hard physical work simply was not possible. Only my mother, one of my younger brothers (not quite sixteen years old at the time), and I could easily earn wages. My father, due to his injuries, could not help out. We needed a different type of employment where most of the family members could participate. After discussions with a federal government employment official, our option was to go to southern Ontario to pick fruits and vegetables. With the assistance of the federal government, we went to Chatham the following summer.

Picking fruits and vegetables was hard and back-breaking labour. We began each day around 6 a.m. and stopped around 9:30 P.M. My dad looked after my youngest brother, who was barely one and a half years old. My younger siblings could not endure the punishing sun. They did as much as they could. My mother and I carried the heavy load. I think we got paid $2.50 for each basket of tomatoes weighing approximately 10 kilograms. We wore long-sleeved shirts, pants, and hats to protect ourselves against an unforgiving sun. I worked in the field seven days a week. My younger brothers usually joined me for part of the Sundays. My mother, usually accompanied by my two sisters, went into town with the farm owner and his family to buy supplies and to do laundry. They would drop off my mother and my sisters at the laundromat before they continued on to the local church.

I am not quite sure what to make of our employment experience in those earlier years. I remain unsure whether we were cheated or exploited when the pay for such hard labour was so little. Perhaps it was the nature of the industry. What I do know, however, is that it was a matter of survival for the family. I swallowed my pride. I sensed that my parents did as well. The life they once had belonged to an already distant past. They were no longer somebody.

One night, my parents and I, along with some of the older siblings, discussed whether we should go back to Mistassini or to Kitchener-Waterloo. The decision was made almost as soon as the discussion began. Besides my three uncles, there was a large ethnic community in Kitchener-Waterloo. Staying nearby would provide easy access to the community for support. On the way back, we spent three nights in Kitchener-Waterloo. My uncles and many community leaders urged my parents not to go back to Mistassini. Relatives living in Detroit, St. Paul (Minnesota), New York, and other places in the United States came up to see my parents and the family. A little bit of urging on their part solidified the decision to stay in Kitchener-Waterloo. My younger siblings were enrolled in school. My mother and I went back to Mistassini to tidy up a few loose ends. Until today, my family has yet to acknowledge and to thank formally those who had so selflessly and generously helped us in Mistassini. We left friends behind.

Living in Kitchener-Waterloo has been both comforting and reassuring to my parents. We have family and the community to rely on. Friends of my parents live only five or six hours away in the United States. For the first two months or so, the community helped us out very generously. They brought us food and vegetables. Struggling to make ends meet themselves, they did the best they could. My mother held down two full-time jobs. One paid $4.25 an hour and the other $3.25. I worked part-time, washing dishes at night and on weekends for $3.25 an hour while attending school.

Speaking very few and broken phrases in English, I began relearning my "ABCs." I enrolled in grade nine. I also attended night classes and summer school. During the summer months, my siblings and I picked fruits during the daytime and worms at night. We got paid about $8 per can of worms weighing about two kilograms. Many immigrants and refugees, including Polish people and other Eastern Europeans, did as well. On average, I could pick about five to eight cans per night. Those who were very fast could fill up to fifteen cans. We prayed for rain every night. With rain, the worms were easily captured. We also went fishing and hunting. We preserved the fruits of our labour for the long winter months.

In 1983, my family became Canadians. We were very anxious, in fact. It had been a very long wait. We went through the interview process and the ceremony. We proudly took the oath of allegiance to Her Majesty, Queen Elizabeth II. We have a new identity and a nationality. We have survived war and conflict. We have escaped oppression, torture, and persecution. We have ceased to be refugees. We sang the national anthem with pride. The generosity of others, along with Canada's abundant resources, picturesque geography, richly endowed landscapes, and sociologically diverse composition, made me one of the luckiest and richest persons alive.

Yet I remained full of mixed emotions. Memories of a painful past, a past filled with images, images of brutality, violence, torture, and deaths ran through my mind. I felt isolated, sad, and helpless. Who would speak on behalf of those Laotians who had disappeared without a trace? Would the world and my new country care about the Laotian killing fields, their trails, and their experience?

During my undergraduate years at the University of Ottawa, I met Francine Bitz, a wonderful French-Canadian lady, fell in love, got married, had children, and bought a house and a car. Dating and marrying a Caucasian person heightened my sense of belonging and sharpened my focus on identity. I used to feel that I was constantly on a stage, being watched and examined every time I turned or twitched. Indeed, when we first started dating, someone close to my wife-to-be told her to stop because the sole purpose of my dating her was to obtain Canadian citizenship. How could she possibly contemplate marriage with an Asian—apparently an "uneducated and inassimilable" people—and "yellow babies"? On the other hand, my parents, too, were upset. How could I, the oldest son, defy them in marrying someone other than a Hmong girl? How would I take care of my parents in their golden age? Would my wife welcome my parents, my siblings, and my relatives? How could I possibly be sure that she would not leave me? How would the children be referred to? Mixed? Half-breed? When our children were born, they were not yellow babies. Each one of them was simply another newly born Canadian.

How to come to terms with the "hyphenated and non-hyphenated" Canadianism? I still have more questions than answers. Whenever I hear arguments that Canada is not as united a country as it should be because there are too many "hyphenated" Canadians, with an overwhelming emphasis on the origin of an individual, I feel that I have not been fully accepted and that my allegiance to Canada is being questioned. I ceased to be a refugee approximately a quarter of a century ago. For me, Canada is home. It is my security. It is my safety. Canada is as precious for me as it is for my children. I am an equal co-proprietor of this country. When will established Canadians stop asking me whether I am a Canadian?

Celebrity Inn

ANNA PRATT

Legal scholar Anna Pratt describes the dark side of the Canadian refugee process.

In the United States, hotels that double as immigration holding centres have been referred to as "Kafka hotels," no doubt because of Franz Kafka's powerful depiction of the absurd, seemingly senseless, though ultimately punitive qualities of modern bureaucracy.

The Celebrity Inn in Mississauga is Canada's own Kafka hotel, complete with Kafkaesque name. It is located in one wing of the fully functioning and busy airport hotel, the Celebrity Budget Inn. Conveniently located less than a kilometre from Toronto's Pearson International Airport, Celebrity promises to "treat all guests as celebrities."

There are two entrances for those who stay at Celebrity, one for those who can leave freely and one for those who cannot. The included and the excluded bunk in different wings of the same hotel, illustrating dramatically the contrasting destinies of those deemed to be deserving and/or desirable and those deemed otherwise who are ushered into this distinct zone of exclusion.

The Celebrity Inn is one of the three principal immigration holding centres in Canada. The other two are located in Vancouver, British Columbia, and Laval, Quebec. In 2004, Vancouver operated a centre for short-term detentions (under seventy-two hours). Laval's facility, officially designated the "Immigration Prevention Centre," is located in a refurbished former prison. Generally speaking, there are between 75 and 100 people detained at Celebrity, which has the capacity to detain 100 people "comfortably." In contrast, Vancouver and Montreal Laval each hold approximately twenty to forty people.

These immigration "holding centres" are for the detention of non-criminal noncitizens, people who have come to the attention of the authorities, who have violated or are suspected of having violated Canadian immigration law, and who are judged, initially by immigration officers and subsequently by adjudicators, to represent a "flight risk." Individuals whose cases involve criminality and who are deemed to be a "danger to the public" are not sent by Immigration to the Celebrity Inn but to provincial jails. Detention is *for* deportation: "The intention with the non-criminal is that detention be as short as possible. In most cases it really is to facilitate removal, so there is not a justification for a long detention."

While one might expect that those confined in more secure correctional institutions for reasons of criminality would likely be subjected to the coercive and punitive dimensions of criminal justice incarceration, "temporary holding centres" for the administrative detention of *noncriminal* immigration cases might reasonably be expected to operate under a different, noncarceral regime. However, notwithstanding the absence of "criminals," and notwithstanding official declarations to the contrary, immigration detention—even in a holding centre for noncriminals located in a busy hotel—is a distinctly carceral experience.

The presence of a secure detention facility in the isolated rear wing of the Celebrity Budget Inn would likely come as a surprise to most of the hotel's paying customers. From the main entrance to the inn, there are few visual clues that it doubles as a medium-security detention centre. Around the side of the building, a keen observer might notice a surveillance camera mounted on the outside wall, just above a steel door entrance with a coded locking mechanism just beside it. This is the visitor's entrance to the detention facility. It is permanently locked. To enter, visitors ring a buzzer, and their images are recorded and transmitted to a security officer within who may then deactivate the lock and allow entry.

The door opens into a large, dingy, yellowish room empty of furniture except for the chairs that line the walls. There is another surveillance camera and a pay phone in this room. One corner of the room has been sectioned off, and a security guard permanently posted behind fortified Plexiglas acts as the facility's "visits officer."

Just behind this security post is the "detainee visiting area" in which detainees sit at cubicles and meet their visitors through Plexiglas barriers and communicate through a telephone. There are twelve visiting "stations."

To enter the inner regions of the centre, the locks on two more steel doors need to be deactivated by security. A metal detector lines the frame of one of these doors. Immediately on the other side are blue tiled stairs that lead up to the second floor of the detention wing. It is a gloomy place indeed: dim lighting, nondescript beige/brown walls, long empty corridors. It is exceptionally clean—not new, not necessarily in good repair, but clean. The detention centre is serviced by the cleaning staff of the Celebrity Inn. The detainees' rooms and every floor of every room are cleaned daily, in the winters sometimes twice or three times a day because of the snow and salt tracked in from outside. The disinfectant smell of ammonia and cleaning fluids hovers throughout. The walls, inside and out, are frequently painted. The air quality within the facility can only be described as terrible due to the permanently sealed windows and lack of ventilation and fresh-air circulation.

Located at the top of the immaculate but gloomy stairway are the separate entrances to the male and female dining and smoking rooms and the cafeteria-style kitchen. A long, dimly lit hotel hallway leads away from the dining rooms to the detainees' rooms. There are security posts at each end of the hallway and at each entrance to the dining areas. There are surveillance cameras in the hallway and in each of the common areas. Escape, not violence, is the primary security concern. Each room has an outside window, which is sealed with reinforced Plexiglas. Beds have also been modified so that the iron frames cannot be removed and used as pry bars or weapons.

The enforcement detention officers (EDOs) who run the facility, and their support staff, work primarily out of three rooms across from the dining areas. In addition to admission and release powers, the EDOs at the Celebrity Inn are responsible for every aspect of the daily management and administration of the facility, including hearing and investigating complaints; taking disciplinary action against unruly detainees; making visitation decisions; managing transportation to and from detention reviews and refugee hearings; managing contracts with private suppliers; and communicating with a range of other agencies, including government departments, law enforcement, airport authorities, the Immigration and Refugee Board (IRB), foreign embassies, legal counsel, community advocates, media, and the public.

Across from the immigration office is a rather sparsely equipped "children's playroom." It was created in response to pressure from members of the Toronto Refugee Affairs Council (TRAC). The detention of minors is a matter of considerable concern and has long been the subject of sustained criticism by nongovernmental advocates. The official response is that it is not the practice to *detain* young children; they are there with their detained parent(s) as *guests* of Immigration.

On the first floor of the detention wing, the rooms that line the hallway are used for a variety of purposes. Several are designated as "meeting rooms" for detainees and their lawyers or other "professional" contacts. In 1999, a few were adapted to function as "video-conferencing" detention review rooms. Before then, all detainees had to be transported off site to attend these reviews. They may now be done at Celebrity with the technology of video-conferencing. This manner of conducting the reviews further undermines a detainee's ability to make a case persuasively. As observed by one of TRAC's case workers, because so much of each detention release decision depends on the perceived credibility of the detainee, the disconnected and impersonal medium of video-conferencing presents a further obstacle to detainees.

In addition to the video-conferencing rooms, the contract community doctor and duty nurses work out of two rooms. There is also a detainee baggage room, a room for the TRAC case worker, and finally several rooms used for segregation and solitary confinement for either health or security/disciplinary purposes. . . . The beige and brown hallway on the first floor of the detention wing leads to the main security (or supervisor's) office, the admissions and discharge office, and the holding room, which form a triangle at the end of the hall. The supervisor of security and the head guard are more or less permanently posted at the main security desk. The supervisor's desk faces a wall of monitors that continuously transmit the images generated by the facility's five internal and seven external surveillance cameras. Here the gaze of surveillance is not coupled with discipline or the collection and classification of information about the detainees.

Across the hall from the security office is the detainee holding room. Of all the rooms at Celebrity, this one most closely resembles and evokes the popular image of a police cell. It is small, no more than eight to ten feet square. It is a dirty shade of pale, institutional yellow and has fluorescent lights, no windows. Wooden benches are bolted to the walls. There is a large Plexiglas window in the door to permit viewing of the room from the outside when the door is closed. Once closed, the door cannot be opened from the inside. The third room in the security triangle is the admissions and discharge office.

Just beyond these rooms is the third entrance to the inn, the detainees' entrance. It opens into the "loading and unloading" area of the compound that forms a corner of the detainees' "exercise yard," which used to be the parking lot for the hotel rooms in this wing. It measures about 25 feet wide by 100 feet long. It is empty save for two picnic benches bolted to the pavement and a poorly situated basketball hoop. The yard is monitored by several cameras mounted to the outside walls of Celebrity. Other than the basketball hoop and the occasional soccer ball, the only exercise equipment provided for those detained are a StairMaster and a fitness bike located in the children's playroom and in dubious states of repair.

The exercise yard and the loading and unloading area are encircled by two wire fences. The outside fence is twelve feet high and is capped with "ordinary" barbed wire as opposed to the "razor" variety. The inside fence is eight feet high and fitted with an inward-leaning overhang covered with mesh to prevent detainees from climbing up and over.

Intelligent Waiting

PIA AND ANDY DIACONESCU

After a two-year negotiation with the Passport Bureau, Pia Diaconescu left Communist Romania in 1988 for a three-week visit to her sister in Canada. She decided to stay. Husband Andy

*and the two children joined her in Ottawa in 1990. Their prior-
ity was "to offer a new place and educational environment to our
two sons." They wrote this sobering advice to immigrants in 2005.*

Immigration is a very demanding process and requires outstanding
motivation in order to be successful. First, one has to clearly know
the reason for taking such a step. Being motivated and knowing exactly why you immigrated helps overcome failures and activates your
desire for success. Secondly, you must be mentally agile and understand that each case is different: nothing about immigration is stan-
dardized.

Visiting a foreign country, even for a long period of time, is not
similar to immigration. Once that decision is taken, different challenges come into play. Among these is the position where the new
world is placing you, always a lower one compared to what you had
in the old country. As an immigrant, you do not change a bit, but
your profile and self-esteem decrease drastically just by passing the
border. It is hard to understand why you cannot get a job because
you don't have "Canadian experience," but at the same time nobody
is hiring you in the first place. The cultural shock, including different habits, values, interests, and the barriers of language, prevent the
newcomer from rapid social integration. It inevitably leads to health
problems, often including depression, weight gain, teeth degradation,
and hair loss. More importantly, there are scars left in your soul, affecting personality. The high rate of divorces we have observed among
new immigrant couples is testimony to the hardship.

When arriving at the new destination, good advice is at a high
price. In general, the people you meet are not capable of understanding the real situation. Consequently, the information received is often
not pertinent. Instead it's usually an amalgam of gossip and easy as-
sumptions, without a sound estimation of results. So, receiving proper
advice in critical situations is paramount. We questioned all advice,
however sincerely offered. We checked everything twice, filtered the
stories we heard, and retained only what was good for us. We constantly tried to meet people who were reliable and clear-minded.
What helped us most during immigration was our involvement with
sports. That taught us how to be successful immigrants—how to

meet new friends, how to lose without quitting, and how to select the right strategy for the next battle.

Successful adaptation to another place implies an intelligent waiting for those things that matter most, and for us they all centred on our family. Perseverance and tolerance worked for parents like us, who cared more for our children's future than our own personal status. Taking jobs under our qualification standards was never considered a demotion. The priority was to generate a sound learning environment for our children. Today, our eldest is a medical doctor in Montreal, while the youngest is a Ph.D. from the California Institute of Technology, working as a senior design engineer at Nortel in Ottawa.

We have helped and continue to help new immigrants arriving in Ottawa and other parts of Canada. Immigration is a rewarding process, but we would never encourage it because it puts such an enormous stress on individuals, families, and relationships. Its wounds can be irreversible.

Hold the Complacency, 2005

MICHAEL VALPY

After ethnic youth rioted in France in the summer of 2005, a leading journalist asked, "Could it happen here?"

For Canadians smug in their mythology of inhabiting the planet's most successful multicultural society, the riots of France have been cause for national tsk-tsking and self-satisfaction. At least, goes the script, we've got social inclusiveness right.

At least—maybe more by luck than by design—we've avoided the creation of racial underclasses: no endless ugly suburbs of brown and black people imprisoned in poverty from which scant hope of escape exists.

At least we've embraced into our national culture the notion of post-ethnic identity, woven the values of anti-discrimination and equality into not only our laws but into our hearts and national idiom.

Well, hold the complacency, eh?

To be sure, a Canadian mirror held up to the car-BQs of France shows no violent mass unrest brewing in, say, Toronto's Jane-Finch or Jamestown neighbourhoods, Montreal's *quartier* St-Michel or patches of Greater Vancouver's Surrey and the Downtown Eastside.

But what recent research reveals is an alarming and disquieting analogue to the demographic portrait of the French suburban *cités*.

It shows an emerging population of Canadian-raised daughters and sons of visible-minority immigrants *à la* France whose accents and cultural reference points are as Canadian as maple syrup, but who in many respects feel less welcome in the country than their parents.

"Their parents came to improve their lives," says University of Toronto sociologist Jeffrey Reitz, one of Canada's foremost academic experts on immigration and multiculturalism.

"They can make comparisons to where they were. They can [move] on. But for their children born in Canada, they don't have the option of going anywhere else. And they expect equality. Therefore their expectations are much higher."

The data show, in fact, a generation raised in the milieu of the Charter of Rights and Freedoms and multiculturalism's rhetoric, who expect to be treated as equals in Canadian society and who angrily are discovering that they are not. Their disaffection has gone largely unnoticed until now in polls and academic research because, unlike in France, the numbers of the visible-minority second generation are statistically small—less than a million.

France's wave of visible-minority immigration occurred in the fifties and sixties; Canada's began only in the seventies. Two-thirds of the Canadian visible-minority second generation are still under 16.

As Prof. Reitz observes, "It is striking that indications of lack of integration into Canadian society are so significant for the Canadian second-born generation, since it is this group which is regarded as the harbinger of the future . . ."

Data collected by Statistics Canada for its 2002 Ethnic Diversity Survey and other studies and then analyzed by scholars such as Prof. Reitz and the Institute for Research on Public Policy show that, for the immigrant second generation in multicultural Canada, all visible minorities have less of a sense of belonging to the country than do whites.

The data show that on virtually all indicators used by sociologists and governments to measure integration into Canadian life, visible minorities rate themselves as less integrated than whites.

Add their perceptions of non-belonging to their socioeconomic rankings—among all ethnocultural groups in Canada, racial minorities clearly have the lowest relative household income and the highest poverty rates—and the outlines of underclass loom menacingly from the mist.

Indeed, Princeton sociologist Douglas Massey, considered the leading scholar on race and economic underclass in the United States, recently told a University of Toronto audience that some of the indicators of racial underclass are appearing in Canadian cities.

It is not, however, just a matter of economics.

As Prof. Reitz points out, "Although visible-minority immigrants have lower earnings than whites, at an individual level, low earnings contribute little to trends in social integration.

"Rather, the negative trends in integration reflect their more pronounced experiences of [broad] discrimination and vulnerability, which become or remain pronounced for the second generation"— experiences felt with more acuity and resulting anger by the second generation.

Listen to the voice of 22-year-old Rahel Appiagyei, a third-year student in international relations attending Toronto's elite bilingual Glendon College at York University.

"No, I don't feel accepted," she says. "The one thing I don't understand—me, personally, and for blacks in general—is why we're still seen as immigrants."

In the Canada of her experience, she says, "the word 'immigrant' is used to mean coloured and the word 'Canadian' is a code word for Caucasian." Her parents emigrated from Ghana in 1988, when she was 5. Immigrants from Ghana—along with those from Ethiopia, Somalia and Afghanistan—have the highest rates of poverty in Canada, between 50 and 80 per cent. She, her parents and five siblings live crowded into a three-bedroom apartment.

Ms. Appiagyei, whose idiom and accent with trademark raised *ou* diphthong are flawlessly Canadian, says with pride that her family has never needed a penny of welfare, that her father has steadily worked since he arrived, and that she is the first in the family to be accomplishing what her mother and father brought their children to Canada to do.

She cites the Toronto school board's policy of zero tolerance for violence and points out its targets are overwhelmingly black students. Something can't be right with a policy that winds up being aimed at a single racial group, she says. "It gives me a lot of messages."

Ms. Appiagyei tells the story of living one summer in Quebec with a family to learn French. The father made clear that he associated blacks with poverty and one day commented that he had never thought blacks attractive until he met her. "It was a compliment and insult at the same time."

The Ethnic Diversity Study found 37 per cent of Canada's visible minorities report discrimination, and for blacks alone the figure is 50 per cent.

Ms. Appiagyei says the more engaged and involved in Canadian life she becomes, the more she encounters gaps between her expectations of what Canadian society should be and the reality she encounters.

She tells of being often asked:

"'You're from Africa, how come you know English so well?' I feel I'm always being assessed with lions and tigers, with remoteness. Why is it we're not allowed to feel we belong here?"

On her sense of remoteness, one of Prof. Reitz's findings from the data carries special weight: "Although most Canadians deny harbouring racist views," he says, "they express 'social distance' from minorities—that is, preferences not to act with members of other racial groups."

And so, Prof. Reitz says, the alienation of today's visible-minority second generation is a harbinger of the future.

"Perspectives on racial discrimination divide racial groups, and such racial divisions do matter for the broader cohesion of Canadian society."

Canada's visible-minority population is rapidly growing and, by

2017, will be 20 per cent of the population, with the percentages significantly higher in Canada's largest cities.

The research data show that about 30 per cent fewer visible minorities than whites have voted in federal elections (although only 20 per cent fewer visible minorities than whites are citizens). The same 30-per-cent gap exists between visible minorities and whites in identifying as Canadian. A smaller percentage of visible minorities than whites report satisfaction with life and trust in others; a smaller percentage engage in volunteer work in their communities.

And, of course, the data show clearly that as second-generation white immigrants nestle comfortably into Canadian life, their visible-minority counterparts lag behind.

What the data also show is that white Canadians tend to discount the claims of discrimination reported by their non-white fellow countrymen and countrywomen. It's not the mythology of multicultural inclusiveness. And yet discounting those claims, Prof. Reitz warns, may make matters worse.

"Lack of [racial] conflict in the present may not be a good predictor of the future."

The Real Immigrant Experience

ANDREW COYNE

Somewhat to his surprise, conservative columnist Andrew Coyne found himself enthusiastically praising the inaugural address of a new governor general, Michaëlle Jean. Her speech went to the heart of the immigrant experience as it really was, Coyne asserted, not as it existed in the blather of official government rhetoric.

Madam, I surrender. Let us forget past criticisms. Let us put aside old quarrels. Your speech has collapsed my defences. You are my Commander-in-Chief.

After the oath of allegiance, after the musical numbers, after the Prime Minister's introduction, I settled in to hear the new Governor-General deliver her first address to the nation, expecting to hear the usual banal bureaucratese, or worse, the coded appeals to regional and racial chauvinism—sorry; diversity—that have become the official language of Ottawa. Indeed, given her own past, I half expected some sly reference to the independence of small peoples or the like.

I had not expected to hear the full-throated song of love to this country that in fact followed, a speech of heartbreaking sincerity and jaw-dropping boldness—the most ringing endorsement of undifferentiated pan-Canadianism, I'm willing to guess, that the capital has heard in years. Nor could anyone have anticipated precisely how she would choose to convey her message, the points she emphasized, the words she preferred. The gesture of renouncing her French citizenship had been welcome enough. But the speech was note-perfect in tone, and transformative in content.

It was uplifting without being pollyanna-ish, tender yet tough-minded, vigorous, audacious, even bellicose in spots.

In place of the usual gooey clichés of Canadian nationalism, the obsession with minor differences, the nursing of ancient grievances, the exaltation of some supposed national predisposition to statism, we heard an invocation of a different Canada, and a different Canadianism—an older, meatier variety, before the Liberals and their bureaucratic accomplices went to work bleaching the life out of it. It was a speech, perhaps paradoxically, that only an immigrant could have given, or could get away with, for it spoke from and to the reality of the immigrant experience, of what immigrants really see in this country, and cherish about it. It is why they come here, and it is worlds away from what the mythmakers would have us believe about it.

The headline-making passage was, of course, her firm declaration that "the time of 'two solitudes' . . . is past." This wasn't a fond hope. It was a brisk directive: not only to the traditional divisions of French and English, but to "all the solitudes." We must learn, she said, "to see beyond our wounds, beyond our differences, for the good of all." Beyond our wounds? Beyond our differences? But, but . . . what about the mosaic? What about the community of communities? What about the Canada "whose strength is its diversity," the Canada that issues weekly apologies for centuries-old slights, that spent 40 years turning itself inside out trying to meet the latest revision of Quebec's "historic demands"? Balls to that, said this descendant of slaves.

Get over yourselves. "We must eliminate the spectre of all the solitudes and promote solidarity among all the citizens who make up the
Canada of today."

On its own, this would make this a remarkable speech. Try to
imagine any elected politician in Canada having the brass to make
such a statement. Or even the inclination—they whose careers have
been built on pandering to those very differences, pouring salt into
those same wounds. She shamed them all. Gilles Duceppe looked
unhappiest when it was over. But I can't imagine any of the assembled dignitaries could have been entirely comfortable at this implied
rebuke.

Yet there was much more. What was the first quality she identified with Canada? What did she spend the first half of her speech
praising? Our tolerance, perhaps? Our health care system, or our devotion to multilateralism? Try freedom. Over and over, she returned
to the theme of "this land of freedom," connecting her own story to
that of the first settlers, each seeking, and finding, freedom on its
shores. Her life, she said, had been "a lesson in learning to be free." As
a refugee from "a ruthless dictatorship," she knew, she said, "how
precious that freedom is," and at what price it must sometimes be
won.

To defend it required courage, even a little orneriness, qualities
she was certain her fellow citizens, contrary to stereotype, possessed
in spades. "Every Canadian woman, every Canadian man prizes that
freedom and would defy anyone who tried to take it away—of that I
have no doubt." The same words might have been uttered by Joseph
Howe or D'Arcy McGee, or any Father of Confederation. But today?
Doesn't it sound a little too . . . American? Would any Canadian
politician so much as mention "freedom" without automatically bal-
ancing it against some equally valid opposite, like order, or equality,
or the notwithstanding clause?

The freedom she prized as a distinguishing feature of Canada, it
was clear, was defined not just as the absence of tyranny, but as a
habit of mind: what she referred to, no less than four times, as
our "spirit of adventure." It was a spirit rooted deep in our history.
"More than four centuries ago," she said, "that spirit of adventure
drove women and men to cross the ocean and discover a new world

elsewhere. . . . Our history speaks powerfully about the freedom to invent a new world, about the courage underlying those remarkable adventures." Indeed, "we are the sum of those adventures."

Think about that: Canada as the creation of individual acts of courage, the accumulated history of millions of private adventures, for which the indispensable ingredient was freedom. This is not the orderly series of public works projects of so many high-school textbooks. It is the secret history of Canada, the one our statists have suppressed.

It is in freedom, she went on, that we find the true source of our unity: not in the heroic acts of statesmen, or in the romanticization of [a] Crown corporation, but in the common experience of liberty. "From Signal Hill to Vancouver Island, from Baffin Land to Thetford Mines, the freedom that is ours unites us all." A century ago, this sort of thing was commonplace. "Canada is free," Sir Wilfrid Laurier said, "and freedom is its nationality." Today it is heresy.

Does that make us different from other countries? Should we make the preservation of national differences, the protection of a distinctive national culture the idée fixe of policy? Not according to Mme. Jean. "I hope to rally our creative forces around those values that unite us all and that are universal in scope." Not the values that make us distinct, note: the values that unite us. And they unite us, because they are universal: they connect us as Canadians, because they connect us as human beings.

Universal values? For decades, our artists and intellectuals, politicians and bureaucrats, have scoffed at the very idea. Apparently Her Excellency didn't get the memo.

Pioneering

SHEEMA KHAN

The daughter of Indian immigrants, seeing herself as a pioneer in a continuing line of Canadian pioneers, Sheema Khan is a Harvard Ph.D. in chemical physics, a patent agent in intellectual property law, and a columnist for the Toronto Globe and Mail. *Hers is a deep connection to Canada—its inclusive opti-*

mism, its compassionate meritocracy, and its love of hockey. Her
Canadian journey, however, is more complex than a joyous
nationalism. It, and her Muslim upbringing, have brought her
closer to her Creator.

My eyes begin to overflow every time I hear it. On Canada Day. At hockey games. My children's schools. First thing in the morning on local TV stations.

"O Canada," our national anthem, captures the essence of my Canadian identity. It begins quietly, with unassuming dignity, and resonates with the expansiveness that characterizes both our glorious landscape and human potential. We *are* intimately connected to the land. It represents all that I love, and have loved about Canada.

In 1965 I came from India to Montreal at the age of three, with my parents. We left chronic Hindu-Muslim strife for an opportunity to prosper in peace. For the first time, we experienced snow, maple syrup, and that most Canadian of passions—hockey. We were welcomed warmly and tried our best to integrate. It was an era on the cusp of Trudeaumania, multiculturalism, and Expo 67's Man and His World. There was an atmosphere of unbridled optimism that infected citizens from Vancouver to St. John. In Quebec, the Quiet Revolution was, well, still quiet.

The most enriching aspects of living in Montreal were the opportunity to learn French and the ability to visit the world without ever having to leave the city. In Canada, my best friend while growing up was Hindu. I had neighbours from countries such as China and Brazil; neighbours who were "pur-laine," and old-stock Brits. My close friends at school were Jewish and Christian; black, white, and many colours in between. Multiculturalism was not merely a policy—it was a force to bind our world together based on mutual respect among members of our diverse human family. A shining example in a strife-torn world. Looking back, if I do have one regret, it is not having had the opportunity to interact with members of our indigenous communities—Aboriginals and the Inuit.

The innocence of childhood changed abruptly in 1970, when the Front de Libération du Québec began its campaign of terror in Quebec. The kidnap and murder of Pierre Laporte left the indelible marks of fear and revulsion—at an early stage of my life, I hated politics. Unbeknownst to me at the time, our warm, jovial neighbour-landlords were none other than the parents of FLQ lawyer Robert Lemieux. I had met their other adult children, who reflected their parents' generosity of spirit. I also learned another valuable lesson—the human dimension of conflict is rarely black and white. English media images presented Quebec nationalism as a dark force, and yet the many French Canadians I met—especially my wonderful neighbours—had a culture, a history which they wished to preserve, without resorting to violence. After all, isn't identity our raison d'être?

The painful memories of October 1970 seemed to recede somewhat in the spring of 1971, when our beloved Montreal Canadiens scored upset wins over the mighty Boston Bruins and the vaunted Chicago Blackhawks to capture the Stanley Cup. A bookish rookie by the name of Ken Dryden won the hearts of Canadiens fans everywhere, stopping puck after puck. And the true grit of players such as Jean Beliveau and Henri Richard restored the pride of "le bleu, blanc et rouge." This particular Stanley Cup win had me hooked on hockey for life.

The emotional roller-coaster ride was repeated in September 1972, when my family and I joined the nation in cheering for Team Canada against the Soviets. Although I never admitted it to any of my friends, one of my favourite players was Valeri Kharmalov—a brilliant, graceful player for the Soviets, who reminded me of one of my other favourites, Yvan Cournoyer. I joined my classmates in cheering Canada during that memorable Game 8, inspired by the gritty comeback of our team. After we had won, I persuaded my father to go to Dorval airport so that we could see the team's plane land. We joined many others. Hockey, it seems, is the uniting factor of this country.

While I was growing up, there were very few Muslims in Montreal. My parents tried their best to have the family adhere to Muslim culture. We did not drink alcohol, did not eat pork, and, come high school, did not date. Twice a year, we joined other members of our small community to celebrate the two Eids—Eid-ul-Fitr (to mark the end of Ramadan) and Eid-ul-Adha (to commemorate the sacrifice of Ibrahim). When we had first arrived in Canada, someone had presented me with a piggy bank in the shape of an Eskimo girl. My parents taught me to save coins in that bank—which I did with great diligence. I had amassed what I thought was a fortune of $50, when my parents informed me that the Muslim community would be building its first mosque. Donations would be needed to help with this project, which would provide all of us a place to pray. In Islam, helping to build a mosque is one of the supreme acts of charity. My parents did not force me, but tried to persuade me of the value of sacrifice. It was one of the best lessons I learned early in life. At first I hesitated, but then I gladly offered my life savings toward a bigger cause.

As I grew up, I saw my father send portions of his savings to help not only his immediate family, but extended relatives in India. They lived in a rural village, with no electricity. Many had no funds to pay for education. My siblings and I were always grateful for the opportunities we had in Canada. And yet we always felt that it was our duty to help those less fortunate in India, through the dignified example of our parents. Charity is also an essential feature of Islamic beliefs, one that unfortunately gets very little media exposure. It forms the fabric of so many Muslim cultures. The generosity of the human spirit is such a powerful force that enhances so much good. Living in Canada, and being the recipient of so much generosity by fellow Canadians, made me realize that such a force is not confined to any particular people or faith—but a gift from the Creator to all human beings.

Perhaps one of the most comforting aspects of my youth was to have my mother at home. She chose not to work outside the home. We were able to come home for lunch for a nice hot meal, prepared with much TLC. It was wonderful to come home after school and share events of the day with her, while sampling her delicious snacks. It made doing homework all the easier. One cannot put a price on the human security that emanates from a mother's presence and love. In today's age, it is hard to find the balance between work and family. Like many other working mothers, I try to provide my own children with that same security and comfort. Struggling to balance work and family, I look back to the serene example of my mother to guide me.

Like many immigrant families, education formed an important part of our upbringing. While we could not afford luxuries, my parents always made sure we would have the educational tools needed to succeed. Books, visits to the library, after-school lessons, and home encyclopedias were never in short supply. We loved to learn, and we loved to study. My parents never pushed us to succeed academically, but encouraged us gently to do our best. I still remember my father telling me not to worry about how others did, but to just concentrate on my own efforts. And he never made a distinction between the male and female children—we were equally encouraged to strive. Honesty and hard work were part and parcel of our household.

The emphasis on education seemed to pay off. My siblings and I did well in school, receiving academic prizes and scholarships. We all went on to higher study—at York's renowned Business School, Harvard, and Princeton.

In addition, I loved sports, and my parents encouraged me to pursue that love. During high school, I played a steady diet of tennis, basketball, volleyball, soccer, and badminton. Upon graduation, I received the award for best female athlete. I continued to play soccer and recreational hockey. During grad school, I was disappointed to find that there were no opportunities to play recreational hockey. Why not start such a venture? So, a Muslim female teetotalling Canuck helped to start Harvard's first female intramural ice-hockey league. Friends who had never laced up were encouraged to experience the thrill of gliding on the ice, all the while holding a hockey stick and chasing a piece of rubber. My friends from California and Florida particularly enjoyed the experience. As Canadians, we should never underestimate the ambassadorial nature of hockey—to bring people together in a spirit of goodwill and gamesmanship.

It was during my graduate school experience that I began to contemplate more about my identity. Who am I? What will happen to me when I die? Are there universal truths? I was also beginning to tire of the dual identities that many experience—behaving one way when immersed in the wider society, and behaving in another in the presence of one's own ethnic or religious community. I was also finding it increasingly difficult to socialize in an atmosphere that emphasized alcohol and sexual relations. I felt a suffocation of the spirit. The rar-ified secular atmosphere of Harvard was quite disdainful of those who expressed faith in God. I began to attend the Friday congrega-tional prayers at Harvard, finding that one hour of the week to be a time of soulful bliss and tranquility. As time passed, I was drawn increasingly to the sense of inner peace of who I was, and my abiding faith in a merciful, compassionate Creator who was the bestower of all provisions.

The quest for identity is an open-ended journey, a path to self-discovery. In my case, this quest has been based on spirituality, rather than ethnicity or nationalism. In looking back, my love for science was part of that spiritual quest—reminiscent of the story of Abra-ham described in the Qur'an. As a boy, Abraham observed the rising and setting of a star, the moon, and finally the sun, each object more dazzling than its predecessor. He realized that no matter how awe-inspiring, each object had no inherent power but was subject to a far greater power. Empirical research and deductive reasoning paved his way towards belief in God. He also understood that it was useless to worship objects created through human agency, inanimate creations that could not respond to the innate spiritual calling of the heart. Some would argue that the West's infatuation with technical achieve-ments is akin to the idol worship of Abraham's time.

Given the tumult of so much of the world, I consider myself immensely blessed to have had the opportunity to pursue this jour-ney in relative peace, with ample time to reflect and exchange ideas with so many people. Canada is a haven—of respect, of opportunity, and of reward. It is a compassionate meritocracy, weaved by count-less women and men of the past and the present.

The first Quebec Referendum provided me with my first oppor-tunity to vote. It was an exciting time for the province, for the nation. I felt part of history in the making—simply by exercising my right to vote, a right that is fragile, if not non-existent, in many parts of the world. That is why I have made a point of voting in every municipal, provincial, and federal election, and bringing along my children to see democracy in action. In June 2004, my husband and I were walk-ing with our kids to the ice-cream store. My seven-year-old daughter asked me about the many campaign signs propped on the sidewalk. I explained that the people on these signs were trying to represent us in government, and that an election meant that people in our neighbourhood would listen to each person's ideas and then vote for whom they thought was the best. The person who received the most votes would win. My daughter seemed to understand. Her next words melted my heart: "Mama, if you were running, I would vote for you."

While we have gone through issues of national unity, the beauty of this nation's evolution has been the willingness to settle our differences through the rule of law. Referendums, parliamentary debates, public commissions, and the courts are the instruments of choice with regard to political dissent—a shining example in a world troubled by increasing resort to violence.

In February 2002 my husband had gone for hajj—the pilgrimage to Mecca, which is one of the five pillars of Islam. I had performed my hajj in 1995. It is an arduous journey, taken for the sake of God, during which an individual joins millions of fellow human beings in the solemn worship of God. In my husband's absence my kids and I were following the Olympic Games, with a keen eye on the Canadian men's and women's hockey teams. First, our women's team avenged their defeat in Nagano by beating the Americans in a gritty performance, led by the poise of head coach Diane Sauvageau. Then, our men's team, with a lucky looney buried at centre ice, captured the gold. We were so happy. And yes, I cried when the maple leaf was raised during the playing of "O Canada."

I waited until my husband had finished the hajj rites, then called him in Mecca a few days later. He had been in spiritual seclusion, with no access to news of the outside world. I told him about the hockey wins. He was so happy, and he spread the news to his fellow Canadian hajjis, who also rejoiced. Imagine—hockey news permeating Saudi Arabia following the performance of one of the most sacred acts of worship. Such is the simple yet powerful allure of hockey. The story doesn't end there. When my husband returned, he greeted us warmly, and promptly asked me: "Who did Canada beat to win the gold?"

Our national passion for hockey may speak to issues about our identity. For me, it speaks to the inclusive optimism that defines this nation. Lace up, grab a stick, and let's play. Or, if you can't skate, no matter. Let's cheer together. The opportunity to participate is so central to our nation's (relative) success at integrating immigrants.

Here is but one example of this simple concept. For years, I had written letters to the editor of Canadian newspapers, explaining basic concepts about Islam and Muslims. At one point, I read the *Globe and Mail* voraciously, writing constantly to the editors—including a few op-ed pieces, straight from the heart. Then one day, I received a call from Patrick Martin, the editorial page editor, who asked to meet me in Ottawa to explore my writing for the paper on a regular basis. I felt humbled and honoured by this opportunity. It's as if I had been accepted by Harvard all over again. Thus unfolded my quintessential Canadian moment: establishment of a freelance contract with the *Globe* at the Chateau Laurier, followed by a celebration of beaver tails and Tim Horton's coffee from the Byward Market. You can't get any more Canadian than that, eh?

My personal encounters with the generosity of spirit that permeates this land were supplanted by a chapter of Canadian history that is still in the making. In September of 2002, I received word that a Canadian Muslim engineer by the name of Maher Arar had been detained in the United States, with the threat of deportation to Syria. Before anyone could provide meaningful assistance to Mr. Arar, the United States shipped him off first to Jordan, and then to Syria as part of its infamous "rendition" program. My immediate thoughts turned to his wife, Monia, and their two small children. The Muslim community in Ottawa is small, and I had occasionally met Monia and Maher at community gatherings. Over the next twelve months, Monia mounted an effective, dignified campaign to free her husband. And Canadians rallied to her support, slowly, but surely. Once Maher was released from his Syrian hell-hole, Canadians demanded accountability of our government and supported Maher and Monia to have the truth come out. In a post-9/11 climate, Muslims ventured into the public arena with trepidation, unsure of how they would be perceived by the wider Canadian public. It has been so heartening to see the support of ordinary Canadians for the dignified effort of Maher and Monia.

My son recently asked me if I had known anything about Canada before I came to this country. No, I responded—I was only three when I immigrated. "Well then, you're a pioneer," he said, adding, "that's what we learned in school today." Pioneers come to a land with little or no knowledge about what lies ahead, he explained. They work the land and build their lives. I loved his analysis, for it replaced the sterile connotation of the word "immigrant" (i.e., one who immigrates) with the dynamic description of a "pioneer." One who arrives with hopes and dreams, ready to work hard and contribute. In that sense, Canada is a land of pioneers, always evolving toward higher ideals. I hope to be a part of this national dream and to pass this sense of identity to my children.

Sophie's New World

MICHAEL DUFRESNE AND KATHERINE LAGRANDEUR

Each year, Canadians adopt more babies from China than from any other foreign country. Between 1993 and 2004, Canadians adopted 8,358 Chinese children, most of them daughters, accounting for approximately 35 percent of all inter-country adoptions by Canadian families during that period. In 2006 Sophie Lagrandeur-Dufresne began to sort out her new world.

It seemed to take forever. One by one, they were carried from the brightly lit hallway into the dull brown ballroom and placed in the arms of their waiting parents. Where was ours? We searched their faces, hoping to find the one that matched our photos, taken seven months before. And then we heard our guides say something familiar. Although we speak few words of Mandarin and understand almost none, we recognized these words immediately. Le Yuan Jin. Our daughter's name.

Born on July 10, 2004, our Jin Jin was discovered two days later on the doorstep of the LePing Social Welfare Institute (SWI) in Jiangxi, a relatively poor, underdeveloped province of China. She was dressed in a blue checked cotton padded jacket and the lower part of her body was wrapped in a purple apron with red patterns. She weighed seven and a half pounds. The orphanage gave her the name Le Yuan Jin (Jin being the first name). After a week of medical tests, our healthy Jin Jin was placed in foster care until she was thirteen months old.

Around the time of her birth, we were in the middle of a home study to determine our suitability to parent an internationally adopted baby. We met with a social worker over the course of several months, discussing the challenges and highlights we experienced in our lives, our health, our families, our education, our parenting philosophy, our reasons for adopting, and why we chose China for our adoption. Several years earlier, we decided to eschew invasive, expensive and often unsuccessful fertility treatments in favour of adoption. We didn't need to spend a lot of time considering it: we knew on a profound level that international adoption was the right way for us to become a family.

We chose China for many reasons. Its policies to minimize population growth and its tradition of bestowing the responsibility for the welfare of elderly parents on sons mean some poor Chinese families cannot keep their baby girls. Around the early 1990s, China made it possible for these babies to be adopted by parents living in other countries, establishing a well-organized and reliable international adoption process. We trusted their program and knew our baby would probably be healthy, and a girl—we really wanted a daughter. We were also excited about embracing Chinese culture and becoming part of its history and heritage through our relationship with our child. Perhaps most importantly, we knew we would be able to connect with other Canadians who shared our experience. Our child would have an immediate sense of belonging by being part of a larger community of daughters born in China and raised in Canada.

We were linked to these families even before Jin Jin was in our lives. While doing our home study, we met other couples who were at various stages of the adoption process at social gatherings, parenting seminars, and adoption information sessions. We participated in online chat groups with parents and parents-to-be in Canada and around the world. But our deepest connection with other families began on the day our adoption file was registered at the China Center of Adoption Affairs (CCCA) in the fall of 2004. Once home studies are approved by provincial governments, they are translated and mailed to the CCCA where they are assigned a log-in date. The CCCA matches parents and children once a month, based on the date the parents' file was registered with them. On average, parents are matched with a child about a year after their file has been logged in at CCCA. Our adoption agency sends a number of files at the same time. With our file registered at CCCA, we were provided with the names and coordinates of others in our group. Suddenly, we were part of a family of Canadians who would probably be receiving their referrals, the term used to describe the part of the adoption process in which parents are offered a child, at the same time. We formed our own online chat group and shared our anticipation during the waiting period, our joy on referral day, and our excitement as we planned our trips to China.

And we were together in the hotel ballroom in Nanchang on "Gotcha Day," the day we met our daughters for the first time. In that moment, our families experienced collectively one of life's most profound moments and became parents together to fifteen beautiful daughters.

Less than an hour before, we had arrived in Nanchang from Beijing, where we had all gathered after flying to China from various parts of Canada. Upon landing, we boarded a bus destined for our hotel, knowing we would receive our babies almost immediately after checking in. The hushed anticipation among us grew as we arrived at the hotel and saw beautiful Chinese babies everywhere. Families had come from around the world to adopt children at the same time as us, and some had already received their daughters earlier in the day or even minutes before our arrival. A few days later, our family ate breakfast with a family from Sweden, who had adopted two daughters from China, a three-year-old adopted a few years before and a baby adopted on the same day as our daughter. Our hotel was a home away from home for families from around the world, all united through the wonder of international adoption.

Tearing ourselves away from the beautiful babies in the hotel lobby, we went up to our room and were overcome with emotion when we opened the door and discovered a crib by our bed and a baby bathtub in the washroom. Our dream was finally coming true. Ten minutes later, we made our way downstairs to the ballroom assigned to our group and waited for our daughter. Jin Jin was one of the last babies to be carried into the room, and even though the whole process took very little time, waiting for her those last few minutes was almost unbearable. We were relieved and grateful when we finally heard her name called and when she was in our arms at last.

We loved her right away. We said hello to her in Mandarin and told her we were her parents. She looked back at us with bewilderment. Then, realizing the people with whom she had come were no longer there, she burst into tears and cried incessantly for over two hours. We grieved with her, knowing how hard it must be for a thirteen-month-old to be left with strangers, especially ones whose looks, smell, and language are unfamiliar to her. She cried herself to sleep that night. But she awoke a few hours later and smiled at us for the first time—it was the most beautiful smile we had ever seen.

We spent the next two weeks in China, finalizing paperwork and visiting tourist attractions, including the Great Wall and the Forbidden City. With each day, Jin Jin became more comfortable with us and started to laugh and play and imitate us. We enjoyed discovering the country where our daughter was born and had lived for the first year of her life. Still, we couldn't wait to introduce her to her new family and friends in Canada and were excited when our departure day finally arrived.

Along with many of the other new "forever families," to use the language of the international adoption community, we flew from Beijing to Vancouver, where we all lined up together in the airport immigration office to fill out more paperwork and receive our daughters' proof of permanent residence in Canada. Afterwards, we all went our separate ways, boarding planes to various parts of the country or heading to hotels until our flights home the next day. The following morning, our family boarded a direct flight to Ottawa, where we were greeted by loved ones who couldn't wait to meet the newest addition to our family and country.

There is a Chinese legend that says there is an invisible red thread that connects us with every person we are going to meet in our lives. We know in our hearts that our daughter was destined to be part of our lives, and we also know that her red thread will always be linked to her birth and foster families in China. We have decided to call our daughter Sophie Jin, hoping that her name will help her feel connected both to the people who love her in Canada and to the people who loved her in China. Our daughter's invisible red thread may have stretched halfway around the world, but it will never break.

Source Acknowledgements

The authors have conscientiously sought out copyright holders. If there are omissions or errors, they will be corrected in future editions. We are grateful to the following for their contribution to this volume:

"Quebec: Canada's Main Path," Samuel de Champlain, "To the King and the Lords of His Council" and "Statement of Persons to Be Brought and Maintained at the Quebec Settlement for the Year 1619," in H.P. Biggar, ed., *The Works of Samuel de Champlain*, vols. II and IV (Toronto: Champlain Society, 1925), with gratitude to Cameron Nish; "Trying Newfoundland, 1622," Edward Wynne to George Calvert, August 17, 1622, in Peter E. Pope, "Six Letters From the Early Colony of Avalon," *Avalon Chronicles* I (1996); "Old France Into New, 1635–36," Paul Le Jeune, in Reuben Gold Thwaites, ed., *The Jesuit Relations and Allied Documents*, vols. VIII and IX (New York: Pageant Book Company, 1959), with gratitude to Cameron Nish; "'La fécondité de ce pays,'" Jean Talon, Fonds d'archives du Séminaire de Québec, Mémoire to Jean-Baptiste Colbert, November 10, 1670, from the website of the Musée de la civilisation de Québec; "Counting Heads, 1671," Port Royal Census 1671, Library and Archives Canada, microfilm c-2572; "Halifax's 'Poor Idle Worthless,' 1749," Governor Edward Cornwallis to Lord Halifax, July 24, 1749, in H.A. Innis, ed., *Select Documents in Canadian Economic History, 1497–1783* (Toronto: University of Toronto Press, 1929), with gratitude to P.B. Waite; "Displacing the Acadians – to Admit the English, 1755," Governor Charles Lawrence to Lieutenant-Colonel Robert Monckton, August 8, 1755, in T.B. Akins, ed., *Selections from the Public Documents of the Province of Nova Scotia: Papers Relating to the Forcible Removal of the Acadian French From Nova Scotia, 1755–1768* (Halifax: Charles Annand, 1869), from the website of Nova Scotia Archives and Records Management; "Fractious Loyalist Tendencies, 1784," Governor John Parr to Lord Shelburne, January 24, 1784, Public Archives of Canada, *Report, 1921* (Ottawa, 1922), with gratitude to P.B. Waite; "Rich Loyalist in Quebec," William Smith to his wife,

October 28, 1786, in L.F.S. Upton, ed., *The Diary and Selected Papers of Chief Justice William Smith, 1784–1793*, vol. II (Toronto: Champlain Society, 1965); "The Implements of Settlement," William Bell, *Hints to Emigrants, In a Series of Letters from Upper Canada* (Edinburgh: Waugh and Innes, 1824); "Island Evils, 1820," William Johnstone, *A Series of Letters Descriptive of Prince Edward Island. . .* (Dumfries: J. Swan, 1822), with gratitude to P.B. Waite; "'Dirty, Gross and Indolent,'" John Howison, *Sketches of Upper Canada: Domestic, Local, and Characteristic* (Edinburgh: Oliver and Boyd, 1821); "The Perils of the Voyage, 1821," John M'Donald, *Emigration to Canada: Narrative of a Voyage to Quebec, and Journey From Thence to New Lanark, in Upper Canada* (1826); "Getting Married," Abraham Gill, diary of December 16, 1870, from www.islandregister.com, with gratitude to David Campbell and David Hunter; "Setting Up in the Woods, 1823," in E.S. Dunlop, ed., *Our Forest Home: Being Extracts from the Correspondence of the Late Frances Stewart* (Montreal: The Gazette, 1902); "New Brunswick Politics, 1829," J. Mulligan to James Mulligan, July 9, 1829, from Centre for Migration Studies, Ulster American Folk Park, Omagh, Northern Ireland, Irish Emigration Database, document no. 9502084, with the permission of the Deputy Keeper of the Records, Public Record Office of Northern Ireland, PRONI D/1757/2/2; "'This Ultra-Republican Spirit,'" Susanna Moodie, *Roughing It in the Bush, or, Life in Canada* (London: R. Bentley, 1852); "Grosse Île, 1831," Henry Deaves, May 27, 1831, in *Montreal Gazette*, June 14, 1834, from http://www.ist.uwaterloo.ca/~marj/genealogy/voyages/mary1831.html; "The Cholera Came," John and Esther Chantler, in Wendy Cameron, Sheila Haines, and Mary McDougall Maude, eds., *English Immigrant Voices: Labourers' Letters from Upper Canada in the 1830s* (Montreal and Kingston: McGill-Queen's University Press, 2000); "Travel Advisory, 1832," *Information Published by His Majesty's Chief Agent for the Superintendence of Settlers and Emigrants in Upper and Lower Canada* (Quebec: Thomas Cary & Co., 1832), from http://www.ist.uwaterloo.ca/~marj/genealogy/emigrants1832.html; "'My Own Wish To Go,' 1833," Elizabeth Wainwright to her mother, August 1833, Wainwright Papers, Toronto Public Library, with gratitude to Aileen Howes and Suzanne Evans; "American Money, Canadian Distances," letters of September 21, 1833, and January 10, 1834, *Counsel for Emigrants* (Aberdeen, Scotland: J. Mathison, 1834); "Highland Scots in Inverness Township, 1834," William Hendry, in Ronald Black, "An Emigrant's Letter in Arran Gaelic, 1834," *Scottish Studies* 31 (1992–23); "Virtues of Upper Canada," letter from George Menzies, November 30, 1834, in *Counsel for Emigrants*; "Duty and Faith, 1837," letters from Ellen Osler, May 1837, Archives of Ontario; "Women's Work, 1841," Robert McDougall, *The Emigrant's Guide to North America* (Glasgow: J. & P. Campbell, 1841): "Much Better Off," James Thomson, in R.A. Preston, ed., *For Friends and Home: A Scottish Emigrant's*

Letters from Canada and the Cariboo, 1844–1864 (Montreal and Kingston: McGill-Queen's University Press, 1974); "'So Many Joyous Beings,'" from *A Cabin Passage* (1848), in J.M. Gibbon, *Canadian Mosaic: The Making of a Northern Nation* (Toronto: McClelland and Stewart, 1938); "The Maritimes Labour Market, 1849," Reverend John G. Mulholland to Reverend George Kirkpatrick, March 21, 1849, from Centre for Migration Studies, Irish Emigration Database, document no. 9004022, with the permission of the Deputy Keeper of the Records, Public Record Office of Northern Ireland, PRONI D1424/11/1; "A Plea for Black Emigration to Canada, 1852," Mary A. Shadd, *A Plea for Emigration, or, Notes of Canada West, in its Moral, Social, and Political Aspect, with Suggestions Respecting Mexico, West Indies, and Vancouver's Island. For the Information of Colored Emigrants* (Detroit: George W. Pattison, 1852); "Trapped in Quebec," in Orm Overland, ed., *Johan Schrøder's Travels in Canada, 1863* (Montreal and Kingston: McGill-Queen's University Press, 1989); "The Settler's Life, 1881," Edward ffolkes, *Letters from a Young Emigrant in Manitoba* (Winnipeg: University of Manitoba, 1981); "Please Decide," William Wallace, in Kenneth S. Coates and William R. Morrison, eds., *My Dear Maggie—: Letters from a Western Manitoba Pioneer* (Regina: Canadian Plains Research Center, 1991); "'Don't Send Any More,'" *Manitoba Free Press*, May 27, June 2 and 9, 1882; "Quarantine Island," Vera Velichkina, in John Woodsworth, ed., *Russian Roots and Canadian Wings: Russian Archival Documents on the Doukhobor Emigration to Canada* (Manotick: Penumbra Press, 1999), courtesy J.L. Black and the Centre for Research on Canadian-Russian Relations; "The Battle of the Pioneer," Sir Clifford Sifton, "The Immigrants Canada Wants," *Maclean's*, April 1, 1922; "Recruiting Americans, 1901," J.E. Blum and J. Grumpper, *Manitoba Free Press*, July 27, 1901; "The Dojack Family," © Thomas S. Axworthy; "'Blue Sky Ahead,' 1903," John Qutle [signature difficult to decipher] to Alexander Taylor, October 30, 1903, from Centre for Migration Studies, Irish Emigration Database, document no. 8910017, with the permission of the Deputy Keeper of the Records, Public Record Office of Northern Ireland, PRONI T/2296/7; "Providence's Choice," Henri Bourassa, House of Commons *Debates*, April 9, 1907; "A Harsh Initiation," Leslie H. Neatby, *Chronicle of a Pioneer Prairie Family* (Saskatoon: Western Producer Prairie Books, 1979), courtesy of the Neatby family; "The 1907 Anti-Asian Riot," *Daily News-Advertiser* (Vancouver), September 8, 1907; "En partant de Saint-Pierre et Miquelon," in *En partant de Saint-Pierre et Miquelon: Autobiographie de Soeur Yvonne Landry*, unpublished document, courtesy of Pierrette Landry; "'How Wisely Should We Care for the Immigrant!'" J.S. Woodsworth, *Strangers Within Our Gates; or Coming Canadians* (F.C. Stephenson, c 1909); "'The Case of the Negro,' 1909," William J. White to Frank Oliver, September 13 and 14, 1909, Library and Archives Canada, RG 76, microfilm reels c-7346-7, with gratitude to Harold Troper; "Macedonian Self Help," Lillian Petroff, *Sojourners and Settlers: The Macedonian Community in Toronto to 1940* (Toronto: University of Toronto Press, 1995); "'Life Was Different Here,'" Andrej Potocký, in Imrich Stolárik, ed., *Spomienky pionierov* (Toronto: Canadian Slovak League, 1978), document translated and edited by M. Mark Stolarik; "In Steerage, 1910," *The Montreal Star*, November 5, 1910; "'I Thought Only of the Music,'" Antonio Funicelli, in Bruno Ramirez, *Les Premiers Italiens de Montréal* (Boréal Express, 1984), document translated by Gillian I. Leitch; "Writing Back to Newfoundland, 1912," John Sparks to *Bay Roberts Guardian*, February 16, 1912; "Rugged British Columbia," Daisy Phillips, reprinted with the permission of the publisher from *Letters from Windermere, 1912–1914* by R. Cole Harris and Elizabeth Phillips, eds., © University of British Columbia Press, 1984, all rights reserved by the publisher; "The CPR's Rough Treatment," Ivan Humenyuk to the Russian consul, Montreal, 1913, Library and Archives Canada, Likacheff-Ragosine-Mathers Collection, document translated by Vadim Kukushkin; "Labouring in British Columbia," Zinovy Peshkov, "Working in Canada," *Novyi mir*, July 25 and August 1, 1913, document translated by Vadim Kukushkin; "Toronto's Jewish Community," interview with Joseph B. Salsberg, June 9, 1978, Multicultural History Society of Ontario; "Three Hundred Barbadians," interview with Dudley Marshall, July 1978, Multicultural History Society of Ontario; "The *Komagata Maru*, 1914," *Vancouver Sun*, July 20, 1914; "Wives Left Behind," letter of Agafia Koval, October 8, 1915, and letter to Vasyl Dohvan, August 1917, Library and Archives Canada, Likacheff-Ragosine-Mathers Collection, document translated by Vadim Kukushkin; "Picture Bride," Tami Nakamura, in Tomoko Makabe, *Picture Brides: Japanese Women in Canada* (Multicultural History Society of Ontario, 1995); "An East Indian's Loneliness," A.P. Ledingham to R.P. MacKay, February 3, 1917, United Church of Canada/Victoria University Archives, Presbyterian Church in Canada Board of Foreign Missions, Records Pertaining to the Central India Mission, General Correspondence, box 14, file 158, with gratitude to Ruth Compton Brouwer; "Life in an Internment Camp," Phillip Yasnowskyi, in Harry Piniuta, ed. and translator, *Land of Pain, Land of Promise: First Person Accounts by Ukrainian Pioneers, 1891–1914* (Saskatoon: Western Producer Prairie Books, 1978); "Unworthy Persecution, 1918," Phillips Thompson, *The Globe*, March 29, 1918; "'They Hated the Germans,'" Bertha Knull, in Tova Yedlin, ed., *Germans from Russia in Alberta: Reminiscences* (Edmonton: Central and East European Studies Society of Alberta, 1984), with gratitude to Tova Yedlin; "Three Hungarians on the Prairies," Sámuel Zágonyi, in N.F. Dreisziger, "Immigrant Fortunes and Misfortunes in Canada in the 1920s," *Hungarian Studies Review* XVII (Spring 1990); "A Home Boy's Shame," Albert O. Lee, in Milly Charon, ed., *Between Two Worlds: The Canadian Immigration Experience*

(Dunvegan, Ontario: Quadrant, 1983), with the permission of Milly Charon; "'Why Orientals Should Be Excluded,' 1922," W.G. McQuarrie, House of Commons *Debates*, May 8, 1922; "An Immigrant Pastor," Eduard Duesterhoeft, in Yedlin, *Germans from Russia in Alberta*; "Jobs Canadians Didn't Want," Nellie O'Donnell, in Shelagh Conway, ed., *The Faraway Hills Are Green: Voices of Irish Women in Canada* (Toronto: Women's Press, 1992); "'There Weren't Many Blacks,'" in Donna Hill, ed., *A Black Man's Toronto: The Reminiscences of Harry Gairey, 1914–1980* (Multicultural History Society of Ontario, 1981); "The Brain Drain, 1927," W.A. Irwin, "Can We Stem the Exodus?" *Maclean's*, May 15, 1927; "Assimilation: A Dissent," Frederick Philip Grove, "Canadians Old and New," *Maclean's*, March 15, 1928; "Ralph Connor's Injustice," Gibbon, *Canadian Mosaic*; "A Word of Warning, 1928," H. Denkers et al., in Herman Ganzevoort, ed., *The Last Illusion: Letters from Dutch Immigrants* (Calgary: University of Calgary Press, 1999), with gratitude to the editor; "Colonial Canada," in Phyllis Knight, *A Very Ordinary Life*, as told to Rolf Knight (Vancouver: New Star, 1974), through the kindness of Rolf Knight; "A Mennonite Family in the Depression," with permission from Arthur Kroeger, *Hard Passage: A Mennonite Family's Long Journey from Russia to Canada*, forthcoming from the University of Alberta Press; "Deporting the Bolsheviks, 1932," *The Globe*, May 9, 1932; "While the Natives Starve," Robert Jackson to R.B. Bennett, October 22, 1934, in L.M. Grayson and Michael Bliss, eds., *The Wretched of Canada* (Toronto: University of Toronto Press, 1971); "Sadness," in Jarmila L.A. Horna, ed., *Alberta's Pioneers From Eastern Europe, Reminiscences: The Story of Anthony (Tonek) Slezina* (Division of East European Studies, The University of Alberta/Central and East European Studies Society of Alberta, 1979); "Concerning Mr. Cohen, 1937," William Lyon Mackenzie King Diary, February 10, 1937, Library and Archives Canada; "Am I Less Canadian?" Esther Thompson, in Gibbon, *Canadian Mosaic*; "Joining Up, 1938," Gus Garber, *Montreal Herald*, September 26, 1938; "'Fellow Subjects of a Beloved Ruler,'" from M.A. Pease, *Echoes* (Imperial Order Daughters of the Empire), in Gibbon, *Canadian Mosaic*; "The *St. Louis*, 1939," George M. Wrong et al., telegram to Mackenzie King, June 7, 1939, from http://www.virtualmuseum.ca; "War and the Enemy Within," Gregory S. Kealey and Reg Whitaker, eds., *R.C.M.P. Security Bulletins: The War Series, 1939–1941* (St. John's: Committee on Canadian Labour History, 1989); "Things Turn Nasty," Karl W. Butzer, "Coming Full Circle: Learning from the Experience of Emigration and Ethnic Prejudice," in Peter Suedfeld, ed., *Light From the Ashes: Social Science Careers of Young Holocaust Refugees and Survivors* (Ann Arbor: The University of Michigan Press, 2001); "Unionizing Galt Malleable, 1943," Garabed Palvetzian, in Isabel Kaprielian-Churchill, *Like Our Mountains: A History of Armenians in Canada* (Montreal and Kingston: McGill-Queen's University Press, 2005), with gratitude to the

Palvetzian family; "A Dutch War Bride," Olga Rains, found at Pier 21 website, with the permission of Olga Rains; "Democratic Living," *This Was My Choice: Gouzenko's Story* (Toronto: J.M. Dent & Sons Limited, 1948), contributed by the estate of Igor and Svetlana Gouzenko, in their memory; "Nobody We Knew: Sachiko's Story," © R.L. Gabrielle Nishiguchi, with the permission of Sachiko Nakamura (née Ohata); "Travelling West, 1947," letter of Robina Evelyn Lee, October 29, 1947, from the Canadian Letters and Images Project, by permission of the Lee family; "Refugee Doctors Need Not Apply," A.D. Kelly, in Jean Bruce, *After the War* (Don Mills: Fitzhenry & Whiteside, 1982); "Our Remnant of a Family," Moses Znaimer, from Passages to Canada, Dominion Institute, with gratitude to Moses Znaimer; "'White Man's Thinking,' 1949," A.L. Jolliffe, in Bruce, *After the War*; "The German Parish," interview with Lucy Amberg, March 22, 1979, in Mina Kuttner, "Oral Biographies of Canadians in Ontario's German Community," Multicultural History Society of Ontario; "Dearest Nia, 1950," letter of William Azzi, August 21, 1950, courtesy of the author; "A Migrant Chain," Nicholas DeMaria Harney and Franc Sturino, eds., *The Lucky Immigrant: The Public Life of Fortunato Rao* (Multicultural History Society of Ontario, 2002); "Time to Adjust," interview with Lillian Sulteanu, in Charon, *Between Two Worlds*, with the permission of Milly Charon; "'Keeping My Faith,'" Tara Singh Bains and Hugh Johnston, *The Four Quarters of the Night: The Life-Journey of an Emigrant Sikh* (Montreal and Kingston: McGill-Queen's University Press, 1995); "The Shadow of Leaving," Helmut Walter Ott, "Immigration: A Personal Retrospective of an Austrian in Canada," in Franz A.J. Szabo, ed., *Austrian Immigration to Canada: Selected Essays* (Ottawa: Carleton University Press, 1996); "Sense of Continuity," © Hartley Janssen; "A Rhodesian in the Army," © Michael Pillar; "Civil Defence, 1955," Tass Grundel to Federal Co-ordinator of Civil Defence, November 7, 1955, Library and Archives Canada, RG 29, volume 102, file 180-8-1; "'You Chose Canada,'" interview with Irene Brown, March 6, 1989, Pauline Greenhill transcripts, Multicultural History Society of Ontario; "From the Kremlin to Cornflakes," © János Máté; "Beyond Civilization," interview with Steve Zaban by Rebecca Sampson, October 2003, with the permission of Steve Zaban; "Such Hardworking People," Franca Iacovetta, *Such Hardworking People: Italian Immigrants in Postwar Toronto* (Montreal and Kingston: McGill-Queen's University Press, 1992); "L'ancrer fermement au Québec," © Yohanna Loucheur; "Aussie Youth," © Valerie Jacobs; "'A Racist Country,'" interview with Reverend Harold Jackman, July 1978, Multicultural History Society of Ontario; "After the Prague Spring," Ivan and Marta Straznicky, in Elizabeth McLuhan, ed., *Safe Haven: The Refugee Experience of Five Families* (Multicultural History Society of Ontario, 1995); "Going North," © Stephen Eaton Hume; "From the Old to the New

Canada," Andrew Faiz, from Passages to Canada, Dominion Institute, with the permission of the author; "'I Was Quite Afraid,' 1970," Dr. Godwin Eni, from Passages to Canada, Dominion Institute, with the permission of the author; "'Frightened Faces,'" interview with Zaven Degirmen, in Milly Charon, ed., *Worlds Apart: New Immigrant Voices* (Dunvegan: Cormorant Books, 1989), with the permission of Milly Charon; "Through the Wire Fence," Lori Weber, "I Am Canadian But My Father Is German," in Carl E. James and Adrienne Shadd, eds., *Talking About Identity: Encounters in Race, Ethnicity, and Language* (Toronto: Between the Lines, 2001), with the permission of Lori Weber; "'Alone in a New Land,'" Neil Bissoondath, "A Question of Belonging: Multiculturalism and Citizenship," in William Kaplan, ed., *Belonging: The Meaning and Future of Canadian Citizenship* (Montreal and Kingston: McGill-Queen's University Press, 1993); "The Junta's Victims, 1973," Farley Mowat, *The Globe and Mail*, December 4, 1973, with gratitude to Farley Mowat; "Escaping Chile," Gabriela Enriquez, in McLuhan, *Safe Haven*; "Always With You, 1978," letter of Ramesh Mehta to Hansa Mehta, March 2, 1978, courtesy of Bina Mehta; "The Vietnamese Boat People," Pham Thê Trung, in McLuhan, *Safe Haven*; "We Portuguese Came to Canada," Domingos Marques and João Medeiros, "Here to Stay," in their *Portuguese Immigrants: 25 Years in Canada* (Toronto: West End YMCA, 1980); "'More Sri Lankan,'" Siva Segaran, in McLuhan, *Safe Haven*; "'Send Them Back!' 1987," from "A Dangerous Backlash," *Maclean's*, August 10, 1987; "Safety and Survival, 1990," Enrique Robert, from Passages to Canada, Dominion Institute, with the permission of the author; "My Beliefs and the RCMP," Sergeant Baltej Singh Dhillon, from Passages to Canada Digital Archive, Dominion Institute, with the permission of the author. "A Cold Paradise," A Somalian, "Allah, Forgive Us," in Ivaylo Grouev, ed., *Bullets on the Water* (Montreal and Kingston: McGill-Queen's University Press, 2000); "The Best Multiethnic State," A Sarajevan, "This Was Not My War," Grouev, *Bullets on the Water*; "An Encounter with ESL," Karishma Kapil, "A Question of Standards," *YORKU* (October 2005), with the permission of the author and gratitude to Berton Woodward; "An Inventory of Belonging," Ken Wiwa, from Passages to Canada Digital Archive, Dominion Institute, with the permission of Ken Wiwa; "Two Sides of the Globe, 1995," Denise Chong, "Being Canadian," in *Canadian Speeches: Issues of the Day* (May 1995), with the permission of Denise Chong; "Lessons in Patience," Layla Sharif, from Passages to Canada Digital Archive, Dominion Institute, with the permission of the author; "Smugglers' Slaves, 2001," Tom Fennell, with Sheng Xue, "The Smugglers' Slaves," *Maclean's*, December 11, 2001; "A Muslim After September 11, 2001," Suhail Abualsameed, from Passages to Canada Digital Archive, Dominion Institute, with the permission of the author; "All Mixed-Up," © Andrew Chung; "We Children of Immigrants, 2003," Madeleine Thien,

"But, I Dream in Canadian," © 2003, reprinted with the permission of Madeleine Thien; "Giving Up on Canada," Marina Jimenez, "A Star Immigrant Gives Up on Canada," *The Globe and Mail*, April 19, 2005, reprinted with permission from *The Globe and Mail*; "My Two Countries," Margaret Wente, "It's True: Life Is Better in Canada," *The Globe and Mail*, July 2, 2005, reprinted with permission from *The Globe and Mail*; "Brazilian and Canadian," © Adriana Rio Branco Nabuco de Gouvêa; "My Disjointed Life," © Tou Chu Dou Lynhiavu; "Celebrity Inn," reprinted with permission of the publisher from *Securing Borders: Detention and Deportation in Canada*, by Anna Pratt, © University of British Columbia Press, 2005, all rights reserved by the publisher; "Intelligent Waiting," © Andy and Pia Diaconescu; "Hold the Complacency, 2005," Michael Valpy, "Could It Happen Here?" *The Globe and Mail*, November 12, 2005, reprinted with permission from *The Globe and Mail*; "The Real Immigrant Experience," Andrew Coyne, "Jean's Siren Song of Freedom," *National Post*, September 28, 2005, reprinted with permission from CanWest MediaWorks Publications Inc.; "Pioneering," © Sheema Khan; "Sophie's New World," © Michael Dufresne and Katherine Lagrandeur.

Index